"CAN WE ALL GET ALONG?"

"CAN WE ALL GET ALONG?"

RACIAL AND ETHNIC MINORITIES IN AMERICAN POLITICS

SEVENTH EDITION

Paula D. McClain
Duke University

and

Jessica D. Johnson Carew
Elon University

WESTVIEW
PRESS

Westview Press
Hachette Book Group
1290 Avenue of the Americas, New York, NY 10104
westviewpress.com
twitter.com/westviewpress

Printed in the United States of America

Seventh Edition: July 2017
Published by Westview Press, an imprint of Perseus Books, LLC,
a subsidiary of Hachette Book Group, Inc.

The Hachette Speakers Bureau provides a wide range of authors for speaking events. To find out more, go to www.hachettespeakersbureau.com or call (866) 376-6591.

The publisher is not responsible for websites (or their content) that are not owned by the publisher.

Print book interior set by Cynthia Young.

Library of Congress Cataloging-in-Publication Data
Names: McClain, Paula Denice, author.
Title: "Can we all get along?": racial and ethnic minorities in American politics /
    Paula McClain (Duke University) with Jessica Carew (Elon University).
Description: Seventh edition. | Boulder, Colorado : Westview Press, 2017. |
    Includes bibliographical references and index.
Identifiers: LCCN 2017007871 (print) | LCCN 2017009357 (ebook) |
    ISBN 9780813350516 (paperback) | ISBN 9780813350691 (ebook) |
    ISBN 9780813350691 (e-book)
Subjects: LCSH: Minorities—Political activity—United States. | United States— relations
    Race relations—Political aspects. | United States—Ethnic—Political aspects. |
    BISAC: POLITICAL SCIENCE / Political Freedom & Security /
    Civil Rights. | POLITICAL SCIENCE / Political Process / General. |
    POLITICAL SCIENCE / Government / General.
Classification: LCC E184.A1 M347 2017 (print) | LCC E184.A1 (ebook) | DDC
    305.800973—dc23
LC record available at https://lccn.loc.gov/2017007871

ISBNs: 978-0-8133-5051-6 (paperback), 978-0-8133-5069-1 (e-book)

LSC-C

10   9   8   7   6   5   4   3   2   1

In February 2016, I lost my mentor, friend, and colleague Dr. Harold M. Rose. Previous editions of the book were dedicated to him, and he got a kick out of it, throwing back his head and giving a hearty laugh as he ran his hand down his face. As I said in previous editions, Harold taught me more about research and the academy than he would ever know. But more important, he taught me how to be a scholar. Harold, I miss you and your sage advice and support. You are always in my thoughts and prayers.

—P. D. Mc.

I dedicate this book to my parents, Elaine C. W. Johnson and Frank O. Johnson Jr. As my first real teachers and mentors, they taught me to never shy away from seeking knowledge and truth and to recognize and challenge injustice, rather than accepting or being bound by it. Thank you for your endless love and support.

—J. D. J. C.

Contents

Illustrations   xi
Acronyms   xv
Preface   xvii

Chapter 1 – America's Dilemmas   1

Terms Used in This Book   3
Race and Ethnicity   6
American Government Foundation and Racial Minorities   8
The Constitution and Black and Indian Citizenship   10
Citizenship and Later Minorities: Latinos and Asians   15
The Constitution and Black and Indian Suffrage   19
Structure of This Book   23
Conclusion   24
▶ DISCUSSION QUESTIONS   25
   NOTE   25

Chapter 2 – Resources and Status of America's Racial Minorities   27

Population Size, Socioeconomic Status, and Concentration   28
Participation in a Civil Rights Movement   42
Voting Rights Law   63
Conclusion   71
▶ DISCUSSION QUESTIONS   71

Chapter 3 – America's Racial Minorities in the Contemporary Political System: *Actors*   73

Group Identity and Perceptions of Discrimination   77

Political Ideology   83

Partisan Identification   92

Voting Behavior   106

The 2000 Elections   115

The 2004 Elections   120

The 2008 Elections   122

The 2012 Elections   128

The 2016 Elections   137

Interest Group Activities   146

Conclusion   150

▶ DISCUSSION QUESTIONS   150

   NOTES   151

Chapter 4 – America's Racial Minorities and the Policymaking Process   153

Agenda Setting   155

Minority Representation in the US Government   156

Minority Representation in the Presidency   157

Minority Representation in Congress   168

Minority Representation in the Supreme Court   174

Minority Representation in the Bureaucracy   177

Federalism   179

State Elective Office   181

Equal Educational Opportunity for Minorities   187

Affirmative Action in Employment   204

Conclusion   208

▶ DISCUSSION QUESTIONS   210

   NOTES   211

Chapter 5: – Intersectional Identity in Racial and Ethnic Politics   213

Intersectionality: Identity Along Multiple Dimensions   215
Salient Dimensions for Racial And Ethnic Intersectional Identities   218
Sociopolitical Experiences When Multiple Identities Intersect   222
Participating in Electoral Politics   226
Social Activism and Protest   237
Conclusion   245
▶ DISCUSSION QUESTIONS   246
   NOTES   247

Chapter 6 – Coalition or Competition?
Patterns of Interminority Group Relations   249

Interminority Group Relations   251
Coalition or Competition Politics?   251
Racial Threat and Competition Theories:
   Memphis, Little Rock, and Durham   256
Conclusion   268
▶ DISCUSSION QUESTIONS   269
   NOTES   269

Chapter 7 – Will We "All Get Along"?   271

The Dilemmas Revisited   274
Targeting Racial and Ethnic Minorities   279
VRA: Looking to the Future   281
Conclusion   284
▶ DISCUSSION QUESTION   286
   NOTES   286

Glossary   287
Time Lines   295
References   335
Index   361

Illustrations

PHOTOGRAPHS

1.1   Lynching of African Americans   *21*

2.1   Civil Rights Protest of Desesgregation Policies   *46*

2.2   Harlington Wood Escorted by AIM   *57*

2.3   Native Hawaiian Activists   *63*

3.1   Julio Martinez   *101*

3.2   Hillary Clinton   *104*

3.3   Barack Obama's Election Night   *129*

3.4   Anti–Black Lives Matter Graffiti   *143*

4.1   Mochida Family   *158*

4.2   Barack Obama at Tribal Nations Conference   *159*

4.3   Representative Shirley Chisholm   *164*

4.4   Nikki Haley   *186*

5.1   Kamala Harris and Women Senators   *233*

5.2   Cofounders of the Black Lives Matter Movement   *237*

5.3   Protesters in Brooklyn, NY   *240*

5.4   Native Americans and the DAPL   *244*

6.1   Rodney King   *250*

6.2   Cesar Alamilla   *257*

6.3   Reverend William Barber   *260*

6.4   Elizabeth Eckford   *263*

MAPS

2.1   African American Population Distribution, United States, 2014   *35*

2.2   Hispanic Population Distribution, United States, 2014   *36*

2.3   American Indian Population Distribution, United States, 2014   *37*

2.4   Asian Population Distribution, United States, 2014   *38*

2.5   Population Patterns, Metropolitan Los Angeles County, 2014   *44*

TABLES

2.1   Selected Characteristics of the Non-Latino Black, Asian American, American Indian/Alaskan Native, and White Populations in the United States, 2015   *29*

2.2   Selected Characteristics of the Latino Population and Selected Subgroups in the United States, 2015   *30*

2.3   Selected Characteristics of Selected Asian American Population Subgroups in the United States, 2015   *31*

2.4   Population Size and Percent of Largest Five American Indian Tribes, and States of Primary Concentration, States with American Indians as Highest Percentage of Population, and States with Largest Number of American Indians and Alaskan Natives, 2010   *40*

2.5   Cities with the Largest American Indian Population, 2010   *41*

3.1   Proportion of Blacks Perceiving That They Share a Common Fate with Other Blacks   *79*

3.2A   Experiences with Discrimination Among Latinos   *80*

3.2B   Perceptions of Discrimination Against Latinos   *80*

3.3   Degree to Which Latino Subgroups Believe That Their Well-Being Is Dependent on the Well-Being of Other Latinos   *81*

3.4   Degree to Which Asian Americans Perceive They Share a Common Fate with Other Asian Americans   *83*

3.5   Black Ideological Identification   *85*

3.6   Latino Ideological Identification   *87*

3.7   Asian American Ideological Identification   *89*

3.8   American Indian Ideological Identification   *91*

3.9   Black Partisan Identification   *95*

3.10   Latino Partisan Identification   *98*

3.11   Asian American Partisan Identification   *102*

3.12   American Indian Partisan Identification   *106*

3.13   Registration and Voting for Blacks and Latinos in Fifty States, 2014   *108*

3.14   Registration and Voting by Race, National Sample Citizens Only: White, Black, Latino, and Asians, 2012 and 2014   *110*

3.15   Registration and Voting by Race and Sex, National Sample Citizens Only: Black, Latino, and Asian, 2012   *114*

3.16   Reported Registration and Voting Among Native and Naturalized Black, Latino, and Asian Citizens, 2012   *115*

3.17   2000, 2004, 2008, and 2012 Presidential Election Results by Race and Gender   *118*

3.18   Latino and Asian American Votes, Presidential Election, 2016   *142*

4.1   Black Members of the 115th Congress, January 3, 2017–January 3, 2019   *170*

4.2   Latino Members of the 115th Congress, January 3, 2017–January 3, 2019   *172*

4.3   Asian–Pacific Islander Members of the 115th Congress, January 3, 2017–January 3, 2019   *174*

4.4   American Indians Who Have Served in the US Senate and House of Representatives   *175*

4.5   Representation of Racial/National Origin Groups in Federal Civilian Workforce and Civilian Labor Force, Fiscal Year 2014   *179*

4.6   Distribution of Racial/National Origin Groups in Federal Civilian Workforce by General Schedule and Related Pay Plans, Fiscal Year 2014   *180*

4.7   Black, Latino, and Asian Governors in the United States   *183*

4.8   Native American State Legislators, 2017   *188*

Acronyms

AAPF	African American Policy Forum
ACLU	American Civil Liberties Union
AIM	American Indian Movement
APILC	Asian Pacific Islander Legislative Caucus
APSA	American Political Science Association
BIA	Bureau of Indian Affairs
BLM	Black Lives Matter
CILS	California Indian Legal Services
COFO	Council of Federated Organizations
CRLA	California Rural Legal Assistance
DAPL	Dakota Access Pipeline
DHH	Louisiana Department of Health and Hospitals
DOS	US Department of State
FBI	Federal Bureau of Investigation
HAVA	Help America Vote Act
HEW	Department of Health, Education, and Welfare
INS	Immigration and Naturalization Services
JACL	Japanese American Citizens League
JCPES	Joint Center for Political and Economic Studies
LAPD	Los Angeles Police Department
LDF	NAACP Legal Defense and Educational Fund
LEAP	Leadership Education for Asian Pacifics
LNPS	Latino National Political Survey
LNS	Latino National Survey

LULAC   League of United Latin American Citizens
MALDEF   Mexican American Legal Defense and Education Fund
NAACP   National Association for the Advancement of Colored People
NARF   Native American Rights Fund
NBES   National Black Election Study
NBPS   National Black Politics Study
NCLR   National Council of La Raza
OCR   Office for Civil Rights
OFCCP   Office of Federal Contract Compliance Programs
PAC   Political Action Committee
PASSO   Political Association of Spanish-Speaking Peoples
PNAAPS   Pilot Study of the National Asian American Political Survey
PRLDEF   Puerto Rican Legal Defense and Education Fund
SCLC   Southern Christian Leadership Conference
SNCC   Student Nonviolent Coordinating Committee
UDL   United Defense League
USACE   United States Army Corps of Engineers
VAP   Voting-Age Population
VRA   Voting Rights Act

Preface

This is the seventh edition of *Can We All Get Along?* and I want to thank Joseph Stewart Jr. for his coauthorship on the previous editions. With this new edition, Jessica D. Johnson Carew, a coauthor on other research and a former student, joins me as a new coauthor. She is now an assistant professor of political science at Elon University. Her expertise in gender, politics, and the politics of women of color add a new dimension to this edition. I am thrilled with her addition. For those who do not know, the first edition of this book was the result of a collaboration between Joe Stewart and me that began over a bottle of cabernet sauvignon at the 1992 American Political Science Association (APSA) meeting in Chicago. What started as an evening devoted to reading papers quickly turned into a discussion of the difficulties of teaching a true minority group politics course.

Some universities, depending on their location, have a course devoted to a particular group—for example, black politics, Latino politics, Asian politics, American Indian politics—or even a more specialized course such as Mexican American politics or Puerto Rican politics. Indeed, we have both taught such courses. But more commonly the demand is for an umbrella course that, ideally, compares the politics of the four principal US racial and ethnic minority groups—blacks, Latinos, American Indians, and Asian Americans—and their relationships with the majority. This is the situation at our current institutions.

Such umbrella courses generally take one of two forms. The less-than-ideal alternative is focused on one ethnic group because that is where the interest and expertise of the instructor lie. In such situations, it is possible for a student to take the same course twice from different instructors, never to encounter overlapping patterns, and never explicitly to consider interminority group relations. The second, preferable form involves undertaking a comparative examination of the politics of the major racial and ethnic minorities of the United States. This is an idealized alternative because, as we can report from personal experience, it is difficult to implement. One must spend countless hours amassing data from various sources in an attempt to draw out the similarities and the differences among the groups and to develop the depth and nuance that characterize a good course.

Toward the bottom of the bottle of wine, we decided that we had sufficient expertise on black and Latino politics and enough familiarity with the literature of American Indian and Asian American politics to write a book for a true junior/senior-level minority politics class. We mentioned our "prospectus from a bottle" to Cathy Rudder, executive director of APSA, who discussed it with Sandy Maisel of Colby College, the editor of Westview Press's new series Dilemmas in American Politics. Sandy contacted us and indicated that this was the book the series' editorial advisory board had decided was a high priority; McClain, a member of the board, had missed the meeting! Sandy convinced us to write a shorter, less-detailed volume for use as a supplement, primarily in American government courses. The larger, upper-division book is still in our plans.

The words for the title are appropriated from Rodney King's first news conference following the acquittals of his attackers and the subsequent Los Angeles riots. His words crystallize the dilemmas faced by the nation, by members of both minority and majority groups.

Response to the first, second, third, fourth, fifth, and sixth editions has been gratifying. To paraphrase Yogi Berra, we would like to thank everyone who made this seventh edition necessary. Sales for all editions suggest there is an interest in learning more about the nation's racial and ethnic politics (or in teachers having their students exposed to more material on the topic). Racial and ethnic politics, like politics in general, is constantly changing. Thus, for this book to fulfill its role, it is necessary to produce a new edition. The basic structure has been altered somewhat to accommodate Jessica's expertise, and materials have been added or updated. Readers will find an analysis of the 2016 elections and data from the 2010 census updates.

We could not have accomplished what turned out to be a larger undertaking than we had imagined—to write the first edition—without the help of numerous people. Steven C. Tauber served as our principal factotum. (Hint: This word appears in the GRE verbal exam. Look it up. Fans of the old TV series *The Fugitive* will have already encountered it.) Steve spent countless hours on numerous tasks, with perhaps the worst being an attempt to get the National Black Election Study data file to run again after a transfer from one computer system to another. Steve served as McClain's teaching assistant for her Minority Group Politics course at the University of Virginia for several years in the early 1990s. His intellectual contributions to the study of racial minority group politics are present throughout the book.

Thanks also to Don Nakanishi of the Asian American Studies Center at UCLA for helping us identify Asian American elected officials; to Larry Bobo of the Department of Sociology at UCLA for sharing his Los Angeles County Survey data with us; to Paul Waddell and his staff at the Bruton Center for Development Studies of the University of Texas at Dallas for generating the maps in Chapter 2 in the first edition; the research staffs of the Joint Center for Political and Economic Studies and the National Association of Latino Elected and Appointed Officials; and to Paula Sutherland, head of government documents, and Linda Snow, reference librarian, McDermott Library, University of Texas at Dallas, for tracking down or pointing us toward valuable information we knew existed somewhere but had no idea where. McClain's and Stewart's colleagues and students over the years, especially those in McClain's Minority Group Politics class, helped by enduring our on-the-job efforts to fashion a coherent, comparative course by asking questions that forced us to seek more answers, and by answering questions we posed.

We are also indebted to Sandy Maisel; to Jennifer Knerr, our acquisitions editor, Shena Redmond, our project editor, and Cheryl Carnahan, our copyeditor, at Westview Press for the first edition; and to the reviewers of a very rough first draft—the late Stephanie Larson of Dickinson College, Roderick Kiewiet of California Institute of Technology, and F. Chris Garcia of the University of New Mexico. Each offered helpful comments, some of which we heeded. Ted Lowi also read the rough draft and gets a special nod for pushing us to put more politics in the book. This book is better for their efforts, and none of them is responsible for any errors that remain. We blame those errors, as has become the convention in our discipline, on Paul Sabatier.

The second edition benefited from the encouragement and suggestions of many individuals in addition to those who helped us in the beginning. We cannot remember everyone who provided helpful suggestions, but some people cannot be forgotten. Working with series editor Sandy Maisel and our Westview editor Leo Wiegman was a joy. Hanes Walton Jr., University of Michigan (who left us far too soon in 2013); Todd Shaw, University of Illinois; and Rick Matland, University of Houston, provided us with detailed insights of their experiences in using the first edition and numerous suggestions for what we should change or not change for the edition. We actually paid attention to some of those suggestions! Several graduate and undergraduate students at the University of Virginia—Stacy Nyikos, J. Alan Kendrick, and Andra Gillespie—tracked down items that helped us update the earlier edition. Stacy, Alan, and Andra are heartened to know that there is life after working with us. Their predecessor, Steve Tauber, now an associate professor of political science at the University of South Florida, would like us to note that it took three people to replace him. Amy Fromer of the Institute for Public Policy at the University of New Mexico produced the maps of the United States, and David Deis of the Department of Geography, California State University–Northridge produced the Los Angeles map found in Chapter 2.

We were gratified to be able to produce the third edition. We noticed an increasing interest in race, ethnicity, and politics as the demographics of the United States continue to change. The importance of the politics of the groups examined in the book cannot be understated. Several graduate students at Duke University—Shayla Nunnally, Monique Lyles, and Jen Merrolla—found much of the information used to update the edition. We thank them for all of their help. We would also like to thank those individuals who reviewed the second edition and offered us valuable suggestions for the third edition; their names remain anonymous to us. Our thanks as well go to David Deis of Dreamline Cartography for producing all of the maps in that edition.

In the publication of the fourth edition, we continued to be buoyed by the tremendous increasing interest in race, ethnicity, and politics. Several graduate students at Duke University—Efren O. Perez, Michael C. Brady, and Niambi M. Carter—found the data and updated most of the tables in this new edition. We owe Mike Brady a tremendous thank you for finding the picture that appeared on the cover of that edition. He included in it pictures of multiracial groups and its sense of irony, authority, and power jumped out at us. We also must thank our editor, Steve Catalano, and our marketing manager, Michelle Mallin, of Westview Press for their continued support and belief in this book. They are our champions and we are truly appreciative.

When we put the fifth edition to rest, we were only weeks away from the inauguration of former senator Barack Obama as the forty-fourth president of the United States. We were still elated that we had seen the election of the first black president of the United States, and still a little stunned that this occurred so quickly between the fourth edition and the fifth edition. As we examined the foundation of presidential politics laid by the late representative Shirley Chisholm in her groundbreaking run for president in 1972, we could not help but think that the slogan for President Obama should be, "Thank you, Mrs. Chisholm," because without her first steps, we are convinced that the path would not have been laid for President Obama. Several graduate students at Duke University—Candis S. Watts, Jessica Johnson Carew, and Eugene Walton Jr.—found the data and updated all of the tables in the new edition. David Deis of Dreamline Cartography produced the new maps with 2006 updated data from the census. We were pleased that the fifth edition's editor, Anthony

"Toby" Wahl, continued the high standard and quality of production set by our previous editor, Steve Catalano.

When we put the finishing touches on the sixth edition manuscript, President Obama had just taken the oath of office for a second term. His reelection continued his historic first victory as he became the first president since 1956 to achieve 51 percent of the vote twice. As in 2008, the mobilization and votes of racial and ethnic minorities were key to the president's 2012 victory. Duke University graduate students continued to be critical to the research needed to produce the sixth edition—Jessica Johnson Carew and Brittany Perry found the data and updated all of the tables and created several new ones for the edition. Paula's youngest daughter, Jessica A. McClain-Jacobson, found all of the pictures used in that edition. Her willingness to pitch in over her holiday break is much appreciated; she came through like a champ. David Deis of Dreamline Cartography once again produced all of the maps with 2010 census data. David has been with this book since the beginning, and we appreciate his sticking with us. We also want to thank our former editor, Anthony "Toby" Wahl, who saw the fifth edition and part of the sixth edition through the process. We miss him! But, we are in very capable hands with our new editor, Ada Fung, and our editorial assistant, Stephen Pinto, for working so closely with us and for believing in this book.

As the seventh edition goes into production, Donald J. Trump has been president for less than two weeks. What that might mean for racial and ethnic minorities, women of all colors, immigrants, Muslims, and other groups that are not part of Trump's coalition is unknown. But, we have some inklings of where these groups fit—or more precisely, do not fit. Protests against his presidency have been regularly occurring since Trump took office. Our hope is that the foundation upon which racial and ethnic minorities have been able to make their voices heard and gain access to the political system will provide the impetus to resist the policies that are surely coming down the pike.

The seventh edition benefitted, once again, from Paula's doctoral students in the Department of Political Science at Duke University—Nura Sediqe, Gloria Ayee, Taneisha Means, and Katelyn Mehling. Jessica also updated many of the tables before coming on as a coauthor. We thank them immensely and hope that their efforts benefitted their intellectual development. David Deis and his students Tom Chen and Amanda Lindgren of California State University–Northridge again created the maps in Chapter 2. We want to thank our editor, Ada Fung, for her commitment to the book and her thoughts and guidance on how to make changes and add material to the seventh edition that keeps it current and ahead of the curve. Finally, we would like to thank those who reviewed the sixth edition and provided us with invaluable feedback, including: Sharon Austin (University of Florida); Clarissa Peterson (DePauw University); Jason F. Kirksey (Oklahoma State University); Kira Sanbonmatsu (Rutgers University); Robert C. Oberst (Nebraska Wesleyan University); and others who wished to remain anonymous.

Perhaps most important, Joe and Paula thank Don Lutz, University of Houston, for giving us the bottle of wine that began this process for the first edition. Paula wants to thank her family—Paul C. Jacobson, Kristina L. McClain-Jacobson Ragland, and Jessica A. McClain-Jacobson Hester. Jessica was two-years old when the first edition came out, and she is now a young woman of twenty-seven. Kristina is now the mother of our grandsons—Jackson (age seven) and Sterling (age two). As in politics, much changes in one's life as well. Jessica also extends her thanks to her family—Khary S. Carew, Jonathan A. Carew (age nine), and Benjamin E. Carew (age three). Khary's support and encouragement has been existential throughout this process. Jonathan and Benjamin help to brighten the world and our home, and they provide a constant reminder of the importance of this work.

Finally, for Paula the book is dedicated to her mentor, Harold M. Rose, an urban geographer at the University of Wisconsin–Milwaukee, who passed in February 2016. They shared close to four decades of research collaboration on black urban homicide and other research projects. While they became intellectual partners, it was in 1977 that Rose befriended the new assistant professor; shared his ideas for a major collaborative project; mentored her in the ways of the academy; and taught her the importance of maintaining one's intellectual integrity, of paying attention to detail, and of being thoughtful and reflective in one's scholarship. Paula affectionately dedicates this book to him and misses him tremendously. There is not a day that passes that I do not see his influence on my career and my development as a scholar.

For Jessica, the book is dedicated to her parents, Elaine C. W. Johnson and Frank O. Johnson Jr. Her parents provided the guidance necessary to better understand history, the present, and the possibilities for the future, by sharing their own experiences and their families' courage in the face of racial segregation and oppression. They also imparted their strong beliefs in the equality of all and the importance of seeing people for who they are, without regard to race. Their unwaveringly high expectations and mantra that, given society's continuing racial beliefs, she would have to work "twice as hard to get half as far" were essential to Jessica's early academic success, and were the bedrock for her later scholarly pursuits in the world of academia. She is forever indebted to them for the love and support they have given and the unwavering example of integrity and meticulousness they provided, and she will continue to pay this forward to her own children and through her work.

Paula D. McClain
Durham, North Carolina

Jessica D. Johnson Carew
Elon, North Carolina

► **CHAPTER 1**

America's Dilemmas

After spending five years questioning whether President Barack Obama was born in the United States, Republican presidential nominee Donald Trump conceded in 2016 that President Obama was indeed born in the United States (Haberman and Rapperport 2016).

The "birther conspiracy" movement began early on, during the 2008 presidential election, when people began asking to see verification of President Obama's birth in the state of Hawaii. The idea channeled into more of a movement when Donald Trump began raising the issue again, beginning in March 2011 (Krieg 2016). The issue gained more traction as it was advanced by Trump as a means to question President Obama's legitimacy as president. For example, in August 2012, Trump took to Twitter to state that, "An extremely credible source has called my office and told me that Barack Obama's birth certificate is a fraud" (Trump 2014). The questioning of President Obama's place of birth is one of the most salient examples of how explicitly racist assumptions have been used as a means to delegitimize the standing of a high-ranking person in the United States.

—DONALD TRUMP'S BIRTHER CAMPAIGN 2011–2016

On April 29, 1992, rioting erupted in Los Angeles after the announcement that a predominantly white jury in a suburban municipality had acquitted police officers who had been videotaped beating black motorist Rodney King. These activities were widely reported as black reactions to an obvious injustice perpetrated by whites against blacks. Indeed, Americans are used to interpreting political and social relations in white-versus-black terms. The facts are more complex. The brunt of property crimes in Los Angeles due to the riots was borne by Korean retailers; the majority of those arrested during the civil disorders was Hispanic (Morrison and Lowry 1994). As the United States proceeds through the twenty-first century, the variety and identity of the actors are changing, but racial and ethnic conflict is an old story.

In his *Democracy in America,* published in 1835, Alexis de Tocqueville, an early French visitor to the republic, noted that the treatment and situation of blacks in the United States contradicted the American passion for democracy. He saw slavery and the denial of constitutional rights and protection to blacks as the principal threats to the US democratic system: "If there ever are great revolutions there [in America], they will be caused by the presence of the blacks upon American soil. . . . It will not be the equality of social conditions but rather their inequality which may give rise thereto" (de Tocqueville 1835 [original], Mayer and Lerner 1966:614). This same disparate treatment was noted more than a century later by sociologist Gunnar Myrdal, who published the first comprehensive scholarly examination of the oppression of blacks in the United States, *An American Dilemma* (1944). Myrdal argues that the contradiction within American society between an allegedly strong commitment to democratic values on the one hand and the presence of racial oppression on the other creates a moral dilemma for white Americans and is the root of the US race relations problems.

Although many doubt that Myrdal's argument is correct—that is, that most white Americans are terribly cross-pressured by the presence of both democratic ideals and racial discrimination—the use of the term *dilemma* is invaluable in an examination of racial minority group politics in the United States. This book focuses on two dilemmas. The first dilemma harkens back to the founding of America, is the subject of de Tocqueville's concern, and continues to resonate today: *How does a governmental system that professes in its Constitution and its rhetoric to be democratic and egalitarian handle the obvious reality of its systematic denial of basic rights and privileges to its own citizens based on color? When forced to confront and correct the inequalities, how does it provide for and protect the rights of identifiable racial and ethnic minority groups?* The questions this reality-versus-rhetoric dilemma engenders are amazingly similar over time: How shall blacks be counted when apportioning congressional seats (1787)? Is it impermissible to draw "funny-shaped" congressional districts in an attempt to enhance minority group representation (2001)?

The second dilemma is less often articulated, perhaps because it exists within the perspective of the minority groups: *What strategy—coalition or conflict—should be used by minority groups in dealing with other minority groups and with the majority group?* In essence, this dilemma poses the "what do we do about it?" question, given the political realities of the first dilemma. In many, if not most, considerations of this second dilemma, members of minority groups are treated as passive subjects in a majoritarian system and as natural allies against members of the majority. The present volume challenges this perspective and considers a broader range of strategic choices that are available to members of racial and ethnic minority groups as actors within the polity.

In focusing on these dilemmas, this book addresses the importance of race and ethnicity in American politics—the decisions about who gets what, when, where, and how—in general and in the politics (historical, legal, attitudinal, and behavioral) of the four principal racial minority groups in the United States: blacks (African Americans), Latinos, Asians, and Indian peoples in particular. These groups are the focus because unlike other ethnic minorities—for example, the Irish, Italians, and Jews—who have also suffered from social discrimination, blacks, Latinos, Asians, and American Indians have lived in the United States *under separate systems of law* for varying periods of time. Because each has a history of differential legal status and because this history has led to special attention in contemporary law in an attempt to remedy the effects of historical discrimination, these groups require special attention in political analysis.

There is a tendency in political science literature to assume that all racial minority groups within the United States share similar experiences and political behaviors. Consequently, blacks, Latinos, Asian Americans, and American Indians are often merged under the rubric "minority group politics." But the increasing recognition of differences among and within these groups has generated debate over whether the concept of minority group politics is useful in thinking about and studying the political experiences of all nonwhite groups in the United States. Although these groups share racial minority group status within the United States, there are fundamental differences in their experiences, orientations, and political behaviors that affect the relationships among the four groups as well as between each of the groups and the dominant white majority. Similarities in racial minority group status may be the bases for building coalitions, but they may also generate conflict. Consequently, this book focuses on the groups separately at times and comparatively at other times.

TERMS USED IN THIS BOOK

Before proceeding, it is important to define the terms used throughout the book. The way individuals identify themselves and how they are identified by others in the polity is of more than semantic interest. Self-identification, often referred to as **group political consciousness**, and other-identification can promote or thwart nation building and can affect, as we shall see later, people's ability and willingness to participate in the political system.

First, the terms *black* and *African American* are used interchangeably. Recent research suggests that among Americans of African descent, there is a 1.1 percent difference in those who prefer to be called black (48.1 percent) and those who prefer to be called African American (49.2 percent) (Sigelman, Tuch, and Martin 2005). We prefer the term *black* for theoretical reasons, however. It concisely describes an identity and a status within American society that are based on color. The black experience in America differs markedly from that of the white ethnics, and the use of *African American* may convey the impression that blacks are just another ethnic group similar to Italian Americans, Irish Americans, or Polish Americans. Blacks have been subjugated and segregated, on the basis of color, from *all* whites regardless of their ethnic backgrounds. Further, after one generation, white ethnics have been able to shed their ethnicity and blend into the mainstream of white America, but blacks, because of their skin color, remain identifiable generation after generation. We also use *black* because it is a convenient proxy term for an insular group that is more or less politically cohesive, that has historically been stigmatized, that is generally depressed economically, and that remains socially isolated.

Similarly, we use *Latino* and *Hispanic* interchangeably as umbrella terms when we cannot distinguish among subgroups of the nation's Spanish-origin population. The largest of the Latino groups are Mexican Americans, Puerto Ricans, and Cuban Americans. The term *Hispanic* is eschewed by many intellectuals because it is Eurocentric—the term literally means "lover of Spain"— which, given the national origins of the overwhelming majority of US Latinos, is inappropriate. Moreover, *Hispanic* is a term devised by the US Census Bureau for classifying individuals and is devoid of any theoretical or political context.

Pew Hispanic Center data from 2012 suggest that Latinos do not primarily identify themselves as members of a Hispanic or Latino community. Although *Latino* is the preferred identifier among the intelligentsia, few Mexican Americans, Puerto Ricans, Cuban Americans, or other Latinos self-identify themselves with either pan-ethnic term. Most prefer their family's country of origin term, such as *Mexican* or *Mexican American* among Mexican Americans, *Puerto Rican* among Puerto Ricans, and *Cuban* among Cubans and so forth (Taylor, Lopez, Martinez, and Velasco 2012).

Third, we use the term *Indian peoples* or *American Indian peoples* rather than *Native Americans*. The reasons for this choice are simple yet profoundly important. The term *Native American* was used during the nativist (anti-immigration, antiforeigner) movement (1860–1925) and the antiblack, anti-Catholic, and anti-Jewish Ku Klux Klan resurgence during the early 1900s (Higham 1963). The rhetoric of these groups was couched in terms of "native-born" white Protestants vis-à-vis those of "foreign" origin, for example, Catholics. There was even a political party known as the Native American Party. Thus, whereas popular culture may refer to Indian peoples as Native Americans, we feel it is important to separate this group from the white supremacist terms used by the nativist movement. Moreover, we seek to defuse the specious argument made by some that if one is born in the United States, one is a native American, thereby dismissing the unique situation and status of American Indian peoples. Indian peoples encompass a variety of tribes, each with its own history and different structural relationships with the US government. Finally, many Native Hawaiians consider themselves Native Americans. Although not grouping Native Hawaiians with American Indians in the 2000 census, the US Census Bureau, after years of grouping Native Hawaiians with Asians, put them in a new category with Pacific Islanders. Our terms separate American Indians from Native Hawaiians.

The question of who is an Indian is central to any discussion of American Indian politics. The essence of the "Indianness" issue rests not with Indian peoples themselves but with the federal government. One of the inherent powers of Indian tribes as sovereign nations is the power to decide who belongs, and historically tribes have focused on allegiance as the deciding factor. Over time, the federal government has increasingly tried to answer the question of who is or is not covered by legislation. As a result, more than thirty different definitions of who is legally an Indian have been produced depending on "blood quantum," federal tribal recognition, residence, descent, self-identification, and miscellaneous other factors. Moreover, the question of who is subject to Indian law also depends on the relationship of the tribe to the federal government and on whether the federal government recognizes the tribe. Federal recognition occurs in a variety of ways: congressional action, presidential executive order, administrative ruling by the Bureau of Indian Affairs (BIA), or judicial opinion. In addition to federally recognized Indians, there are more than one hundred groups who used to be recognized as Indians but have had their status "terminated" by the federal government and more than fifty tribes who are recognized by state, but not federal, governments (Wilkins 2002:13–27).

Finally, the term *Asian American* envelops a multiplicity of ethnic origin groups—Japanese, Koreans, Chinese, Filipinos, Southeast Asians, and East Indians (Kitano 1981). Each of these groups has a different history of entrance into the United States, but "Asian Americans have been here for over one hundred and fifty years, before many European immigrant groups" (Takaki 1993:7). The Chinese arrived first in significant numbers, followed by the Japanese, Koreans, Filipinos, Asian Indians, and, later, Southeast Asian refugees. We find no local, contemporary survey data that address ethnic identity for

Asian Americans, but the historical record suggests a situation even less unified than that of Hispanics. National rivalries often survived the immigration process, so that, for example, early Japanese immigrants were as anti-Chinese as any of their non-Asian counterparts (Ichioka 1988). Furthermore, unlike Latinos, first-generation immigrant Asians have not shared a common language, a situation that provides a formidable barrier to any pan-Asian identification (Espiritu 1992).

RACE AND ETHNICITY

Although this is not a book about **racism**—the belief in and practice of using race as a justification for discrimination among individuals—per se, each of the groups considered has been affected by racism, albeit differently. Some of this racism is on an individual level, in which individuals discriminate against other individuals because of their membership, real or perceived, in a racial group. More problematically, some of the racism is institutionalized, which is more complex, less obvious, more routinized, and more difficult to eradicate than discrimination based on individual racism. Individual racism is usually more conscious, and perhaps more blatant, whereas discrimination based on institutional racism is more likely to be subtle, unconscious, and rationalized on the basis of nonracial criteria (Feagin and Feagin 1978). Furthermore, social class and gender differences are variables that both compound the effects of racism and affect the way group members can and do respond to the situations in which they find themselves. When information is available to allow us to take these factors into account, we shall do so. But over and above class and gender, race has been and continues to be a central theme of the American polity and society.

Race—initially construed in terms of white, black, and Indian—has never been a benign concept in the United States. We should remember that the first Africans to arrive at Jamestown, Virginia, in 1619 were indentured servants, not slaves. Slavery was not instituted on a broad scale until 1661 in Virginia (twenty years after slavery had first been incorporated into colonial law in Massachusetts) as the need for labor increased and whites found Indian servitude and slavery inadequate and the supply of white indentured servants insufficient. The permanent enslavement of Africans and African Americans was the answer to a "vexing" labor problem. The supply of blacks appeared to be endless, and "if they ran away they were easily detected because of their color. If they proved ungovernable they could be chastised with less qualms and with greater severity than in the case of whites, because Negroes represented heathen people who could not claim the immunities accorded by Christians" (Franklin 1969:72).

With the institution of slavery and the mass importation of black slaves, whites—although solving their labor problems—began to fear the mixture of races and to be concerned that growing numbers of blacks would rebel against the institution of slavery. These fears and the whites' disdain and contempt for blacks created a dynamic of white oppression of blacks that manifested itself in a multiplicity of ways. Many states, concerned about the purity of the white group, codified into law the degree of black ancestry that qualified one to be legally defined as black and thus subject to legal restrictions. Louisiana and North Carolina used the one-sixteenth criterion (one great-great-grandparent); one-eighth (one great-grandparent) was the standard in Florida, Indiana, Maryland, Mississippi, Missouri, Nebraska, North Dakota, South Carolina, and Tennessee; Oregon used a one-quarter standard (one grandparent) (Spickard 1989:374–75).

This obsession with "black blood" was also codified into legal restrictions on marriage partners, which were referred to as **antimiscegenation laws**. Throughout most of their history, twenty-nine states maintained laws forbidding interracial marriage between blacks and whites. Over time, many of these laws were amended to include a prohibition on marriages between other racial combinations in addition to blacks and whites. The fourteen states with additional prohibitions included California, between white and Mongolian; Georgia, between white and American Indian, Asiatic Indian, or Mongolian; Nebraska, between white and Chinese or Japanese; and Arizona, between white and Mongolian or Indian. The penalties for interracial marriages ranged from maximum imprisonment of more than two years in fourteen states to no penalty in California. These antimiscegenation laws were not nullified until the US Supreme Court decision *Loving v. Virginia* in 1967 (Spickard 1989:374–75). Clearly, the black-white dynamic is the most ingrained in the American political system and is the relationship that has formed much of our thinking about race in the United States. Although the importance of the black-white dynamic cannot be diminished, issues of race and the complexity of the racial dynamic extend beyond black and white today.

We are also concerned with issues of ethnicity—in a specific sense of the term. We use the term **ethnicity**—generally meaning the grouping of people on the basis of learned characteristics, often associated with national origin—because we recognize that within the four groups addressed in this book there are different ethnic origin groups that may have different political attitudes and behaviors. Issues of ethnicity are particularly pertinent within the Latino, Asian, and Indian groups. The US Census Bureau used five racial categories for the 2010 Census—white, black or African American, Asian, American

Indian or Alaska Native, and Native Hawaiian or Other Pacific Islander. Those who do not feel that they fall within the five racial categories could check a sixth category—"Some other race." The 2010 Census also allowed people to check more than one race, which resulted in the addition of fifty-seven additional racial categories, for a total of sixty-three. Hispanic, however, was used as an ethnic, rather than a racial, category. Although many Hispanics view themselves as a separate nonwhite race, they are forced to classify themselves as one of the five races listed above. This practice has caused consternation among several of the groups, particularly Mexicans, who are a mixture of Indian, African, and European—principally Spanish—races. In the 2010 Census, 36.7 percent of Hispanics checked the "some other race" category, while 53 percent identified as white. The confusion on the part of Latinos about checking one of the racial categories has led the US Census Bureau to consider adding Latino or Hispanic as a racial category on the 2020 census. As of this writing, a decision has not yet been made, and there have been mixed reactions to this proposed change, as the racial differences within the larger Latino population might be lost with the addition of a single Latino racial category. Until Hispanic is deemed to be a racial category, we will continue to use ethnicity in conjunction with racial minorities in recognition of the idiosyncratic situation of Latinos vis-à-vis the US Census Bureau.

Such formal identification may define who is included in and who is excluded from the political system. In official terms, the issues are citizenship and voting rights. We now consider the key values in the foundation of the US Constitution, including citizenship and suffrage, and their application to the nation's original minorities—blacks and American Indians.

AMERICAN GOVERNMENT FOUNDATION AND RACIAL MINORITIES

April 13, 1993, marked the 250th anniversary of the birth of Thomas Jefferson, the third president of the United States and author of the Declaration of Independence. Despite all of the celebrations around the world, the contradictions and inconsistencies between Thomas Jefferson the man and Thomas Jefferson the statesperson were not lost. The man who wrote in the Declaration of Independence that "all men are created equal and are endowed by their Creator with certain inalienable rights . . . and among these are life, liberty, and the pursuit of happiness" was also a slave owner. The tension that existed between the venerated values of the American political foundation—democracy, freedom, and equality—and the enslavement of a sizable segment of its population was not limited to Thomas Jefferson. It is an ever-present tension and a continuing struggle for the citizens of the United States and the values contained in the organizing document, the Constitution, which is the nation's foundation.

The political values contained in the Declaration of Independence in 1776 and spelled out later in the US Constitution, drafted in 1787 and ratified in 1789, have their origins in classical liberal theory. **Classical liberalism** refers to a particular body of Western European political thought that sought to justify the liberation of the individual from feudal positions and to deride those who benefited from feudalism. In classical liberal theory, private interests are given priority over public or governmental authority, and the economy receives priority over the polity. Liberalism finds expression in the writings of John Locke and others, writings with which Thomas Jefferson was very familiar. The free individual in Locke's liberalism was free from the confines of the state—free to seek private ends. States and governments were coercive; despite declarations that they should be representative, their main purpose was to control and to regulate the conduct of individuals. To paraphrase Locke, if individuals are to be free, mechanisms must be developed to limit government's powers and to ensure that those limits will be preserved. Classical liberal thought runs throughout the *Federalist Papers,* the essays written to justify the ratification of the Constitution. Government's responsibility to protect private property and to provide an environment in which the pursuit of private property can be facilitated is a fundamental principle of the papers.

Given the emphasis on property in classical liberal theory in general, and in the *Federalist Papers* in particular, it is not surprising that the 1787 Constitution was explicitly intended not to apply to blacks and Indians. Article I, Section 2, of the original Constitution states: "Representatives and direct Taxes shall be apportioned among the several States which may be included within this Union, according to their respective Numbers, *which shall be determined by adding to the whole Number of free Persons, including those bound to Service for a Term of Years, and excluding Indians not taxed, three-fifths of all other Persons*" (emphasis added). "Other Persons" refers to the 92 percent of the black population held in slavery in the United States in 1790, the year the government began the census; the remaining 59,557 blacks were free individuals (Pohlman 1991:34; Jarvis 1992:21). In fact, there was no ambiguity regarding the founders' views on slavery or their position regarding the legal status of blacks within the United States.

Jefferson's original draft of the Declaration of Independence included an indictment of King George III for "violating the most sacred rights of life and liberty in the persons of a distant people who never offended him, captivating and carrying them into slavery in another hemisphere or to incur miserable death in their transportation hither" (quoted in Jarvis 1992:20). However, this

indictment of slavery was unacceptable to both Southern and Northern delegates because the Southerners argued that slavery was fundamental to the economy of the new nation, and the Northerners viewed slavery as a business that
needed to be regulated.

The issue of slavery and the ensuing debate influenced the final compromise contained in Article I, Section 2, of the Constitution quoted earlier. The
framers were cognizant of the fact that slavery would affect the "issues of
representation, apportionment among the states, direct taxation, and commerce" (Jarvis 1992:20). *Compromise* was the watchword of the individuals
who drafted the Constitution, and several important compromises were
struck over the issues of slavery and suffrage requirements. Whereas Article I,
Section 9, mandated a twenty-year time period before Congress could limit
the importation of African slaves, Article IV, Section 2, maintained that es-
caped slaves would not be freed from slavery but should be returned to their
owners (the fugitive slave clause). The **three-fifths compromise**, in which
the delegates decided to count a slave as only three-fifths of a person, resolved
the issue of how to count slaves for representational and direct taxation
purposes.

Although blacks were counted for representational and taxation purposes,
they were not considered citizens of the United States: "Slaves were persons,
but they were also property, which meant that a Negro's right to liberty conflicted with his master's right to property. In the colonial ideology, the right of
property was central" (Robinson 1971:86). The compromise was momentous
because it gave Constitutional sanction to the fact that the United States was
composed of some persons who were "free" and others who were not. And it
established the principle, new in republican theory, that a man who lived
among slaves had a greater share in the election of representatives than the man
who did not. With one stroke, despite the disclaimers of its advocates, it acknowledged slavery and rewarded slave owners. It is a measure of their adjustment to slavery that Americans in the eighteenth century found this settlement
natural and just (Robinson 1971:201).

This twisted logic satisfied the issue of apportionment but failed miserably
in settling the right of blacks, particularly those who were not enslaved, to vote
(Jarvis 1992:21).

THE CONSTITUTION AND BLACK AND INDIAN CITIZENSHIP

After ratification of the Constitution, two important issues remained to be
addressed—suffrage and citizenship. Issues of **suffrage**—voting eligibility—
were left to the states because reconciling differences in voting qualifications at
the national level was thought to be too difficult. Moreover, and critically

important, the criteria for **citizenship**—determining who was and was not a citizen of the United States or of a state—were also left to the states. The fact that these two important issues were left up to the states set the stage for the systematic exclusion from the political process of blacks, Indian peoples, women of all colors, and other racial minority groups.

Prior to the Declaration of Independence, the Continental Congress defined the colonies' citizens as "all persons abiding within any of the United Colonies and deriving protection from the laws of the same owe allegiance to the said laws, and are members of such colony" (Franklin 1906:2). Several events surrounding the institution of the Declaration of Independence and the Articles of Confederation indicate that initially "the right to citizenship was to be opened to all white people who were willing to identify with the struggle against the King" (Robinson 1971:135). Among the complaints against King George III contained in the Declaration was that "He has excited domestic Insurrections amongst us, and has endeavoured to bring on the Inhabitants of our Frontiers, the merciless Indian Savages, whose Known Rule of Warfare, is an undistinguished Destruction, of all Ages, Sexes, and Conditions." After the advent of the Articles of Confederation, the committee—consisting of Benjamin Franklin, John Adams, and Thomas Jefferson—that had been appointed to devise a new national seal proposed that the seal be representative of the countries from which the peoples of the new nation had originated: England, Scotland, Ireland, France, Germany, and Holland. "Apparently neither the Africans nor the Indians were thought, even by this cosmopolitan committee, worthy of representation" (Robinson 1971:135).

Another event that lends credence to the contention that citizenship was reserved for whites was the manner in which a committee of Congress under the Articles of Confederation, of which Thomas Jefferson was also a member, wrestled with the issue of Indian inclusiveness in the new country. The initial committee report advised Congress to urge the states to make it easy for Indians to become citizens. After all, the colonists had enjoyed generally friendly relations with the American Indian nations with which they had come into contact. Most Indians traded with, protected, and supported European settlers until conflict erupted over control of land. The support of the Iroquois Confederacy, a government that at the time was more than seven hundred years old, in the French and Indian War had been crucial to the English victory. Likewise, two of the six tribes—including the most powerful, the Oneidas—had sided with the colonists against Great Britain in the Revolutionary War.

This report, however, was tabled. A subsequent report by a different committee "referred to the Indians, not as potential citizens, but as possible allies"

(Robinson 1971:136). These events, combined with others, led to the conclusion "that the 'one people,' to whom Jefferson referred in the opening paragraph of the Declaration of Independence, were the white people of the thirteen colonies" (Robinson 1971:136). In addition, the Articles of Confederation, when discussing privileges and immunities, continually referred to "free inhabitants" and "free citizens" (Franklin 1906:1–18).

Although the US Constitution, which replaced the Articles of Confederation, used the word *citizen* in several places, it did not confront citizenship directly; it assumed it. The assumption was that if individuals met the conditions of citizenship developed by the states, they were entitled to the rights and privileges extended in the Constitution. For example, Article I, Section 2, when discussing voting qualifications for election of members to the House of Representatives, states that if an individual meets the voting requirements in the state in which he resides, he is eligible to vote for members of the House of Representatives. Article IV, Section 2, states that "the Citizens of each State shall be entitled to all Privileges and Immunities of Citizens in the several States." The result was that each state was free to determine citizenship as well as voting requirements.

Following the ratification of the Constitution, Congress passed the Naturalization Act of 1790 in response to the Constitution's granting congressional power to pass a uniform rule to deal with the process by which foreigners could be "admitted to the rights of citizens" (Franklin 1906:33). This act granted citizenship as a matter of right to free white aliens who had lived in the United States and had shown good behavior for two years, who expressed the intention of remaining in the United States, and who took an oath of allegiance. Between 1790 and 1854, Congress passed fifteen laws concerning **naturalization** and retained the phrase "free white person" in all of these laws without discussion: "The reason for the adoption of the phrase 'free white person' was manifestly the conviction that Indians and slaves, since they did not understand our life and political system, were not freemen and, therefore, were not fitted to be members of the body politic, nor to exercise the duties and responsibilities of citizenship" (Gulick 1918:55–56). Only after the Civil War, in the Naturalization Act of 1870, were naturalization laws "extended to aliens of African nativity and to persons of African descent" (Gulick 1918:56).

Although it could be argued that the Constitution, as it was framed, only excluded enslaved blacks from being citizens, the citizenship status of free blacks was debatable. Whatever doubt existed about the citizenship status of blacks under the Constitution was clarified with the Supreme Court decision in *Dred Scott v. Sanford* (1857). Writing for the majority in its attempt to settle the most explosive political issue of the time, Chief Justice Roger Taney said the question was

> whether the provisions of the Constitution, in relation to the personal rights and privileges to which the citizen of a State should be entitled, embraced the negro African race, at that time in this country, or who might afterwards be imported, who had then or should afterwards be made free in any State; and to put it in the power of a single State to make him a citizen of the United States and endue him with the full rights of citizenship in every other State without their consent? Does the Constitution of the United States act upon him whenever he shall be made free under the laws of a State, and raised there to the rank of a citizen, and immediately clothe him with all the privileges of a citizen in every other State, and in its own courts? . . . It becomes necessary, therefore, to determine who were citizens of the several States when the Constitution was adopted. (*Dred Scott v. Sanford* 1857:406–7)

Taney argues that on the surface the words of the Declaration of Independence that state "that all men are created equal" and "are endowed by their Creator with certain unalienable rights" would appear to apply to blacks. Yet, he concludes, "it is too clear for dispute, that the enslaved African race were not intended to be included, and formed no part of the people who framed and adopted this declaration" (*Dred Scott v. Sanford* 1857:393, 410) and that this exclusion extended to the Constitution when ratified. Taney argues that two clauses in the Constitution, the right of the states to ban the importation of slaves after twenty years and the return of fugitive slaves (property) to their owners, provide evidence that the framers of the Constitution excluded blacks as "people" or citizens of the states in which they resided and thus as citizens of the United States. The Supreme Court thus declared that Dred Scott was not a citizen of the state of Missouri "in the sense in which that word is used in the Constitution" and that blacks, whether free or enslaved, "had no rights that the white man was bound to respect" (*Dred Scott v. Sanford* 1857:454, 407).

The issue of defining national citizenship and citizenship for blacks was not confronted directly until the ratification of the Fourteenth Amendment to the Constitution in 1868. Section 1 of that amendment says, in part, that "all persons born or naturalized in the United States, and subject to the jurisdiction thereof, are citizens of the United States and of the State wherein they reside." Thus, the issue of the citizenship status of African Americans was resolved, and national citizenship was added to the Constitution. Yet the rights, privileges, and immunities granted to blacks by this amendment were illusionary, as is discussed later. (The ratification of the Fourteenth Amendment to the Constitution also modified the three-fifths provision in Article I, Section 2. The Fourteenth Amendment implied that blacks would be counted equally with whites for purposes of representation.)

Although the Fourteenth Amendment established the citizenship status of blacks, American Indian peoples were still not considered citizens. In *Cherokee Nation v. State of Georgia,* the Supreme Court had ruled that Indian tribes "are in a state of pupilage [a minor child under the care of a guardian], and the relationship between the Indian tribes and the United States government [is] likened to that of 'a ward to his guardian'" (1831:16). Based on this wardship status, Indian peoples were considered to be "domestic subjects" and were not entitled to be thought of as citizens. Thus, they could be denied civil, political, and economic rights because "the framers of our constitution had not the Indian tribes in view, when they opened the Courts of the union to controversies between a state or the citizens thereof" (*Cherokee Nation v. Georgia* 1831:16). In fact, the Supreme Court in *Elk v. Wilkins* (1884) refused to extend the right of citizenship conferred in the Fourteenth Amendment to Indian peoples. The decision said, in part:

> Indians born within the territorial limits of the United States, members of, and owing immediate allegiance to, one of the Indian tribes (an alien, though dependent, power), although in a geographical sense born in the United States, are no more "born in the United States and subject to the jurisdiction thereof," within the meaning of the first section of the Fourteenth Amendment, than the children of subjects of any foreign government born within the domain of that government or the children born within the United States, of ambassadors or other public ministers of foreign nations. (*Elk v. Wilkins* 1884:102)

The court ended its decision by stating:

> The plaintiff, not being a citizen of the United States under the Fourteenth Amendment of the Constitution, has been deprived of no right secured by the Fifteenth Amendment and cannot maintain this action. (*Elk v. Wilkins* 1884:109)

Thus, Indian peoples were left in a status much like that of slaves prior to the Civil War—they were neither aliens nor citizens.

Citizenship came to Indians only in piecemeal fashion. In response to a Supreme Court ruling that Indian peoples who left their tribes voluntarily were not US citizens, Congress passed the Dawes Act in 1887, which granted citizenship to those who received individual allotments of tribal land (a new procedure meant to destroy the tribes and make Indians private property owners) and to those who voluntarily left their tribe. Tribal Indian peoples remained noncitizens.

In 1901, Congress formally granted US citizenship to the "five civilized tribes," originally of the Southeast—Cherokee, Chickasaw, Choctaw, Creek, and Seminole—who had been displaced to "Indian territory," centered in Oklahoma.[1] In 1919, citizenship was granted to American Indians who had served in the US armed forces in World War I. It was not until the Indian Citizenship Act of 1924, however, that citizenship was conferred on all American Indian peoples.

CITIZENSHIP AND LATER MINORITIES: LATINOS AND ASIANS

Although citizenship denial was the most egregious in the cases of blacks and Indian peoples, an exclusion purposely crafted in the Constitution and upheld by the Supreme Court, other racial groups faced similar situations as they entered the United States. Citizenship for the various Latino groups—Mexicans, Puerto Ricans, and Cubans—came at different times and in different ways. In 1836, Anglos and dissident Mexicans in Texas revolted and seceded from Mexico, creating the Republic of Texas. Hostilities between Texas and Mexico continued for nearly a decade until 1846, when the United States declared war on the Republic of Mexico. The Treaty of Guadalupe Hidalgo in 1848 officially ended the war, and Mexico ceded what are now the states of Arizona, New Mexico, California, Colorado, Texas, Nevada, Utah, Kansas, Oklahoma, and Wyoming to the United States. Mexican citizens living in the territories that were ceded who chose to stay on the land and live under US rule had one month from the date the treaty took effect to state their preference either for retaining Mexican citizenship and living under US rule or for becoming US citizens.

The treaty supposedly provided Mexicans who decided to become US citizens all the rights, protections, and guarantees of citizenship, but the reality was quite different. Problems with the citizenship status of Mexicans arose as early as 1849, when California, in trying to deal with blacks and Indians who were citizens of Mexico prior to the treaty and entitled to US citizenship under the provisions of the treaty, decided that Mexicans were not citizens of the United States and that further action from Congress was necessary to confer citizenship (Griswold del Castillo 1990). The property rights of Mexicans also were unprotected. Boards were set up to determine the validity of Mexican land claims, routinely resulting in Mexicans losing their land to the Anglo newcomers. (The unfulfilled promises of the Treaty of Guadalupe Hidalgo were central to the Chicano movement, discussed in Chapter 2.)

Spain granted autonomy to the island of Puerto Rico in 1897, but when the Spanish-American War began in 1898, US troops landed on the island. With the ratification of the Treaty of Paris in 1899, which ended the Spanish-American War, the United States annexed Puerto Rico. The 1900 Foraker Act made Puerto Rico an unincorporated US territory with a presidentially appointed governor. Puerto Rico remained an American colony until 1952, when it became a commonwealth of the United States. Immediately after the US acquisition, Puerto Ricans were in a political netherworld; they were not citizens of the United States nor of Spain nor of an independent nation. However, with the passage of the Jones Act in 1917, Puerto Ricans became citizens of the United States, although citizenship was conferred over the objections of the island's legislature (Hero 1992). Puerto Ricans residing on the island are subject to the military draft, when there is one, but do not pay US income taxes and do not participate fully in federal social service programs (Moore and Pachon 1985). But Puerto Ricans who live on the mainland are not distinguished from other US citizens for taxation and government assistance purposes.

US involvement with Cuba can be traced to the Monroe Doctrine of 1823. In 1895, with the help of the United States, Cuba launched a war of independence against Spain. Intense US involvement, as with its involvement with Puerto Rico, stems from the time of the Spanish-American War, after which Cuba achieved its independence from Spain although it was still under US military rule. In 1901, Congress passed the Platt Amendment, granting Cuba conditional independence, with the United States reserving the right to intervene—militarily and otherwise—on "Cuba's behalf."

Although many think Cuban Americans first came to the United States after 1959, the 1870 US Census indicates that just over five thousand persons living in the United States had been born in Cuba (Boswell and Curtis 1983:39). In the 1860s and 1870s, several Cuban cigar manufacturers relocated their operations to the United States, settling principally in Key West, Tampa, and New York City. However, the majority of Cubans arrived in the United States after 1959. Census data indicate that in 1960 there were approximately 124,500 Cubans, just over one-third of whom were second- or third-generation Americans. Just a decade later the Cuban population had increased to more than 560,000 persons, slightly over 78 percent of whom had been born in Cuba.

Little is known about the naturalization of the early Cuban immigrants to Florida, but until the 1980s, 96 percent of the Cuban immigrants were considered to be white (Boswell and Curtis 1983:102). Thus, it is possible that they were also considered white under the naturalization acts and thus were eligible for citizenship. Cubans entering the United States after Castro's rise to power in 1959 generally enjoyed handsome financial support from the US government and were encouraged to seek US citizenship.

The citizenship status of Asian Americans—primarily the early Chinese and Japanese immigrants—although similar to that of Latinos, also has close parallels with the legal status of blacks and Indians under the various naturalization acts. Two events—the Treaty of Guadalupe Hidalgo (1848) and the California gold rush—precipitated Chinese immigration to the United States, which began in 1848. With the annexation of California under the treaty, a plan was sent to Congress for expansion of the railroad to the Pacific coast. The plan proposed that Chinese laborers should be imported to build the transcontinental railroad as well as to cultivate the land in California. At the same time, gold was discovered in California, thus generating the need for both Mexican and Chinese miners, who were seen as the best sources of cheap labor. Consequently, the 1850s saw a substantial increase in the number of Chinese immigrants to the United States, principally, but not exclusively, to California. By 1870 there were sixty-three thousand Chinese in the United States, 77 percent of whom lived in California (Takaki 1993:192–94).

At first the Chinese were welcomed because their labor was essential to the expansion into California and the development of the territory. But in 1850, the California legislature enacted, then quickly repealed, a foreign miners' tax designed to eliminate Mexican miners (Takaki 1993:194). In 1852, the legislature passed another foreign miners' tax, this one targeted at Chinese miners. This tax required that every foreign miner who did not wish to become a US citizen pay a monthly fee of three dollars. "Even if they had wanted to, the Chinese could not have become citizens, for they had been rendered ineligible for citizenship by a 1790 federal law that reserved naturalized citizenship for 'white' persons" (Takaki 1993:195). The exclusion barred most Chinese from citizenship, but the interpretation of who was "white" was left to administrative officials. Thus, a small number of Chinese were able to be naturalized. The first Chinese applied for citizenship in 1854, another was naturalized in New York in 1873, and thirteen applied for citizenship in California in 1876 (Gulick 1918:59).

But anti-Chinese and Chinese immigration antipathy and nativist sentiments were on the rise. President Rutherford B. Hayes warned Americans about the "Chinese problem," saying that "the present Chinese invasion . . . should be discouraged. Our experience in dealing with the weaker races—the Negroes and Indians . . . —is not encouraging. . . . I would consider with favor any suitable measures to discourage the Chinese from coming to our shores" (quoted in Takaki 1993:206). Acceding to anti-Chinese agitation and violence in the 1870s and 1880s, Congress passed the Chinese Exclusion Act in 1882, which reduced Chinese immigration to a trickle (Higham 1963:25; Takaki 1993:200). Additionally, part of the act mandated "that even those Chinese who might otherwise qualify should not be given citizenship privileges" (quoted in Gulick 1918:59). Section 14 of the Chinese Exclusion Act stated that "hereafter no State Court or Court of the United States shall admit Chinese to citizenship; and all laws in conflict with this act are hereby repealed" (quoted in Gulick 1918:59).

As a result of World War II and the participation of Chinese Americans in the war effort, in 1943 Congress repealed the Chinese exclusion laws and extended the right of naturalized citizenship to Chinese immigrants: "At last after almost one hundred years in America, Chinese immigrants could seek political membership in their adopted country" (Takaki 1993:387). Although Chinese immigrants were initially denied citizenship, their children who were born in the United States were considered US citizens. The Supreme Court decided this issue in *United States v. Wong Kim Ark* in 1898 when it ruled that a child of Chinese immigrants was entitled to US citizenship under the jus soli (by birth) clause of the Fourteenth Amendment. The Court found that the constitutional prescription of citizenship by birth superseded the Chinese Exclusion Act of 1882 (Ueda 1997).

The first known Japanese immigrants arrived in the United States in 1843, yet the need for labor on Hawaiian plantations in the mid-1860s precipitated the search for labor from Japan. (The United States officially acquired the Hawaiian Islands in 1898 as a territory.) The first Japanese contract workers arrived in Hawaii in 1868, and in 1885, the Japanese government officially allowed Japanese workers to migrate to Hawaii and to the US mainland. Between 1885 and 1924, "200,000 [Japanese] left for Hawaii and 180,000 for the United States mainland" (Takaki 1993:247).

On the mainland, Japanese were initially employed as migrant workers in agriculture, railroad construction, and canneries (Takaki 1993:267). Eventually, the Japanese—primarily those in California—became farmers with extensive land holdings, and their success and increasing presence engendered great animosity. In 1908 the US government pressured Japan to prohibit the emigration of Japanese laborers to the United States, and in 1913 the California legislature passed the California Land Act, which prohibited aliens—principally the Japanese—from owning and leasing land. Other states passed similar legislation. Drawing on the 1790 act, which limited naturalization to "white" persons, these restrictive alien land laws were based on the Japanese ineligibility to become naturalized US citizens: "In 1922, the United States Supreme Court affirmed that Takao Ozawa, a Japanese immigrant, was not entitled to naturalized citizenship because he 'clearly' was 'not Caucasian'" (Takaki 1993:273). Moreover, in 1924 Congress passed the Immigration Quota Act—which was aimed specifically at the Japanese but also covered other Asians—and which excluded all aliens who were ineligible for citizenship (those who were not "white," as stated in the 1790 and subsequent naturalization laws, or "African," as the naturalization laws were amended after the Civil War). Once again, however, although Japanese immigrants were denied citizenship, their children born in the United States were citizens. Only with the passage of the McCarran-Walter Act in 1952 were the racial restrictions contained in the 1790 Naturalization Act rescinded and Japanese immigrants allowed naturalization rights.

THE CONSTITUTION AND BLACK AND INDIAN SUFFRAGE

The Constitution left voting requirements to the individual states and did not specifically prohibit free blacks from exercising the franchise (Foner 1992:57). Moreover, the concepts of citizenship and voting were not linked in colonial and postrevolutionary America (Kleppner 1990). Because the thirteen original colonies were settled primarily by the British, it is not surprising that they adopted the British system of restricting the franchise to property owners. Voting qualifications varied from colony to colony and were based on criteria such as property ownership, status ("freeman"), race (white), gender (male), age, religion, and length of residence (Jarvis 1992:18). Although only Georgia and South Carolina adopted state constitutions that expressly limited voting to white males on the basis of race, voting restrictions based on race were soon instituted in other states as the number of black slaves increased following the introduction of slavery. At the time the Constitution was framed, "free black men could vote in some of the original states, including the southern one of North Carolina" (Davidson 1992:7).

As the black slave population increased in the South, white colonists became concerned about their ability to control slaves and prevent slave insurrections. Thus, numerous slave codes were introduced. As a result, free blacks in the South saw their political and social access restricted and eventually curtailed. Free blacks were forced to carry certificates of freedom or risk being captured and sold as slaves. In addition, "they could no longer vote (except in Tennessee until 1834 and North Carolina until 1835), hold public office, give testimony against whites, possess a firearm, buy liquor, assemble freely (except in a church supervised by whites), or immigrate to other states" (Jarvis 1992:19). Free blacks in the Northern regions fared better and lived under less restrictive conditions, but they were regarded as inferior and undesirable, and their employment opportunities were limited. In some instances, Northern jurisdictions prohibited their immigration to other regions through the threat of punishment or enslavement (Jarvis 1992:19). By the time of the Civil War, free blacks were denied suffrage everywhere in the United States except in New York and the New England states (except Connecticut).

Following the Civil War and in response to the Southern states' refusal to extend suffrage to blacks, numerous actions were taken by the Radical Republican–dominated Congress. For example, the Civil Rights Act of 1866 "anticipated the Fourteenth Amendment by making United States citizens of all native-born people except untaxed Native Americans, and guaranteeing to all citizens regardless of race or previous servitude the right to enforce contracts, file lawsuits, testify in court, own property, and enjoy all benefits of law to which white citizens were entitled" (Jarvis 1992:25). However, neither these laws nor the Fourteenth Amendment explicitly prohibited racial discrimination in the area of voting. This prohibition was not achieved until the ratification of the Fifteenth Amendment in 1870, which states, "the right of citizens of the United States to vote shall not be denied or abridged by the United States or by any State on account of race, color, or previous condition of servitude."

Although in theory the Fifteenth Amendment provided a constitutionally protected guarantee of black male suffrage, resistance—often violent—by white Southerners to black voting was evident. And although three Enforcement Acts (1870, 1871, and 1875) were passed in an attempt to put teeth into the amendment, white resistance was not overcome (Davidson 1992:10). Moreover, two Supreme Court decisions undercut the effectiveness of the Fourteenth and Fifteenth Amendments. In *United States v. Cruikshank* (1876), in a case involving white defendants who had killed approximately one hundred blacks in a mob attack, the Supreme Court ruled that because these individuals were private actors and were not acting on behalf of the state, the Fourteenth and Fifteenth Amendments did not apply to them. Although it did not find the Enforcement Act of 1870 unconstitutional, the court severely limited the act's application.

In the other decision, *United States v. Reese* (1876), in a case involving Kentucky election officials' refusal to accept the votes of a black person in a municipal election, the court ruled that Congress could protect against interference only in congressional elections and not in state elections. Thus, Sections 3 and 4 of the Enforcement Act of 1870 were ruled unconstitutional because they went beyond the Fifteenth Amendment's prohibition against the denial of suffrage. The end of a national commitment to protect the suffrage and other constitutional rights of blacks came with the compromise of 1877 in which Rutherford B. Hayes, to gain the support of the Southern states in the

PHOTO I.I *On June 15, 1920, three African American circus workers, Elias Clayton, Elmer Jackson, and Isaac McGhie, suspects in an assault case, were taken from jail, attacked, and lynched by a white mob of thousands in Duluth, Minnesota. The picture is from a postcard that was created of the event and sold for souvenirs. The assault and rape that the three were accused of was later determined never occurred.* (Courtesy of the Library of Congress, Prints & Photographs Division, Visual Materials from the NAACP Records LC-USZ62-35349.)

contested presidential election of 1876, agreed to remove federal troops and protection from the former states of the Old Confederacy and then leave the South free to deal with "the Negro problem" as the states saw fit.

After the removal of federal protection, the Southern states moved quickly to disenfranchise blacks. This disenfranchisement was achieved through a combination of structural discrimination (e.g., gerrymandering, annexations, at-large election systems, and appointive offices), violence, voting fraud, and eventually through disenfranchising conventions that rewrote state constitutions with clauses to prohibit blacks from voting or participating in politics. By the 1890s, blacks—primarily in the South but in some Northern jurisdictions as well—had been legally and very effectively removed from the electoral process (Kousser 1992).

Additionally, in 1896 the Supreme Court, in *Plessy v. Ferguson,* upheld Louisiana's practice of racial discrimination, essentially declaring that separation of the races was allowable under the US Constitution as long as the facilities were "equal." This reasoning became known as the **separate but equal doctrine.** The end of the nineteenth century and the beginning of the twentieth century constituted the nadir of black political history (Logan 1954).

Although American Indians were the first "Americans," they were the last large group to be granted voting rights and citizenship (Sigler 1975:156). The ruling in *Elk v. Wilkins* (1884) that Indians were not citizens of the United States under the Fourteenth Amendment kept "all Indians unable to prove that they were born under United States jurisdiction from registering to vote" (McCool 1985:106). Moreover, because Indians were not made citizens until the Indian Citizenship Act of 1924, the Fifteenth Amendment, which extended the right to vote to all male citizens regardless of race, did not apply to Indians until that time.

Even after the conferring of citizenship, many states—including Arizona, New Mexico, and Utah—through their state constitutions continued to deny Indians the right to vote. These states argued that because Indians were in a "guardianship" relationship with the federal government and were subject to federal rather than state jurisdiction, Indian reservations could not be considered part of the state in which they existed.

Therefore, Indians were not state citizens and were not eligible to vote in state and local elections. Beginning in 1927, federal as well as state courts began to reject this argument, but many states continued to find mechanisms to deny Indians the right to vote. The twin issues of state residency and federal guardianship were used in a long series of court cases in various states in attempts to keep Indians from voting. Indians in Arizona, through a series of court challenges, won the right to vote in 1948, and Indians in New Mexico won their case shortly thereafter.

Challenges continued. For example, in 1956 the Utah state attorney general issued an opinion based on an 1897 state law "that withheld residency from anyone who lived on an 'Indian or military reservation' unless that person had previously established residency in an off-reservation Utah county" (McCool 1985:109). In effect, this ruling denied Utah Indians the right to vote. The Utah Supreme Court upheld the attorney general's interpretation of the law, so the state legislature had to amend state statutes to allow Indians to vote. In another case in 1962, a defeated non-Indian candidate in New Mexico challenged the validity of Indian voting rights, claiming Indians were not residents of the state. In this instance, the Utah Supreme Court upheld the right of Indians to vote (McCool 1985:109).

STRUCTURE OF THIS BOOK

This chapter has articulated the dilemmas we address in this book. Furthermore, it shows that the roots of the first dilemma, the clear presence of racial inequality in a nation that promises equality, precede the founding of the current constitutional system. The remainder of the book elaborates on this dilemma and sets the stage for a consideration of the second dilemma, the choice between coalition or conflict as a strategy.

Chapter 2 provides a brief survey of some of the political resources and the status of each of the groups treated in this book. Several key variables—relative size and geographic concentration, socioeconomic status, degree of participation in a civil rights movement, and coverage by contemporary voting rights legislation—are highlighted to provide both comparable data and a context within which to discuss the contemporary political situations of racial and ethnic minorities, both as individual groups and comparatively. The chapter also discusses the importance of the Voting Rights Act of 1965 and its extensions for the ability of various racial and ethnic groups to gain elective office.

Chapter 3 explores the attitudes that members of racial and ethnic minority groups bring to the public policymaking process and the ways they choose to participate. The aspects of political participation we address are (1) perceptions of discrimination; (2) political ideology; (3) partisan identification; (4) voting behavior; and (5) interest group activities. For each of these areas, when applicable, class and gender differences are noted.

When a government chooses to undertake a purposive course of action in an effort to address a problem, that decision can be affected by whether members of racial and ethnic minority groups are present in policymaking positions. Furthermore, the effect of that decision is unlikely to be uniform across all racial and ethnic groups. Chapter 4 employs a sequential model of the policymaking process to explore the ways members of racial and ethnic minority groups can affect what government does and does not do and what difference these policies make for these groups. The representation of these groups within policymaking institutions offers another perspective on the continuing manifestation of the first dilemma. Analysis of the efforts made to achieve policy goals should provide evidence to help articulate a response to the second dilemma.

Chapter 5 is a new chapter examining the concept of intersectional identity. The chapter calls for the recognition that race and ethnicity are identity dimensions that are inextricably linked with other salient identities—such as gender, class, religion, sexuality, and physical ability—and, as such, cannot be examined in an isolated fashion. Further, this chapter provides an overview of sociopolitical experiences that differ at various intersectional identities, such as experiences with the criminal justice system, the immigration system, and employment. Finally, there is an examination of electoral and activist participation at the intersection of multiple identities. Using an intersectional analytical lens allows for more in-depth sociopolitical examination and critique of race and ethnicity in the American political system.

Chapter 6 uses the question posed by Rodney King at his first postverdict news conference, which we have appropriated for the title of this book, in an attempt to address squarely the second dilemma. This chapter focuses on the tensions among minority groups and between minority groups and the majority. What options are available to members of minority groups within the American political system, and what are the consequences of pursuing each of these options? The bulk of the discussion compares the viable alternatives of coalition and competition and the arguments, both theoretical and practical, for and against each position. The consequences for both the nation and minority groups of following either track are explored. Finally, Chapter 7 discusses the future of American minority groups' politics and the authors' perspective on the resolution of the dilemmas.

CONCLUSION

This chapter shows that certain groups have been treated differently in our legal system based on their race or ethnicity. Thus, who is identified as being a member of one of these groups has had important legal implications, at times extending so far as to classify individuals as property rather than as citizens and to impose restrictions upon whom one could marry. This unequal treatment began before the current Constitution was adopted, with the nation's original minorities—blacks and American Indians. The treatment was applied as other racial and ethnic minorities—Latinos and Asians—immigrated, and it continues despite a common rhetoric of equality.

▶ DISCUSSION QUESTIONS

1. The authors argue that there is evidence of the continuing salience of race and ethnicity in the American political fabric. Do you agree with this assessment? Why or why not?

2. Thomas Jefferson, a student of classical liberal theory, opposed slavery but owned slaves. Theoretically, given the tenets of that theory, what justification could Jefferson have devised to explain his holding of slaves? Also from a classical liberal framework, what would be the weaknesses of his rationalization?

3. Citizenship is a primary criterion for participation in the American political system. What are the similarities and differences in the barriers to US citizenship faced by blacks, Latinos, Asians, and American Indians? What are the important landmarks in these groups' efforts to attain citizenship? How was the Constitution changed to accommodate the inclusion of these groups?

4. Following citizenship, the ability to vote is central to participation in the political process. Yet gaining the franchise was not easy for racial minorities in the United States. How have the requirements for voting eligibility evolved since the ratification of the Constitution? How did blacks, Latinos, Asians, and American Indians each gain the franchise?

5. How does Donald Trump's "birther conspiracy" to delegitimize Barack Obama's presidency fit into a broader understanding of the continued salience of race in the American political system?

NOTE

1 The term *civilized* came about because historically these tribes had associated with whites and adopted the culture of whites—especially their commercial culture. The fertile Southeast land coupled with a commercial mind-set enabled these tribes to amass great wealth, furthering their image as "civilized." It should be noted that the fertility of the land of the Southeast was not lost on whites, who coveted the territory. Beginning in the 1830s, the US government, especially under the administration of President Andrew Jackson, removed the Five Civilized Tribes from their land to reservations in the relatively barren Oklahoma Territory.

CHAPTER 2

Resources and Status of America's Racial Minorities

President Barack Obama's eldest daughter, Malia Obama, recently shared her decision to enroll in Harvard College for her undergraduate studies. The backlash created by her decision was seen primarily in the comments sections of news articles. Comments on an article posted online by *Fox News* provided the clearest example of racist commentary (Roussi 2016). They included "I wonder if she applied as a muDslime . . . or a foreign students . . . or just a N——" and "Sounds like black privilege to me." There were also many pointing to affirmative action assisting Malia in the admissions process (Willis 2016). *Fox News* subsequently shut down the comments section in light of these remarks (The Grio 2016).

—MAY 2 AND 3, 2016

The fact that all American racial and ethnic minority groups have not been treated according to the rhetoric of the nation's founding principles has resulted in differences in these groups' contemporary political status based on differential resources, histories of political activism, and levels of access to political participation. The size, economic well-being, and geographic concentration of the group's population; the extent to which the group has participated in a civil rights movement; and the amount of protection that is provided under contemporary voting rights law all affect the way members of each of the groups will be treated within the American polity, what kind of role members of the group will be expected to play in the political system, and what kind of strategy—cooperation or conflict—will be chosen. A consideration of these factors identifies the commonalities and the differences among the various groups that are often lumped together under the rubric "minority group politics."

POPULATION SIZE, SOCIOECONOMIC STATUS, AND CONCENTRATION

The number of people and where they are located are important pieces of data in the US political system. The population of a certain location affects important factors, such as the number of members each state will have in the US House of Representatives, the way electoral districts will be drawn, the number of votes each state will have in the Electoral College to choose the president, and the way some government resources will be distributed. The latest population surveys (2015) provide a detailed picture of the populations with which we are concerned. Tables 2.1, 2.2, and 2.3 present these data and provide basic information about the populations of each group, the groups' age structures, and some indicators of **socioeconomic status**—the general social and economic conditions of these groups—a variable that is related to political participation. In addition, we are able to see the variations that exist within the Latino and Asian communities.

Despite the growth in the populations of the various minority groups, non-Latino whites constitute slightly more than three-fifths of the nation's population (61.5 percent). Latinos, as of the 2015 Census update, are the next-largest single group, at more than one-eighth of the nation's population, but less than one-fifth (17.6 percent), while blacks are slightly less than one-eighth of the population (12.3 percent). Latino attainment of the status of the nation's largest racial/ethnic minority has occurred over a relatively short period of time—increasing 63 percent between 1970 and 1980, 53 percent between 1980 and 1990, 58 percent between 1990 and 2000, and 43 percent between 2000 and 2010. (Yet, growth from immigration slowed significantly between 2010 and 2014 [Stepler and Brown 2016].) Thus, in any political issue in which raw population counts matter, from a national perspective whites will clearly maintain an upper hand for the foreseeable future. Even with rapid Latino population growth, and with Latinos projected to be the primary component of national population growth for the next century, Latinos are predicted still to be a clear minority—around 29 percent of the population by 2060. Yet the US Census Bureau estimates that minorities, now roughly one-third of the US population, are expected to become the majority in 2042. By 2060, non-Hispanic whites are estimated to compose only 43.65 percent of the total population (US Census Bureau 2014 National Population Projections).

At the same time the Latino population has been growing, it has been diversifying. Immigration from Central and South America and the Caribbean

TABLE 2.1 Selected Characteristics of the Non-Latino Black, Asian American, American Indian/Alaskan Native, and White Populations in the United States, 2015

	BLACK	ASIAN AMERICAN	AMERICAN INDIAN & ALASKAN NATIVE	WHITE
Population (in thousands)	39,598	17,081	2,070	197,534
% of Total US Pop.	12.3	5.3	0.6	61.5
Median Age (yrs.)	34.0	36.8	33.5	43.3
% ≥ 18 Yrs. Old	74.7	79.9	73.6	80.9
% H.S. Grad (of Pop. > 25 yrs.)	84.8	86.5	82.3	92.3
% Unemployed (of Pop. > 16 Yrs. Old)	7.0	3.3	6.9	3.1
Males	7.7	3.6	8.0	3.5
Females	6.4	3.0	5.9	2.7
Median Family Income (In 2015 Inflation-Adjusted Dollars)	$45,055	$89,136	$46,734	$77,072
% Owning Home	41.1	57.9	55.4	71.0
% Living in Poverty	25.4	12.0	26.9	10.4
% without Health Insurance	11.0	7.8	21.0	6.3

Source: Figures reflect data from the US Census Bureau, 2015 American Community Survey 1-Year Estimates (Selected Population Profiles), http://factfinder.census.

Population Data: "Total Population"; age data: "Median Age (Years)" and "18 Years and Older"; education data: "High School Graduate or Higher"; unemployment data (found or computed): "Employment Status: Unemployed"; median income data: "Income in the Past 12 Months: Median Family Income (Dollars)"; homeownership data: "Housing Tenure"; poverty data: "Poverty Rates: All People"; health insurance coverage data: "No Health Insurance Coverage."

has reduced the proportion of Latinos of Mexican, Puerto Rican, and Cuban origins among Latinos; Colombians, Dominicans, Ecuadorians, Guatemalans, El Salvadorans, and those from other countries now are more than one-third of the Latino population in the United States (Stepler and Brown 2016).

Electoral politics, however, depends not just on the number of bodies but also on the number of those who vote. The one consistent legal restriction on

TABLE 2.2 Selected Characteristics of the Latino Population and
Selected Subgroups in the United States, 2015

	PUERTO RICAN	MEXICAN	CUBAN	OTHER	TOTAL LATINOS[1]
Population (in thousands)	5,373	35,797	2,107	13,219	56,496
% of Total US Population	1.7	11.1	0.7	4.1	17.6
% of Total US Latino Pop.	9.5	63.4	3.7	23.4	–
Median Age (yrs.)	29.5	26.9	40.8	31.7	28.7
% ≥ 18 Yrs. Old	69.0	65.4	79.9	72.5	67.9
% H.S. Grad (of Pop. ≥ 25 Yrs.)	78.9	60.9	79.2	70.8	66.0
% Unemployed (of Pop. ≥ 16 Yrs. Old)	5.9	4.9	3.9	4.7	4.9
Males	6.3	4.9	4.1	4.7	5.0
Females	5.5	4.9	3.7	4.7	4.8
Median Family Income in 2015 Inflation-Adjusted Dollars)	$45,693	$45,616	$51,105	$49,812	$46,690
% Living in Poverty	24.6	23.5	17.6	20.0	22.6
% Owning Home	36.1	47.7	52.3	41.9	45.2
% Total Population Non-Citizens	0.9	23.5	23.7	29.0	22.6
% without Health Insurance	8.5	21.5	13.9	19.5	19.5

[1] Total Latinos includes aggregate data on the following Census groups: "Puerto Rican," "Mexican," "Cuban," and "Other Hispanic or Latino," all of which include respondents of any race.

Sources: Figures reflect data from the US Census Bureau, 2015 American Community Survey 1-Year Estimates (Selected Population Profiles), http://factfinder.census.gov. Population data: "Total Population"; age data: "Median Age (Years)" and "18 Years and Older"; education data: "High School Graduate or Higher"; unemployment data (found or computed): "Employment Status: Unemployed"; median income data: "Income in the Past 12 Months: Median Family Income (Dollars)"; homeownership data: "Housing Tenure"; poverty data: "Poverty Rates: All People"; citizenship data: "Not A U.S. Citizen"; health insurance coverage data: "No Health Insurance Coverage."

TABLE 2.3 Selected Characteristics of Selected Asian American Population Subgroups in the United States, 2015

	CHINESE	JAPANESE	KOREAN	FILIPINO	ASIAN INDIAN	VIET-NAMESE	TOTAL ASIANS
Population (in thousands)	4,134	757	1,460	2,848	3,700	1,739	17,081
% of Total US Population	1.3	0.2	0.5	0.9	1.2	0.5	5.3
% of US Asian Population	24.2	4.4	8.6	16.7	21.7	10.2	–
Median Age (in Years)	38.4	50.3	39.5	41.4	33.6	38.5	36.8
% Age 18 and older	82.4	89.8	83.4	83.2	76.6	79.1	79.9
% H.S. Grads (of Pop. ≥ 25 yrs.)	82.8	95.5	92.5	92.6	92.1	73.4	86.5
% Unemployed (of Pop. > 16 yrs.)	3.0	1.6	2.9	3.6	3.4	3.1	3.3
Males	3.2	1.7	3.3	4.1	3.1	4.0	3.6
Females	2.8	1.5	2.6	3.2	3.7	2.3	3.0
Median Family Income (in 2015 inflation-adjusted dollars)	$88,788	$95,779	$79,646	$92,122	$115,291	$64,931	$89,136
% Living in Poverty	15.4	8.3	13.4	6.5	7.5	14.5	12
% Owning Home	62.1	66.2	47.7	59.4	54.6	66.1	57.9
% without Health Insurance	7.3	3.5	11.6	6.6	5.7	9.2	7.8
% Non-Citizens	30.5	28.0	28.6	21.0	36.8	17.0	28.1

Sources: 2015 US Census Bureau, American Community Survey (Selected Population Profiles), http://factfinder.census.gov. Population data: "Total Population"; age data: "Median Age (Years)" and "18 Years and Older"; education data: "High School Graduate or Higher"; unemployment data (found or computed): "Employment Status: Unemployed"; median income data: "Income in the Past 12 Months: Median Family Income (Dollars)"; homeownership data: "Housing Tenure"; poverty data: "Poverty Rates: All People"; health insurance coverage data: "No Health Insurance Coverage"; citizenship data: "Not A U.S. Citizen."

the right to vote is age. In no US jurisdiction can one vote until one is eighteen years old. If each group's age distribution is approximately the same, the translation of the potential power of numbers into the actual power of votes becomes an issue of mobilization. But as the tables show, there are broad variations in age structures. In general, the non-Latino white population is older than the other groups, and a higher proportion of its population is over age eighteen. The only exceptions to this pattern are the Japanese, whose median age is higher than that of non-Latino whites, and Japanese, Korean, and Filipinos, whose proportion of those eighteen years and older is also higher than that of non-Latino whites—who cumulatively account for only about 1.6 percent of the nation's population. Thus, whites not only continue to constitute the overwhelming majority of the population nationwide, but they also maintain an advantage over most other racial and ethnic groups in the proportion of their population that is old enough to vote. Minority groups' numerical disadvantage is therefore exacerbated by the relative age distributions.

Beyond the numbers and age structure, socioeconomic status has been found to be important in determining levels of participation. Simply put, people who fare better economically have a greater stake in the system and are more likely to be able to afford the time to participate in politics, to engage in activities that stimulate political participation, and to have peers who are politically active. If one is struggling to subsist, political participation—even the simple act of voting—may be perceived as a luxury, a not very profitable investment of one's time and energy.

Tables 2.1, 2.2, and 2.3 also present some selected indicators of socioeconomic status taken from the latest data released by the US Census Bureau. These indicators reflect a number of different perspectives on such status, and the picture that emerges from these data is clear. Only Asian Americans approximate, and in some instances surpass, the educational attainment levels of whites, and as Table 2.3 shows, there is significant variation within the Asian American community. Blacks are the next closest group, but even they only come within 7.5 percentage points of whites' educational attainment levels.

Only Asian Americans approach whites' unemployment levels. The rates for Chinese, Japanese, and Korean are lower and the rates for Filipino and Asian Indian are higher than that for whites, while the rate for Vietnamese is the same as that for whites. The rates for other groups, however, are noticeably higher than the rate for whites. Thus, it should not be surprising that the median white family enjoys at least a $30,000 advantage over any other group, with the exception of Asian Americans. Asian Americans report a median family income almost $12,064 higher than that of whites. Moreover, this difference is more than the $5,327 difference measured in the 2000 Census. It must be remembered that the US Census Bureau median family income measure takes into account all persons in the household who are working. Some Asian American families, many with small businesses, have more persons in the household working than white families do.

In spite of the family income advantage enjoyed by Asian Americans, a smaller proportion of whites lives below the poverty line than does any other major group. Asians are about 1.2 times more likely, Cubans are slightly more than 1.9 times more likely, and each of the other groups is slightly more than 2 times more likely than whites to live in poverty. Whites clearly overshadow all of the other groups when we look at homeownership. White homeownership is 1.73 times the rate of black homeownership, 1.23 times the rate of Asian American homeownership, 1.28 times the rate of American Indian homeownership, and 1.57 times the rate of homeownership for Latinos in general. The meltdown in the subprime mortgage market between 2007 and 2010, to which racial minorities were more often steered than were whites, and the rising number of home foreclosures as a result, increased the disparity in homeownership between whites and racial and ethnic minorities. Clearly, by whatever measure one wants to use, the numerical and age distribution disadvantages of racial and ethnic minority groups in the United States are generally compounded by the lack of resources that may be used to compensate for these disadvantages. Only Asian Americans have some apparent equity with or advantage over whites on some of the variables, but there are several areas of disadvantage. Further, Asian Americans make up only 5.3 percent of the US population. Additionally, for Latinos and Asian Americans, the high proportion of noncitizens in the various subpopulations reduces their ability to use what resources they may have available to them.

Despite these apparently cumulative disadvantages, there are clearly examples of each of these communities mobilizing for political success. How is this possible? The answer lies in looking lower than the national level. Just as the population figures must be considered in light of age structure and socioeconomic resources, we must also look at the way these groups' populations are distributed geographically. Although the figures suggest that minority groups are certain to be overwhelmed in any type of national contest, if former US House Speaker "Tip" O'Neill's dictum, "All politics is local," is correct, we should be looking at the subnational level.

Maps 2.1 through 2.4 display the concentration by county within the United States of each of the groups considered here. These maps confirm that each of the minority groups has very different geographic distribution patterns and that areas exist in which each of the "minorities" either is a majority or has the potential to be an important political player.

On each of the maps, we have identified areas in which the group is totally or virtually nonexistent (because the maps use natural breaks in the population, the scales differ for each group). Because our data are aggregated at the county level, it is possible and even likely that subcounty-level jurisdictions (e.g., cities, school districts) exist in which minorities may constitute majorities but do not appear on our maps. Likewise, there are areas within what appear on our maps as heavily minority that maintain a majority white population. Still, these maps give us some sense of where minority group members are most likely to be found in our nation and where potential minority group political power exists.

Map 2.1 reveals that the African American population is concentrated in a crescent that runs from Maryland down the Atlantic seaboard across the Deep South to east Texas. The heaviest concentrations of black population are found in the traditional "Black Belt," where blacks were concentrated during the days of slavery. The overwhelmingly black counties in the nation are found in rural Alabama and Mississippi. There are, however, more than token populations of blacks scattered throughout most US regions, with the exception of the upper Great Plains. Much of the non-South concentration of blacks consists of residents in predominantly black central cities ringed by "whiter" suburbs; therefore, the county populations depicted here do not adequately reveal the black concentration.

Map 2.2 shows a similar pattern for Hispanics but in a different area of the country. The Hispanic crescent runs along the United States–Mexico border from the Rio Grande Valley in south Texas through New Mexico and Arizona and into Southern California. An appendage of this crescent juts up through New Mexico into southern Colorado, and separate pockets of significant concentrations appear in central Washington State. The overwhelmingly Hispanic counties in the nation are found along the Rio Grande in south Texas and in northern New Mexico. The only significant Hispanic concentrations east of Texas are found in urban areas, particularly around New York City and in south Florida. This pattern reflects the different settlement patterns of the three major Latino groups. Although Hispanics of different origins are found in each of the three major areas of concentration, in general Mexican Americans are concentrated in the southwestern states that were added after the Mexican War, Puerto Ricans are concentrated in the New York metropolitan area, and Cubans are concentrated around Miami. Indeed, a majority of Cuban Americans in the United States live in Dade County, Florida. Of particular note are the increasing numbers of Latinos in such states as Iowa, North Carolina, Georgia, and Alabama. These states had extremely small Latino populations in the 1990 Census, but because of increased Latino immigration coupled with jobs in the

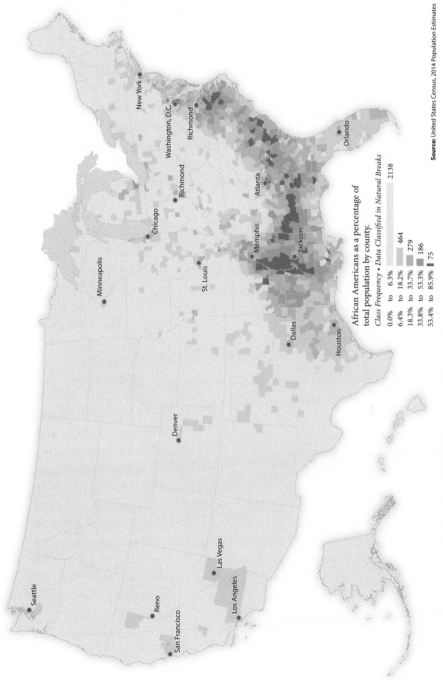

Source: United States Census, 2014 Population Estimates

African Americans as a percentage of
total population by county.
Class Frequency • Data Classified in Natural Breaks

0.0%   to   6.3%   2138
6.4%   to   18.2%   464
18.3% to   33.7%   279
33.8% to   53.3%   186
53.4% to   85.9%   75

MAP 2.1 *African American Population Distribution, United States, 2014*

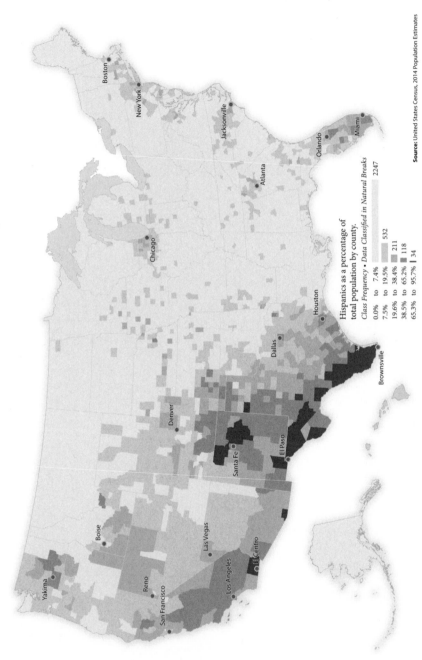

MAP 2.2 *Hispanic Population Distribution, United States, 2014*

Hispanics as a percentage of
total population by county.

Class Frequency • Data Classified in Natural Breaks

0.0%	to	7.4%	2247
7.5%	to	19.5%	532
19.6%	to	38.4%	211
38.5%	to	65.2%	118
65.3%	to	95.7%	34

Source: United States Census, 2014 Population Estimates

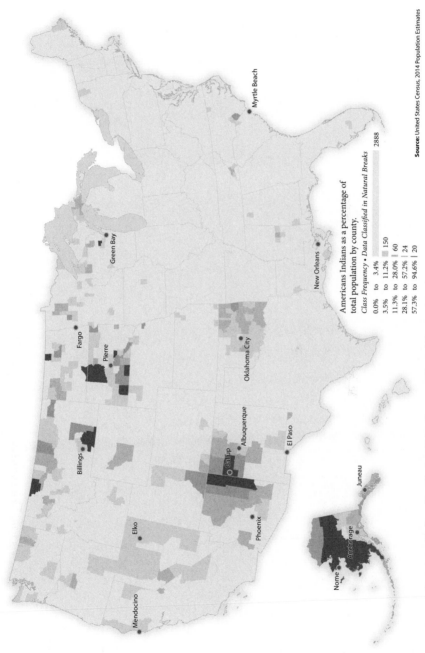

Americans Indians as a percentage of
total population by county.
Class Frequency • Data Classified in Natural Breaks

0.0%	to	3.4%	2888
3.5%	to	11.2%	150
11.3%	to	28.0%	60
28.1%	to	57.2%	24
57.3%	to	94.6%	20

Source: United States Census, 2014 Population Estimates

MAP 2.3 *American Indian Population Distribution, United States, 2014*

38

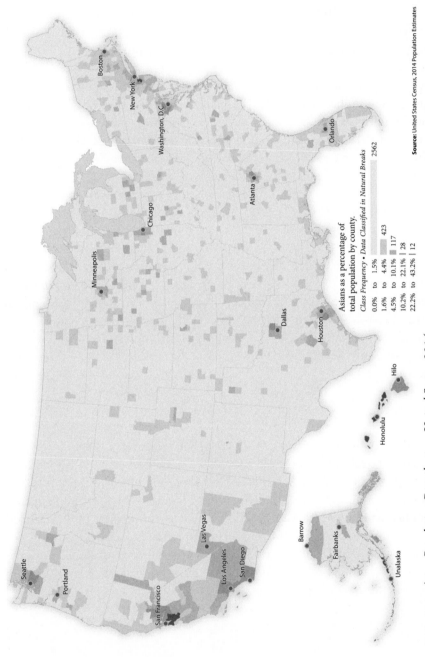

Asians as a percentage of
total population by county.
Class Frequency • Data Classified in Natural Breaks

0.0% to 1.5%   2562
1.6% to 4.4%   423
4.5% to 10.1%   117
10.2% to 22.1%   28
22.2% to 43.2%   12

Source: United States Census, 2014 Population Estimates

MAP 2.4 *Asian Population Distribution, United States, 2014*

poultry, meat-packing, and farming industries they are finding significant increases in their Latino population as demonstrated by the 2000 and the 2010 Census, and the 2014 Census updates. This has also resulted in a dispersion of the Hispanic population. In 1990, the Hispanic population topped 5 percent in only fifteen states and was the largest minority group in sixteen of the fifty states. The 2000 Census revealed that in twenty-three states, Hispanics exceeded 5 percent of the population and were the largest resident minority group. And in the 2010 Census, Hispanics exceeded 5 percent of the population in thirty-six states, although they were not always the largest resident minority. In 2010, 41 percent of Latinos lived in the West and 36 percent lived in the South. It is possible that by the 2020 census, the largest proportion of Latinos in the country might live in the South rather than in the West.

The distribution of the American Indian population, shown in Map 2.3, reflects the effects of the group's push westward. Although there are pockets of Indian concentration in the eastern states, the areas of greatest concentration are found in the Great Plains and westward. This map shows the continuing effects of putting Indians on reservations in rural areas where whites showed little demand for the land. Because of the numbers, however, the map hides the fact that over one-half of American Indians live in metropolitan or suburban areas. Table 2.4 shows the populations of the five largest American Indian tribes and the states in which they are primarily concentrated. Also listed are the states with the highest number of American Indians as a proportion of the state population.

As of 2010, Cherokees, concentrated largely in Oklahoma, California, and North Carolina, were the largest tribe, accounting for 14.1 percent of all American Indians. The Navajo, whose nation occupies the corners of Arizona, New Mexico, Colorado, and Utah, were concentrated in Arizona, New Mexico, and Utah and were the second largest, with 15.2 percent of the total American Indian population. Alaska had the highest proportion of American Indians (including Eskimos and Aleuts) of any of the US states—14.6 percent of its total population. New Mexico and South Dakota were next, with 9.4 and 9.0 percent of their respective populations being American Indians.

Finally, Map 2.4 illustrates the intense concentration of the Asian American population. Except for some pockets in eastern urban areas, such as Washington, DC; New York; and Boston, and areas just outside Chicago, Minneapolis, Dallas, Las Vegas, and Houston, Asian Americans are concentrated in the Pacific coast states, particularly in California, Washington, and Hawaii.

County-level data obscure the fact that blacks, Latinos, and Asian Americans are concentrated in urban areas. Latinos now represent the largest minority

TABLE 2.4 Population Size and Percent of Largest Five American Indian Tribes,[1] and States of Primary Concentration,[2] States with American Indians as Highest Percentage of Population,[3] and States with Largest Number of American Indians and Alaskan Natives,[4] 2010

TRIBE		% OF TOTAL	STATES OF PRIMARY CONCENTRATION
Total American Indian Tribes, Specified	2,022,931	–	
Cherokee	285,476	14.1	Oklahoma, California, North Carolina
Chippewa	115,859	5.7	Minnesota, Michigan, Wisconsin
Navajo	308,013	15.2	Arizona, New Mexico, Utah
Sioux	131,048	6.5	South Dakota, North Dakota, California
All Specified Other American Indian	1,182,535	58.4	California, Oklahoma, Arizona

STATES WITH HIGHEST PERCENTAGE OF POPULATION		TEN STATES WITH LARGEST NUMBER OF INDIANS	
	% of State Population		Size of Population
Alaska	14.6	Arizona	285,768
New Mexico	9.4	California	281,908
South Dakota	9.0	Oklahoma	261,746
Oklahoma	7.0	New Mexico	195,162
Montana	6.2	Texas	129,162
North Dakota	4.9	North Carolina	111,756
Arizona	4.5	Alaska	104, 539
Wyoming	2.6	Washington	99,736
Washington	1.5	South Dakota	73,601
Idaho	1.4	New York	71,792

Sources:
[1] Table C02005, "American Indian and Alaskan Native Alone for Selected Tribal Groupings," for United States, 2010 American Community Survey.
[2] Table C02005, "American Indian and Alaskan Native Alone for Selected Tribal Groupings," for all states, 2010 American Community Survey.
[3] Table R0203, "Percent of the Total Population Who Are American Indian and Alaskan Native Alone," 2010 American Community Survey.
[4] Table S0201, "Selected Population Profile in the United States," for all states, 2010 American Community Survey.

group in urban areas in the United States. Well over half of America's cities are now majority nonwhite. More than half of all minority groups in large metro areas, including blacks, now reside in the suburbs. The share of blacks in large metro areas living in suburbs rose from 37 percent in 1990, to 44 percent in 2000, to 51 percent in 2010. Higher shares of whites (78 percent), Asians (62 percent), and Hispanics (59 percent) in large metro areas live in suburbs (Frey 2011, 1). In 1940, only 5 percent of American Indians lived in urban areas. In the 1950s, the federal government instituted a program to relocate reservation Indians to urban centers. The Bureau of Indian Affairs (BIA) offered employment assistance to Indians who would voluntarily leave their reservations and relocate in urban communities where job opportunities were more plentiful. The Voluntary Relocation Program, renamed the Employment Assistance Program in 1954, provided a one-way bus ticket, temporary low-cost housing, and new clothing to Indians willing to relocate. As a result of this program, in 1990, 51 percent of American Indians lived in urban areas (Hirschfelder and de Montaño 1993). Table 2.5 shows the ten cities with the largest American Indian populations as of 2010. New York City headed the list, with slightly less than 1.8 times the number of the next city, Phoenix, Arizona, which had the second-largest number. This represents a shift from 2000, when Los Angeles had the second-largest American Indian population. In 2010, Los Angles was number three, behind Phoenix.

Historically, cities have been magnets for new immigrants, having offered greater employment prospects than have rural areas, as well as established immigrant communities into which newcomers could integrate. Between the 1860s (the Civil War) and World War I, the populations of major US cities swelled as Europeans from Scotland, Ireland, Germany, and England—and later, southern and eastern Europeans, such as Poles, Czechs, Slovaks, Greeks, and Russian Jews—immigrated and settled en masse in these urban areas (Lineberry and Sharkansky 1978). During this period, early Asian immigrants settled primarily in cities

TABLE 2.5 Cities with the Largest American Indian Population, 2010

City	Size of Population
New York, NY	57,512
Phoenix, AZ	32,366
Los Angeles, CA	28,087
Albuquerque, NM	25,087
Anchorage, AK	20,817
Tulsa, OK	20,817
Oklahoma City, OK	20,533
Houston, TX	14,997
Tucson, AZ	14,154
Chicago, IL	13,337

Source: "Profile of General Population and Housing Characteristics," for Selected Cities, 2010 Decennial Census.

on the West Coast, particularly in California. More recently, Asians, Latinos, and the overwhelming majority of other newcomers have continued this pattern of predominantly urban settlement. As a result, US cities today have large populations of these immigrant groups.

It was not only immigrants, however, who were drawn to cities by the promise of greater economic opportunity. Large numbers of native blacks, Latinos, and Asians also migrated to urban areas in search of economic and political advancement. Between 1910 and 1930, nearly one million blacks—one-tenth of the black population in the South—moved to cities in the North (Judd 1979). The migration of blacks to northeastern states was followed by another black migration to selected manufacturing centers of the Midwest, which continued into the post–World War II era. Many of these migrants were seeking increased economic opportunities as well as escape from the harsh conditions of segregation and racial discrimination in the South. By 1960, socioeconomic trends had resulted in a concentration of blacks in most of the nation's urban centers outside the South (Rose 1971). Coupled with this migration of blacks and other racial minorities into the cities was the exit of a sizable number of whites to the newer suburbs surrounding the cities.

Yet urban centers were not the havens of opportunity that immigrants and migrants had envisioned. Blacks, Latinos, and Asians routinely encountered racial discrimination in employment and housing. Many cities enacted racial zoning ordinances to ensure that racial minorities would be confined to "separate cities" within the larger city, making it virtually impossible for these groups to move out of these segregated areas (Silver and Moeser 1995; Sugrue 1996). Lenders, real estate agents, school boards, city governments, and the federal government, among other individuals and institutions, participated in segregating blacks, Latinos, and Asians not only from whites but from one another. Los Angeles is an example of the racial segregation present in many US cities. Map 2.5 shows the racial and ethnic geographic distribution of blacks, Latinos, and Asians in the city and county of Los Angeles. Yet in many cities the concentrations of minority populations in certain areas could be used by these groups as powerful political and economic resources. How well have these population resources been mobilized? We now turn to this question.

PARTICIPATION IN A CIVIL RIGHTS MOVEMENT

With the level of resources just described, even without a knowledge of the history depicted in this text in the timelines, one would guess that these minority groups are at a disadvantage in the political system. They fit under the rubric "**dominated groups**"—groups that have generally been excluded from participation in the decision-making process by which society's benefits are distributed. "Because of this exclusion, dominated groups at different times attempt to change their situation of powerlessness by engaging in nontraditional and usually nonlegitimized struggles with power holders" (Morris 1984:282). These overt efforts by groups to empower themselves constitute **social movements**.

Certain prerequisites appear necessary for a social movement to have a chance to enhance the group's power. First, successful social movements generally tap a reservoir of social organizations for experienced leaders, potential followers, communication networks, money, and labor. The ability to draw from preexisting organizations minimizes start-up costs and provides stability in the early, tenuous days when the movement is vulnerable to a serious countereffort by the dominant group.

Second, successful social movements require catalytic leadership—social activists who create or recognize opportunities to protest the groups' subordinate status. Furthermore, they must be able to organize and motivate people to engage in the effort over what may be an extended period of time.

The movement will be stronger if these two prerequisites are combined— that is, if the leadership is taken from preexisting organizations. These organizations have already demonstrated their ability to raise money and to organize people sufficiently that, at the least, they still exist. If the leadership arises from such organizations, the task becomes one of redirecting energies toward a new goal rather than of having to create an entirely new organization.

Third, successful movements tap outside resources. They elicit money and personnel from the environment that is not immediately affected by their struggle. These resources, although they may be sporadic and may come with strings attached, can be valuable in sustaining the movement and in expanding the scope of conflict. As part of a dominated group, people active in social movements have little to lose by getting others involved. The existing social, political, and economic decision-making apparatus does not yield positive results for them. They see change—any change—as likely to yield an improvement.

Finally, the social movement must have a plan—a set of tactics and an overall strategy it can use to confront the existing power structure. An effective set of tactics and strategies will disrupt the existing order; educate others about inequities, injustices, and civil wrongs; provide some sense of hope or efficacy for movement participants; and push the system—if at times imperceptibly— toward change.

Each of the groups considered in this book has participated to some extent in a social movement in an attempt to improve its situation. But the level, scope, and forms of activity have varied across groups. We now discuss the movements of the respective groups.

Asian

Population DIstribution

Los Angeles County,
California • 2014

Asian as a percentage of total
population by census tract.

Class Frequency • Data Classified In Natural Breaks

0%	to	7.3%	1007
7.4%	to	18.1%	779
18.2%	to	33.8%	314
33.9%	to	54.1%	151
54.2%	to	88.2%	92

Source: 2014 United States Census • American Community Survey

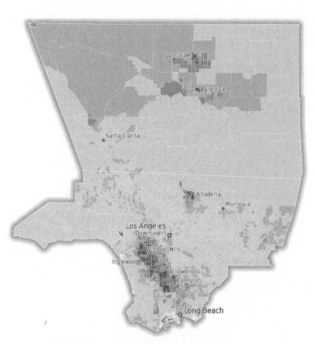

African
American

Population DIstribution

Los Angeles County,
California • 2014

African American as a percentage of total
population by census tract.

Class Frequency • Data Classified In Natural Breaks

0%	to	5.2%	1442
5.3%	to	14.9%	543
15%	to	30.4%	212
30.5%	to	54.0%	95
54.1%	to	90.0%	51

Source: 2014 United States Census • American Community Survey

MAP 2.5 *Population Patterns, Metropolitan Los Angeles County, 2014*

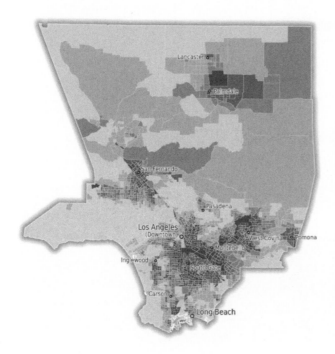

Hispanic

Population Distribution

Los Angeles County,
California • 2014

Hispanic as a percentage of total
population by census tract.

Class Frequency • Data Classified in Natural Breaks

0% to 19.5%		565
19.6% to 38.5%		473
38.6% to 59.2%		407
59.3% to 79.7%		463
79.8% to 100%		435

Source: 2014 United States Census • American Community Survey

PHOTO 2.1 *About fifty-five members of civil rights organizations protested desegregation policies in public schools at a meeting of the Board of Education in downtown St. Louis on June 11, 1963. Among those protesting were members of the National Association for the Advancement of Colored People, the Congress of Racial Equality, and St. Louis parent groups.* (AP Photo: 6306110534)

The Black Civil Rights Movement

The black Civil Rights Movement of the 1950s and 1960s is the best known and most studied of such movements, and in many ways it has served as a model for other groups. As with most movements, it was not one overall movement led from the top but instead constituted a collection of local movements that when added together produced massive social change. In recognition of the localized nature of the black Civil Rights Movement, this section examines three small but vital parts of this movement as illustrations of the way it operated and what it was and was not able to achieve.

Baton Rouge. The Baton Rouge bus boycott, which began on June 19, 1953, is often used as the starting point of the modern black Civil Rights Movement. The boycott sought to have the city enforce its ordinance allowing black riders to be seated in city buses on a first-come, first-served basis—in essence, to force the city to make reality match rhetoric. The city refused to discipline drivers who failed to enforce the ordinance, so Reverend T. J. Jemison, minister of Mt. Zion Baptist Church—the city's largest black church—broadcast a radio appeal for blacks to boycott the city bus system.

The United Defense League (UDL) was formed to direct the mass boycott. This confederation of organizations held mass rallies, which drew up to three thousand people, each of the seven nights of the boycott. A movement "police department" was organized to patrol the black community and to provide security for movement leaders. A free carpool was organized with volunteer drivers to help boycotting blacks get to and from work. Even the black community's drunks and winos were organized to "open up the car doors of movement participants as they arrived" at the mass meetings (Jemison, quoted in Morris 1984:19).

Such an effort, of course, is not free of cost. Reverend Jemison asked for and received permission to redirect $650 he had been given for a business trip to help support the boycott. Following his example, his church gave an additional $1,500 to the effort. Other churches in the community followed, donating $3,800 to give the movement its initial capital. The nightly mass meetings provided an opportunity to collect operating expenses. As a result, all of the volunteer drivers' expenses were covered, and the expenses of the movement's police department, as well as the costs of miscellaneous goods and services necessary to run the boycott, were paid as they were incurred.

The dominant white power structure in Baton Rouge quickly offered a compromise, reserving only the two front side seats for whites and the long bench seat in the rear of the bus for blacks and leaving all other seats open on a first-come, first-served basis. After much debate, and with the approval of a mass meeting of eight thousand blacks, on June 25, 1953, Reverend Jemison announced the end of the boycott and the dismantling of the free carpool.

Although the subsequent Montgomery bus boycott became more famous, probably because the recalcitrance of the white power structure there resulted in a more extended and complex effort, the Baton Rouge boycott is instructive. First, this boycott drew on the black churches for the masses of people needed to implement and carry out the boycott, communications networks, leadership, and money. But the successful operation of the boycott also necessitated the creation of an umbrella organization. Without the UDL, there was too much danger that the purposes of the individual churches would have superseded those of the movement.

Second, in Jemison the movement had an educated, articulate leader who had the ability to recognize the potential for effective social action and to organize and motivate people to take advantage of that opportunity. In a pattern that was repeated with Dr. Martin Luther King Jr. in Montgomery, Reverend Jemison was a relative newcomer to Baton Rouge and was unencumbered by any history of personal or organizational conflicts with other potential leaders or by any residual level of distrust.

Third, in the Baton Rouge movement the movement leader was an insider in an existing social organization—the largest black church in town—whose resources the movement needed to tap. The advantage this gave the movement was best exemplified by the ease with which Jemison redirected to the movement coffers the $650 from the canceled business trip. His dual status as both a movement and a church leader placed him in a unique position to make an almost effortless, yet vitally important, contribution to the initiation of the movement.

Fourth, there is limited evidence that external resources were tapped (Jemison reported that "a few whites" contributed; see Morris 1984:23), but the brevity of the boycott made these resources less necessary than would have been the case in a prolonged effort. It is important to note, however, that if the movement had been dependent on external resources, it is doubtful that they could have been amassed quickly enough to allow the leadership to mobilize against this grievance.

Finally, the tactic chosen in this case—an economic boycott—was well suited for its task of disrupting the status quo. It allowed—in fact, required—the concerted effort of the masses, giving them a feeling of solidarity while simultaneously inflicting great financial losses on the bus company. This tactic demonstrated the economic clout of the black community to both whites and blacks and also served to broaden the conflict and perhaps to recruit some unwilling, or unwitting, allies. Individuals who had never thought about the seating arrangements on buses, or who, if they had thought about the issue, might have preferred the status quo, may have been willing to tolerate change if their insistence on continued segregation would have meant the loss of bus service or the loss of a job if the bus service had been forced out of existence.

The Baton Rouge bus boycott was only the opening skirmish in the black civil rights movement, but it provided some valuable lessons. The leaders of other, later bus boycotts—Martin Luther King Jr. and Ralph Abernathy in Montgomery (1955–1956), the Reverend C. K. Steele in Tallahassee (1956), and the Reverend A. L. Davis in New Orleans (1957)—were all church-based movement leaders who were keenly aware of the experience of Reverend Jemison in Baton Rouge (Morris 1984).

Of course, the black Civil Rights Movement continued to evolve, new issues were addressed, other leaders emerged. One major area in which the Baton Rouge boycott is not very instructive is in promoting a movement over time. The experience in Mississippi from summer 1961 through summer 1964 sheds more light on the way the black civil rights movement was able to accomplish what it did.

Mississippi. It is an understatement to say that Mississippi was the stronghold of segregation. As late as 1964, a black attorney who was active in the civil rights movement saw the movement as a "no-fail" situation because "it was impossible for things to have grown worse" (Holt 1966:13).

The black Civil Rights Movement came to Mississippi in 1961 in the form of Freedom Riders, individuals who challenged the state's refusal to desegregate buses and bus stations and who viewed the state through bus windows and jail bars. Late that summer field secretaries from the Student Nonviolent Coordinating Committee (SNCC) also arrived, led by Robert Moses, a Harvard-educated schoolteacher from Harlem. Moses sought to organize black Mississippians based on the idea that they would need to be self-reliant when SNCC left. Rather than taking an obvious leadership role, Moses worked to develop local leaders and to discourage "outside" involvement. His fear was that outsiders who played a major role in the movement would leave at some point without having equipped indigenous leaders for the continuing struggle.

The development of leadership is a slow process, and there is a risk of stalling or stopping the movement if such development is arrested. Continued and increasing white resistance threatened to do just that. With the assassination of the National Association for the Advancement of Colored People (NAACP) field secretary Medgar Evers in June 1963 and the continuing violence against civil rights workers with no protection from federal authorities (local and state authorities were often involved in perpetrating the violence or allowing it to continue), Moses began to reconsider his opposition to outside, episodic assistance. In particular, he thought the presence of Northern white students might insulate civil rights workers from the most blatant discrimination and might raise Northern white consciousness about the racist system that existed in the South. It had become clear to Moses that violence against, and even murders of, Mississippi blacks had been insufficient to arouse national sympathies, much less to inspire protest or action.

Local white officials generally argued that blacks did not vote because they did not want to, because they were apathetic. The first tentative use of white students occurred during the fall 1963 "Freedom Vote," which was designed to reveal the state's hypocrisy and to puncture the apathy myth. Essentially, the idea was to put forth a slate of candidates and to have black voters cast "votes," not at the normal polling places but at less threatening locations and not for any official candidates but for individuals who supported the Civil Rights Movement; further, the blacks knew these votes would not count. If black Mississippians bothered to cast "ballots" under these conditions, the apathy myth could be dispelled.

Allard Lowenstein, a white activist and attorney, organized white students—mainly from Stanford and Yale—to assist in this project. The project accomplished four things. First, with a turnout of more than eighty thousand black "voters," no one could seriously argue that black Mississippians were apathetic. Second, and as a result of the first accomplishment, local blacks gained confidence. Not only had they taken a courageous step, but so had many of their fellow black citizens. Third, white Mississippians became hysterical over both the idea of a Freedom Vote and the presence of the white students in support of the black Civil Rights Movement. America's best and brightest students were threatened, beaten, shot at, and arrested for the heinous crime of attempting to attend a performance of the Jackson Philharmonic as part of an interracial group. Thus, and fourth, the student volunteers came to understand clearly what life was like in Mississippi, and they communicated this reality outside of the state. The white volunteers wrote to their parents, friends, and representatives in Congress; national attention became focused on Mississippi, and news coverage of the movement increased. The symbolic exercise, therefore, was not meaningless (Chafe 1993).

Based on the Freedom Vote experience, Robert Moses became convinced that bringing in more students from prominent white Northern families would either restrain white violence or highlight it for national attention, thus increasing pressure on federal authorities to become involved. An umbrella organization, the Council of Federated Organizations (COFO), was formed to coordinate the civil rights movement efforts. Under COFO auspices, more than one thousand college student volunteers were brought to Mississippi for the 1964 Summer Project. The underlying logic was correct but disheartening. The movement had discovered a tactic that would help it to expand the audience for its struggle and, it was hoped, bring federal intervention on its behalf. The bad news was that the tactic was predicated on the notion that threatening, beating, and shooting at affluent white Northern students was a serious offense, but that doing the same to black Mississippians was not.

This logic proved all too true. At the very beginning of the Summer Project, three participants—James Chaney, Michael Schwerner, and Andrew Goodman—disappeared while on a trip to investigate the bombing of a black church. Their disappearance prompted a massive investigation by the Federal

Bureau of Investigation (FBI) that eventually led to the discovery of the men's bodies. The important lesson for the movement was that the murder of white civil rights workers (Schwerner and Goodman) resulted in federal attention, whereas the numerous attacks on black Mississippians that had been reported previously had not done so.

Although the Summer Project did not change Mississippi overnight, it provided an important first step in the process. For example, "freedom schools" enhanced the academic skills of black children, better preparing them for future political and economic participation. And building on the Freedom Vote, the racially integrated Mississippi Freedom Democratic Party, which pledged allegiance to the national Democratic Party ticket, was formed to challenge the still segregated regular Mississippi Democratic Party. Although it was unsuccessful in achieving its goal of replacing the "regulars" as the official Democratic Party, the project's efforts foretold a major increase in black political participation in the state that had been the most resistant to any such participation of any state in the nation. Perhaps because of the length of their effort, or perhaps because of the more resistant environment, the movement leaders in Mississippi—unlike those in Baton Rouge—used outside resources to further their cause. The lessons of the black civil rights movement were not lost on other racial and ethnic minority groups.

Black Lives Matter. Although not a social movement in the classic definition, Black Lives Matter (BLM) can be considered one of the latest chapters in the black Civil Rights Movement. BLM began in 2012, after the shooting of seventeen-year-old Trayvon Martin (Garza 2014). The suspect, George Zimmerman, shot Martin, but claimed he had done so under Florida's "stand your ground" law, and he was later acquitted at trial. Martin's death generated a national discussion on racial profiling and gun control, and Zimmerman's acquittal spurred widespread uproar as many perceived that justice for Trayvon Martin had not been served (Smith 2014).

Patrisse Cullors, Opal Tometi, and Alicia Garza, three community organizers, began discussing whether black lives matter and calling attention to the lack of accountability when unarmed African Americans are murdered. Cullors developed the hashtag #BlackLivesMatter on social media, and they began a national conversation on the disparate treatment of black Americans by law enforcement, particularly the deaths of young black males as a result of encounters with the police (Zyra 2015). As the deaths of unarmed black Americans continued, Black Lives Matter began to gain national attention. The death of Michael Brown at the hands of police officer Darren Wilson in Ferguson, Missouri, on August 9, 2014, became an important flash point (Smith 2014).

More vocal leaders, including DeRay McKesson, a public school administrator, became active in BLM, speaking out and criticizing the police response to the events that transpired in Ferguson. Protests increased across the nation, as more young black individuals were killed by police, including Freddie Gray in Baltimore and Sandra Bland in Texas. Between August of 2014 and August of 2015, over 950 demonstrations occurred nationwide (Ruffin n.d.).

BLM's main platform for activism is online organizing through social media platforms such as Twitter and Facebook. It mobilizes through the "Black Twitter" community, a term that refers to black activists who utilize Twitter as a means to develop collective action around issues of concern for the black American community. While their members are primarily African American, BLM's growth has caught national and international attention.

Two points about the origins of BLM need to be emphasized. One is that the organizers have specifically worked to include members of the black American community who are typically on the margins—queer black women, undocumented people, and the working poor. The organizers stress that the effort is meant to include and uplift traditionally marginalized experiences. In a magazine interview, cofounder Opal Tometi emphasized, "It's not just about black heterosexual lives. . . . It's about all black lives" (Zarya 2015). Second, the BLM effort has spread internationally, with chapters now in Canada and Ghana. Activists in Toronto, Canada, shut down a major highway to protest the deaths of two black Canadians at the hands of police (Johnson 2016). Additional international campaigns included the #Palestine2Ferguson campaign, where protestors in Ferguson began a conversation with Palestinians residing in Gaza, later resulting in an international convention between organizers in Ferguson with activists in Gaza (Tamari 2015).

In addition to protesting the deaths of unarmed black men and women, Black Lives Matter activists have highlighted the issue of police brutality by organizing nonviolent protests during the 2015–2016 campaign cycle and by boycotting Black Friday shopping (Henderson 2015). During the 2016 Democratic presidential primaries, BLM pressured Bernie Sanders and Hillary Clinton, and as a result of these efforts, both Sanders and Clinton incorporated more conversations around the issues that BLM championed (Patterson 2015). Events during the summer of 2016—the police shootings of Alton Sterling in Baton Rouge and Philando Castile in Minneapolis and the murder of five police officers in Dallas by a lone black Army veteran shooter after a peaceful march to protest the deaths of Sterling and Castile—brought the issues of police killing of black men and of support for police officers front and center. The unanswered question is whether these two positions will be able to find common ground or if the debate will continue to be viewed as zero sum—support for one means opposition to the other.

BLM remains a salient part of the national conversation, and some black celebrities have highlighted the effort through their art. The imagery and lyrics in Beyoncé's "Formation" music video, released on February 6, 2016, the day before Super Bowl 50, highlighted her support for BLM. The music video, and her performance of the song at the Super Bowl, which referenced BLM elements, renewed and reinvigorated national conversation around the movement and its platform.

The Chicano Movement

Social movements among Latinos have been limited, and there has been no overarching pan-Hispanic effort. Young Puerto Ricans in New York and Chicago have participated in a Puerto Rican nationalist movement. César Chávez emerged as a leader of the National Farm Workers Association, which joined with Filipinos to protest pay inequities in the agricultural labor force. But the most wide-ranging, significant Latino movement was the Chicano power movement of the 1960s among Mexican Americans in the Southwest.

The Chicano movement was influenced both directly and indirectly by the black civil rights movement. The direct influence came through the participation of a few Mexican Americans in that movement. Such individuals as Maria Varela and Elizabeth Sutherland Martinez gained both valuable experience and a realization that the black movement was not concerned with the plight of Mexican Americans. Indirectly, however, the Chicano movement emerged from the general activism of the 1960s, which was spearheaded by the black civil rights movement.

At the core of the Chicano movement were Mexican American students, male and female, who sought more attention for the needs of their people. They wanted to move beyond the efforts of the more conservative Mexican American interest groups. The movement's most dramatic early political success came in Crystal City, Texas, in 1963, when the Political Association of Spanish-Speaking Organizations (PASSO) was formed and coalesced with a predominantly Mexican American local chapter of the Teamsters Union to defeat all of the white candidates for the city council, replacing them with Mexican Americans. This "Crystal City Revolt" was important because it demonstrated the possibilities for local Mexican American political mobilization. This was the first time Mexican Americans had taken political control of a municipal government in the US Southwest. Furthermore, it highlighted the important role young people were to play in the movement.

This role was further highlighted in the March 1968 Mexican American student walkout at Lincoln High School in East Los Angeles. Acting on an idea of Sal Castro, a teacher at the school, more than one thousand students staged a week-and-a-half-long strike that was "the first major mass protest explicitly against racism undertaken by Mexican Americans in the history of the United States" (Muñoz 1989:64). This action served as a catalyst to increase political awareness, revitalize existing community organizations, generate new political organizations, and mobilize young Mexican Americans, who became the heart of the Chicano movement.

Unlike the black civil rights movement, the Chicano movement relied less on established organizational resources and more on the energies of young people. By doing so, it found an energetic reservoir of leaders and skilled organizers—including Rodolfo "Corky" Gonzáles, José Angel Gutiérrez, and Reies López Tijerina—who minimized the need to tap outside resources. Furthermore, by emphasizing the need to win local political and economic control of Mexican American communities, the movement adopted a strategy in which there was a possibility of a visible payoff in an effort to attract new supporters.

The spirit of the Chicano movement is best expressed in the autobiographical writing of Gutiérrez (1998:11).

My generation of Chicano activists made events happen. We were determined, motivated, political actors in the Chicano movement. As proud militants and ready activists . . . we sought group ascendancy; we wanted to uplift our people, *la raza,* as a group. . . . [We] were in solidarity with one another. . . . We asserted our right to a homeland, Aztlan. My generation began the struggle to make a reality of Aztlan, building community in a serious way. Nation building begins at the neighborhood level, and we were the epitome of community development. To date, our generational struggle and creativity is manifest in the numerous Chicano institutions we created while making community. We took the Chicano movement from sporadic unrest to social protest to social movement to political party to governance and left Chicano institutions in place to keep vigil and shepherd over our gains.

We created more organizations and programs for all Chicanos than any previous generation of activists. Our record as builders of the Chicano community remains unmatched and unchallenged by the present generation of Hispanics.

The Asian American Movement

The Asian American movement is a clear example of a civil rights movement that was spawned by the black civil rights movement. Until the time of the black movement, each group of Asians in the United States had organized, litigated, and participated in politics when such participation was permitted, but they had done so as Japanese Americans, Chinese Americans, Filipino Americans, Korean Americans, or whatever their country of ancestry rather than as Asian Americans. The example of the black civil rights movement, which heightened sensitivity to racism, in combination with the anti-Vietnam movement, changed that situation. A generation of middle-class college students was suddenly aware of its "Asianness" as it questioned the nature of the Vietnam War. The students were in a unique position to raise questions about the racial implications of US military policy. Thus, much like the Chicano movement, the Asian American movement was youth-oriented and drew less on established organizations than did the black movement.

Perhaps because of the attempt to bridge such a broad spectrum of diversity, no single national leader or strategy emerged. Leaders were prominent only within a specific geographic area or a particular Asian ethnic group. Thus, it is not surprising that no single plan of action was ever formulated. The unifying principle of the various localized movements seems to have been the pursuit of equality (Wei 1993).

The American Indian Movement

The 1960s and 1970s also marked the reemergence of American Indian activism from the seventy-year hiatus that had followed the Wounded Knee Massacre of December 28, 1890. The group that came to symbolize this renewed activism was the American Indian Movement (AIM), a protest group modeled after black protest groups, formed in Minneapolis in 1968 to deal with the problems faced by urban Indians, especially the problem of police brutality. Within two years, AIM had expanded its concerns and addressed tribal and Indian issues regardless of the Indians' place of residence. Unlike other social movements, AIM and related Indian interest groups have sought "to retain their political and cultural exclusion from absorption or incorporation in the American polity" (Wilkins 2002:201).

Leadership of AIM came not from established groups but from Clyde Bellecourt and Dennis Banks, two of the cofounders of the movement, and

Russell Means—the most outspoken of the AIM leaders, who became a symbol of American Indian resistance. This leadership allowed AIM to attract bright, energetic young Indians from all parts of the country.

AIM became best known for its participation in dramatic events to highlight injustices. For example, in 1972 AIM was a major actor in the takeover of the headquarters of the Bureau of Indian Affairs (BIA) in Washington, DC. And in 1973, AIM activists protested tribal government corruption on the Pine Ridge Reservation, US violations of the 1868 Fort Laramie Treaty, and continuing federal controls over American Indians by seizing the village of Wounded Knee and holding it for ten weeks against a force of hundreds of federal officers. But AIM's use of confrontation triggered the concerted opposition of the BIA, the FBI, and other federal agencies. These agencies engaged in an effective, organized campaign of surveillance, infiltration, and intimidation against American Indian activists—including AIM—which diverted their energies from pursuing policy changes to squabbling internally.

Standing Rock Sioux and the Dakota Access Pipeline Protest. Like Black Lives Matter, the Lakota Sioux protest against the Dakota Access Pipeline is not a classic social movement, but it can be considered the next chapter in the American Indian Movement. The Lakota Sioux have a long history of struggling against encroachment on their ancestral lands. The Fort Laramie Treaties of 1851 and 1868 established the increasingly smaller boundaries of the Sioux Nation as settlers, prospectors, and railroad companies pushed farther and farther west (History n.d.). Despite the treaties, the Sioux sovereignty and lands were consistently violated. Conflict enveloped the second half of the nineteenth century (History n.d.) In 1890, the Sioux Act was passed, breaking the twenty-five million acres of the Sioux Nation into six separate, much smaller reservations—one of those was the Standing Rock Reservation for the Lakota Sioux (History n.d.).

Standing Rock Reservation is approximately 2.3 million acres, of which less than half is owned by tribe members. Their primary occupations are farming and ranching; water needed for these operations is drawn primarily from the Missouri River. The Sioux fight against the Dakota Access Pipeline is not the first time they have fought with the US Army Corps of Engineers (USACE). In 1948, the Sioux tried and failed to prevent the creation of the Oahe Dam (relevant to the current conflict), as the confluence of the two rivers previously there were considered sacred by the Sioux (History n.d.).

The Dakota Access Pipeline Project, which is being developed by Dakota Access LLC and constructed by Michels Pipeline Construction and Precision Pipeline LLC (Dakota 2015), is over eleven hundred miles of underground

PHOTO 2.2 *Harlington Wood, assistant U.S. attorney general (third row center without hat) is escorted into the village of Wounded Knee by militant Indians of the AIM group, March 13, 1973. Russell Means, one of the AIM leaders, and Carter Camp, another leader walka beside Wood. Wood was sent to the reservation in an effort to find a solution to the problem.* (AP Photo: 3714410322)

pipes that will connect the production areas of Bakken and Three Forks in North Dakota and an oil tank farm in Patoka, Illinois. The end point in Patoka serves as a crude oil distribution point for refineries throughout the Midwest and along the Gulf of Mexico. The bulk of the pipeline is being built on private land, but the pipeline will pass under a number of major waterways (Dakota n.d.); the effect on the environment in the event of a leak is a major worry. Though the pipeline will not pass directly through reservation land, it is within one-half mile of the northern edge of Standing Rock. More importantly, in the case of the Standing Rock Reservation eight thousand people and their livelihoods depend on the Missouri River for water (Heim and Berman 2016). There are also objections to the pipeline on the basis of violations to sacred American Indian ancestral lands, specifically with regard to the area surrounding Lake Oahe, though the Sioux object to the pipeline in its entirety (Civil 2016).

Individuals have been protesting the pipeline since April 2016 (Northcott 2016). As of this writing, members from all seven Sioux tribes have arrived and made their home at what has come to be called Red Warrior Camp. The American Civil Liberties Union (ACLU) claims representatives from as many as two hundred tribes have joined the protest. The estimated number of protestors varies from several hundred to a couple thousand and includes children who travelled to the site with their families (Northcott 2016). The protests are mostly peaceful, individuals standing in prayer, blocking the main road to the construction site with their bodies. There has been episodic violence, however, between the American Indians and the private security company protecting the workers and construction site (Healy 2016, Peralta 2016). As a result, North Dakota governor Jack Dalrymple declared a state of emergency, which has produced a highway roadblock, first by police, then by the National Guard, thirty miles south of the protest camps (Cook 2016).

In late July 2016, the Standing Rock Sioux filed a lawsuit against the USACE to block the permits issued for the Dakota Access Pipeline, claiming that the pipeline threatened their economic and environmental prosperity. The Sioux further claimed the Dakota Access Pipeline posed a risk to lands of "cultural and historical significance" (Civil 2016). The Standing Rock Sioux also filed a preliminary injunction to halt construction on the pipeline near the area of contestation for USACE violation of Section 106 of the National Historic Preservation Act (NPHA). Briefly, this section mandates that the USACE consult with American Indian peoples on projects that may pass through and potentially damage or destroy sacred or tribal lands (Civil 2016).

A federal judge denied the Standing Rock Sioux's request for a preliminary injunction to halt construction of the pipeline. But shortly after the judge's decision, the Obama administration issued a federal order to stop construction until the USACE could revisit its previous decision about the placement of the pipeline (Heim and Berman 2016). The work on the pipeline near Lake Oahe was halted as a result of the order, and the USACE was ordered to follow the procedure that required consultation with American Indian tribes for permitting infrastructure projects ("Joint" 2016). In early December 2016, the Department of the Army announced that it would not allow the pipeline to be drilled under a dammed section of the Missouri River, and said that it would look for an alternative route. As of this writing, it is unclear if this decision will stand in the Trump administration, given President Trump's support for the pipeline. He also owns stock in the company building the pipeline, Energy Transfer Partners, although he has said that his stock ownership will not play any part in his decision on the issue (Healy and Fandos 2016).

The Native Hawaiian Movement*

A little known and excluded history is that of the push by Native Hawaiians for full inclusion into their original homeland, now the state of Hawaii. In 1893, the American military overthrew the constitutional Hawaiian government headed by Queen Lili'uokalani. This was the final disposition that began in the early 1800s, when white missionaries began the systematic destruction of Native Hawaiian culture by getting the legislature to outlaw the Native Hawaiian language and the hula dance, which they viewed as idleness, debauchery, and leading to unproductive workers (Imada 2004:117). Despite Native Hawaiian resistance, an all-white puppet government was established in 1894, which evolved into the Republic of Hawaii. Native Hawaiians lost all political and economic power, and their Hawaiian citizenship was nullified. In 1898, the United States formally accepted the cession of sovereignty of Hawaii, although the Hawaiian people never had an opportunity to vote on whether they favored or opposed annexation by the United States. After the annexation, Native Hawaiians were officially citizens of the United States, but did not have the right to vote and remained inferior to the white "*haoles*" (Halualani 2002).

From 1898 to 1959, Hawaii was a territory of the United States. During this time, the United States refused to enter any formal treaties with the native peoples whose land had been taken from them during the annexation. In 1900, Congress passed the Organic Act, removing limitations on Native Hawaiian voting rights in the new Republic. Because Asians were denied citizenship in the United States, the passage of the Organic Act left Native Hawaiians as the majority of voters on the islands. Nonetheless, voting rights did nothing to improve the life chances and economic circumstances of native peoples.

In an attempt to alleviate the economic hardships of Native Hawaiians, in 1921, Congress enacted the Hawaiian Homes Commission Act (HHCA), which set aside two hundred thousand acres of lands the United States received in 1898 to provide residences and farm lots for natives. The HHCA provided long-term inalienable leases to "native Hawaiians"—as defined as "any descendant of not less than one-half part blood of the races inhabiting the Hawaiian islands prior to 1778" (The Hawaiian Homes Commission Act 1921). While the HHCA was designed to improve the economic circumstances of Native Hawaiians, it provided only marginal benefits, partially because of pressure

---

*The research and some of the writing in this section were done by Brittany Perry, doctoral candidate in political science, at Duke University at the time this was written. She is now Dr. Perry and is on the faculty of Texas A & M University.

from sugar interests, who wanted to keep the best lands for themselves (Levy 1975). In addition, the program was never properly funded; and to this day, many HHCA lands remain undeveloped and unavailable for many waiting applicants.

One significant outcome of the HHCA was that it constructed and imposed a definition of what it meant to be a "Native Hawaiian." Even today, the 50 percent blood quantum rule is used in the islands to manage and evaluate claims to indigeneity (Kauanui 2008). As Kēhaulani Kauanui explains, after 1921 "blood quantum began to stand in for race, indigeneity, and nationhood and it is now used to mean any or all of these depending on the specific political agenda of any given moment" (6). In many cases, the blood criterion emerged as a way to avoid recognizing Native Hawaiian entitlement to the specific lands that were desired for the leasing program. During debate over the HHCA, *need* was redefined in racial terms by using blood quantum as an indicator of social competency, where those defined by the 50 percent rule were deemed incapable of looking out for themselves.

In 1959, Hawaii was admitted as a state, and responsibility for the HHCA was transferred to Hawaii's new state government. At that time Congress also conveyed, in trust to the state, 1.2 million acres to be used for five listed purposes, including "the betterment of the conditions of Native Hawaiians." The truth was that no benefits were actually given to Native Hawaiians until the state constitution was amended in 1978 (Van Dyke 1998). This amendment provided that 20 percent of the funds received from ceded lands would go to a new entity, the Office of Hawaiian Affairs (OHA), for the benefit of natives (Office of Hawaiian Affairs [OHA] 2016).

Overall, statehood did not remedy the injustices imposed by colonization, and many Native Hawaiians remained staunchly opposed to joining the United States as the fiftieth state. When it came to voting on statehood, the vote of the indigenous peoples was essentially nullified by the nonindigenous Hawaiian settlers, who were given an equal vote if they had lived in Hawaii for one year (Anaya 1993). Additionally, the statehood ballot did not afford indigenous individuals the choice of sovereignty. Instead, voters only had two choices: to become a state or remain a territory, neither of which met the immediate interests of Native Hawaiians.

Hawaiian statehood was followed by a period of uncontrolled growth in Hawaii (McGregor-Alegado 1980). The tourism industry expanded, and farms were shut down to make room for hotels, resorts, and condominiums. The cost of living increased tremendously and left many Native Hawaiians dependent on welfare. According to a government survey conducted in 1970, 80 percent of Hawaii's people were priced out of the housing market (Thompson 1971).

In response to deteriorating standards of living, many Native Hawaiians began to organize and protest for better economic opportunities. Natives who worked in union-organized industries actively participated in efforts for higher wages and better working conditions. The forty-one-day United Public Workers strike in 1979 most significantly influenced the labor issue in the Hawaiian community.

In the 1970s, many Hawaiians also began to organize advocacy groups for welfare recipients. They established the Welfare Recipients Advisory Coalition for Welfare and Employment, which fought against major cutbacks to the welfare program under the Nixon administration. In many instances, Native Hawaiians also joined forces with many other ethnic groups to obtain certain benefits. As an example, during the 1970s, many Native Hawaiians joined with Filipinos, Okinawans, Portuguese, Japanese, and even a few whites to promote low-income housing, long-term farm leases, and access to Hawaiian fishing villages (McGregor-Alegado 1980).

Native Hawaiians also organized to protect certain aspects of their culture, and they continue to do so today. As an example, Native Hawaiians have worked to protect the tradition of surfing. Surfing has been a part of Native Hawaiian life since 500 CE, and since 1778, this tradition has been threatened by outsiders (Helekunihi-Walker 2005). Pro surfers from around the world have come to Hawaii and exploited native surfing beaches. In response, some Native Hawaiian surfing groups, including the Hui O He'e Nalu, have organized in protest. Despite efforts to peacefully protest the International Professional Surfing (IPS), the Hui were portrayed as terroristlike savages in the national media during the 1970s and 1980s. In the movie *North Shore* (1987), Hui members are shown as uncivil men who carry cane knives and threaten white "*haoles.*" Although the media and Hollywood stigmatized Native Hawaiians, the positive effect of such attention was that Native Hawaiians were finally visible to the public and they were not viewed as weak and emasculated, as they had been in the past. Today, the Hui are seen as an anticolonialist group and continue to work to protect Native Hawaiian culture and Native Hawaiian land. They hold yearly Native Hawaiian paddleboard races and beach cleanup operations and have helped push legislation to recognize surfing as a sport in Hawaii's public schools.

On a broader scale, the Hawaiian Renaissance, founded in the 1970s, was a collective Native Hawaiian movement designed to restore traditional Hawaiian culture and language. Influenced by global culture and civil rights movements on the American mainland, the Renaissance spurred various forms of political and social activism. Leaders of the Renaissance included musicians, scholars, and even hula instructors. The movement led to the resurrection of the Hawaiian language and the founding of Hawaiian immersion schools (Tsai 2009).

During the 1970s, many Native Hawaiians were also working to protest the presence of the US military in Hawaii. Many were particularly concerned with US Navy bombing exercises being conducted on Kaho'olawe Island at the time. Natives organized what was called the Kaho'olawe movement and successfully stopped the bombing and won a partial cleanup and return of the island. Today, such organizations as DMZ Hawaii continue to work to counter the military's negative social, cultural, and environmental effects on the islands (DMZ Hawaii/Aloha Aina 2008).

On the one-hundredth anniversary of the overthrow of Hawaii, thousands of Native Hawaiians gathered to put pressure on Hawaii's congressional delegation to take their grievances surrounding the unauthorized overthrow of Hawaii to Washington. The result was the 1993 Apology Resolution, introduced by Senator Daniel Akaka, Native Hawaiian Democrat from Hawaii, and approved by Congress and President Clinton. In signing this resolution, the US government formally acknowledged its complicity in the overthrow of Hawaii. Today, Hawaiian leaders are continuing to press the US government to also acknowledge the illegality of annexation and statehood.

In 1994, Congress passed the Native Hawaiian Education Act, which extended equal privileges and rights afforded to other Native Americans to Native Hawaiians. Essentially, what this law did was establish the special responsibility of Congress toward Native Hawaiians as a result of the US overthrow of Hawaiian sovereignty in the 1800s.*

It was because of this act that Native Hawaiian groups have since argued that they have a right to self-determination under international law (Ah Nee-Benham and Heck 1998). Many worked to pressure the US government to adopt the United Nations Declaration on the Rights of Indigenous Peoples, which recognizes the individual and collective rights of indigenous peoples as well as their rights to culture, identity, language, employment, health, education, and other issues. Although the second Bush administration refused to support this declaration, President Obama agreed to sign it in December 2010. However, the terms of the declaration only apply to federally recognized Indian tribes, not Native Hawaiians. Efforts have been made to recognize Native Hawaiians as indigenous peoples with a status similar to

---

*Yet this law did not recognize Native Hawaiians as having a relationship with the US government that was akin to that of American Indians. This reality was drawn out distinctly in *Rice v. Cayetano* (2000).

PHOTO 2.3 *Native Hawaiian activists march during a Hawaiian independence protest in Honolulu on Friday, August 21, 2009.* (AP Photo/Marco Garcia; ID: 090821035772)

that of American Indian tribes, but to date they have been largely unsuccessful. One example of such a failure is the National Hawaiian Government Reorganization Act (known as the Akaka Bill), last proposed in 2009 by Hawaiian senator Daniel Akaka. This bill sought to establish a process for indigenous Hawaiians to gain federal recognition similar to that of an Indian tribe. Although both the House and Senate were looking to pass this bill, in the end, they could not completely agree on its content and thus it failed in the 111th Congress.

VOTING RIGHTS LAW

One of the goals of each of these movements has been to attain political power. Casting a vote is the most basic formal act of participation in a polity, and this simple act has important symbolic and practical ramifications. The right to cast a ballot separates the insiders (citizens) from the outsiders (noncitizens) and dependents (the underaged). When aggregated, votes determine who the nation's public policymakers, the people who allocate public resources, will be. In short, the vote is seen as a tool for protecting other rights and achieving other goals—as a means rather than an end. In this section, we consider the contemporary status of voting rights for minority groups.

For most Americans the right to vote is assumed, and Americans assume all other citizens have the same right. After all, in the wake of the Civil War, the Constitution was amended to ban intentional discrimination by public officials based on race or previous condition of servitude (the Fourteenth Amendment) and to prohibit the denial or abridgment of the right to vote by officials at all levels of government on the basis of race, color, or previous condition of servitude (the Fifteenth Amendment). But within a few years, the Supreme Court declared much of the legislation designed to enforce the Fifteenth Amendment unconstitutional, and Congress repealed other such legislation. Thus, when federal supervision of Southern elections ended in 1877, the states were effectively free to structure and operate their electoral processes as they saw fit.

What followed was the systematic disenfranchisement of the black electorate. Through a variety of devices—discriminatorily administered literacy tests, poll taxes, white primaries—Southern states passed some of the most effective legislation ever enacted. For example, between 1896 and 1900, the number of black Louisianans registered to vote dropped from 130,334 to 5,320. Likewise, at the end of the nineteenth century, only 9 percent of Mississippi's black voting-age population was registered to vote; three decades earlier the figure had been 70 percent (US Commission on Civil Rights 1968).

In the early part of the twentieth century, some legal progress was made in attacking various methods of disenfranchisement. In 1915 the Supreme Court, in *Guinn v. United States,* declared unconstitutional the **grandfather clause**—a device used by Southern states to deny the vote to those whose grandparents were slaves—which circumvented the Fifteenth Amendment. In 1944, in *Smith v. Allwright,* the Court invalidated Texas's **white primary** as a violation of the Fifteenth Amendment. This primary had been based on the logic that the state's Democratic Party was a private organization and, thus, that its means of nominating candidates—the "white primary"—was not covered by the equal protection clause of the Fourteenth Amendment. The Democratic Party was the dominant party in Texas, and the individual who won the primary was the predetermined winner of the general election. If the Democratic Party were a private organization, and if only members of the party could vote in the primary, black voters were effectively blocked from participation. In spite of these victories, the Supreme Court rarely changed day-to-day realities for black citizens. It was against this backdrop that the black civil rights movement pressed for the right to vote as a top priority. The belief was that the ballot could be a tool for achieving other changes sought by the movement.

The federal legislation that was passed at least partially in response to the black civil rights movement was the **Voting Rights Act (VRA) of 1965**, which was amended in 1970, 1975, 1982, and 2006. Much of the law continues in perpetuity, unless specifically repealed, and the act was extended without major changes in 2006 for another twenty-five years. The extension passed the Senate 98–0 (Babington 2006). Basically, the act, as amended,

1. prohibits "tests or devices" that had been used in the past to dilute racial minorities—for example, literacy tests, education requirements, tests of good character, racial gerrymandering, and English-only elections in jurisdictions in which a single linguistic minority constitutes more than 5 percent of the voting-age population;

2. makes clear that if the effect of a practice is discriminatory, it is unlawful, regardless of the intent of its originator;

3. defines the jurisdictions covered by special provisions of the law as those which used a "test or device" to limit voting and in which less than half of the voting-age population (VAP) were registered or voted in either the 1964, 1968, or 1972 presidential elections (Section 4 of the VRA);

4. requires that "covered" jurisdictions gain federal permission to implement any changes in election laws or procedures to assure that such changes are not "retrogressive," that is, do not make it more difficult for protected minorities to elect representatives of their choice (Section 5 of the VRA);

5. allows the attorney general to assign federal examiners to register voters who must be accepted as qualified by local authorities and to appoint federal poll watchers in the jurisdictions in which examiners have been used to attempt to detect irregularities in the conduct of elections.

6. requires jurisdictions with significant language minority populations who have limited proficiency in English and higher than the national illiteracy rate to provide voting materials in the language of the applicable minority group as well as in English.

The fourth, the "preclearance" provision, applies only in those political jurisdictions in which fewer than half of those who were eligible to vote were registered or voted in the 1964, 1968, or 1972 presidential elections *and* in which a discriminatory "test or device" was used in registration or voting. Thus, the states of Alabama, Alaska, Arizona, Georgia, Louisiana, Mississippi, South Carolina, Texas, and Virginia, as well as five counties in California, five counties in Florida, two towns in Michigan, ten towns in New Hampshire, three counties in New York, forty counties in North Carolina, and two counties in South Dakota are covered jurisdictions. These jurisdictions remain covered today.

This legislation has been fairly effective in dealing with vote denial. Although gaps still exist between the political participation rates of the various racial and ethnic populations and the rate of the white population, these gaps have narrowed since the passage of the VRA. And the number of successful office seekers from groups previously denied the vote is increasing—particularly for blacks.

More work remains, however, in the area of **vote dilution**. Vote dilution involves "the impairment of the equal opportunity of minority voters to participate in the political process and to elect candidates of their choice" (McDonald and Powell 1993:27). Drawing on Supreme Court decisions that mandate that voting power must be apportioned equally based on population (the one person, one vote decisions), the logic has been extended to mandate that voters have the right to cast ballots that have the potential to elect candidates of their choice. At various times, at-large elections, racially gerrymandered districting schemes that unnecessarily fragment or unnecessarily concentrate minority group voters, laws that prohibit single-shot voting, discriminatory annexations or deannexations, and the abolition of elected or appointed offices or the changing of the means of selection have been used to dilute minority voting strength. These practices are not necessarily dilutive, but when they are combined with other social and historical circumstances, they may create an unequal opportunity for minority groups or white voters to elect their preferred candidates.

The determination of whether a jurisdiction is engaging in minority vote dilution requires an examination of the "totality of circumstances." The circumstances that courts examine include racial bloc voting; a history of discrimination; depressed minority socioeconomic status; a paucity of elected minority officials; the use of racial campaign appeals; the existence of formal or informal "slating" groups, which are groups of candidates who band together or who are endorsed as a group by other organizations; and the employment of devices that enhance the possibility for discrimination, such as numbered positions, where electoral offices are designated by number and political candidates are essentially running for separate offices in separate elections, which requires each candidate to specify the position for which he or she wants to be elected.

Although much of the voting rights legislation was designed to vindicate the suffrage rights of blacks, other groups have also used the law to attempt to enhance their own political power. For example, American Indians used litigation pursuant to modern voting rights legislation in such attempts. Indians have the same right to vote as all other citizens, and election districts in which they vote must be apportioned under the one person, one vote principle. All four nonblack minority groups—Hispanics, Asian Americans, American Indians, and Alaskan Natives—are recognized as language minority groups under the VRA, and election administrators must take that into account in affected jurisdictions.

A common remedy applied when vote dilution is found or when legislators are reapportioning or redistricting following the census is to draw districts in which a protected minority constitutes a majority of the residents—"majority minority" districts. Both the creation of such districts and the shape of some of them are matters of continuing controversy. A series of US Supreme Court decisions about the appropriateness of considering race in the drawing of congressional districts, raised in the context of a number of oddly shaped districts, has apparently limited the drawing of majority minority districts. The first such case heard by the court, *Shaw v. Reno* (1993), focused on a congressional district drawn in North Carolina in response to Justice Department pressure to give effect to potential minority voting strength in certain parts of the state. The plan that was adopted created a district in the north central part of the state that linked urban black population concentrations with a 160-mile-long "bridge," at times no wider than the I-85 right-of-way. The court subjected this arrangement to strict scrutiny and ultimately struck down the majority black district as an example of racial gerrymandering (*Shaw v. Hunt* 1996). Specifically, the court found that when districts' shapes are "bizarre"—that is, when they are inexplicable on grounds other than race—strict scrutiny by the court is required. Building on and clarifying this decision, the court struck down districting plans in Georgia (*Miller v. Johnson* 1995) for three majority black congressional districts and in Texas (*Bush v. Vera* 1996) for two majority black districts and one majority Latino district, requiring that congressional districts in both states be redrawn. Subsequently, federal district courts declared the majority black Third District in Virginia and the majority Latino Twelfth District in New York unconstitutional. These rulings meant that in the 2001 round of redistricting, following the 2000 Census, the crafting of new majority minority districts was severely constrained.

The issue is important because of what majority minority districts mean relative to the ability of blacks and Latinos to be elected to office. There is substantial evidence that racism persists in American society, that voting is still racially polarized, and that racial appeal tactics are still used in political campaigns (Grofman, Handley, and Niemi 1992; Davidson and Grofman 1994; Reeves 1997). Nevertheless, controversy surrounds the creation of majority minority districts because some believe that the VRA has become an affirmative action tool to get minorities elected, thereby making representation an entitlement; that racism among whites has decreased; and that racially polarized voting is no longer a problem (Thernstrom 1987). From the latter viewpoint, if minorities are not elected in white majority districts, it is for reasons other than racial ones, and therefore the drawing of districts to maximize minority electoral prospects is unnecessary (Reeves 1997).

Such controversy is part of the ongoing struggle over whether and, if so, how to merge the reality of racial minorities' political status with the rhetoric of American democracy, and its resolution will have a tremendous impact on the strategies chosen by minority political activists. At its heart, this controversy centers on the notion of representation and what it means. The structure of our electoral process, and of who wins and loses in the process, affects who will raise the questions and what positions will be taken.

Lani Guinier, Harvard University law professor and President Clinton's failed nominee for assistant attorney general for civil rights in 1993, has ideas on representation and power that are not as outlandish as her opponents and the media portrayed them to be (Guinier 1994). Her questioning of whether it is fair in a majoritarian system for a majority—50 percent plus one—in any given election to hold 100 percent of the power is gaining currency. What about the other 50 percent minus one? Should they, because they are in the minority, be excluded from the governing body? It should be understood that whereas Guinier is concerned with the electoral representation of racial minorities, in her view "minority" refers not only to racial minorities but to gender minorities, and to Republican or Democrat minorities as well. She also questions whether concentrating racial minorities in majority minority districts is the best approach to rectifying the exclusion of such minorities from the political process.

One of Guinier's solutions to this imbalance is the concept of cumulative voting. **Cumulative voting**, a technique used until recently by the state of Illinois in its legislative races, is a mechanism that benefits numerical minorities, whether they are blacks, Latinos, Asians, Indians, women, Democrats, or Republicans. The concept is simple. At present, if there are seven seats on the city council, each voter votes for one individual in each of seven contests. In essence, each voter has seven votes but can vote for only one candidate in each contest. Under cumulative voting, each voter has seven votes and can assign them however he or she wants. The voter can give five votes to one candidate and one each to two others or can give all seven votes to one candidate. In this manner, numerical minorities could give all of their votes to a particular candidate, thus increasing their chances of electing members of their own group. Cumulative voting systems have allowed the Sisseton Sioux Indians in South Dakota to elect a representative to the local school board; and in Chilton County, Alabama, allowed blacks to elect a black to the County Council, along with two white Republicans who, until the implementation of cumulative voting, had never been able to overcome the Democratic registration and voting majorities. In May 2000, as a result of the settlement of a voting rights lawsuit, cumulative voting was used in Amarillo, Texas, to elect members of the school board. Despite constituting a significant portion of the city's population, blacks and Latinos had not been elected to the school board in more than two decades. Under cumulative voting, both a black and a Latino were elected to the seven-member school board. More than one hundred jurisdictions have adopted alternative voting systems, with cumulative voting among the most preferred. Although cumulative voting is often mentioned in relation to the four groups that are the subject of this book, it would also benefit whites who are increasingly becoming numerical minorities in many urban centers. Clearly, a serious yet highly charged discussion of the concepts of majority and the access of numerical minorities will take place in the future.

After the 2010 elections, Republicans controlled both chambers in state legislatures in twenty-six states, and controlled the redistricting process in seventeen of those states. As a result, Republicans were able to draw congressional districts that benefited their party and disadvantaged Democrats. (It should be noted that both political parties draw lines to benefit their own partisan goals. Democrats controlled the redistricting process in six states, courts controlled redistricting in eight states, five states have independent redistricting commissions, four states have split control between Republicans and Democrats, and two have politician-appointed commissions.) According to the Brennan Center, Republicans redrew the lines for four times as many congressional seats as Democrats did (Iyer and Gaskins 2012). In some states, Republicans drew districts that packed black and Latino voters into excessive population majority minority districts or, in others, diluted minority voting power. Lawsuits challenging the redistricting maps were filed in thirty-eight states. For example, in Texas, suits were filed over vote dilution of Latino populations in federal congressional seats, as well as state House and Senate seats. The federal district court in Washington, DC, found that the maps violated the VRA and that the dilution of Latino voting was intentional. The federal court in San Antonio had to draw its own maps in order for the 2012 congressional elections to occur. The court-drawn maps increased black and Latino voting power, but those maps were to be used for the 2012 elections only. Interestingly, the legislature adopted them, with only minor changes, as permanent maps in 2013, and they have been used in two election cycles, including 2016. Despite legislative action to adopt the court's maps, litigation is still ongoing on the congressional and state House districts. State Senate boundaries were settled in court.

The Voting Rights Act has been subjected to a number of legal challenges since its implementation in 1965, particularly Section 5 of the VRA. Section 5, referred to as the preclearance portion of the VRA, requires state, county, and local governments that have a history of discrimination and marginalization against some members of the community to submit all proposed changes to voting laws to federal authorities (Rutenberg 2015). Section 5 was ratified to halt changes in election practices or procedures in specified jurisdictions until it could be determined that the new procedures did not have a discriminatory purpose or effect (US Department of Justice 2015). Such determinations would be made following administrative review by the attorney general, or a lawsuit before the US District Court for the District of Columbia (US Department of Justice 2015).

In *South Carolina v. Katzenbach* (1966) the state of South Carolina challenged the constitutionality of Section 5 of the VRA. In 1969, the state of Mississippi attempted to alter voting regulations, but the US Supreme Court held that the state could not implement any voting provisions unless these provisions were approved under Section 5 of the VRA (*Allen v. State Board of Elections*). In *Oregon v. Mitchell* (1970) the Supreme Court held that Congress could establish rules regarding voter age requirement for federal elections, but not for state and local elections. In *Georgia v. Ashcroft* (2003), the Supreme Court had to determine if a redistricting plan in the state of Georgia should have been precleared under Section 5 of the VRA.

A case from Shelby County, Alabama, became one of the most important challenges to the Voting Rights Act. The county argued that Congress exceeded its authority in 2006 when it reauthorized Section 5 of the VRA, requiring that states and localities with a history of discrimination receive federal approval before making any changes to their voting laws. On June 25, 2013, in a landmark ruling, the US Supreme Court held that "it is unconstitutional to use the coverage formula in Section 4(b) of the Voting Rights Act to determine which jurisdictions are subject to the preclearance requirement of Section 5 of the Voting Rights Act." Thus states are no longer required to apply for preclearance before changing their voting laws (Bondl 2015; US Department of Justice 2015).

Although the Supreme Court did not actually rule on the constitutionality of Section 5, the court's decision in *Shelby County v. Holder* nullified Section 5 of the Voting Rights Act, since Section 4 outlines the formulas for how the US Department of Justice must implement Section 5 of the VRA (Fuller 2014; Rutenberg 2015). Without Section 4 of the VRA, the Justice Department has fewer legal resources at its disposal for challenging voting laws that are deemed to be discriminatory (Fuller 2014). Following the Supreme Court's ruling, North Carolina's Republican-led legislature implemented a revised, and highly restrictive, voter ID law. In July 2016, a federal appellate court struck down this law, ruling that North Carolina's Republican lawmakers had enacted new voting restrictions to suppress black voter turnout and "intentionally blunt the growing clout of African American voters" (Barnes and Marimow 2016; Wine and Blinder 2016).

The effects of changes in voter ID laws can be difficult to measure, but evidence suggests that voter turnout can be affected by restrictive and discriminatory voting laws. The Moral Monday movement started by the North Carolina NAACP was directly involved in protesting the racially discriminatory provision of HB 589, North Carolina's legislation that included the voter ID requirement put in place after the *Shelby* decision. Other states with new voting legislation, including Florida, Georgia, and South Carolina, also began similar protests.

CONCLUSION

Political success has not been attained without struggle. Civil rights movements have been necessary for each group openly to challenge the system not only in which it was at a disadvantage, but in which the rules were structured to keep it that way. One of the goals of each of these movements has been to achieve the right to vote, which it hopes it can use as a tool for winning political victories and protecting the fruits of those victories. The Voting Rights Act, as amended, has provided some protection for each of the groups. But the gutting of Section 5 of the Voting Rights Act puts access to one of the core elements of a democracy, the vote, at risk for communities of color. In Chapter 3 we address the way members of these groups have been able to play a role in the US political system.

- -

DISCUSSION QUESTIONS

1. A group's size is important in a majoritarian system, but population means different things depending upon the political issue under consideration. How do demographic characteristics affect actual and potential political power?

2. "Minorities" by definition are at a disadvantage in national politics. But in some areas, groups that are in the minority nationally constitute a near majority or a majority. What are the implications of this pattern for minority politics?

3. Why are some political movements successful, whereas others fail? Choose a group that suffers from a disadvantage within the US political system and explain how you would design a political movement to try to alleviate this situation.

4. What kind of protection is afforded to racial and ethnic minorities under contemporary voting rights law, and why was such a law thought to be necessary when it was passed and extended?

5. Do you agree with Lani Guinier's questioning of whether a majoritarian system means that 51 percent of the people control 100 percent of the power?

6. How have social media platforms altered the way in which social movements and political activism organizations operate? Consider this question in the context of Black Lives Matter particularly.

7. How do the protests at the Standing Rock Sioux Reservation fit into our broader understanding of civil rights movements and activism? What are the similarities and differences between Standing Rock activism and other instances of political activism?

▶ CHAPTER 3

America's Racial Minorities in the Contemporary Political System
Actors

Mississippi-based regional bank BancorpSouth (BXS) paid a $10.6 million settlement after evidence mounted of its discriminatory lending practices. After investigations by the Department of Justice and Consumer Financial Bureau, these government agencies filed a complaint that bank officials directed loan officers to turn down minority mortgage applicants more quickly than whites, and to avoid giving "borderline" applicants credit assistance that other mortgage seekers might receive (McCoy 2016). While the bank denied the allegations, an audio recording of an internal meeting of BXS provided evidence that such statements were made. The Consumer Financial Bureau also sent individuals as testers to several bank branches to ask about mortgages. Their findings highlight that the bank's process "harmed the people who were overcharged or denied their dream of ownership based on their race" (McCoy 2016). In addition to denying mortgages and loan applications to African Americans, it was also found to charge African Americans a higher annual percentage rate for loans than it did whites with similar loan qualifications (DOJ 2016). Moreover, it was illegally redlining in Memphis, Tennessee, whereby it was structuring business practices in order to avoid and discourage applications for mortgages from customers who resided in minority areas.

—WASHINGTON, DC, JUNE 29, 2016

James Madison, in *Federalist No. 10,* envisioned the United States as a society in which conflict rather than consensus would predominate. The citizenry would be divided into many groups, parties, and factions that would compete for benefits they felt to be rightly theirs. For Madison, the chief cause of these divisions was economic in origin, but, as we well know, race has emerged as a major dividing factor in American society. Madison's concept of US society is represented in political science by pluralist theory. **Pluralism**, the reigning paradigm in political science, states in part that if citizens participate in the political process by voting and other means, the political system will produce electoral and policy outcomes favored by the participants.

Yet many of pluralism's assumptions do not favor the participation of, or acknowledge the barriers to, participation in the political process by America's racial minorities. Pluralism assumes that many centers of power exist and that different groups have access to a variety of power centers; thus, if a group is blocked from one center of power, it will always have access to another. Therefore, although groups may differ in their levels or types of political resources—for example, population size versus financial means—on balance the government will play a neutral role, and the resource differential will be balanced through the competition process. Pluralism also assumes that every group has equal access to the political process and that not every group will win all of the time, but will win or lose depending on the issue and on its ability to use political resources.

Despite its preeminence in political science, pluralism has numerous critics. Pluralism assumes that interests will become diversified across economic, social, and political issues, resulting in little need for racial and ethnic groups to organize around group-based issues. Race and ethnicity will thus be obscured as these other issues take precedence. Pluralism also states that once groups realize their subjective interests, they will become incorporated into the political system. Critics argue that these notions of interest diversification and incorporation dismiss the fact that racial minorities are treated as groups; no individual achievement improves the status of the individual or changes the position of the group (Pinderhughes 1987:38).

Another criticism is that pluralism has a class bias: Upper-income individuals are better situated to compete for political outcomes. Despite pluralism's contention that political resources are counterbalanced, with one group's financial resources being neutralized by another group's population base, pluralism tilts political outcomes in favor of those with economic and political resources. As E. E. Schattschneider (1960:34) observed, "The flaw in the pluralist heaven is that the heavenly chorus sings with a strong upper-class accent."

There is a great deal of conflict in the scholarly literature over the utility of the pluralist framework in explaining the political behaviors of, and outcomes for, America's racial minorities. Nevertheless, African Americans, Latinos, American Indians, and Asian Americans are players—albeit often unequal players—in the US political system. What we have not done is use any particular conceptual framework to study these groups. It may be impossible to use one particular framework to guide the analysis of all four groups, or a chosen framework may work better in guiding analysis of a particular group at one point in time rather than at another. Regardless of which framework one uses, it is important to remember that if one is to undertake serious, empirical study of racial and ethnic politics in the United States, one inevitably adopts some type of conceptual framework that affects what one studies, which in turn affects the conclusions one reaches about the status of and the prospects for the future evolution of these politics.

Here we provide brief sketches of frameworks that have been used to study racial and ethnic politics or particular groups within the American context. We cannot do justice to these approaches in the confines of this book, but we provide at least a core reference.

- *The Moral Dilemma Framework.* Gunnar Myrdal (1944) posited that the basic problem in US racial and ethnic relations was an alleged contradiction between commitment to a democratic creed and the presence of racial discrimination. One possible implication of this framework was that racial conflict would disappear when whites' attitudes changed, suggesting a strategy of persuasion rather than of confrontation.
- *The Power Relations Framework.* Sociologist Hubert Blalock (1967) has argued that race relations in the United States can be characterized as power contests between dominant whites and subordinate minorities. If power is the product of multiplying "total resources and the degree to which these resources are mobilized" (Blalock 1967:110), then change will occur when minorities' resources are enhanced or are more effectively mobilized.
- *Two-Tiered Pluralist Framework.* Pluralism promises change through individual and collective participation in the existing political regime. As we noted, there are problems with this framework. An innovative attempt to adapt the concept to fit the situation in which minorities find themselves is "two-tiered pluralism," devised by Rodney Hero (1992). Based on his analysis of the situation of Latinos in the US political system, Hero describes "two-tiered pluralism" as a system "in which there is formal legal equality on the one hand, and . . . actual practice that undercuts equality for most members of minority groups" (1992:188–90). Thus, the pluralist solution to racial and ethnic

conflict cannot work efficiently or effectively because there is only marginal inclusion of minority group members within the political system.

• *The Modernization/Developmental Framework.* Advocates of this approach see racial and ethnic relations corresponding to specific levels of socioeconomic development and improving as greater socioeconomic development occurs. For example, Harry Holloway (1969) employed this approach in his study of blacks in Southern politics.

• *Black Utility Heuristic.* Michael Dawson (1994) introduces the black utility heuristic for analyzing the political choices and policy positions of black Americans. Using the concept of linked fate (the feeling on the part of many black Americans that their fate is linked to the fate of other members of the group), Dawson suggests that the black utility heuristic for African American political behavior leads an individual to use the social standing of the group as a proxy for the well-being of the individual. Linked fate for African Americans stems from a common and specific history and a set of shared experiences.

• *The Internal Colonialism Framework.* This final framework draws an analogy to the colonial experience in world history. In this instance, the colonized people reside within the political and social system of the United States. As developed by Robert Blauner (1972), this framework emphasizes the political powerlessness, economic dependence, and deculturation of minority populations within the United States.

None of these frameworks has proven to be the one best way of examining racial and ethnic politics in the United States. A variety of perspectives, however, can be useful, and as you explore the topics and issues raised in this volume more thoroughly, you may find one of these lenses helpful in clarifying or magnifying your chosen focal point.

This chapter explores approaches to the second dilemma—what is to be done—by examining ways in which racial and ethnic minorities participate in the political system. The aspects of political attitudes and participation addressed are: (1) **group identity or cohesion**—an individual's awareness of belonging to a certain group and having a *psychological attachment* to that group based on a perception of shared beliefs, feelings, interests, and ideas, as well as perceptions of discrimination with other group members (McClain et al. 2009); (2) **political ideology**, the underlying beliefs and attitudes of a group, which shape its opinions and actions on political issues; (3) **partisan identification**, the attachment to and intensity of feeling for a particular political party; (4) **voting behavior**, the way people vote in elections and the forces that influence these votes; and (5) **interest group activities**, actions taken by organized groups seeking to influence public officials and policies.

For each of the areas, when applicable, discussion is broken down along gender lines so that differences in the attitudes and behaviors of women and men within a group, as well as those between groups, are highlighted. These distinctions are important for a variety of reasons. We often hear about the political behavior and feelings of groups, but group feelings and actions may vary in intensity or even in kind when broken down into responses by men versus women. The salience and importance of gender for women in framing their political attitudes and behaviors may result in different attitudes and behaviors from those of men. Further, we cannot assume that gender issues will resonate similarly for all women. It is reasonable to expect that the beliefs of black women may differ not only from those of black men but also from those of Latinas, Indian women, and Asian women. The same expectation holds true for various combinations of women. Moreover, women from one racial or ethnic minority may have views similar to those of men in other ethnic or racial categories. As has been and will continue to be demonstrated throughout this book, race and its effects on the political system may be different for different racial groups.

The best data sources for identifying the political attitudes of blacks, Latinos, and Asians include: the National Black Election Study, 1984–1988 (NBES); the National Black Politics Study, 1993 (NBPS); the National Black Election Study, 1996 (NBES96); the Joint Center for Political and Economic Studies 2008 National Opinion Poll (JCPES2008); the Latino National Political Survey, 1990 (LNPS); the *Washington Post*/Kaiser Family Foundation/Harvard University Survey Project, National Survey on Latinos in America, 1999; the Pew Foundation 2002, 2004, 2007, 2010, and 2011 National Surveys of Latinos; the Latino National Survey 2006; the Pilot Study of the National Asian American Political Survey, 2000 (PNAAPS); the National Asian American Survey 2008, The Pew Research Center's 2012 Asian American Survey; the American National Election Study, 2008 and 2012; and the General Social Survey, 2010. These sources are national probability samples of the appropriate populations and represent the most comprehensive basis to date for determining the political attitudes of these groups. Data on American Indian political attitudes are much more limited. To date, we have no national surveys exclusively devoted to this population. Thus, we must rely on the results from a small number of local surveys from various cities and areas around the country and aggregate the small number of American Indians in national surveys.

GROUP IDENTITY AND PERCEPTIONS OF DISCRIMINATION

Actual or perceived group cohesion (group solidarity) has been identified in political science research as being strongly associated with increased levels of political participation among racial and ethnic minority groups in the United States (Olsen 1970; Verba and Nie 1972). The more individuals identify with other members of a group, the more likely they are to participate in politics and to coalesce around candidates and policy issues they perceive as being beneficial to the group. One of the measures of group cohesion among racial and ethnic minorities is the degree of perceived discrimination against both the individual and one's group. Another measure of group cohesion is the degree of closeness an individual feels to other people in the group with respect to ideas and feelings about issues.

According to a Pew Research Center study on the views of black, Latino, and white Americans on inequality, conducted between February 29 and May 8, 2016, blacks are more likely than whites to say racial discrimination (70 percent vs. 36 percent), lower quality schools (75 percent vs. 53 percent), and lack of jobs (66 percent vs. 45 percent) are major reasons that blacks may have a harder time getting ahead than whites. About 84 percent of black Americans say blacks in this country are treated less fairly than whites in dealing with the police, and majorities also say blacks are treated less fairly in the courts (75 percent), when applying for a loan or mortgage (66 percent), and in the workplace (64 percent). Regarding closeness, 93 percent of the black respondents in the 1984 NBES data reported being close to other blacks in terms of feelings and ideas (Gurin, Hatchett, and Jackson 1989:75–81), and a majority felt that what happens to the group affects them personally. As Table 3.1 exhibits, fully three-fourths of blacks surveyed in the 1984 and 1988 NBES (Tate 1993:25), the 1993 NBPS, and the 1996 NBES felt that what happens to black people in general will shape their lives. The number dipped in the 2005 National Politics Survey (65 percent), and again in the 2007 Center on African American Politics and Society Survey (59.7 percent), but rose slightly again in the 2008 Black Politics and Society survey (66.7 percent). It stayed about the same in the 2012 American National Election Study (65.3 percent). Despite the dips, close to two-thirds of black respondents believed they share a common fate with other blacks in the United States.

The level of cohesiveness among Latinos, as measured on these dimensions, is very different from the pattern found among African Americans. As seen in Tables 3.2a and 3.2b, according to the 2010 Pew Foundation National Survey of Latinos, regardless of national origin, the majority of Latinos believed they had *not* personally been discriminated against because of their ethnicity. Puerto Ricans, Mexicans, and other Latino groups were more likely than Cubans to report instances of discrimination. In fact, slightly more than four-fifths (81.2 percent) of Cubans indicated that they had not had personal experiences with discrimination. Yet when queried about their perceptions of

TABLE 3.1 Proportion of Blacks Perceiving That They Share a Common Fate with Other Blacks

	1984 (%)[a]	1988 (%)	1993 (%)[b]	1996 (%)[c]	2005 (%)[d]	2007 (%)[e]	2008 (%)[f]	2012 (%)[g]
Yes	73.5 (796)[h]	77.4 (339)	77.9 (904)	83 (954)	65 (601)	59.7 (261)	66.7 (661)	65.3 (677)
No	26.5 (287)	22.6 (99)	22.1 (256)	17 (196)	35 (318)	40.3 (176)	33.3 (330)	34.7 (360)
Total	100 (1,083)	100 (438)	100 (1,160)	100 (1,150)	100 (919)	100 (437)	100 (991)	100 (1,037)

[a] Preelection sample, 1984 and 1988 National Black Election Studies.
[b] 1993 National Black Politics Study.
[c] 1996 National Black Election Study, preelection sample.
[d] 2004–2005 National Politics Survey.
[e] 2007 Center on African American Politics and Society Survey.
[f] *ABC News/USA Today*/Columbia University Poll: Blacks, Politics, and Society (September 23, 2008).
[g] 2012 American National Election Study.
[h] Figures in parentheses represent the number of respondents.

Sources: Authors' computations from the 1984 and 1988 National Black Election Studies; 1993 National Black Politics Study; 1996 National Black Election Study; 2004–2005 National Politics Survey; 2007 Center for African American Politics and Society Survey; 2008 *ABC News/USA Today*/Columbia University Poll: Blacks, Politics, and Society; and 2012 American National Election Study.

discrimination, majorities of all Latino groups perceived discrimination against their ethnic origin group to be a major problem. Still, despite a majority perceiving discrimination as a major problem, Cubans were more likely to see discrimination as a minor problem or not a problem at all. This finding is consistent with Cubans indicating that they had not had personal experiences with discrimination.

Cubans clearly have a different pattern of perceptions than do Mexican Americans, Puerto Ricans, and other Latinos. This may partially stem from the fact that most Latinos from the various groups do not believe that all Latinos in the United States share a common culture. Nearly seven in ten (69 percent) Latinos say Latinos in the United States have many different cultures; only 29 percent say Latinos in the United States share a common culture (Taylor, Lopez, Martinez, and Velasco 2012). In terms of self-identification, only about a quarter (24 percent) of the Latinos in the 2011 survey identified themselves with the pan-ethnic terms Latino or Hispanic. A majority of all groups prefer to identify themselves with their family's country or original place of origin,

TABLE 3.2A Experiences with Discrimination Among Latinos

ETHNICITY	YES	NO	TOTAL
Mexican	34.4% (284)	65.6% (541)	100% (825)
Puerto Rican	33.3% (37)	66.7% (74)	100% (111)
Cuban	18.8% (13)	81.2% (56)	100% (69)
Other	32.7% (110)	67.3% (226)	100% (336)

Source: Adapted from Pew Hispanic Center, 2010 National Survey of Latinos.
Question wording: During the last five years, have you, a family member, or close friend experienced discrimination because of your racial or ethnic background, or not?

TABLE 3.2B Perceptions of Discrimination Against Latinos

ETHNICITY	MAJOR PROBLEM	MINOR PROBLEM	NOT A PROBLEM	TOTAL
Mexican	62.8% (509)	23.8% (193)	13.4% (109)	100% (811)
Puerto Rican	69.4% (75)	17.6% (19)	13.0% (14)	100% (108)
Cuban	56.3% (36)	21.9% (14)	21.9% (14)	100.1% (64)
Other	63.4% (225)	23.1% (82)	13.5% (48)	100% (355)

Source: Adapted from Pew Hispanic Center, 2010 National Survey of Latinos.

for example, Mexican or Mexican American, Cuban, Puerto Rican, El Salvadoran and so forth (Pew Research Center 2012:9).

Nevertheless, Table 3.3 shows that on the question of whether one Latino group's doing well depends on other Latino groups' also doing well, we do see a sense of connection. Almost half (46.8 percent) of Mexican Americans feel that their well-being depends on other Latinos' also doing well. This sense of doing well is highest among El Salvadorans and Dominicans and lowest among Puerto Ricans. Whether this measure might be a substitute for group cohesion is not clear and deserves further study, but it does give us a sense that on some level the various Latino groups think there is a connection among them.

TABLE 3.3 Degree to Which Latino Subgroups Believe That Their Well-Being Is Dependent on the Well-Being of Other Latinos

	MEXICAN	PUERTO RICAN	CUBAN	EL SALVADORAN	DOMINICAN
Nothing	7.1% (407)	11.9% (98)	13.3% (56)	5.4% (22)	5.7% (19)
Little	13.1% (749)	13.8% (113)	8.6% (36)	11.3% (46)	11.6% (39)
Some	25.8% (1,469)	29.1% (239)	22.1% (93)	17.4% (71)	19.4% (65)
A Lot	46.8% (2,666)	37.4% (307)	43.6% (183)	59.0% (240)	55.5% (186)
DK/NA	7.2% (413)	7.9% (65)	12.4% (52)	6.9% (28)	7.8% (26)
Total	100% (5,704)	100% (822)	100% (420)	100% (407)	100% (335)

Source: 2006 Latino National Survey (LNS).

Question wording: How much does [ethnic subgroup's] "doing well" depend on how other Hispanics or Latinos also doing well? A lot, some, a little, or not at all?

According to the Pew Research Center's 2012 Asian American Survey, Asian Americans, for the most part, do not believe that discrimination is a major problem for their communities. About one in five Asian Americans say they have personally been treated unfairly in the past year because they are Asian, and one in ten say they have been called an offensive name. Older adults are less likely than young and middle-aged adults to report negative personal experience with bias. Compared to blacks, and to a lesser extent Latinos, Asian Americans appear to be less inclined to view discrimination against their group as a major problem. Just 13 percent of Asian Americans say it is a major problem, while about half (48 percent) say it is a minor problem, and a third (35 percent) say it is not a problem. Of the various ethnic origin groups, Korean Americans are more likely than other groups to say that discrimination is a major problem (24 percent), while Japanese Americans are the least likely to see discrimination as a major problem (8 percent). Yet discrimination was not dismissed as a problem, as substantial portions of all groups—Koreans, Chinese, Vietnamese, Asian Indian, Filipino, and Japanese—saw it as a minor problem. Only in the case of Filipinos and Japanese did almost half not see discrimination as a problem at all (Pew Research Center, Asian American

Survey 2013). Earlier analysis of data collected in 1984 in California found that perceptions of discrimination among Asian Americans have a generational dimension. Second-generation Asian Americans are far more likely than are first-generation individuals to perceive discrimination (Cain and Kiewiet 1986). But this does not explain the attitudes of Filipino and Japanese Americans, as both of these groups are among the oldest in the United States, while Vietnamese are the most recent immigrants to the United States.

Similar to Latinos, Asian Americans do not find the "Asian American" label itself appealing. Only about 19 percent say they most often describe themselves as Asian American or Asian. A majority (62 percent) say they most often describe themselves by their country of origin (e.g., Chinese or Chinese American, Vietnamese or Vietnamese American, and so on), while just 14 percent say they most often simply call themselves American. Among US-born Asians, the share who most often call themselves American rises to 28 percent. The 2008 National American Survey suggests that the lack of identification with a pan-ethnic identity might contribute to what could be perceived to be a lack of group cohesion for Asian Americans. On the question of whether Asian Americans perceive that they share a common fate with other Asian Americans, miniscule proportions of Asians in all ethnic origin groups—Chinese, Asian Indian, Vietnamese, Korean, Filipino, and Japanese—feel that they share a strong common fate with other Asian Americans (see Table 3.4). More believe there is some common fate, but the greater portion of Asian Americans feel they do not share a common fate with other Asian Americans. Filipinos and Asian Indians have the highest belief in not sharing a common fate, followed by Vietnamese, Japanese, and Chinese Americans. When asked if they share a common fate with other Asian Americans from their ethnic group (data not shown), there are some shifts, with half (50 percent) of Korean Americans believing that they share a lot and some common fate with other Korean Americans. Increases are also seen among the Vietnamese (48.4 percent) and Japanese Americans (45.1 percent). But there are still large portions of each group that believe that they do not share a common fate with others of their ethnic-origin group.

What should we make of the different patterns among blacks and Latinos on the one hand and Asian Americans on the other? Does this mean that political cohesion among the latter groups does not exist? Scholars studying the political behavior and attitudes of nonblack racial minority groups suggest that the relationship of group consciousness to political behavior "should be treated as a hypothesis rather than an assumption," for "making the connection from shared classification in a racial category to group-based political behavior is neither simple nor obvious for nonblack minorities, particularly those whose

TABLE 3.4 Degree to Which Asian Americans Perceive They Share a Common Fate with Other Asian Americans

	CHINESE	INDIAN	VIET-NAMESE	KOREAN	FILIPINO	JAPANESE
A Lot	9.1% (121)	7.7% (85)	7.5% (54)	14.6% (89)	8.6% (51)	7.9% (42)
Some	31.3% (417)	28.3% (314)	27.1% (194)	37.9% (231)	17.7% (105)	29.9% (158)
Not Very Much	7.1% (95)	5.1% (56)	5.0% (36)	2.5% (15)	12.8% (76)	7.0% (37)
None	43.0% (573)	50.1% (555)	47.8% (343)	37.9% (231)	55.6% (329)	45.2% (239)
Don't Know	9.5% (127)	8.8% (98)	12.6% (90)	7.2% (44)	5.2% (31)	10.0% (53)
Total	100.0% (1,333)	100.0% (1,108)	100.0% (717)	100.1% (610)	99.9% (592)	100.0% (529)

Source: Adapted from National Asian American Survey, 2008.

Question wording: Do you think what happens generally to other Asians in this country affects what happens in your life? Will it affect you a lot, some, or not very much?

population growth is attributed to new immigration" (Junn and Masuoka 2008, 729). Junn and Masuoka (736) suggest that Asian American group identification can be either enhanced or diminished depending on the context, which research on blacks and Latinos suggests might not be at play.

High levels of group cohesion may translate into increased levels of political participation, especially registering to vote and actually voting, by racial minority groups. Blacks have higher levels of group cohesion and share more of a common destiny than do Latinos and Asians. Lower levels of voter registration and actual voting among Asians and Latinos may be partly explained by the lack of group cohesion, although other factors also contribute to this outcome (see "Voting Behavior" section in this chapter).

POLITICAL IDEOLOGY

In popular culture and the news media, racial minorities are often described as ideologically and politically "liberal" on a conservative-to-liberal continuum. Yet those who study black and Latino political attitudes argue that it is inappropriate to use the standard political ideology labels of "liberal," "moderate," and "conservative," which were developed from national studies that contained few nonwhites, and apply them to the black and Latino populations. This simple application of labels misses the complexity and variability of attitudes within the various racial communities. Moreover, the application of the labels implies that there is an agreed-upon definition of their meaning and that individuals who identify themselves by these labels are able to define what they mean (Hero 1992; Smith and Seltzer 1992; Tate 1993).

Are we safe in saying that if an individual or a predominant portion of a group believes the federal government should take a more active role in reducing unemployment, providing services for the poor, and improving the socioeconomic position of blacks and other racial minorities, that individual or group is liberal? Similarly, are we safe in saying that if an individual or the majority of a group supports prayer in public schools, the individual or group is conservative? Based on popular notions of liberal and conservative, the answer would be yes to both questions. Yet we commonly find such responses within African American public opinion, which raises doubts about the assignment of stereotypical labels such as liberal and conservative.

Contrary to popular wisdom, blacks are spread across the ideological spectrum, with only an approximately 10-percentage-point gap between the number of blacks self-identifying as some degree of liberal and those identifying as some degree of conservative in 1988 NBES data, and an approximately 4-percentage-point gap between the same categories in the 1993 NBPS and the 1996 NBES data (see Table 3.5). The distance increased a little in 2004 and 2008 between blacks self-identifying as liberals and those identifying as conservatives—6.7 percent in 2004 and 6.5 percent in 2008, but the distance increased significantly, 19.2 percentage points, in 2012. The difference appeared to be an increase in the proportion of individuals identifying as moderate, and a considerable drop-off of blacks identifying themselves as conservative. The percentages identifying as moderates fluctuates among the data sets, with the largest portion (48.5 percent) in the 2004 CBS/BET data dropping to 36.6 percent in the 2008 American National Election Study, then bouncing back up again to 44.4 percent in the 2012 American National Election Study. But the meaning behind these labels is unclear. When asked to define what they meant by *liberal* or *conservative* when identifying themselves as such, some respondents were unable to do so. In fact, in the 2008 American National Election Study, 44.8 percent (257) of blacks responded that they "haven't thought much about" where they were positioned on a liberal/conservative ideology scale. Moreover, higher-income blacks were no more likely than lower-income blacks to identify themselves as conservatives, but older blacks were far more likely than younger blacks to identify themselves as liberal. Regardless of self-identified ideological labels,

TABLE 3.5 Black Ideological Identification

Ideology	1988 (%)[a]	1993 (%)[b]	1996 (%)[c]	2004 (%)[d]	2008 (%)[g]	2012 (%)[j]
Extremely liberal	–	–	–	–	9.1 (28)	4.7 (41)
Strongly liberal	18.5 (63)[e]	23.9 (241)	18.4 (181)	–	–	–
Liberal	–	–	–	29.1 (268)	15.2 (47)	18.5 (162)
Not very strongly liberal	18.0 (61)	11.9 (121)	13.5 (133)	–	–	–
Slightly liberal	18.0 (61)	–[f]	–	–	10.7 (33)	14.2 (125)
Moderate/ leaning liberal	–	15.4 (155)	–	–	–	–
Moderate	1.8 (6)	2.4 (24)	41.1 (406)	48.5 (446)	36.6 (113)	44.4 (390)
Moderate/ leaning conservative	–	22.7 (219)	–	–	–	–
Slightly conservative	22.1 (75)	–	–	–	12.0 (37)	7.7 (68)
Not very strongly conservative	10.2 (35)	9.3 (94)	11.5 (113)	–	–	–
Conservative	–	–	–	22.4 (206)	10.7 (33)	7.9 (69)
Strongly conservative	11.4 (39)	15.4 (155)	15.5 (153)	–	–	–
Extremely conservative	–	–	–	–	5.8 (18)	2.6 (23)
Total	100 (340)[h]	100 (1009)	100 (986)	100 (920)	100 (309)[i]	100 (878)[i]

[a] Postelection sample, 1984 and 1988 National Black Election Studies.
[b] 1993–1994 National Black Politics Study.
[c] 1996 National Black Election Study, preelection sample.
[d] 2004 *CBS News*/Black Entertainment Television (BET) Monthly Poll (ICPSR 4154).
[e] Figures in parentheses represent the number of respondents.
[f] Differences in response categories between National Black Election Studies and National Black Politics Study.
[g] 2008 American National Election Study.
[h] Totals may not sum to 100 due to rounding.
[i] In the 2008 American National Election Study, 44.9 percent (257) of blacks responded that they "haven't thought much about" where they are positioned on a liberal/conservative ideology scale; in the 2012 American National Election Study, 16.5 percent (173) of blacks responded that they "haven't thought much about" placement on this ideological scale.
[j] 2012 American National Election Study.

Source: Authors = computations from the 1984 and 1988 National Black Election Studies, 1993–1994 National Black Politics Study, 1996 National Black Election Study, 2004 *CBS News*/Black Entertainment Television (BET), 2008 American National Election Study, 2012 American National Election Study.

blacks' policy preferences are generally fairly liberal across a variety of issues, but, with the exception of capital punishment, they are relatively conservative on a range of social issues (Tate 1993:31–32, 38).

The meanings of the terms *liberal* and *conservative* do not resonate well with Latinos or accurately reflect the attitudes of various Latino groups (Hero 1992). Table 3.6 shows the range of ideological orientations among Latinos. In the 1989/1990 LPNS, the 1999 *Washington Post,* and the 2006 Latino National Survey (LNS) data, Mexican Americans were almost equally likely to describe themselves as some degree of liberal, as moderate, and as some variant of conservative. Puerto Ricans in the 2006 data were more conservative and moderate and less liberal than they reported in the 1990 and 1999 data. Cubans were far more likely to identify themselves as liberal or moderate than conservative in 1990 and 1999, but shifted slightly more conservative in 2006. Yet about one-third still identified themselves as moderate. The drop occurred in those Cubans who identified as some form of liberal. Regardless of their self-identified ideological label, large majorities of all three groups supported what could be characterized as core elements of a liberal domestic agenda (de la Garza et al. 1992; Pew Hispanic Survey 2007).

The 1999 *Washington Post* and the 2006 LNS data provide information on the ideological orientations of other subgroups of Latinos that were not surveyed in the earlier LPNS survey. El Salvadorans in 1999 appeared to be more conservative than moderate or liberal and in 2006 appeared to be even more conservative. Almost equal percentages of Central Americans and Dominicans identified themselves as liberal or as conservative in 1999 but also appeared to be more conservative in 2006. Among the catchall category "Other Latinos," almost equal percentages identified as liberal, moderate, and conservative in both years, although slightly more identified as conservative in 2006 than did in 1999.

The 2000 collection of the Pilot Study of the National Asian American Political Survey (PNAAPS) data, the 2008 National Asian American Survey (NAAS), and the Pew 2012 Asian American Survey (AAS) provide us with information on the ideological orientations of Asian Americans. Prior to these data, we had to rely on local survey results that did not break down the Asian population into specific ethnic groups to infer their ideological orientations. The 1984 Cain and Kiewiet survey of political attitudes of California's three principal minority groups—blacks, Latinos, and Asian Americans—found that Asians generally supported a liberal domestic agenda: increased support for welfare programs, support of the equal rights amendment, and support of a ban on handguns. Moreover, they were far more likely than were blacks and Latinos in California to take a prochoice position. Data from the PNAAPS, the

TABLE 3.6 Latino Ideological Identification

Ideology	Mexican			Puerto Rican			Cuban			Central Americanc		Dominican		El Salvadoran		Other	
	1989/1990a	1999b	2006d	1989/1990	1999	2006	1989/1990	1999	2006	1999	2006	1999	2006	1999	2006	1999	2006
Very Liberal	4.9% (42)	–	11.6% (327)	7.0% (40)	–	15.2% (73)	3.7% (16)	–	11.6% (28)	–	20.8% (35)	–	15.2% (27)	–	10.1% (21)	–	21.4% (60)
Liberal	11.6% (100)	26.3% (204)	–	12.3% (71)	34.6% (104)	–	13.0% (4)	34% (98)	–	29.8% (118)	–	28.7% (27)	–	26% (40)	–	33.6% (77)	–
Slightly Liberal	12.1% (104)	–	11.7% (329)	9.2% (53)	–	9.8% (47)	6.3% (19)	–	7.4% (18)	–	9.5% (16)	–	9% (16)	–	6.3% (13)	–	17.4% (49)
Moderate	35.4% (304)	38.5% (299)	35.5% (999)	24.7% (142)	32.9% (99)	30.7% (147)	22.5% (69)	36.8% (106)	31.5% (76)	38.4% (152)	26.2% (44)	36.2% (36)	28.7% (51)	31.2% (48)	21.7% (45)	35.4% (81)	34.2% (96)
Slightly Conservative	14.8% (128)	–	12.7% (61)	16.3% (93)	–	12.7% (61)	14.3% (44)	–	16.6% (40)	–	14.3% (24)	–	21.3% (38)	–	32.4% (67)	–	24.2% (68)
Conservative	15.4% (133)	35.3% (274)	–	22.7% (130)	32.6% (98)	–	34.2% (106)	29.2% (84)	–	31.8% (126)	–	29.2% (31)	–	42.9% (66)	–	31.0% (71)	–
Very Conservative	5.8% (50)	–	22.7% (639)	7.8% (45)	–	31.5% (151)	5.2% (18)	–	32.8% (79)	–	29.2% (49)	–	25.8% (46)	–	29.5% (61)	–	24% (67)
Total	100% (863)	100% (777)	100% (2,818)	100% (574)	100% (301)	100% (479)	100% (439)	100% (288)	100% (241)	100% (396)	100% (168)	100% (94)	100% (178)	100% (154)	100% (207)	100% (229)	100% (281)

Sources:
a "Latino National Political Survey," in Latino Voices: Mexican, Puerto Rican, and Cuban Perspectives on American Politics by Rodolfo O. de la Garza et al. (Boulder, CO: Westview Press, 1992), 84.
b The Washington Post/Kaiser Family Foundation/Harvard University Survey Project, National Survey on Latinos in America, 1999.
c Central Americans, Dominicans, El Salvadorans, and other Latinos were not surveyed in the 1989–1990 Latino National Political Survey.
d Latino National Survey (LNS), 2006. ICPSR (20862).

Figures in parentheses represent the number of respondents.

NAAS, and the Pew AAS (see Table 3.7), indicate that in 2000 Japanese Americans were just as likely to self-identify as some form of liberal (34 percent) as they were to identify themselves as moderate or middle of the road (37 percent). In 2008, more Japanese Americans saw themselves as some form of liberal (24 percent) than conservative (15 percent), and a smaller portion saw themselves as moderates (28 percent), but almost a quarter (23 percent) said that they had not thought about where they would place themselves on a liberal/conservative ideological scale. The 2012 data just had the categories liberal, moderate, and conservative, so we put those indicating liberal in the "somewhat liberal" category, and the conservative in the "somewhat conservative" category. The pattern for Japanese Americans in 2012 was closer to the distribution in 2000 than in 2008—just as many identified themselves as liberal (29 percent) as they did conservative (28 percent), with about one-third (36 percent) identifying themselves as moderate. Chinese Americans were more likely to identify themselves as moderates (42 percent) in 2000, with slightly less than one-third (30 percent) identifying as some form of liberal. Interestingly, 15 percent of Chinese Americans either did not identify with the labels of liberal or conservative or did not attach those labels to their political views. In 2008, a pattern similar to that observed for Japanese Americans also appeared from Chinese Americans. More identified as liberal (18 percent) than conservative (11 percent), a smaller proportion identified as moderate (33 percent), but one-quarter (25 percent) said that they had not thought much about where they would place themselves on a liberal/conservative ideological scale. In 2012, more Chinese Americans identified as liberal (31 percent) than conservative (21 percent), with almost two-fifths (39 percent) identifying as moderate. The absence of the "other response" category in the 2012 data forced respondents to choose one of the three categories or not respond to the question.

In 2000, Koreans appeared to be almost evenly distributed across the ideological spectrum. About one-third of Koreans identified as either some form of liberal (33 percent) or some form of conservative (31 percent), with slightly less than a third (28 percent) identifying as moderates. But in the 2008 data, the pattern shifts. Fewer Koreans saw themselves as liberal (22 percent), but the same proportion (33 percent) saw themselves as conservative and moderate (29 percent). The difference appears to be in the 11 percent who did not feel the labels applied to them. Yet, in 2012 the pattern appears to shift back to what was found in 2000—almost equal numbers identify themselves as liberal (30 percent), moderate (30 percent), or conservative (33 percent). In 2000, Filipinos were slightly more liberal than the other groups, with two-fifths (40 percent) classifying themselves as some form of liberal. They also had the smallest

TABLE 3.7 Asian American Ideological Identification

		JAPANESE			CHINESE			KOREAN			FILIPINO			INDIAN	VIETNAMESE	ALL[a]		
IDEOLOGY		2000/2001 %	2008 (%)	2012 (%)	2000/2001 %	2008	2012	2000/2001 %	2008	2012	2000/2001 %	2008	2012	2012 (%)	2012 (%)	2000/2001 %	2008	2012
Liberal	Very liberal	9	–		4	–		4	–		8	–				8	–	
	Strong liberal	–	9	29	–	7	31	–	9	30	–	6	20	37	34	–	10	31
	Somewhat liberal	25	–		26	–		29	–		32	–				28	–	
	Not so strong liberal	–	15		–	11		–	13		–	10				–	11	
Moderate	Middle of the road/Moderate	37	28	36	42	33	39	28	29	30	18	32	42	39	34	32	33	37
Conservative	Not so strong conservative	–	9	28	–	7	21	–	24	33	–	11	33	18	19	–	9	24
	Somewhat conservative	20	–		11	–		27	–		29	–				18	–	
	Strong conservative	–	6		–	4		–	9		–	12				–	6	
	Very conservative	4	–		2	–		4	–		5	–				4	–	
Other Responses	Not sure	4	–		15	–		8	–		6	–				10	–	
	Haven't thought much about this	–	23		–	25		–	11		–	19				–	21	
	Don't know/Refused	–	8		–	12		–	4		–	9				–	8	
	Total[b]	99	98	93	100	99	91	100	99	93	98	99	95	94	87	100	98	92

[a] Included are also the 2000/2001 and 2012 responses for Vietnamese and South East Asians, and the 2008 responses for nineteen other Asian ethnic origin groups, which are not reported here.

[b] 2000/2001 totals do not sum to 100 because those who refused to answer the strength of their ideological identification. 2008 totals do not sum to 100 due to the exclusion of those refusing to answer the strength of their ideological identification. 2012 totals do not sum to 100 due to unavailability of data from those who did not answer questions about the strength of their ideological identification.

NOTE: 2012 percentages do not include information about the strength of ideological identification.

Sources: 2000/2001 data: Pilot Study of the National Asian American Political Survey (PNAAPS); 2008 data: National Asian American Survey (NAAS); 2012 data: the Pew Research Center's 2012 Asian American Survey.

proportion identifying as moderate (18 percent), with about one-third (34 percent) identifying as some form of conservative. By 2008, those identifying as liberal (16 percent) dropped substantially, those self-identifying as moderate increased significantly (32 percent), those identifying as conservative remained about the same (33 percent), but almost one-fifth (19 percent) did not feel that the labels liberal and conservative applied to them. Those identifying as liberal in 2012 ticked up a bit from 2008 to 20 percent, as did the proportion identifying as conservative (33 percent), but the biggest increase was in Filipinos putting themselves in the moderate category (42 percent).

The 2012 data include South Asian Indians and Vietnamese. In these data, Indian Americans appear to have the largest share (37 percent) of its population identifying as liberal and the smallest (18 percent) identifying as conservative. This suggests that this group is the most liberal and the least conservative of the various groups, at least in 2012, although we do not want to overstate small differences. Vietnamese Americans seem to be equally spilt between liberal (34 percent) and moderate (34 percent), with a much smaller portion (19 percent) identifying as conservative.

While research on the political participation of American Indians is increasing, data on the ideological leanings of American Indians are rare. We identified only two studies. One (Ritt 1979) concluded that Indians are ideologically moderate, but this was based on only 151 American Indian respondents to a national survey. The other study (Hoffman 1998), based on a slightly larger sample, found that Indians more likely identified themselves as moderate or conservative rather than as liberal. In the absence of large numbers of American Indians in national probability samples and in an effort to move us further along on identifying ideological orientations of American Indians, we combined all Native American data in the American National Election Studies 1990 to 2012 into a single file. This resulted in a sample of approximately 171 American Indians.* Table 3.8 shows that, of those individuals who responded to the question, slightly more than a quarter (27.98 percent) identified as some form of conservative, whereas another quarter (27.38 percent) identified as moderate. About a fifth (19.05

---

*In past editions of this book, we have listed a larger number of individuals, 445, in the 1990 to 2008 ANES data indicating that they are American Indian. When we included the 2012 data and reran the data, the number dropped to 171 respondents identifying as American Indian. Recognizing the discrepancy, we tried to figure out what had happened. Thus, we examined the 1948–2008 ANES cumulative data set and the 1948–2012 ANES cumulative data set, and there is something strange going on with the data that we have not been able to figure out. The former data set uses a percent) identified as some form of liberal. Interestingly, a quarter (25.6 percent) did not answer the question, indicating again that these particular ideological categories did not resonate with American Indians. These results appear to contradict somewhat the earlier findings of Ritt and Hoffman. Nevertheless, the small samples in Ritt's, Hoffman's, and our analyses suggest that we must be circumspect in discussing this group's ideology.

This section has revealed the complexity and range of the ideological identifications of blacks, Latinos, Asians, and, to a lesser extent, Indians. This range of orientations has implications for one strategy of the second dilemma—it makes the formation of interminority group coalitions more difficult. As Chapter 6 discusses,

TABLE 3.8 American Indian Ideological Identification

IDEOLOGICAL IDENTIFICATION	1990–2012 (%)
Extremely liberal	2.98% (5)[a]
Liberal	10.71% (18)
Slightly liberal	5.36% (9)
Moderate	27.38% (46)
Slightly conservative	10.71% (18)
Conservative	13.10% (22)
Extremely conservative	4.17% (7)
Don't know/Haven't thought much about it	25.60% (43)
Total[b]	100% (n=168)

[a]Figures in parentheses represent the number of respondents.
[b]Total does not add to 100 due to rounding.

Source: American National Election Studies Cumulative Data File (1948–2012). All respondents who identified as Native American in the 1990–2012 American National Election Studies were combined into a single file in order to obtain a sufficient sample size to identify partisan identification. These data do not allow for the tribal affiliation of the respondents.

ideology is one of the bases on which interracial coalitions are formed. Shared racial minority group status in the United States does not mean that all minority groups occupy the same end of the ideological spectrum. Blacks, Latinos, and Asians are dispersed all along the ideological continuum, but the meanings of the terms *liberal, moderate,* and *conservative* for these groups differ from the popular culture definitions of the terms.

---

race variable (VCF0106– "Respondent Race 6-category") that indicates that there are 445 American Indians among the respondents from 1990–2008. The 1948–2012 data set does not include this variable, and instead has the VCF0105a– "Race-ethnicity summary: 7 categories" variable. This indicates that the total number of American Indian/Alaskan Native respondents from 1990–2012 is 171. This is what is accounting for the significant difference in the sample size for American Indians when we compare the current tables with the previous tables.

PARTISAN IDENTIFICATION

As each presidential election nears, the media point to the heavily Democratic orientation and voting within the African American community. Many assume that because blacks vote heavily Democratic, all racial minority groups do likewise. Despite the acknowledgment of this orientation among African American voters, the media never ask the reasons for the orientation and how it came about. The Republican Party, in attempting to appeal to black voters, conveniently ignores the history of the relationship between blacks and the party dating from the party's inception in 1856. Many believe it was the policies of the Democratic Party rather than the pressure from the Republican Party that resulted in the present configuration of black partisan identification. Moreover, the media never explore the issues of the strength of blacks' commitment to the Democratic Party and whether other racial minority groups have different points of view.

Blacks

A little of the complex history of the relationship between blacks and the political parties in the United States must be reviewed before we can place the current identification of African Americans with the Democratic Party in perspective. Blacks were heavily involved in the Republican Party from its inception in 1856 around the issue of the abolition of slavery. Before the end of Reconstruction, sixteen blacks were elected to Congress, all as Republicans. Blacks were actively involved in the party organization, with John R. Lynch, a state legislator from Mississippi, serving as temporary chair of the 1884 Republican Convention. At the 1892 Republican Convention, 13 percent of the delegates were black (Gurin, Hatchett, and Jackson 1989).

After the compromise of 1877, in which Rutherford B. Hayes promised to remove federal troops from the South and to allow the former Confederate states to deal with the "Negro problem" in their own way if he were elected president, the Democratic Party became the party of white supremacy, and the Republican Party became the party of blacks. In attempts to rebuild the Republican Party in the South, successive Republican presidents pursued a strategy aimed at drawing more Southern whites into the party while at the same time pushing out or alienating black Republicans. The conflicts between the **Lily White Republicans** and the **Black and Tan Republicans** (the anti– and pro–civil rights wings of the party, respectively) continued until the 1956 election. Between 1877 and the complete shift of blacks to the Democratic Party in the 1964 elections, numerous pejorative acts and perfidious behaviors toward black Republicans by white Republicans at the national, state, and local levels resulted in the change of blacks' allegiance.

It was not just the push of the Republican Party but also the pull of the Democratic Party that resulted in this shift of allegiance. The neglect and hostility of Republican administrations led some prominent blacks, including W. E. B. DuBois, to support Woodrow Wilson in the 1912 presidential election. However, Wilson's subsequent segregation of the federal government and the city of Washington, DC, and his limited attention to black concerns resulted in blacks returning to the Republican Party in subsequent elections. The perception that Herbert Hoover was pursuing an overtly racist strategy in his administration policies and his explicit overtures to Lily White Republicans, coupled with the Depression and the election of Franklin D. Roosevelt in 1932, set the stage for the beginning of the black party realignment.

Although the implementation of many of Roosevelt's New Deal policies was tinged with racial discrimination, and many blacks were still uncertain about Roosevelt's commitment to addressing issues of concern to blacks, many blacks were persuaded enough to vote Democratic in large numbers. Roosevelt's informal formation of a group of black government advisers, commonly referred to as the Kitchen Cabinet—which included such prominent individuals as Robert C. Weaver, Ralph J. Bunche, Mary McLeod Bethune, and Rayford W. Logan, among others—was a first for any presidential administration.[1] Moreover, the visibility of Roosevelt's wife, Eleanor, on issues of importance to the broader black community raised blacks' confidence in Roosevelt. Thus, by Roosevelt's 1944 reelection, blacks voted overwhelmingly Democratic and provided the margin of victory in seven states: Pennsylvania, Maryland, Michigan, Missouri, New York, Illinois, and New Jersey (Gurin, Hatchett, and Jackson 1989:36).

Harry Truman, however, found that black loyalty to the Democratic Party was tied to Franklin Roosevelt and realized that he could not automatically count on black votes in the 1948 election. Both Truman and the Republican candidate, Thomas Dewey, knew they would need black votes in the major urban areas to win. Dewey, as governor of New York, had a very good record on issues of concern to blacks. Prior to the 1948 election, Truman had made his civil rights recommendations, based on a report from a commission he had established, to Congress. In addition, a civil rights plank was inserted into the Democratic platform at the 1948 Democratic Convention, which resulted in the walkout of Southern Democrats—led by then governor Strom Thurmond—and in the formation of the Dixiecrats. The controversy surrounding Truman and his civil rights initiatives led many to assume that Dewey would win the election, but Truman was victorious.

In the 1952 election, in protest of the Dixiecrats' influence and the connection between the Dixiecrats and the Democratic Party in the South, many Southern blacks voted for Dwight Eisenhower. Eisenhower's appointment of Earl Warren as chief justice of the Supreme Court and the subsequent ruling on *Brown v. Board of Education of Topeka* in 1954 led many blacks to credit Eisenhower with the victory.[2] An estimated 38 percent of the black vote went to Eisenhower in the 1956 election (Gurin, Hatchett, and Jackson 1989). During his second term, however, Eisenhower's administration was viewed as less committed to civil rights and equality, as was evidenced by Eisenhower's reluctance to implement the 1957 Civil Rights Act and to enforce school desegregation in Little Rock. The Eisenhower administration's reluctance played to the Democrats' advantage in the 1960 presidential election contest between John F. Kennedy and Richard M. Nixon, although both parties actively campaigned for the black vote. The black vote shifted in large numbers to the Democrats in that election primarily because Kennedy's telephone call to Coretta Scott King, to express his concern over the jailing of her husband Martin Luther King Jr. in Georgia, got through before Nixon's call. This shift solidified in 1964 when Republicans nominated Arizona senator Barry Goldwater as their presidential candidate. Goldwater's extreme conservative positions and his opposition to civil rights legislation alienated many blacks who previously had supported the Republican Party. Black voters have remained solidly Democratic since 1964.

In the 1984 NBES data, 83.5 percent of blacks surveyed considered themselves Democrats, but less than half (45.8 percent) identified as strong Democrats. The 2012 American National Election Study (ANES) data show that 57.8 percent reported themselves as strong Democrats and 87.8 percent identified as some strength of Democrat (see Table 3.9). It should not be a surprise that in the 2012 reelection of President Obama the proportion of blacks that identified as strong Democrats increased substantially. The number of blacks that identified as pure independents, not leaning toward one party or the other, seems to have peaked in the 1996 National Black Election Study at 20.4 percent. This figure remained relatively stable in the 2004 CBS data and the 2008 JCPS data, but began to drop off in the 2010 General Social Survey, to 13.9 percent, and dropped off significantly to 7.6 percent in the 2012 ANES data. Again, this shift is probably related to Barack Obama being on the ticket in 2012. African American Voter Poll data, collected during the 2016 presidential election, provide support for the contention that President Obama at the top of the ticket made a difference—54 percent of the respondents were more excited about voting in 2012 than they were in 2016. While 50 percent of that group said that their lack of enthusiasm in 2016 was that they did not like

TABLE 3.9 Black Partisan Identification

Partisan Identifi- cation	1984 (%)[a]	1988 (%)[a]	1994 (%)[b]	1996 (%)[c]	2004 (%)[d]	2008 (%)[e]	2010 (%)[f]	2012 (%)[j]
Strong Democrat	45.8 (521)[g]	57.0 (260)	49.5 (597)	49.8 (583)	–	–	40.9 (124)	57.8 (650)
Democrat[h]	–	–	–	–	77.7 (725)	76.1 (548)	–	–
Weak Democrat	23.5 (267)	21.5 (98)	20.7 (249)	20.1 (236)	–	–	23.4 (71)	15.5 (174)
Indep./ Lean Dem.	14.2 (162)	10.3 (47)	12.4 (149)	–	–	–	11.2 (34)	14.5 (163)
Independent	4.8 (55)	10.3 (47)	6.5 (78)	20.4 (239)	18.8 (175)	19.7 (142)	13.9 (42)	7.6 (85)
Indep./ Lean Rep.	–[i]	–	3.3 (40)	–	–	–	4.0 (12)	1.8 (20)
Repub. (all)	7.8 (88)	6.3 (29)	3.7 (45)	4.0 (47)	3.5 (32)	4.2 (30)	5.9 (18)	2.9 (33)
Other/ Apolitical	3.8 (44)	2.0 (9)	3.9 (47)	5.7 (67)	–	–	0.7 (2)	–
Total	100 (1,137)	100 (456)	100 (1,205)	100 (1,172)	100 (932)	100 (720)	100 (303)	100 (1,125)

[a]Preelection sample, 1984 and 1988 National Black Election Studies.
[b]1993–1994 National Black Politics Study.
[c]1996 National Black Election Study, preelection sample.
[d]2004 *CBS News*/Black Entertainment Television (BET) Monthly Poll (ICPSR 4154).
[e]Joint Center for Political and Economic Studies, 2008 National Opinion Poll.
[f]2010 General Social Survey.
[g]Figures in parentheses represent respondent totals for a particular cell.
[h]Response categories were Democrat, independent, and Republican; no measurement of strength.
[i]Differences in response categories between National Black Election Studies and National Black Politics Study.
[j]2012 American National Election Study.

Sources: Authors' computations from the 1984 and 1988 National Black Election Studies; 1993–1994 National Black Politics Study; 1996 National Black Election Study; 2004 *CBS News*/Black Entertainment Television (BET) Monthly Poll (ICPSR 4154); Joint Center for Political and Economic Studies, 2008 National Opinion Poll; 2010 General Social Survey (Roper Center for Public Opinion Research); and 2012 American National Election Study.

either the Democratic (Hillary Clinton) or Republican (Donald Trump) candidate, 18 percent said that it was because President Obama was not at the top of the ticket.

The proportion of blacks identifying as some form of Republican appears to have reached a low point of 2.9 percent in 2012, down from the peak of 7.4 percent in 1984. Both the 1984 and 1988 NBES data suggest a gender split within the black electorate—black women were more likely to identify strongly with the Democratic Party than were black men; the latter were more likely to be weak or independent Democratic supporters, political independents, or Republicans (Tate 1993:64). The 1993 NBPS data suggest that the gender split may have dissipated—black men appeared just as likely as black women to identify strongly with the Democratic Party. Yet the 1996 data indicate that the gender split had returned, with black women far more likely to identify with the Democratic Party than were black men. In 2008, however, the JCPES data suggest, the gender gap had disappeared completely, with almost equal proportions of black women (84 percent) and black men (83 percent) indicating a preference for the Democratic candidate, Barack Obama. 2004 JCPES data also indicated the absence of a gender gap, so the absence of a gender gap in 2008 with a black Democratic presidential nominee does not appear to be an anomaly. Yet, the 2012 ANES data, despite President Obama running for reelection, indicated the reappearance of the gender gap. Black women were more likely to identify as strong Democrats (65.6 percent) than were black men (47.7 percent)—a 17.9 percentage point difference. While both groups were small in number, black men were more likely to be strong or not very strong Republicans (3.8 percent) than were black women (2.3 percent). Still, it appears that black men and women have moved closer together in their assessment of presidential candidates in recent elections.

There also appears to be a generational split among blacks. In past studies, older blacks tended to be more strongly Democratic than were younger blacks. Yet the 2004 and the 2008 JCPES data suggest that young blacks (ages 18–25) were more Democratic (71 percent in 2004; 81 percent in 2008) than older blacks. Only 55 percent of those ages 51–64 and 66 percent of those over age 65 identified as Democrats in 2004, and 75 percent (ages 51–64) and 77 percent (ages 65 and over) in 2008 identified as Democrats. By 2012, however, the ANES data suggest that young blacks (ages 17–24) were the least likely (55.7 percent) to identify as Democrats than did any other age group. Blacks aged 65–74 (83 percent) and 75 and older (84.9 percent) were the most likely to identify as Democrats. In an earlier period, it appeared that whatever shift might have occurred toward the Republican Party within black America was from this older cohort. In 2002, JCPES data indicated only 5 percent of blacks 51 to 64 years of age and 7 percent of blacks over 65 years of age identified as Republicans. In 2004, however, the proportions had jumped to 15 percent and 12 percent, respectively. But by 2008, whatever attraction the Republican Party had for those two age groups had dissipated, as only 5 percent and 4 percent, respectively, identified themselves as Republican. The other age cohorts' identification with the Republican Party in both 2004 and 2008 either remained the same or declined. In the 2012 ANES data, the numbers of black Republicans in the 65 to 74 age group remained at 4.8 percent, but completely disappeared among those 75 and older. The largest proportion of black Republicans was among blacks aged 35–44 (5.3 percent).

Latinos

The history of Latinos and the two political parties is not as well documented as that of African Americans. Overall, Latinos tend to lean Democratic, but they do not equal blacks in their strength of identification with the Democratic Party. In the 1990 LPNS data, two-thirds of Mexican Americans indicated that they were Democrats of varying strengths (see Table 3.10). In 1999, however, only two-fifths (41.58 percent) self-identified as Democrats, but close to two-fifths (38.21 percent) identified themselves as independents. This is a substantial increase from the 11 percent who identified as independents in the LPNS data a decade earlier. By 2006, however, a majority of Mexican Americans (55.7 percent) identified as Democrat, and the proportion identifying as independent declined by almost 10 percentage points. Interestingly, the proportion of Mexican Americans who identified as Republicans remained relatively constant during the 1990 to 1999 interval but decreased by 5 percentage points in 2006. The 2008 National Survey of Latinos (not shown in Table 3.10), collected by the Pew Hispanic Center, indicates that one-half (50 percent) of the Mexican American sample identified themselves as Democrats, with 18 percent as Republican and 22 percent as independent. Although the numbers differ somewhat between the 2006 and 2008 data, both indicate a preference for the Democratic Party among Mexican Americans. Given Puerto Ricans' tendency to self-identify across the ideological spectrum, popular wisdom would predict a more Republican identification among those who identify as conservative. Once again, the data run counter to conventional wisdom. Nearly three-fourths (71 percent) of Puerto Ricans in 1990, two-fifths (60 percent) in 1999, and close to two-thirds (64.1 percent) in 2006 identified themselves as Democrats of varying strengths. The 2008 National Survey of Latinos showed a similar percentage (61 percent) of Puerto Ricans also identifying as Democrats.

TABLE 3.10 Latino Partisan Identification

PARTISAN IDENTIFICATION	MEXICAN			PUERTO RICAN		
	1989/1999[a]	1999[b]	2006[c]	1989/1990	1999	2006
Democrat[d]	–	41.6 (284)	55.7 (1,916)	–	60.0 (165)	64.1 (415)
Strong Democrat	31.1%[f] (252)	–	–	37.2 (205)	–	–
Not Strong Democrat	28.6 (232)	–	–	26.4 (145)	–	–
Closer to Democrat	7.2 (59)	–	–	7.4 (40)	–	–
Independent/Other	11.6 (94)	–	–	11.5 (63)	–	–
Independent (only)	–	38.2 (261)	29.3 (1,006)	–	24.0 (66)	15.6 (101)
Closer to Republican	5.5 (45)	–	–	3.6 (20)	–	–
Not Strong Republican	11.6 (94)	–	–	7.2 (40)	–	–
Strong Republican	4.4 (36)	–	–	6.7 (37)	–	–
Republican	–	20.2 (138)	15 (517)	–	16.0 (44)	20.2 (131)
Total	100 (811)	100 (683)	100 (3,439)	100 (550)	100 (275)	100 (647)

Sources:

[a]"Latino National Political Survey," in *Latino Voices: Mexican, Puerto Rican, and Cuban Perspectives on American Politics*, Rodolfo O. de la Garza et al. (Boulder, CO: Westview Press, 1992): 127.

[b]The *Washington Post*/Kaiser Family Foundation/Harvard University Survey Project, National Survey on Latinos in America, 1999.

[c]Data are taken from the Latino National Survey (LNS), 2006. ICPSR(20862).

[d]Central Americans, Dominicans, El Salvadorans, and other Latinos were not surveyed in the 1989–1990 Latino National Political Survey.

[e]Response categories were Democrat, independent, and Republican.

[f]Table figures are percentages, and figures in parentheses represent the number of respondents. In addition, column totals are subject to rounding error.

TABLE 3.10 **Latino Partisan Identification** (*Continued*)

	Cuban			Central American[a]		Dominican		El Salvadoran		Other	
	1989/ 1990	**1999**	**2006**	**1999**	**2006**	**1999**	**2006**	**1999**	**2006**	**1999**	**2006**
	–	34.3 (95)	32.4 (103)	48.2 (176)	50 (98)	66.7 (58)	73.2 (156)	45.4 (64)	57 (134)	46.0 (92)	59.5 (263)
	14.4 (45)	–	–	–	–	–	–	–	–	–	–
	5.1 (16)	–	–	–	–	–	–	–	–	–	–
	5.8 (18)	–	–	–	–	–	–	–	–	–	–
	5.8 (18)	–	–	–	–	–	–	–	–	–	–
	–	25.6 (71)	20.1 (64)	40.0 (146)	27.6 (54)	23.0 (20)	17.4 (37)	39.0 (55)	30.2 (71)	29.5 (59)	23.1 (102)
	4.9 (15)	–	–	–	–	–	–	–	–	–	–
	16.2 (50)	–	–	–	–	–	–	–	–	–	–
	47.8 (147)	–	–	–	–	–	–	–	–	–	–
	–	40.1 (111)	47.5 (151)	11.8 (43)	22.4 (44)	10.3 (9)	9.4 (20)	15.6 (22)	12.8 (30)	24.5 (49)	17.4 (77)
	100 (309)	100 (277)	100 (318)	100 (365)	100 (196)	100 (87)	100 (213)	100 (141)	100 (235)	100 (200)	100 (442)

Cubans departed significantly from this partisan pattern in the early data. In 1990, more than two-thirds of Cubans identified themselves as Republicans. In fact, more Cubans self-identified as strong Republicans than did the proportion of Mexicans and Puerto Ricans who identified themselves as strong Democrats. Once again, however, we must caution that Cuban identification with the Republican Party stems more from foreign policy concerns, particularly US relations with Cuba, than from concern with social policy issues. The LNPS demonstrated that the majority of Cubans favored increased government spending on health, crime, drug control, education, the environment, child services, and bilingual education. In essence, a majority of Cubans supported what could be characterized as core elements of a liberal domestic agenda, even though they were more likely to self-identify as conservative (de la Garza et al. 1992:14).

By 1999, Cuban identification with the Republican Party had dropped to around two-fifths (40.07 percent), whereas the proportion of independents and Democrats had increased. In 2006, the percentage identifying as Republicans (47.1 percent) increased about 7 percentage points from 1999. But the 2008 National Survey of Latinos data suggest a dramatic drop in identification as Republicans among Cuban Americans (20 percent) and a substantial increase in Cubans identifying themselves as Democrats (50 percent). Nevertheless, until we see more survey data on Cuban partisan identification, we must consider the 2008 data on Cuban identification with the Democratic Party to be anomalous at this point. Data on the newer Latino groups also suggest a preference for the Democratic Party, especially among Dominicans (66.67 percent in 1999 and 73.2 percent in 2006), or for remaining independent of both political parties. The increasing proportion of Latino independents indicates that these voters are susceptible to appeals from both political parties.

The Pew 2016 National Survey of Latinos, while not breaking down Latinos by ethnic-origin group, showed that 64 percent of all Latino registered voters identified with the Democratic Party in some form, while only 24 percent identified with the Republican Party in some form. The research on the political behaviors, attitudes, and experiences of Latinas is growing, and a few studies suggest that there are gender differences within the Latino groups (Montoya 1996; Montoya, Hardy-Fanta, and Garcia 2000; Fraga and Navarro 2007). On partisan identification, Cain and Kiewiet (1984) found that Latinas are more likely to identify as Democrats than Latino men are, and Welch and Sigelman (1992) found Latinas to be more liberal and more Democratic than Latinos. Gender differences appear in partisan identification in the 2016 data, with Latinas more likely to identify with Democrats than Latino men. Fifty-five percent of Latino men identify as Democrats or leaning Democratic and 30 percent identify as Republicans or leaning Republican. By comparison, 73

PHOTO 3.1 *Julio Martinez, a seventy-three-year-old Vietnam War veteran who came to the United States from Cuba in 1954, has voted Republican since 1961 and is supporting Donald Trump. Martinez said of Trump, "He is the only person who can improve the situation in this country.... I defended this flag with my life, and this man (Trump) will, too."* (AP Photo/Alan Diaz; ID: 16305618167910)

percent of Latina women identify as Democrats or leaning Democratic, while 18 percent identify as Republican or leaning Republican. Latina women were more likely (60 percent) to say that Democrats have more concern for Latinos than Republicans, compared with 48 percent of Latino men. About one-third (35 percent) of Latino men say there is no difference between the parties on concern for Latinos, compared with 23 percent of Latina women voters (Lopez et al. 2016: 25–26).

As with blacks, there are some age-related differences in Latinos' views of the political parties. Older Latinos are more likely than younger Latinos to say the Democratic Party has more concern for Latinos than the Republican Party does. Among registered voters, nearly six in ten (59 percent) non-Millennial Latinos (ages thirty-six and older) say Democrats have more concern, compared with 48 percent of Latino Millennials (ages eighteen to thirty-five). Interestingly, Latino Millennial voters are more likely than non-Millennial Latino voters to say there is no difference between the parties, 38 percent compared with 21 percent.

Asians

Until recently, research had indicated that in the aggregate, Asian Americans appeared to be more Republican than Democratic, with Chinese Americans being more strongly Republican than other groups (Cain and Kiewiet 1986; Stokes 1988; Cain, Kiewiet, and Uhlaner 1991). Partisan attachment was weak, however, and either party could benefit from Asian American support. More recent research based on survey data from Asian American populations finds that the patterns of the early research have changed significantly and appear more fluid than those of other racial and ethnic minority groups (Wong et al. 2011).

Data from the 2016 National Asian American Survey of 1,694 Asian American registered voters (Ramakrishnan et al. 2016) suggest that a shift appears to have occurred within all Asian groups—they are now more likely to identify with the Democratic Party than with the Republican Party (see Table 3.11). Filipino and Japanese Americans are the most Republican of all of the Asian groups. The finding for Japanese Americans is interesting, as it represents a 20 percent increase from the proportion (14 percent) that identified as Republicans in the 2008 National Asian American Survey. Although early research indicated that Chinese Americans leaned Republican, these data do not confirm that finding. Only 18 percent of Chinese Americans in the sample self-identified as Republicans. About one-quarter of Koreans identified as Republicans, but more than two-thirds identified as Democrats. In the 2008 data a significant number of all Asians indicated that they did not think in partisan terms, and a significant number identified themselves as political independents. For instance, about 40 percent of Chinese Americans said

TABLE 3.11 Asian American Partisan Identification

	ALL ASIANS			CHINESE	JAPANESE	KOREAN
		Male	*Female*			
Democrat	57%	53%	61%	51%	59%	70%
Republican	24%	25%	22%	18%	34%	27%
Pure Independent[a]	18%	21%	15%	30%	7%	3%
Total[b]	99%	99%	98%	99%	100%	100%

[a]Not leaning toward one party or another.
[b]Refused not listed, so totals do not equal 100 percent.
Source: 2016 National Asian American Survey, October 5, 2016 (adapted from Ramakrishnan et al. 2016).

that they did not think of themselves in partisan terms, and another 28 percent saw themselves as independents, for a total of 68 percent not connected to either political party. A similar pattern seemed to run through the other Asian American groups. In 2016, however, it appears that the proportion of Asian American groups that saw themselves as independents had decreased significantly. Only 30 percent of Chinese Americans viewed themselves as purely politically independent.

The 2008 data suggest that Asian Americans represented prime groups to be recruited into one party or the other, and, based on the 2016 data, it appears that had happened for some of the groups. Take Asian Indian Americans, for example. In 2008, 39 percent identified as Democrats, while 54 percent either identified as independents or did not think of themselves in partisan terms. In 2016, 71 percent identified as Democrats, and only 14 percent saw themselves as pure independents, not leaning toward one party or the other. A similar pattern is apparent among Korean Americans. In 2008, 38 percent identified as Democrats, while 44 percent either identified as independents or did not think of themselves in partisan terms. But by 2016, 70 percent of Korean Americans identified as Democrats, while only 3 percent saw themselves as pure independents. Republicans made some gains as well. In 2008, 7 percent of Asian Indian Americans and Chinese Americans identified as Republicans, and in 2016 those numbers had risen to 13 percent for Asian Indian Americans and 18 percent for Chinese Americans.

There is a gender difference for Asian Americans as a whole, with Asian American women more likely to identify as Democrats (61 percent) than Asian American men (53 percent). Asian American men were slightly more likely (25

TABLE 3.11 Asian American Partisan Identification (*Continued*)

	Filipino	Asian Indian	Vietnamese	Cambodian	Hmong
Democrat	52%	71%	45%	68%	76%
Republican	33%	13%	29%	26%	6%
Pure Independent[a]	13%	14%	25%	6%	18%
Total[b]	98%	98%	99%	100%	100%

PHOTO 3.2 *Democratic presidential candidate Hillary Clinton, left, is welcomed by Rep. Judy Chu, D-CA, before addressing Asian American and Pacific Islander supporters in San Gabriel, California, Thursday, January 7, 2016.* (AP Photo/Damian Dovarganes; ID: 281541639189)

percent) to identify as Republican than were Asian American women (22 percent). Asian American men also had a larger proportion who identified as pure independents (21 percent) than did Asian American women (15 percent).

For the first time in a national survey, the 2016 National Asian American Survey included a small sample of Native Hawaiians and Pacific Islanders. This is a boon for our research on this population. Looking at partisan identification, 57 percent of Native Hawaiians identify as Democrats, as do 45 percent of Other Pacific Islanders. Twenty-nine percent of Native Hawaiians and 24 percent of Other Pacific Islanders identify as Republican. A larger portion, 29 percent, of Other Pacific Islanders identify as pure independents (not leaning toward any political party) compared to a much smaller portion of Native Hawaiians, 13 percent. The Democratic leanings of Native Hawaiians is in keeping with the history of the two political parties in Hawaii and the Democratic Party's dominance on the islands (Schultheis 2014).

Gender differences also are present within these groups. Among all, Native Hawaiians and Other Pacific Islanders, women are more Democratic than are men, 61 percent to 36 percent, with men being just as Republican, 34 percent, as they are Democratic. Only 17 percent of women identify as Republican. Men are also more likely to identify as pure independents, 26 percent, than are women, 22 percent, but women are more likely to say that they are independents than that they are Republican.

American Indians

There is a small but growing literature on the political behavior of American Indians in nontribal elections. Earlier studies indicated that Indian peoples were not strongly tied to either political party but tended to lean toward the Democrats, although significant differences in party affiliation are found across tribes. For example, over time the Navajos have shifted from voting Republican to voting Democratic and, during the Reagan years, slightly back to voting Republican in national elections, yet they remain fiercely supportive of Democrats in Arizona state politics. Since the 1956 presidential election, the Papagos have consistently voted Democratic (Ritt 1979; McCool 1982). Most of the recent literature finds that American Indians are more likely to identify as Democrats rather than as Republicans (Ritt 1979; McCool 1982; Deloria 1985; Turner 2002; Wilkins and Stark 2011; Min and Savage 2014). An examination of the partisan preferences of American Indian voters in the Upper Midwest (Wisconsin, Minnesota, and North and South Dakota) in elections from 1982 through 1992 reveals a strong preference for Democrats (Doherty 1994). Hoffman (1998) also found that American Indians were more likely to be Democrats or independents than Republicans. Personnel from the Democratic National Committee credited Indian voters with providing the margin of victory for the Clinton-Gore ticket in Arizona in the 1996 presidential election (Michel 1998). Table 3.12 shows that more than half (54.11 percent) of American Indians identified either as Democrats or leaning Democratic, whereas about a third (33.93 percent) identified either as Republican or leaning Republican. Approximately one-tenth (11.9 percent) of the sample identified as independents.

One of the factors that has determined Indian party affiliations at the national level has been an administration's stance on Indian issues. Min and Savage (2014) suggest that some tribes support the Democratic Party because they feel that it has is a more genuine interest in and support for American Indian issues. During Richard Nixon's administration, many Indians, such as the Navajos, voted Republican because Nixon was viewed as having a strong stance regarding American Indian policy. But they shifted to Jimmy Carter during his years in office because he was also viewed as being "good for Indians." Bill Clinton enjoyed strong American Indian support because of his policies and his outreach to American Indian tribes and their leaders. President Obama

TABLE 3.12 American Indian Partisan Identification

Partisan Identification	1990–2012 (%)
Strong Democrat	19.05% (32)[a]
Weak Democrat	18.45% (31)
Independent Leaning Democrat	16.67% (28)
Independent	11.90% (20)
Independent Leaning Republican	12.50% (21)
Weak Republican	11.31% (19)
Strong Republican	10.12% (17)
Total[b]	100% (n = 168)

[a] Figures in parentheses represent the number of respondents.
[b] Total does not add to 100 due to rounding.

Source: American National Election Studies Cumulative Data File (1948–2012). All respondents who identified as Native American in the 1990–2012 American National Election Studies were combined into a single file in order to obtain a sufficient sample size to identify partisan identification. These data do not allow for the tribal affiliation of the respondents.

enjoyed large American Indian support in the 2008 and the 2012 elections because of his support for Indian country and policies important to Indian peoples. The more recent data appear to be more definitive on American Indian partisan identification than do earlier data, but we still need to remember that we need to take into account reservation compared with nonreservation Indians and a party's stance on federal Indian policy.

VOTING BEHAVIOR

Prior to the Voting Rights Act, only 6.7 percent of blacks in Mississippi were registered to vote; by 1967, 59.8 percent of voting-age blacks were registered. It is estimated that in the seven states originally covered by the act, black registration increased from 29.3 percent in March 1965 to 56.6 percent in 1971–1972. Moreover, "the Justice Department estimated that in the five years after passage, almost as many blacks registered in Alabama, Mississippi, Georgia, Louisiana, North Carolina, and South Carolina as in the entire century before 1965" (Davidson 1992:21). Table 3.13 shows the 2014 registration and voting figures for all fifty US states showing the black and Latino portion of the citizen voting-age population. Increases of Latino populations in some states, like Utah and Idaho, necessitate that we list all fifty states rather than just the states with the highest proportion of black and Latino populations. Because "most American national elections are won by 5 percent or less," blacks and Latinos have the potential to be a significant force in determining the outcome of these elections (Williams 1987:101). Moreover, in some states the ability of blacks, Latinos, Asians, and American Indians to decide electoral outcomes is very strong.

In 2012, approximately 235 million Americans were eligible to vote. Non-Latino African Americans accounted for 12.20 percent of the total voting-age population, and Latinos for 14.96 percent of that population. Non-Latino Asians constituted 5.31 percent of the total voting-age population. The US Census Bureau did not report data for American Indians, Aleuts, and Eskimos for the 2012 election. The US Census Bureau will not release the official figures from the 2016 election until sometime in late 2017. Even though data from the 2014 midterm elections are available, voter registration and turnout are always lower in nonpresidential election years than in presidential election years. Data from 2014 will give an incomplete view of voting and participation by racial and ethnic minority citizens, which is why we largely report 2012 presidential election results, rather than 2014 midterm data in this section. Table 3.14 shows the differences in voting and registration data for the 2012 presidential election year and the 2014 midterm elections by racial groups. As you can see, the numbers are lower for all groups in nonpresidential election years.

In 1968, the gap between black and white voter registration rates was 9.2 percentage points; this had narrowed to only 3.3 percentage points in 1984 (Williams 1987). As Table 3.14 demonstrates, by 2012, the gap had narrowed considerably to less than 1 percentage point—73.7 percent of non-Latino white voting-age citizens were registered to vote compared with 73.1 percent of non-Latino blacks. The gap between non-Latino white and Latino and non-Latino Asian voter registration rates was wide, with the difference of 15 percentage points between non-Latino whites and Latinos and 17.4 percentage points between non-Latino whites and non-Latino Asians. Stated differently, only 58.7 percent of voting-age Latino citizens and 56.3 percent of voting-age non-Latino Asian citizens were registered to vote. Although these are wide differences, it should be noted that each of these differences is a drop from those present in 2004, when the difference between non-Latino whites and Latinos was 17.2 percent, and the difference between non-Latino whites and Asians was 23.3 percent. They are also similar to differences in 2008. While the differences between non-Latino whites and blacks seem to be decreasing overall, why are the numbers of Latinos and Asian Americans registered to vote at levels significantly below those of blacks and whites?

Since 1964, black registration rates have followed general national trends, going up in the 1960s, down in the 1970s, and up again in the 1980s

TABLE 3.13 Registration and Voting for Blacks and Latinos in Fifty States, 2014

State	% OF TOTAL ELECTORATE (CITIZENS ONLY)		% OF VOTING AGE CITIZENS REGISTERED		% OF REGISTERED THAT VOTED	
	Black	Latino	Black	Latino	Black	Latino
Mississippi	35.9%	1.5%	83.3%	NA	55.9%	76.5%
Georgia	31.8%	3.1%	62.3%	48.1%	69.1%	62.6%
Louisiana	30.9%	3.0%	70.5%	56.7%	73.1%	54.4%
Maryland	29.1%	4.6%	70.8%	63.6%	67.9%	48.3%
South Carolina	26.4%	3.0%	67.9%	45.1%	65.5%	29.2%
Alabama	25.9%	1.2%	65.4%	NA	91.8%	17.6%
North Carolina	22.3%	3.0%	68.1%	52.3%	70.7%	49.5%
Delaware	20.9%	4.7%	66.1%	NA	64.8%	35.7%
Virginia	19.6%	4.0%	61.7%	47.4%	55.3%	53.6%
New York	16.2%	13.1%	62.6%	55.8%	55.0%	50.5%
Tennessee	16.2%	2.2%	60.5%	39.8%	51.6%	31.0%
Florida	15.2%	17.9%	64.3%	60.2%	68.4%	59.7%
Illinois	14.8%	10.0%	57.8%	45.9%	69.7%	53.2%
Arkansas	14.7%	2.7%	60.7%	NA	63.0%	70.0%
Michigan	13.3%	4.1%	71.0%	60.6%	63.9%	45.8%
New Jersey	13.2%	13.6%	63.6%	61.7%	55.6%	55.1%
Texas	13.0%	29.0%	60.7%	46.2%	58.2%	48.4%
Ohio	11.6%	1.8%	68.7%	58.9%	59.3%	38.7%
Missouri	10.8%	1.1%	67.9%	NA	54.5%	53.6%
Nevada	10.3%	18.9%	65.2%	53.9%	49.2%	51.3%
Pennsylvania	9.7%	5.7%	53.5%	48.1%	69.3%	45.8%
Connecticut	9.6%	8.6%	49.2%	52.6%	68.6%	58.6%
Indiana	8.2%	3.8%	58.8%	43.1%	63.3%	44.9%
Kentucky	8.2%	1.7%	70.0%	NA	63.6%	67.6%
California	7.3%	28.0%	58.4%	48.0%	51.3%	51.8%
Oklahoma	7.1%	5.8%	50.3%	53.8%	58.3%	33.3%
Massachusetts	6.4%	6.5%	45.4%	49.7%	56.7%	34.2%
Kansas	6.1%	6.3%	59.8%	55.8%	72.6%	62.9%
Rhode Island	6.1%	5.9%	NA	NA	57.1%	59.1%
Wisconsin	5.4%	4.0%	56.8%	45.8%	72.1%	68.8%

TABLE 3.13 Registration and Voting for Black and Latinos in Fifty States, 2014

STATE	% OF TOTAL ELECTORATE (CITIZENS ONLY)		% OF VOTING AGE CITIZENS REGISTERED		% OF REGISTERED THAT VOTED	
Arizona	4.5%	26.0%	60.3%	60.0%	55.0%	53.0%
Nebraska	4.1%	5.0%	NA	NA	58.3%	50.0%
Minnesota	3.9%	2.5%	53.6%	47.8%	41.0%	70.8%
Alaska	3.6%	4.8%	NA	NA	66.7%	66.7%
Colorado	3.5%	14.3%	57.0%	60.1%	74.7%	67.9%
Washington	3.3%	7.9%	46.6%	44.8%	71.6%	56.2%
New Mexico	2.8%	35.5%	NA	60.0%	28.6%	59.3%
West Virginia	2.8%	1.1%	NA	NA	29.4%	27.3%
Iowa	2.7%	2.3%	NA	NA	64.5%	52.4%
Wyoming	2.1%	4.7%	NA	NA	60.0%	67.7%
Hawaii	1.9%	6.5%	NA	NA	87.5%	67.8%
South Dakota	1.8%	1.6%	NA	NA	60%	NA
Oregon	1.7%	6.4%	NA	57.7%	48.3%	58.5%
New Hampshire	1.2%	2.1%	NA	NA	57.1%	66.7%
North Dakota	1.1%	2.6%	NA	NA	100.0%	40.0%
Idaho	0.9%	8.7%	NA	24.0	NA	73.9%
Utah	0.8%	8.1%	NA	35.6%	100.0%	50.0%
Vermont	0.8%	0.6%	NA	NA	NA	100.0%
Maine	0.7%	1.0%	NA	NA	60.0%	75.0%
Montana	0.4%	2.0%	NA	NA	NA	72.7%

NA – Base in Data Sample was too small to make an estimate.

Source: U.S. Census Bureau, Current Population Survey, November 2014. "Table 4b. Reported Voting and Registration, by Sex, Race, and Hispanic Origin, for States: November 2014." http://www.census.gov/hhes/www/socdemo/voting/publications/p20/2014/tables.html

TABLE 3.14 Registration and Voting by Race, National Sample Citizens Only: White, Black, Latino, and Asians, 2012 and 2014

2012					
Race	% of VAP[a]	% Citizens	% of Citizens Registered	% of Citizens Reported Voting	% of Registered Voting
Non-Latino White	66.15%	98.2%	73.7%	64.1%	87.0%
Latino[b]	14.96%	66.3%	58.7%	48.0%	81.7%
Black	12.20%	93.8%	73.1%	66.2%	90.5%
Asian	5.31%	66.1%	56.3%	47.3%	84.0%
2014					
Race	% of VAP[a]	% Citizens	% of Citizens Registered	% of Citizens Reported Voting	% of Registered Voting
Non-Latino White	65.22%	98.3%	68.1%	45.8%	67.2%
Latino[b]	15.34%	68.2%	52.3%	27.0%	52.7%
Black	12.37%	94.1%	63.4%	39.7%	62.6%
Asian	5.63%	70.4%	48.8%	27.1%	55.5%

[a]VAP = voting age population (population 18 years and older).
[b]Latinos may be of any race.

Source: US Census Bureau, Current Population Survey, November 2012 (released May 2013). "Table 4b. Reported Voting and Registration, by Sex, Race, and Hispanic Origin, for States: November 2012," http://www.census.gov/hhes/www/socdemo/voting/publications/p20/2012 /tables.html.

Source: US Census Bureau, Current Population Survey, November 2014. "Table 2. Reported Voting and Registration, by Race, Hispanic Origin, Sex, and Age: November 2014," https://www .census.gov/hhes/www/socdemo/voting/publications/p20/2014/tables.html.

(Williams 1987). The 1990s exhibited a mixed pattern. Drops in black registration rates from the rates in 1984 and 1988 seemed to parallel similar drops in white registration from the rates for the 1984 to 1988 period. Although white registration in 1992, at 70.1 percent, was higher than the 67.9 percent registration rate in 1988, by 1994, the rate had dropped again significantly, to 64.6 percent, but had climbed again to 69.3 percent in 1998. Black registration rates fluctuated much like that of whites. Jesse Jackson's 1984 presidential campaign and the resultant voter registration drives apparently increased voter registration, but Jackson's 1988 run, although more successful in terms of primary outcomes, may not have had the same effect on national black registration efforts (Tate 1993). In 1992, black registration stood at 63.9 percent, dropping to 58.5 percent in 1994, rebounding to 63.7 percent in 1998, and increasing significantly in 2008, at 69.7 percent. Latinos and non-Latino Asians have considerably lower registration rates than do non-Latino African Americans. Latino registration rates have also dropped since 1984, when they stood at 40.1 percent of the voting-age population, declining to 35.5 percent in 1988, 35.1 percent in 1992, and 31.3 percent in 1994.

Recent data that look only at voting-age citizens, rather than the entire voting-age population, which includes noncitizen Latinos, provide a much different portrait of Latino registration rates (see Table 3.14). Using the voting-age population in 1994, only 31.3 percent of Latinos were registered. Yet in 2012, using Latino citizen voting-age population, 58.7 percent were registered to vote. Although this number is lower than are black and white registration rates, it is significantly higher than the 1994 rate is. Latinos are disproportionately younger, poorer, and less educated than the general population, which may suggest that the labyrinth of laws and administrative procedures that exist have a greater suppressive effect on Latino registration than the 9 percent effect estimated for the population in general (Calvo and Rosenstone 1989; Hero 1992). Other reasons for lower registration might include difficulty with the English language (Calvo and Rosenstone 1989; Meier and Stewart 1991) and difficulty in understanding US politics and the US political system (Vigil 1987:43).

With 1992 being the first year the US Census Bureau included Asian Americans in the survey, we can observe changes only from 1992 to 2012. Again, the early data included all voting-age Asians regardless of citizenship, and those data indicated that the percentage of Asian Americans registered to vote declined from 31.2 percent in 1992 to 28.7 percent in 1994. Examining data for Asian citizens of voting age in 1998 and 2012 presents a picture of a substantial increase in voter registration over the figures for all Asians, regardless of citizenship status: 49.1 percent of Asian voting-age citizens were registered to vote in 1998, and, as Table 3.14 indicates, a slightly larger percentage (56.3 percent) were registered to vote in 2012. Yet the numbers are still below registration rates of other groups.

Again, American Indian voting and registration data were not reported by the US Census Bureau for 2012. But 1998 data from the US Census Bureau for American Indians suggest a continuation of the pattern identified in the 1994 data. In 1994, 55.5 percent of the American Indian population of voting age was registered to vote, and in 1998, 58 percent of voting-age American

Indian citizens were registered to vote. American Indian voter registration rates almost parallel those of blacks, but they are slightly lower.

Although 73.1 percent of the black voting-age citizen population was registered to vote in 2012, 90.3 percent of those blacks who were registered to vote reported voting in the 2012 presidential election (see Table 3.14). This figure states that although non-Latino blacks were registered in a slightly lower proportion than non-Latino whites, a higher proportion of non-Latino blacks who were registered to vote actually voted than did non-Latino whites. The difference is 3.5 percent. In 2008, black citizens voted at higher levels than in any presidential election since the US Census Bureau began consistently measuring citizenship status in 1996 (File and Crissey 2012). It would not be a stretch to suggest that the candidacy of then senator Barack Obama as the Democratic nominee was one of the factors responsible for the increased black voter registration and voting. The US Census Bureau report for the 2012 election finds that for the first time black voter turnout (66.2 percent) was higher than non-Latino turnout (64.1 percent). In fact, voting rates for blacks were higher in 2012 than in any recent presidential election, even higher than in 2008. The national citizen voter turnout rate for the 2012 presidential election was approximately 61.8 percent. This is an increase over the citizen voter turnout rate of 59.5 percent for the 2000 presidential election, but a decrease from the turnout rate for 2008 (63.6 percent).

The voting levels for Latinos and Asian citizens in 2012 were again substantially lower than those for African Americans. Only 48 percent of voting-age Latino citizens and 47.3 percent of voting-age Asian citizens actually voted. This represents a gap between Latino and white voting rates and Asian and white voting rates of 16.1 percentage points and 16.8 percentage points, respectively. The differences between black and Latino voting rates and black and Asian voting rates were 18.2 percentage points and 18.9 percentage points, respectively. Looking at the behavior of registered voters, however, presents a better picture of Latino and Asian voting. Of those Latino and Asian citizens who were registered to vote, 58.7 percent and 56.3 percent, respectively, overwhelming majorities of Latinos (81.7 percent) and Asians (84 percent) registered to vote actually voted. These numbers are still less than those for non-Latino whites and non-Latino blacks, but not by much in some instances. The difference between registered black and white voters who voted and registered Asian voters who voted is 6.5 percent and 3.3 percent, respectively. But the difference between registered black and white voters who voted and registered Latino voters who voted is substantially greater, 8.8 percent and 5.3 percent, respectively.

Again, using the 1998 data, American Indian voting levels are below those of all of the racial groups in 2012, with 61 percent of American Indians registered to vote having voted in the 1998 congressional elections. This level is far above the limited data available on earlier American Indian voting which suggest that for the six elections from 1982 through 1992, turnout averaged approximately 40 percent. Clearly, in 1998, American Indian voter turnout was higher than that for Latinos, but lower than that for non-Latino whites, non-Latino blacks, and Asian Americans. Some data from the 2012 elections provide additional information, at least for American Indians in Montana and New Mexico, on registration and voting. In both of those states, American Indians are registered to vote at a higher rate than is any other racial or ethnic group. In Montana, 64.1 percent of American Indians are registered, compared to 63.6 percent of whites. In New Mexico, 77 percent of eligible American Indians are registered to vote, compared to 73 percent of blacks, 70 percent of whites, and 68 percent of Latinos (Trahant 2012 Elections 2012: Look at the Numbers and Indian Country Outperformed). Given the scarcity of data, it is difficult to be definitive on levels of American Indian registration and voting, so we must be circumspect in making any claims about the voting and registration patterns of this large umbrella group.

Of particular interest are the differences in registration and voting rates between men and women in the three groups—non-Latino blacks, Latinos, and non-Latino Asians—shown in Table 3.15. In 2012, black women, Latina women, and Asian women had higher registration rates than did black men, Latino men, and Asian men. In addition, black women, Latinas, and Asian women maintained that advantage in voting—a higher percentage of black, Latina, and Asian women voted than did black men, Latino men, and Asian men. Although the US Census Bureau did not report data for 1998 for American Indian men and women separately, 1994 data indicated that American Indian women had higher registration and higher voting rates than did American Indian men.

The reasons for higher levels of registration and voting among black women than among black men may stem from the higher levels of education and the labor force distribution of black women in more white-collar and fewer blue-collar jobs than is true for the black male labor force, although black women have higher turnout rates than black men within the same occupation, income, education, and employment status group. Survey data on group consciousness reveal that another possible reason for the differences may be that black women perceive discrimination on the basis of both race and gender. This dual consciousness, therefore, may foster participation of black women to a greater degree than racial consciousness alone stimulates that of black men (Williams 1987). The same argument could be made for the higher levels of registration and voting of Latinas and Asian women, although no survey data are available to support this contention.

TABLE 3.15 Registration and Voting by Race and Sex, National Sample Citizens Only: Black, Latino, and Asian, 2012

	BLACK		LATINO[b]		ASIAN	
Category	Male	Female	Male	Female	Male	Female
% VAP[a]	5.5%	6.7%	7.5%	7.5%	2.5%	2.8%
% Citizens Registered	69.4%	76.2%	56.7%	60.6%	54.5%	58.0%
% Citizens Reported Voting	61.4%	70.1%	46.0%	49.8%	46.0%	48.5%
% Registered Voting	88.5%	91.9%	81.1%	82.2%	84.4%	83.6%

[a]VAP = Voting Age Population (population over eighteen years old).
[b]Latinos may be of any race.

Source: US Census Bureau, Current Population Survey, November 2012, *Voting and Registration in the Election of November 2012,* Internet release table (May 2013), "Table 2. Reported Voting and Registration, by Race, Hispanic Origin, Sex, and Age, for the United States: November 2012," http://www.census.gov/hhes/www/socdemo/voting/publications/p20/2012/tables.html.

Given the high levels of immigrants within the broader Latino and Asian populations, one question that is often raised is whether these immigrant populations, once naturalized, will register and vote in similar or higher numbers than do the native-born populations. It is assumed that given the increasing size of the Latino population in particular, Latino political strength will increase substantially as soon as these new immigrants become naturalized citizens. Although we are unable to answer this question definitively, the data presented in Table 3.16 may be suggestive of future trends. Asian and Latino naturalized citizens are registered to vote in proportions higher than the native-born population. This differs from the pattern for blacks, where native-born blacks are registered in higher proportions than are naturalized blacks. When we look at voting behavior in the 2012 elections, native-born blacks once again voted in higher proportions than did naturalized blacks, 66.5 percent to 62.8 percent. The same does not appear to be the case for native-born Asians and Latinos, who voted in smaller proportions than did naturalized Asians and Latinos—43.9 percent to 49.3 percent and 46.1 percent and 53.6 percent, respectively. Data from the 2000, 2004, and 2008 elections also reveal a similar pattern—naturalized Latinos reported voting in greater proportions than did native-born Latinos—49.6 percent, and 43.6 percent, and 48.4 percent, respectively. But the 2002 midterm election data showed a different pattern—native-born Latinos and Asians registered and voted in greater numbers than did naturalized members of each group. Given the

TABLE 3.16 Reported Registration and Voting Among Native and Naturalized Black, Latino, and Asian Citizens, 2012

RACE		REPORTED REGISTERED	REPORTED VOTING	REGISTERED VOTING
Black	Native-born	73.5%	66.5%	90.4%
	Naturalized	68.3%	62.8%	92.0%
Asian	Native-born	52.4%	43.9%	83.7%
	Naturalized	58.6%	49.3%	84.1%
Latino	Native-born	57.9%	46.1%	79.7%
	Naturalized	61.3%	53.6%	87.4%

Source: US Census Bureau, Current Population Survey, November 2012, *Voting and Registration in the Election of November 2012,* Internet release table (May 2013), "Table 11. Reported Voting and Registration Among Native and Naturalized Citizens, by Race and Region of Origin: November 2012," http://www.census.gov/hhes/www/socdemo/voting/publications/p20/2012/tables.html.

contradictory findings from 2002, but the similarity in patterns among 2000, 2004, 2008, and 2012, we are not in a position to settle the question of whether naturalized Latinos register and vote in greater numbers than do native-born Latinos. But we might be getting close to an answer, especially if the 2016 data continue the trend. What we can say, however, is that newly naturalized Latino citizens add to an increased Latino political strength.

THE 2000 ELECTIONS

The 2000 presidential election was the closest and most contentious in recent memory. The outcome of the race between Vice President Al Gore and Texas governor George W. Bush turned on the outcome of the popular vote in Florida, which would determine which candidate would receive the state's 25 electoral votes, giving one candidate the 270 required electoral votes. On election eve, fewer than 1,700 votes out of 6 million votes cast separated Bush and Gore, with Bush holding the advantage. The less than 1 percent difference triggered an automatic recount under Florida law. At the end of the automatic recount and the counting of absentee ballots, Bush led by 535 votes. Both parties filed a number of suits in state and federal courts, and Bush filed an appeal with the US Supreme Court. After thirty-six days of differing court decisions that favored Bush at one moment and Gore at another, the US Supreme Court, in a five-to-four decision, stopped the full statewide recount ordered by the Florida Supreme Court, effectively giving the election to Governor Bush. Although Bush won the electoral vote and thus the presidency, he lost the popular vote to Gore by 500,000 votes.

The controversy surrounding the election and its aftermath resonated with racial minorities. A December 2000 Gallup Poll found that almost seven in ten blacks (68 percent) said that they felt "cheated" after the election, compared to 55 percent of white Democrats in the sample. Moreover, 50 percent of blacks polled felt that Bush stole the election. This feeling of injustice among blacks is related to the fact that a substantial majority of blacks (64 percent) felt that fraud was involved in Florida's voting procedures. Additionally, of blacks across the country, 68 percent of those polled felt that black voters in Florida were less likely to have their votes counted fairly than were white Floridian voters. Blacks' negative perception of the election system extended beyond Florida, with 76 percent of blacks saying that the election system in the United States is discriminatory (Gallup 2000).

Questions of possible violations of voting rights arose in various locations around the state before ballots were cast. The weekend before the election, many black Floridians received calls saying that the caller was with the National Association for the Advancement of Colored People (NAACP) and urged them to vote for George W. Bush. The NAACP, which was involved in a massive nationwide get-out-the-vote campaign, is a nonpartisan, nonprofit organization and does not officially endorse candidates. Similar calls were reported in Virginia and Michigan.

On Election Day, roadblocks were set up within a few hundred yards of voting places in predominantly black communities in Volusia County, where police asked black males to get out of their cars and show identification. In Hillsborough County, a disproportionate number of black voters were turned away from polls. Additionally, sheriff's deputies checking voter identification turned people away by saying that the race indicated on the voter identification did not match the race of the person standing in front of them. Clearly, the determination of the race of the people was based on the subjective visual judgment of the sheriff's deputies. Other blacks claimed that they were told that polling places had run out of ballots and that the polls were closed (Bayles 2000). Similar complaints of interference with the right of blacks to vote were registered from black voters around the country.

Other complaints from Florida concerned the high number of votes of minority citizens that were not counted. Ballot errors were very high in a number of Florida black precincts. In Miami-Dade County, about 2.7 percent of ballots were discounted because of overvoting; that is, voting for more than one candidate for president. But in about two dozen inner-city neighborhoods, between 8 and 11 percent of ballots were invalidated (Robles and Dougherty 2000). At least fifty Miami-Dade precincts, including Liberty City, Goulds, Overtown, and part of Coconut Grove, had rates of 7 percent or higher. One hundred of the county's 617 precincts had overvote rates of 5 percent or higher (Robles and Dougherty 2000). A precinct-by-precinct analysis of Florida counties by the *Washington Post* found that heavily Democratic and African American neighborhoods lost many more presidential votes than did other areas because of outmoded voting machinery and rampant confusion about ballots. In fact, the analysis identified a racial component to Florida's election process—counties with high proportions of black voters were more likely to have outmoded voting machinery than were counties with predominately white populations (Mintz and Keating 2000).

Table 3.17 presents trends in racial minority voting in presidential elections from 2000 to 2012. In 2000, Bush took a majority of the white vote (54 percent) to 42 percent for Gore. What kept the race at a 48 percent tie were the votes of racial minorities. Blacks supported Gore in higher proportions (90 percent) than they did Bill Clinton in 1996. In fact, Bush received a smaller proportion of black votes (8 percent) than did Bob Dole in 1996, 12 percent. Exit poll data from Texas indicate that even though Bush pulled 27 percent of the black vote in Texas in his reelection bid for governor in 1998, for his presidential bid in 2000, only 5 percent of black Texans voted for him. Ninety-one percent of black Texans voted for Gore (CNN 2000). After two years in his second term as governor, Bush lost considerable support among black Texans.

A majority of Latinos (67 percent) supported the Democratic presidential candidate, Al Gore. Although this represents a drop from Clinton's 72 percent in 1996, it is higher than Clinton's initial 61 percent of Latino votes in 1992. Even though he did not receive a majority of the Latino votes, Bush pulled more Latino votes (31 percent) than did Bob Dole (21 percent) in 1996, and the elder George Bush (25 percent) in 1992. Of interest is the Latino vote in Texas. In 1998, when Bush ran for reelection for governor, 49 percent of Latino Texans voted for him. That percentage dropped to 43 percent in the 2000 presidential election (CNN 2000). Although the drop in support is not close to the drop in black support, Bush did lose some Latino support in the two years after his gubernatorial reelection. And for the first time, a majority of Asian Americans voted for the Democratic presidential candidate. This is a reversal from the 1992 pattern, where a majority of Asian Americans (55 percent) voted for the Republican candidate, George H. W. Bush. This new voting pattern is consistent with the Asian partisan identification data—Asians on the whole are becoming more Democratic in their voting patterns.

Despite black anger and bitterness over the outcome of the presidential election, if there was a winner in the 2000 election, it was minority voters, especially black voters. In many ways, this is a similar story to that of the 1998 midterm elections. Massive voter registration and get-out-the-vote drives

TABLE 3.17 2000, 2004, 2008, and 2012 Presidential Election Results by Race and Gender

	2000			2004		2008			2012	
	Gore	Bush	Nader	Kerry	Bush	Obama	McCain	Nader	Obama	Romney
Total Vote (%)	48	48	2	48	51	53	46	1	51	47
Whites (%)	42	54	3	41	5a8	43	55	0	39	59
Blacks (%)	90	8	1	88	11	95	4	0	93	6
Latinos (%)	67	31	2	53	44	66	32	2	71	27
Asians (%)	54	41	4	56	44	61	35	–	73	26
Black Men (%)	85	12	1	–[a]	–	95	5	–	87	11
Black Women (%)	94	6	0	–	–	96	3	–	96	3
Latino Men (%)	–	–	–	–	–	64	33	–	65	33
Latina Women (%)	–	–	–	–	–	68	30	–	76	23

[a]Edison/Mitofsky exit polling did not provide information on detailed categories of the black sample in 2004.

Source: *New York Times* News Service exit polling, 2000; CNN Edison/Mitofsky exit polling, 2004; 2008 Edison Media Research/Mitofsky International; 2012 CNN Edison Research exit polling.

across the country made a significant difference in black voter turnout. In Florida, the black share of the vote grew from 10 percent in 1996 to 15 percent of the vote in 2000 (Bositis 2000). This increased black voter turnout helped lift Democrat Bill Nelson over Republican Bill McCollum in the US Senate race. McCollum, a former House of Representatives manager during the impeachment of President Bill Clinton, took the majority of the white and Latino vote (53 percent in each case), but Nelson's 88 percent share of the increased black turnout gave him his margin of victory (51 to 46 percent). Even the presence of Willie Logan, a Democratic black state senator who experienced problems with the state Democratic Party in 1998 and was running as an independent in the 2000 Senate race, did not pull substantial black votes from Nelson; only 4 percent of black voters cast a ballot for Logan.

In Missouri, the black share of voters on Election Day climbed from 5 percent in 1996 to 12 percent in 2000 (Bositis 2000). This significant increase in black voter turnout contributed directly to the defeat of Senator John Ashcroft. Ashcroft's Democratic opponent, Governor Mel Carnahan, died in a plane crash several weeks before the election, but because state law prevented substitution of another candidate, Carnahan's name remained on the ballot. The Democratic governor of Missouri stated that if voters "elected" Mel Carnahan, he would appoint his widow, Jean, to the Senate seat. Black Missourians were furious with Ashcroft for torpedoing the nomination of Ronnie White, a black Missouri Supreme Court justice, to a position on the federal bench. Blacks conducted massive voter registration and voter turnout drives that resulted in the substantial increase in black voting on Election Day. Despite Ashcroft's carrying the majority of the white vote (53 percent to 46 percent), black Missourians gave the deceased Carnahan 82 percent of their votes, which gave Carnahan a 51 to 47 percent victory over Ashcroft (CNN 2000).

At the state level, Latinos in California continued to make significant strides politically. Latinos were 14 percent of those who turned out to vote on Election Day, with blacks and Asians making up 7 percent and 6 percent, respectively. In other words, 27 percent of California voters were racial minorities. Latinos increased their number of representatives in the state Assembly by four, bringing their total to twenty: sixteen Democrats and four Republicans. They maintained their eight seats in the state Senate. In other states with sizable Latino populations, Latinos picked up two additional seats in New Mexico and one additional seat each in Arizona and Colorado. In states with smaller Latino populations, Latinos won state House seats in Rhode Island, bringing the total to two, and in New Hampshire, Latinos picked up their first state legislative seat (NALEO 2000).

Asian Americans also elected four members to the California Assembly, a record high. In January 2001, the assembly members formed the first Asian Pacific Islander Legislative Caucus (APILC) in California history. Democrat Mike Honda, who in 1998 was elected to the California State Assembly, was elected to the US Congress, bringing the number of Asian Americans in the House of Representatives, excluding nonvoting delegates, to four. This trend in increased Latino and Asian American representation at the state level will continue as the demographics in California and other parts of the country continue to favor increased Latino political influence. According to the 2000 census, Latinos now comprise about one-third of the California population, with Asians representing 12 percent and blacks constitute 6 percent.

THE 2004 ELECTIONS

George W. Bush was elected president in 2000 while losing the popular vote—a majority of white voters supported Bush, while a majority of nonwhite voters supported his opponent, Al Gore. Furthermore, as stated above, Gallup (2000) reported that almost 70 percent of blacks felt "cheated" after the 2000 election, one-half felt that Bush stole the election, and more than three-quarters said that the US election system was discriminatory. With that background, it is not surprising that the 2004 election between Democratic senator John F. Kerry and George W. Bush was hotly contested and produced a massive mobilization effort, especially among racial and ethnic minorities. Although nonwhites increased their proportion of all voters, President Bush was able to achieve a decisive reelection by growing his margin of victory among white voters, particularly among white women.

If, as DeSipio and de la Garza (2002:398) assert, "with each presidential election, the media and the punditocracy discover Latinos anew," 2004 took this phenomenon to new heights. Spurred perhaps by the census reports of Latinos becoming the nation's "largest minority" earlier than anticipated and by President Bush's self-proclaimed success at making inroads into this traditional Democratic constituency, speculation about the Latino vote was the rage during the campaign—and after. Postelection speculation was fueled by Election Day exit polls that reported the Latino vote for Bush to be as high as 44 percent—higher than any preelection poll showed and thus suspect. These polls showed broad support for Kerry across a range of demographic categories, with only non-Catholic Latinos favoring Bush (Leal et al. 2005:43–44). Leal and his colleagues (48) concluded that 39 percent is a more likely figure, which would be similar to the Latino support garnered by Ronald Reagan in 1984. They also concluded that whatever the accurate figure, it represented "not the beginning of a Latino realignment but the electoral ceiling for Republican presidential candidates with appealing personalities" (48).

The same exit polls that may have overreported Latino voting for Bush attributed only 11 percent of the black two-party vote to the GOP incumbent. This represented a 3-percentage-point increase over the 8 percent of blacks who voted for Bush in 2000. The 2004 percentage is similar to the partisan margins observed in previous presidential elections, with the exception of 2000. One difference in 2004 was Bush's ability, through his policy to send federal funds to church-based social service programs, to bring a small number of conservative black clergy actively to support him in the 2004 election. Their influence helped Bush increase his percentage of the black vote in two battleground states—Florida and Ohio. Despite the increase in the Republican share of the black vote in a couple of states, the real story about black voters in the 2004 presidential election is the increase in turnout. Blacks turned out at such a rate that they came close to approximating their proportion in the population in the electorate.

If Asian Americans made news in 2000 by, for the first time, supporting the Democratic presidential candidate with a majority of their votes, the 2004 exit poll results giving John Kerry 58 percent of the Asian American vote suggest the beginning of a trend. Exit polls focusing on Asian Americans in eight states, conducted by the Asian American Legal Defense and Education Fund in twenty-three languages or dialects, found a record turnout among Asian American voters, with Bush collecting not quite one-fourth of their votes. American Indians, according to the National Congress of American Indians, turned out in record numbers. Most notably, the number of Indian people voting in Minnesota is estimated to have doubled over previous levels. From the limited information available, American Indians appear to have continued their recent historical preference for the Democratic presidential candidate.

After the 2000 election fiasco in Florida, Congress passed the Help America Vote Act of 2002 (HAVA). It provides money for states to replace outdated voting machines; mandates the availability of provisional ballots in all states, a process that allows people who believe they are registered to vote but do not appear on voter rolls to cast a ballot; reforms voter registration procedures; and provides better access to voting for people with disablilities and better training for poll workers. The act also makes it easier for new voters to register. Despite HAVA, many Florida residents voted on the same machines in 2004 that caused so many problems in 2000.

Whereas Florida was the hot spot in 2000, Ohio was at the center of the 2004 elections, with the outcome of the election hinging on its twenty electoral votes. John Kerry did not concede Ohio until the day after the election, but that did not quell the complaints and concerns about Ohio's voting process. Prior to the election, Secretary of State Kenneth Blackwell, a black Republican, who was also cochair of the state's Bush-Cheney campaign, made several decisions that appeared to be aimed at helping George Bush win Ohio. For example, voter registration drives were in full force in Ohio, and more Democrats were being registered than Republicans when Blackwell instructed the county board of elections, only a few weeks before the registration deadline, to reject registrations on paper less than 80-pound weight, the type used for covers of paperback books and postcards. He said his concern was with registrations being mangled in the mail, but his directive applied to all registration forms, even those delivered by hand to election boards. The criticism that arose was so fierce that Blackwell had to back off, but it was impossible to know how many people had their registrations rejected before the directive was lifted (*New York Times* 2004). He also ruled that voters who had requested but not received absentee ballots could not vote by provisional ballot, supposedly to prevent double voting. Blackwell was sued in federal court, and the court ordered Blackwell to advise election officials that they had to issue provisional ballots to all who appeared at a polling place and claimed to be eligible to vote (Liptak 2004).

Electoral problems on Election Day kept thousands of Ohio voters from voting. Bipartisan estimates say that in Columbus, five to fifteen thousand voters left the polls in frustration without voting because of long lines due to election officials allocating too few voting machines for urban precincts. Similarly, voters in Cincinnati and Toledo and on college campuses stood in line for as long as ten hours, with many leaving without voting, because there were too few voting machines (Powell and Slevin 2004). In Cleveland, poorly trained poll workers gave voters faulty instructions that led to the disqualification of thousands of provisional ballots and misdirected hundreds of others to third-party candidates. And in Youngstown, twenty-five electronic machines transferred an unknown number of votes for Senator Kerry to Bush (Powell and Slevin 2004). Another area of contention was the ninety-six thousand ballots that registered no vote for president, seventy-seven thousand of which were cast on punch-card voting machines. The problem was most pronounced in minority precincts. An analysis by the *New York Times* of zip codes in Cleveland, which is approximately 85 percent black, found that one in thirty-one ballots registered no vote for president, more than twice the rate of predominately white zip codes, where one in seventy-five registered no vote for president (Dao, Fessenden, and Zeller 2004).

THE 2008 ELECTIONS

History in American politics and in the United States was made on November 4, 2008, when then Illinois senator Barack Obama was elected the forty-fourth president of the United States—the first African American to be so. He was elected with 52.9 percent of the vote and 365 electoral votes. Obama's keynote address at the 2004 Democratic National Convention launched him onto the national stage, and he was elected to the US Senate as the junior senator from Illinois in November of that year. On February 10, 2007, Obama announced his intention to run for the presidency, on the steps of the State Capitol in Springfield, Illinois. At the time, his quest for the presidency was viewed as a quixotic venture because he was little known and, of course, he was black. For many Americans, particularly black Americans, the thought that the United States would elect a black man as president was wishful thinking, a pipe dream, something that would happen in someone's else's lifetime, given the history of race in the country and the political process.

Obama entered a field of ten other declared Democratic candidates, and the foregone conclusion was that Senator Hillary Rodham Clinton (D-NY) would be the Democratic Party's nominee. Senator Clinton was not only a former First Lady but also had an incredible political and fund-raising machine that few could approach or compete with. Not only did the polls indicate that Clinton would be the nominee, but Senator Clinton believed that the political winds and public support were behind her. Obama was seen as the least likely of the Democrats to gain the nomination. Former senator John Edwards (D-NC), a vice presidential candidate in 2004, was viewed as a more credible, albeit distant, threat to Clinton than any of the other candidates.

Senator Obama put together a formidable campaign operation that was underestimated by all of his Democratic opponents. In the presidential primaries, he focused a lot of attention on states that chose delegates through a caucus system, while still concentrating on states with presidential primaries. Obama won the first Democratic caucus in Iowa on January 3, 2008, with 38 percent of the caucus votes, and Clinton came in third. This win was significant for Obama because Iowa's population is predominately white, and he demonstrated that he could attract white voters. The next primary was New Hampshire, a noncaucus state, and Clinton won that primary with 39 percent of the vote. The next two contests were Michigan (primary) and Nevada (caucus). Although Clinton won both, the Michigan contest was considered a nonevent because it had violated Democratic National Committee rules by moving its primary up. None of the Democratic candidates campaigned in the states, and only Hillary Clinton's name was on the ballot because the other Democrats had removed their names. Obama then won the South Carolina primary. Hillary Clinton then "won" Florida, which had also violated party rules by moving its primary up.

Then came Super Tuesday, February 5, 2008, when twenty-two states and American Samoa held either Democratic caucuses or primaries. Obama and Clinton basically split the contests, with Obama winning thirteen (Utah, North

Dakota, Missouri, Minnesota, Kansas, Illinois, Idaho, Georgia, Delaware, Connecticut, Colorado, Alaska, and Alabama) and Clinton winning ten (Tennessee, Oklahoma, New York, New Mexico, New Jersey, Massachusetts, California, Arkansas, Arizona, and American Samoa). By this time, it was clear that the contest for the nomination was between Obama and Clinton, and the other candidates dropped out. The nomination battle between the two continued into the summer of 2008 and became quite contentious. Obama had the delegate lead, but Clinton argued that she had won the bigger states, and issues of race became apparent through comments made both by Clinton and her husband, former president Bill Clinton, and by some of her supporters. The tenor of the comments was that Obama, as a black man, could not win and that Clinton could appeal to working-class whites who would not vote for a black man. Clinton finally dropped out, and Obama became the official presidential nominee of the Democratic Party at the August 2008 Democratic National Convention.

Obama's success in winning the Democratic nomination was not serendipity; rather, it was the result of a brilliantly planned campaign strategy and political events that played to Obama's strengths. First, Obama, unlike Clinton, had opposed the war in Iraq from before the 2003 invasion. In October 2002, at an antiwar rally in Chicago, Obama, then an Illinois state senator, delivered a speech where he argued against the impending United States invasion of Iraq. Obama was able to claim the antiwar mantle—as opposed to Clinton, who had voted for the invasion—and generated early support from antiwar Democrats.

Second, until Obama's win in Iowa, most black Americans were not convinced that whites would vote for him. Thus, most supported Hillary Clinton. After his win in the South Carolina primary and comments by President Bill Clinton that were perceived as being racially insensitive, the overwhelming majority of blacks shifted support to Obama. After his former pastor, the Reverend Jeremiah Wright, became a campaign controversy because of the inflammatory nature of some of his sermons, Obama gave a major speech on race in Philadelphia on March 18, 2008. This showed that Obama was not afraid to confront race but that he was not going to put the issue at the center of his campaign.

Third, while Obama shied away from overt references to race, he understood the importance of black and Latino voters. His campaign knew the strategic importance of registering large numbers of black and Latino voters in key Southern states (e.g., South Carolina, North Carolina, and Virginia) and in the Southwest (e.g., New Mexico and Nevada). His campaign strategy was to increase substantially the registrations, then to mobilize these two groups to turn out in the primaries and then the general election in numbers that would put Obama over the top in states where he was not deemed to be competitive. Democratic candidates have consistently not received the majority of the white vote, so large numbers of racial minority voters, combined with the minority of the white vote, would be a winning combination. This strategy was successful in shifting nine formerly Republican states (North Carolina, Virginia, Nevada, Colorado, New Mexico, Florida, Indiana, Iowa, and Ohio) into Obama's column on Election Day.

In 2004, only 59 percent of registered black voters in North Carolina voted, compared with 66 percent of white voters. In 2008, however, a record 74 percent of blacks registered to vote turned out and voted, surpassing the 66 percent rate for whites for the first time (*News and Observer* 2008). Blacks were 23 percent of those who turned out to vote on Election Day, which is higher than their proportion (21 percent in 2006) of North Carolina's citizen voting-age population. Thus, blacks overperformed in voting turnout, and Obama won North Carolina by 14,177 votes.

A similar pattern was present in New Mexico among Latino voters. Latinos, primarily Mexican Americans, were 41 percent of those who turned out to vote on Election Day, although they represented 33.4 percent of the citizen voting-age population (as of 2006). The number of Latinos voting increased by 37 percent over 2004, and 69 percent of Latinos voted for Obama, turning New Mexico from red to blue (Gordon 2008). Obama also focused efforts on states with early voting like North Carolina and New Mexico, where 41.7 percent of New Mexicans voted early in person and another 21 percent by mail, with only 37.7 percent actually turning out to vote on Election Day (Nonprofitvote.org 2008). In North Carolina, 52 percent of black voters voted early, compared to 40 percent of white voters (North Carolina Board of Elections 2008). Obama also actively reached out to Asian American and American Indian voters, using the same strategy to increase registration and voting in key areas. In May 2008, Obama became an honorary member of the Crow Nation in Montana, taking on a native name and honorary parents in a traditional ceremony (Mason 2008). He also wrote a column in *Indian Country Today* on October 26, 2008, where he promised to appoint an American Indian policy adviser to his senior White House staff and to host an annual summit of tribal leaders at the White House to develop an agenda that worked for tribal communities (Obama 2008).

In the general election, Obama received 95 percent of the black vote (95 percent of black men and 94 percent of black women), 66 percent of the Latino vote (64 percent of Latino men and 68 percent of Latina women), and 61 percent of the Asian American vote. John McCain took the majority of the white vote (55 to 43 percent), but the smaller white percentage, coupled with the huge vote margins among black, Latino, and Asian voters, were sufficient to give Obama 53 percent of the popular vote to McCain's 46 percent. Blacks increased their proportion of the electorate from 11 percent in 2004 to 13 percent in 2008, as did Latinos, who went from 6 percent in 2004 to 8 percent in 2008 (Bositis 2008).

Fourth, Obama strategically reached out to young voters, using modern technology to make and maintain contact with this core constituency. His campaign used text messaging, Facebook, and other social networking sites; e-mails; and campaign ads in video games. The campaign also organized thousands of young volunteers to supplement his large paid campaign staff. Obama decided against taking federal campaign funds, thus freeing him to raise as much money as legally permissible. He used technology to get millions of individuals to contribute online. Although he still had big donors, he amassed more than 3.95 million individual donors who gave small amounts multiple times. In the end, Obama raised more than three-quarters of a billion dollars for his campaign (Overby 2008).

Fifth, Obama and his campaign were disciplined, far more disciplined than any presidential campaign in modern history. Obama's campaign was the only one that between the primaries and general election did not change personnel; the same top people who were with him at the beginning were with him in victory. They stuck to a game plan and did not deviate from it based on calls or complaints from nervous Democrats arguing that he needed to fight back more or be tougher or be meaner.

Finally, unlike Obama's disciplined campaign, John McCain's campaign could not agree on a consistent message and appeared to be disorganized and inconsistent. His choice of Alaska governor Sarah Palin as his running mate was very popular with the conservative Republican base, but the ticket's stance on cultural issues (e.g., abortion, religion, and challenges to the patriotism of Senator Obama) turned moderate whites and some Republicans off. McCain could not win without moderate voters, and his campaign techniques and tactics pushed this group away from him. The reaction to Senator McCain's gracious concession speech after his defeat suggested that if he had approached his campaign through the lens of that speech, he might have drawn more moderates to his side.

Despite Obama's desire to keep race peripheral to the campaign, issues of race and racist instances were interjected on numerous occasions. An Inland (California) Republican women's group published the "Obama Buck's" welfare coupon in its October 2008 newsletter. Obama was pictured surrounded by a watermelon, ribs, and a bucket of fried chicken, playing on the worst stereotypes some Americans have of black Americans. In Minnesota, racist flyers were mailed to the predominately white constituents in Representative Betty McCollum's (D) district, stating that property values would decrease as low-income blacks would be moving into their neighborhoods if Obama was elected.

There were also numerous instances of voter suppression techniques and tactics. For example, a phony state board of elections flyer was posted around the Hampton Roads area in Virginia, stating that Republicans vote on Tuesday, November 4, and Democrats vote on Wednesday, November 5. Deceptive flyers about the consequences of voting were distributed in a predominately African American neighborhood in Philadelphia. In California, dozens of voters reported that a firm hired by the California Republican Party tricked them into registering with the GOP when signing a petition they believed to toughen penalties against child molesters. The Los Angeles County registrar-recorder reviewed nine thousand registration affidavits submitted by the firm to determine whether any of the party affiliation changes were involuntary. The owner of the firm was subsequently arrested on felony voter registration fraud and perjury charges. Michigan illegally purged its voter rolls and sent nonforwardable mailings to recently registered voters, according to a federal court ruling. The court ordered the restoration of about 1,400 voters who had been removed because their voter identification cards were returned as undelivered (Weiser and Chen 2008). Four to five million voters were not able to cast ballots in the presidential election because of registration problems or not receiving absentee ballots. An additional two to four million registered voters were discouraged from voting because of long lines and voter identification requirements. Although improvements had been made in the voting process (e.g., new voting technology), little progress had been made in removing the barriers to registration and absentee voting (Urbina 2009).

Below the presidential level, racial minorities also made gains. The election of Ben R. Lujan (D-NM) brought the total number of Latinos in the House of Representatives to twenty-seven in the 111th Congress. (That number dropped to twenty-six when Representative Hilda Solis became Obama's secretary of labor.) Latinos gained seats in the state senates of Wyoming, Tennessee, Massachusetts, and Utah, while also picking up the first seat in the Oklahoma House of Representatives; increasing their number from six to eight in the Connecticut House of Representatives; and increasing their total to thirty-two members in the New Mexico House of Representatives, the largest state House delegation in the nation (NALEO 2008).

One black incumbent member of the US House of Representatives, William Jefferson (D-LA), was defeated in his bid for reelection by Republican

Anh "Joseph" Cao, who became the first Vietnamese American to serve in Congress. Jefferson's indictment on bribery charges and low voter turnout allowed Cao to beat Jefferson 50 to 47 percent in a district that was drawn specifically to give blacks an electoral advantage and where two of every three voters were registered Democrats (Krupa and Donze 2008). There were nine black Republican House candidates, most opposing black Democratic House incumbents; none of them won. There were also two black US Senate candidates—Vivian D. Figures (D) opposing incumbent Jeff Sessions (R) in Alabama, and Erik Fleming (D) opposing incumbent Thad Cochran (R) in Mississippi—but neither of them won (Bositis 2008).

The Joint Center for Political Studies indicates that in 2007, there were 622 black state legislators, of which, according to the Center for American Women and Politics (2008), 239 were black women. There was one notable election in 2008. Pearl Burris Floyd was elected the first black Republican woman to the North Carolina State Legislature. She joins only three other black female Republican state legislators—Representative Jennifer S. Carroll of Florida, Representative Jane E. Powdrell-Culbert of New Mexico, and State Senator Jackie Winters of Oregon.

All of the Asian American incumbents in the US House of Representatives were reelected and were joined by Anh "Joseph" Cao. Three Asian Americans—David Chiu, Eric Mar, and Carmen Chu—were elected to the San Francisco Board of Supervisors. Irvine, California, elected its first nonwhite and first Asian mayor, Democrat Sukhee Kang, a Korean immigrant and city councilman (Barboza 2008).

THE 2012 ELECTIONS

Another historic event occurred on November 6, 2012, when President Barack Obama was reelected president of the United States. He received 51.1 percent of the popular vote and 332 electoral votes, making him the first president since Republican Dwight D. Eisenhower in 1952 and 1956 to win at least 51 percent of the national popular vote twice, and the first Democrat to do so since Franklin D. Roosevelt in 1944 (Giroux 2013). By any measure, this win was not close (his Republican opponent, former Massachusetts governor Mitt Romney, received 47.2 percent of the national popular vote and 206 electoral votes), but prior to the election most analysts and pundits considered President Obama vulnerable and Republicans were certain that they and their candidate would beat him. When President Obama came into office in 2009, the unemployment rate was 7.8 percent; it then rose to 10 percent in October 2009, falling to 7.7 percent in November 2012. Also, the country had lost approximately 4.5 million jobs in the year prior to his taking office, and lost another

PHOTO 3.3 *President-elect Barack Obama and his wife, Michelle, and their daughters, Malia and Sasha, arrive on stage during his election night party at Grant Park in Chicago, Tuesday night, November 4, 2008.* (AP Photo/Pablo Martinez Monsivais; ID: 08110504796)

4.3 million before hitting bottom in February 2010. Obama is the second president since World War II (Ronald Reagan was the first) to win reelection with unemployment above 6 percent (Giroux 2013).

On the very day that Obama took his first oath of office, January 20, 2009, a group of Republican lawmakers and consultants, including representatives Eric Cantor of Virginia, Paul Ryan of Wisconsin, and Pete Sessions of Texas; Frank Luntz, a consultant; and Newt Gingrich, former Speaker of the House, met for dinner. The upshot of the meeting, according to Robert Draper (2012), was to attack President Obama at every turn, oppose his economic policies to revive the economy, and attack some of his cabinet officers and vulnerable

House Democrats. The goal was to take control of the House of Representatives in the 2010 midterm elections, and take back the White House and the Senate in 2012. In October 2010, Republican senator Mitch McConnell of Kentucky said that "the single most important thing we want to achieve is for President Obama to be a one-term president" (Memoli 2010).

Coupled with the obstructionist attitude adopted by the Republicans, some individuals and groups who could not accept President Obama's election filed multiple lawsuits, challenging President Obama's citizenship and right to hold the office. Those challenging President Obama's citizenship have become known as "birthers," because they argued that he was born not in the United States but in Kenya. President Obama was born in Hawaii and released his short- and long-form birth certificates, but despite evidence to the contrary, some individuals continue to believe that he was not born in the United States. A July 2009 poll by Daily Kos/Research 2000 found that 14 percent of whites said that he was not born in the United States and 15 percent were not sure. Conversely, 97 percent of blacks said that he was born in the United States; only 1 percent said he was not and 2 percent were not sure. A majority of Latinos (87 percent) also believed he was born in the United States. When broken down by region, 23 percent of those in the South said that he was not born in the United States and 30 percent were not sure. (There was no racial breakdown of respondents by region.)

Another element opposed to President Obama was a loosely affiliated group that became known as the Tea Party, which began in 2009 in opposition to the bank bailout and economic stimulus package. The membership of the various Tea Party groups consists primarily of conservative Republicans, and one of their aims was to purge the Republican Party of moderates and those who were not sufficiently conservative. Some Republican senators and representatives aligned themselves with the group, particularly South Carolina senator Jim DeMint and Minnesota representative Michelle Bachmann. The Tea Party was instrumental in the 2010 midterm elections, which saw the Republicans regain control of the House of Representatives. The election was after Congress passed President Obama's signature health care reform law, the Patient Protection and Affordable Care Act of 2010, which infuriated the Tea Party even more. Repealing the act became a primary goal of the Tea Party and the Republicans.

The road to the Republican nominee went through thirteen primary debates beginning on May 5, 2011. Republican primary voters tend to be far more conservative than the general voting population, and the Tea Party and its supporters pushed the primary candidates to the extreme right on many public policy issues including immigration, contraception, abortion, revenues, and taxes. Among the candidates were Newt Gingrich; Mitt Romney, former governor of Massachusetts; Michelle Bachmann; Herman Cain, a businessman; John Huntsman, former ambassador to China and former governor of Utah; Ron Paul, representative from Texas; Rick Santorum, former senator from Pennsylvania; and Rick Perry, governor of Texas. The lead shifted numerous times, with Gingrich winning several primaries and being declared the front-runner, only to see Rick Santorum emerge as the front-runner after other primaries. In the end, Mitt Romney secured the nomination in early June 2012, passing the requisite 1,144 delegates for nomination at the Republican National Convention. Romney chose Wisconsin Republican representative Paul Ryan as his running mate.

Romney enjoyed support from a number of conservative super Political Action Committees (PACs) that either supported his candidacy directly or spent considerable money attacking Obama. The largest pro-Romney super PAC was Restore Our Future (cumulative $97 million; 15 percent of total raised), most of which came from the financial industry, including private equity executives and hedge fund managers. The US Supreme Court's 2010 decision in *Citizens United v. Federal Election Committee* ruled that corporations and unions have the same political speech rights as individuals under the First Amendment, and are thus able to donate directly to political candidates and PAC. Yet, despite the huge financial support from outside groups, Romney made a number of errors and misjudgments that removed the edge on handling the economy that his campaign and Republicans had counted on to defeat Obama.

Because President Obama did not have a primary challenge, his campaign spent a good deal of time during the Republican primaries defining the candidates thought most likely to be the Republican nominee. Romney was assumed to be the odds-on favorite, so the Obama campaign focused on him, using Romney's career at Bain Capital and his vast wealth to paint him as out of step with the majority of the American public. The Obama campaign drew on comments made by other Republicans during the presidential primaries to define Romney, such as describing him as a "vulture capitalist." Romney did not help his case by refusing to release more than two years of his tax returns and by making comments that showed his disconnect—for example, entering a horse he owned in the 2012 Olympics, highlighting that equestrian sports were the "sport of the rich." These actions, coupled with his unease with voters, made him seem aloof and out of touch.

In another devastating and possibly fatal comment, Romney was surreptitiously recorded on video at a fund-raiser in May 2012 where he referred to those supporting President Obama as "forty-seven percent who are with him, who are dependent upon government, who believe that they are victims, who believe that government has a responsibility to care for them, who believe that they are entitled to health care, to food, to housing, to you name it" (Corn 2012). The backlash to these comments was intense, immediate, and long lasting. The story was carried by all of the major news outlets, and many people were offended by the idea that they were being labeled as lacking a sense of personal responsibility because they did not earn enough money to be required to pay federal income taxes, even while contributing to payroll taxes, among many other forms of taxation. Further, many found it distasteful that a presidential candidate would outright say that he does not need to concern himself with a significant portion of the population, all within a setting where he clearly had the expectation that his comments were not made for the broader public but rather were for a specific subset of the wealthier population of the United States to which Romney belonged. The Obama team formulated a campaign advertisement strategy meant to highlight the fact that Romney's comments labeled teachers, senior citizens, college students, and individuals in the military as people who saw themselves as victims in search of handouts from the government. Some of these ads solely used Romney's own voice from the secret recording, while showing pictures representing the aforementioned groups. Later Obama ads stated more directly that Romney did not worry about these groups and that therefore they should not vote for the Republican candidate.

But Romney did not lose a race that he was supposed to win; he was beaten by a far superior campaign organization, changing economic conditions, and a changing electorate that had been missed, dismissed, or alienated by the Republican Party. First, the economy began to improve, albeit slowly, and all indicators, while not great, were heading upward. This undercut the Republican claims that President Obama was failing on the economy and the recovery.

Second, the Obama campaign organization was far superior and better organized than Romney's. The Obama campaign's skill in messaging, fund-raising, strategic planning, micro-targeting voters, and getting out the vote swamped Romney's efforts (Feldman 2012). Of the states that Obama won in 2008, he lost only Indiana and North Carolina in 2012. His campaign also understood the changing demographics of the nation and, as in the 2008 campaign, focused detailed attention on women, blacks, Latinos, Asian Americans, and American Indian voters. Exit polling showed that President Obama took the majority of the female vote (55 percent) but only 46 percent of the white female vote. His margin of victory among women came from the votes of black women (96 percent), Latinas (68 percent), and Asian and other nonwhite women (64 percent). As Table 3.17 (p. 118) demonstrates, although Romney took the majority of the white vote (59 percent),

Obama took 93 percent of the black vote, 71 percent of the Latino vote, and 73 percent of the Asian vote. These numbers, coupled with the smaller portion of the white vote (39 percent), secured Obama's clear and substantive victory over Romney.

Looking at a couple of the battleground states also shows the power of black, Latino, and Asian voters. In Virginia, a state Obama won in 2008 and held in 2012, Obama beat Romney with 51 to 47 percent of the vote. Whites represented 70 percent of those who voted in the election, and an overwhelming majority (61 percent) voted for Romney, compared to 37 percent who voted for Obama. But blacks were 20 percent of the electorate that day, Latinos were 5 percent, Asians were 3 percent, and other nonwhites were 2 percent, for a total of 30 percent. Within these groups, Obama took 93 percent of the black vote, 64 percent of the Latino vote, and 66 percent of the Asian vote (the exit polls did not report the other nonwhite vote distribution). Black voters turned out in numbers slightly more than their portion of the voting-age population in Virginia, 19.4 percent in the 2010 US Census, which means they overperformed their voter turnout. But Latinos voted in smaller numbers than their portion of the Virginia voting-age population, which is 6.9 percent. Nevertheless, these numbers, coupled with the 37 percent of the white vote, made up Obama's 51 percent, which put Virginia's thirteen electoral votes in his column.

A similar pattern was present in Ohio, another battleground state, which some might consider the Holy Grail of battleground states, with its eighteen electoral votes. There, Obama beat Romney 51 to 48 percent. Whites were 79 percent of the electorate on Election Day, and a majority (58 percent) voted for Romney, with 41 percent voting for Obama. (This is 4 percentage points more of the white vote for Obama in Ohio than in Virginia.) Black voters were 15 percent of the electorate, Latinos were 3 percent, Asians were 1 percent, and other nonwhites were 2 percent, for a total of 21 percent. Obama took 96 percent of the black vote and 53 of the Latino vote. (No vote breakdown for Asians and other nonwhites was calculated.) Black voters were 11 percent of the 2010 voting-age population in Ohio, but were 15 percent of those who voted. Latinos, who were 2.5 percent of the voting-age population in 2010, were 3 percent of those who turned out to vote. This overperformance on the part of blacks and Latinos, added to the two-fifths of the white vote, gave Obama 51 percent of the vote. Obama's support of the bailout of General Motors and Chrysler and Romney's opposition to it, along with strong union support, proved critical to Obama's winning Ohio. Exit polling in Ohio showed that 59 percent of voters supported the bailout compared to 36 percent who opposed it (Feldman 2012). There were numerous other factors that contributed to Obama's win in 2012, but these are just a few highlights.

Black votes were also critical to Democratic victories in several US Senate races. Blacks provided the margin of victory to Joe Donnelly in Indiana, representing 15.6 percent of his total vote. In Missouri, blacks helped reelect Senator Claire McCaskill, representing 27.8 percent of her vote total. Blacks were 28.5 percent of the vote total that reelected Senator Sherrod Brown in Ohio, 22.3 percent of the vote total for the reelection of Senator Bob Casey in Pennsylvania, and more than one-third (34.7 percent) of the vote total that elected Tim Kaine in Virginia to the Senate (Bositis 2012).

The votes of American Indians were crucial to the victory of two Democratic senators who were supposed to be defeated by Republicans—Senator Jon Tester of Montana and Heidi Heitkamp of North Dakota. Montana is a solidly Republican state, and Tester was considered vulnerable to a challenge by Representative Denny Rehberg. Prior to the election, Tester told Indian Country Today Media Network that he was relying on American Indian votes from the reservations to help him defeat Rehberg (Capriccioso 2012). American Indian organizers canvassed the state and reservations highlighting Tester's efforts on behalf of Indians. Election results found that counties in Montana dominated by reservations voted overwhelmingly for Tester, and those votes are seen as having helped him retain his seat (Woodard 2012).

In North Dakota, a number of tribes held get-out-the-vote rallies for Heidi Heitkamp on reservations and got residents to the polls to vote for Heitkamp. In Sioux County, for example, American Indians are 84.1 percent of the population and voted 83.9 percent for Heitkamp. In Rolette County, Indians make up 77.2 percent of the population, and 80.3 percent voted for Heitkamp (Trahant 2012 Elections 2012: Look at the Numbers and Indian Country Outperformed). In the end, Indian votes provided the margin of victory for Heitkamp. The expectation for both Tester and Heitkamp from American Indian voters was that they would give significant attention to issues of importance to Indians within their states.

Most of the black members of Congress were reelected, and five new members would join the House. Two black representatives, Laura Richardson (D-CA) and Hansen Clarke (D-MI), lost their seats to white Democrats when their districts were merged during redistricting. Republican Allen West (R-FL) also lost reelection to a white Democrat, Patrick Murphy (D-FL), and Republican congressional candidate Vernon Parker lost his bid for a newly created congressional seat in Arizona to former Democratic state senator Kyrsten Sinema. Probably the most surprising loss was that of Mia Love, a black Mormon Republican, in Utah. She had been expected to win, but lost to Democratic incumbent Jim Matheson. She underperformed in actual votes to what preelection polls suggested she would receive. If she had been elected, she would have been the first black Republican female to serve in the House of Representatives.

Nine new Latino members were elected to the House of Representatives, and Ted Cruz (R-TX) became the third Latino, and second Republican Latino, in the US Senate. A race of note was the defeat of Republican representative Mary Bono Mack by Democrat Dr. Raul Ruiz in the Thirty-Sixth Congressional District in California. In New Mexico, Democrat Michelle Lujan Grisham became the first Latina to represent New Mexico in the House of Representatives. Five Asian Americans were elected to the House of Representatives, including Iraq War veteran Tammy Duckworth (D-IL), who is Thai American, and Tulsi Gabbard, a Samoan American from Hawaii. Democrat Mazie Hirono won the Senate seat from Hawaii vacated by Native Hawaiian former Democratic senator Daniel Akaka. Hirono previously served in the House of Representatives. American Indian Markwayne Mullin (R-OK) was elected to the House of Representatives. Mullin is a member of the Cherokee Nation. Denise Juneau (D-MT) was reelected state superintendent of public instruction, a post she won initially in 2008. Juneau is a member of the Mandan and Hidatsa tribes.

Despite Obama's solid win, there were attempts, primarily by Republicans, to make it difficult for people to vote, principally voters who supported President Obama in 2008. The push for voter ID laws began in 2003, when Alabama, Colorado, Montana, North Dakota, and South Dakota passed new laws. These laws were the result of provisions in the 2002 Help America Vote Act that required that new registrants provide their driver's license number or the last four digits of their Social Security number with their registration application. In addition, states that allowed individuals to register by mail had to obtain identification from first-time voters. These early laws did not require photo identification to vote and allowed for the use of a number of pieces of identification. For example, in Montana voters could use a driver's license, tribal photo identification, a current utility bill, bank statement, paycheck, government check, or any other document that showed the person's name and current address (National Conference of State Legislatures 2013).

Heading into the 2008 and particularly the 2012 elections, states began to pass stringent photo voter identification laws that were criticized as being aimed at reducing and suppressing the votes of racial and ethnic minorities that tend to vote Democratic. The argument made by the legislatures was that these laws would prevent in-person voter fraud, a problem for which a number of studies have found little to no evidence exists. These charges were aimed particularly at states controlled by Republican legislatures whose voter ID laws required voters to present state government– or federal government–issued photo ID cards. A study by the Brennan Center for Justice (Weiser and Kasdan 2012) identified that 11 percent of voting-age Americans—or 21 million citizens—do not have a driver's license or other nondriver's state-issued ID. Those without photo IDs are disproportionately seniors (18 percent), African Americans (25 percent), the poor (15 percent), and students or people with disabilities (Weiser and Kasdan 2012:2).

Several of these restrictive laws were blocked by courts before they were able to be implemented. For example, Pennsylvania's highly restrictive photo ID law was blocked by a state court on October 2, 2012, after a video surfaced of the state Republican House majority leader Mike Turzai saying that the photo ID law was passed not to prevent in-person voter fraud but to give the state's electoral votes to Romney. This statement was not the only factor in the injunction, but the state of Pennsylvania actually stipulated in court "Respondents will not offer any evidence in this action that in-person voter fraud has in fact occurred in Pennsylvania or elsewhere; . . . Respondents will not offer any evidence or argument that in-person voter fraud is likely to occur in November 2012 in the absence of the Photo ID Law" (State of Pennsylvania Stipulation, July 12, 2012).

In addition to restricting the type of ID acceptable to be able to vote, six states (Florida, Illinois, Maine, Ohio, Texas, and Wisconsin) passed legislation making it harder for citizens to register to vote, and Florida, Illinois, and Texas put restrictions on voter registration drives. For example, in Florida, restrictions shut down such groups as the League of Women Voters and Rock the Vote from registering people to vote. These restrictions were aimed at cutting down on the number of blacks and Latinos that would register to vote, as these groups register through voter drives at twice the rate of whites (Weiser and Kasdan 2012). (Florida's restrictions stood for a year, but a preliminary injunction on May 31, 2012, and then a permanent injunction on August 20, 2012, was issued, removing restrictions on community-based voter registration drives.)

Five states cut back on early voting, with Ohio and Florida both eliminating early voting on the Sunday before the election—a day when many African American and Latino churches had organized successful "Souls to the Polls" voting in 2008. The shortening of the early voting days in Florida meant that many early voters had to wait in line as long as nine hours to vote (*Huffington Post* November 5, 2012). The long lines and delays continued on Election Day, November 6, with researchers at Ohio State University estimating that across central Florida as many as forty-nine thousand people were discouraged from voting. About thirty thousand of those discouraged voters would likely have voted for President Obama, while about nineteen thousand would have likely backed Mitt Romney (Damron and Powers 2012).

In addition to these instances, there were a number of instances of voter suppression techniques and tactics in 2012. In Florida, fraudulent letters on fake letterhead and with the signature of Kathy Dent, elections supervisor, informing recipients that their citizenship and right to vote was in question were sent to residents in at least twenty-eight counties (though the actual number is thought to be small). Elderly voters in Virginia received phone calls from unidentified individuals, informing them that they could vote by phone and did not need to go to the polls on November 6. Billboards in black and Latino neighborhoods in Pennsylvania, Ohio, and Wisconsin were erected on boards owned by Clear Channel and Norton Outdoor Advertising, warning residents that voter fraud was a felony. After complaints from residents and civil rights groups, the billboards were taken down. There were fifty-eight such billboards in Philadelphia and Pittsburgh alone. In Maricopa County, Arizona, which includes Phoenix, the county recorder's office printed two separate Spanish-language voter information guides listing Election Day as November 8, although the English-language versions had the correct date of November 6.

THE 2016 ELECTIONS*

The 2016 Republican primary and presidential general election was rife with race issus and racism. One of the key undertones to Donald Trump's success in the primaries was his attack of nonwhites. These included explicitly anti-immigrant commentary and suggestions of policies and travel bans meant to profile and target Muslim Americans. As a result of such rhetoric, white nationalists, typically marginalized by the Republican Party, emerged and were more vocal in their support of Donald Trump than they had been for any candidate in past campaigns (Confessore 2016).

On June 16, 2015, Donald Trump announced his candidacy for the Republican nominee for president (Aaron and Dewan 2016). In the one-hour speech, he addressed issues from Chinese oligarchs to ISIS. Most prominent was his discussion on immigration policy and Mexico. Trump stated, "When Mexico sends its people, they're not sending their best—they're not sending you. They're not sending you. They're sending people that have lots of problems and they're bringing those problems with us [sic]. They're bringing drugs.

---

*Parts of this section are drawn from Paula D. McClain and Steven C. Tauber, *American Government in Black and White: Diversity and Democracy* (Oxford: Oxford University Press, 2017).

They're bringing crime. They're rapists. And some, I assume, are good people" (Burns 2016). On July 11, at one of his major rallies in Phoenix, Arizona, Trump explicitly called out the issue of illegal immigration (Rupar and Dewan 2016). Trump had invited to the rally Maricopa County sheriff Joe Arpaio, who is notorious for his racial-profiling tactics targeted toward the Latino community. Most notably in his speech, Trump suggested building a wall at the US-Mexico border (Lee 2015). This idea led to his supporters chanting "Build That Wall!," a chant that would become a defining feature of his rallies. On August 25, at a press conference in Iowa, Trump had anchor Jorge Ramos of Univision forcibly removed from the beginning of the press conference when he tried to ask a question (CNN.com 2015; Finnegan 2015). Ramos was escorted from the room by a member of Trump's private security. In the hallway, a middle-aged white man with a Trump sticker on his lapel, his face flushed with anger, accosted Ramos, jabbing a finger at him. "Get out of my country," he said. "Get out." Ramos told him that he, too, was a US citizen. Ramos was eventually let back into the room.

Many other instances of racial statements and racial insensitivity occurred during Trump's campaign, including Trump acting as if he did not know the background of David Duke, the former grand dragon of the Ku Klux Klan group and neo-Nazi sympathizer who had endorsed him. One of the more sensational events that went on for several weeks was Trump's attack in June 2016 on the Mexican American judge Gonzalo Curiel, who was overseeing the fraud case against Trump University in San Diego. Trump began referencing Curiel's Mexican American background and implying that because of it, he could not be fair in his rulings on Trump University because Trump wanted to build a wall on the Mexican border (Totenberg 2016). The number of instances of racist, misogynist, xenophobic, anti-Muslim, and other types of statements and behaviors were so numerous that it would take an entire chapter to list them.

The outcome of the 2016 presidential contest was unexpected and counter to virtually every public opinion and tracking poll available, but it was in keeping with the unorthodox and surprise-filled campaign that characterized the general election. Just before the second presidential debate on Sunday, October 9, 2016, Trump's campaign appeared to be coming apart. An audiotape of Trump making vulgar comments about women and bragging about sexually assaulting them had surfaced, causing more than two dozen Republican leaders to disavow their support of the GOP presidential nominee (NPR Staff 2016). Although Trump issued an apology for his grossly inappropriate comments, he brushed his words off as "locker room talk" and denied groping or sexually assaulting women. Hours before the debate, Trump held a press conference with four women who accused former president Bill Clinton of sexual assault, and during the debate itself, Trump attempted to deflect questions regarding his own assaultive behavior by launching a verbal attack against first Bill Clinton and then Democratic presidential nominee Hillary Clinton. Trump noted, "If you look at Bill Clinton, far worse. Mine are words, and his was action. His was—what he's done to women, there's never been anybody in the history of politics in this nation that's been so abusive to women. . . . Hillary Clinton attacked those same women and attacked them viciously" (Keneally et al. 2016).

Hillary Clinton's primary campaign had largely been overshadowed by the Federal Bureau of Investigation's (FBI) inquiry into her use of a private e-mail server when she was secretary of state. In the summer, after the conclusion of a full investigation, the FBI announced that it would not recommend filing any criminal charges against Clinton (Nakashima, Horwitz, and Zapotosky 2016). The day after the third debate, however, just two weeks before the presidential election, FBI director James Comey told legislators that the bureau was resuming its investigation as a result of newly discovered e-mail messages found on a laptop seized during a separate criminal investigation of the estranged husband of Clinton aide Huma Abedin (Edwards 2016; Gerstein 2016). Comey's letter set off a Republican assault on Clinton, and Trump and his supporters insinuated that the reopening of the investigation indicated that Clinton had, indeed, done something criminal.

In a second letter, dated November 6, Comey told lawmakers that FBI agents upheld their previous findings and stood by their determination that they would not recommend filing charges against Hillary Clinton, issuing the following statement: "Based on our review, we have not changed our conclusions that we expressed in July" (Bradner, Brown, and Perez 2016). Whereas the Clinton campaign welcomed Comey's announcement as a way to finally put to rest concerns about the e-mail scandal, Trump completely rejected it, questioning how it was possible for FBI agents to thoroughly investigate the new e-mails in such a short period of time (Nakashima et al. 2016). Comey's reopening of the investigation in late October created a firestorm, so his announcement, coming just two days before the November 8 election, was arguably an attempt by the agency to clear "the cloud of suspicion that he had publicly placed" over Clinton's campaign in the last leg of the election (Gerstein 2016). His announcement also renewed skepticism and concern from both Republicans and Democrats about the FBI's handling of the e-mail controversy (Schultheis 2016). Although the FBI should remain politically neutral, the organization played a central role in the 2016 presidential election cycle, leading to widespread questions about the agency's integrity (Apuzzo, Schmidt, and Goldman 2016).

Clinton appeared to rebound in the polls after the initial dip seen following the release of Comey's October letter. Before the letter's release, early voting had already begun in many states, and by November 8 more than forty-six million individuals had already cast their ballots. The projections of which candidate was being helped by early voting were mixed. For example, more than six million Florida registered voters voted early, but, although Democrats had cast more ballots than Republicans, the number of Democrats voting was lower than in 2012, which was good news for Trump. The early voting statistics favored Clinton in Nevada, where Latinos turned out in large numbers, and in North Carolina, where Democrats jumped ahead of Republicans. North Carolina was a critical swing state for both Clinton and Trump, as was Nevada for Clinton.

Virtually all of the polls and election models indicated that Clinton was going to win the election and become the first female president of the United States. As the votes began to come in on the evening of November 8, Clinton appeared to be doing well and pulled ahead in several key states, especially Florida. As the night wore on, however, it became clear that although Clinton was leading in the popular vote, the states that had been historically Democratic, her Midwest "blue firewall," were moving in Trump's direction. Three states that had been reliably Democratic in the past—Michigan, Wisconsin, and Pennsylvania—appeared to be leaning toward Trump. Trump ultimately won Wisconsin and its ten electoral votes by about 1 percent of the votes cast, or 27,000 votes (Bosman and Davey 2016). In Pennsylvania, Clinton took Philadelphia and its suburbs by a healthy 635,000 vote margin over Trump, improving on President Obama's margin in the suburban counties in 2012, but falling behind in Philadelphia itself. This was not enough to offset Trump's strength in the rest of the state, however, including three counties that went for Obama in 2012 but flipped to Trump in the 2016 cycle. Trump won Pennsylvania and its twenty electoral votes by 73,224 votes (Panaritis et al. 2016). Trump won Michigan and its sixteen electoral votes by 13,000 votes, a 0.28 percent difference over Clinton—47.6 percent to 47.33 percent of the total vote. Macomb County, a traditionally Democratic county, went for Trump, whereas heavily Democratic Detroit and Flint, as well as Wayne County, voted for Clinton (Livengood, Wayland, and Feighan 2016).

Trump's messages apparently resonated with white voters in rural areas who believed they had been left behind by the economic recovery. Seven counties that voted for Obama in North Carolina supported Trump in 2016, primarily because the economic growth experienced by the urban areas had bypassed these counties, many of which had some of the state's highest unemployment rates and low incomes. Many of these rural communities had closed factories, and most residents had lost their jobs (Campbell 2016).

Overall, turnout for the 2016 election was the lowest in twenty years, with only 55.4 percent of eligible voters participating. The overall rate in 2012 was 61.8 percent, down from 63.8 percent in 2008. Thus, amid all of the drama and controversy surrounding the 2016 election, fewer voters cast their ballots. Clinton took the majority of the popular vote by more than three million votes, 48.2 percent (65,844,954) to Trump's 46.1 percent (62,979,879), but Trump received 306 electoral votes to Clinton's 232.

According to the exit polls, Trump took the majority of the white vote (58 percent), whereas Clinton took 88 percent of the black vote, 66 percent of the Latino vote, 65 percent of the Asian vote, and 56 percent of the vote of those in other categories. Yet Clinton's margins among these groups was smaller than that of President Obama in 2012, when he received 93 percent of the black vote, 71 percent of the Latino vote, 73 percent of the Asian vote, and 58 percent of the vote of those in other racial categories.

Clinton needed to carry women in general, and white educated women in particular, in large numbers. She did take the majority of the female vote, 54 percent, but only 43 percent of the white female vote. These percentages are similar to those of Obama in 2012, when he took 55 percent of the female vote, but only 42 percent of the white female vote. Clinton's margin of victory among women came from the votes of black women (94 percent) and Latina women (68 percent). Clinton received 51 percent of the votes of college-educated white women (data not shown), but Trump took 54 percent of college-educated white men, 62 percent of non-college-educated white women, and 72 percent of non-college-educated white men.

Based on the polling methods and that only twenty-eight states were included in their polling, there is debate about the accuracy of Trump's support from Latino and Asian American voters as reported in the exit polls. Edison/Mitofsy Election System, which conducts the exit polls for a consortium of news organizations, acknowledges that its sampling frame is not ideal to provide estimates of small, geographically clustered demographic groups. Latino Decisions, a polling organization that specializes in surveying Latino populations, conducted an election eve national survey of Latinos (n = 5,600) and state-level samples in eleven states and interviewed in both English and Spanish. Its data, as reported in Table 3.18, indicate that Clinton received 79 percent of the Latino vote, rather than the 66 percent reported in the exit polls, and Trump received 18 percent rather than 29 percent. According to Latino Decisions, 71 percent of Latino men voted for Clinton compared to 24 percent who voted for Trump, and 86 percent of Latina women voted for Clinton compared to 12 percent for

TABLE 3.18 Latino and Asian American Votes, Presidential Election, 2016

	CLINTON	TRUMP	OTHER
Latinos	79%	18%	3%
Latino men	71%	24%	4%
Latina women	86%	12%	2%
Asian Americans	75%	19%	5%
Asian American men	72%	21%	7%
Asian American women	79%	17%	4%

Source: Latino Decisions, 2016 Latino Election Analysis; and Asian American Decisions, the Asian American Vote, 2016.

Trump. Latinos were 7 percent of the electorate in 2000; their proportion increased to 8 percent in 2004, 9 percent in 2008, 10 percent in 2012, and approximately 12 percent in 2016 (Krogstag 2016).

Asian American Decisions, a polling group that specializes in surveying Asian Americans, also conducted an election eve national survey of Asian Americans (n = 863), as well as state samples in eight states. Its data, also in Table 3.18, indicate that Clinton received 76 percent of the Asian American vote, rather than the 65 percent reported in the exit poll, and Trump received 16 percent, rather than 29 percent. According to Asian American Decisions, 72 percent of Asian American men voted for Clinton compared to 21 percent for Trump, whereas 79 percent of Asian American women voted for Clinton compared to 17 percent for Trump.

There were concerns that the number of black voters turning out differed from that of 2012 around the country; a comparison of exit polls for both elections suggests this is correct. The black proportion of the electorate increased from 10 percent in 2000 to 13 percent in 2008; that share was maintained in 2012. In 2016, the black percentage had declined 1 percentage point, to 12 percent. This 1 percent decline might have made a difference for Democrats, but the assumption is, rather, that black voters chose not to vote. What appears to be lost on commentators is the effect the gutting of Section 5 of the Voting Rights Act has had on black voters in many states that were formerly covered by Section 5. A November 2016 report by the Leadership Conference Education Fund indicated that formerly covered jurisdictions had 868 fewer polling places than in 2012 (Leadership Conference Education Fund 2016).

North Carolina dealt with many legal battles regarding voter access during the 2016 election cycle. These lawsuits were filed because of concerns about

PHOTO 3.4 *Graffiti was spray painted next to a popular black-owned restaurant close to a busy intersection in Durham, North Carolina, the night of Donald Trump's election as president-elect. Many in the city took the message as an expression of hate and not a reflection of the values of the city.* (Courtesy of Derrick Lewis)

voter suppression tactics that would primarily affect black voters in the state. On November 4, 2016, a federal court issued a preliminary injunction barring three North Carolina counties from revoking the voting rights of thousands of residents whose voting eligibility had been challenged by Republican activists and political operatives (Wines and Blinder 2016). The ruling held that voters from the three counties—Beaufort, Cumberland, and Moore—whose voter registrations had been canceled in recent months because of the "individual challenge law" must have their voting privileges reinstated (De Vogue 2016). The NAACP had filed a lawsuit alleging that the three counties had purged voter rolls through a process that disproportionately targeted black voters. The judge's ruling was based on the National Voter Registration Act, a federal law that prohibits the cancelation or blanket removal of voter registrations in the ninety days prior to an election. In the ruling, the judge noted that "electoral integrity is enhanced, not diminished, when all citizens who are eligible to vote are allowed to exercise that right free from interference and burden unnecessarily imposed by others." The North Carolina State Board of Elections revealed that since the 2014 election, officials had removed from voter registration rolls the names of nearly 6,700 voters registered in eight counties (Associated Press 2016). As previously discussed, in August, the Supreme Court issued a decision preventing the state of North Carolina from implementing a strict voting law during the November election. A lower court had previously established that the law was enacted "with almost surgical precision" to specifically target and disenfranchise black voters (Barnes 2016).

Several of North Carolina's counties interpreted the Fourth Circuit and Supreme Court decisions to require them to open only one early voting site, with the decision's language of "at least one site." Guilford County, for example, which includes Greensboro, opened only one early voting site in the first week of early voting, cutting the number of sites from sixteen in 2012 to just one in 2016—a whopping 94 percent cut. As a result, just 12 percent of the 2016 ballots were cast in the first week compared to those cast during the same period in 2012. This was a very successful voter suppression tactic (Newkirk II 2016).

There were many other reports of voter suppression tactics around the country. The responsibility for combatting voter suppression tactics falls on the various election boards or civil rights groups. Often, however, there is not enough time remaining for these groups to go to court and get an injunction against those who are attempting to suppress nonwhite voters. In Arkansas, for example, a Republican election commissioner was accused of voter intimidation after he harassed individuals who were voting early. In a lawsuit filed against the Republican Party of Arkansas and the Jefferson election commissioner Stu Stoffer, Stoffer was accused of yelling at voters, interfering with the voting process, and preventing voters from voting (KTHV 2016.) In Florida, a political advisory committee known as the Florida Citizens for Honest Elections placed newspaper ads across the state offering a $5,000 cash reward for information that could lead to "the arrest and felony conviction of dishonest persons involved in voter fraud" (Dion 2016). In Texas, a Republican political consultant promoted an "Election Integrity Tip Hotline" offering a $5,000 reward for any fraud-related tips that led to a felony conviction. In response, some Democrats expressed concern that tips about election fraud should go to election officials instead, emphasizing concerns that the hotline was "a systematic and deliberate attempt to suppress votes in the Latino community, specifically targeting the elderly" (Tinsley 2016).

American Indians also experienced difficulty in voting in some jurisdictions. The Department of Justice sent election monitors into San Juan County, Utah, which includes a portion of the Navajo Nation. San Juan County has been sued numerous times since 1980 over American Indian voting rights, including by the Department of Justice itself. Recently, a federal court ruled in favor of the Navajo Nation in a lawsuit claiming that the county's school districts were drawn in ways that violated the equal protection clause and that the county had intentionally discriminated against Navajo citizens in setting up commission districts (Indian Country Today 2016). San Juan County has a population of fifteen thousand, almost evenly split between whites and Navajos, yet the county commission has always been majority white. In 2014, the county began to conduct all elections by mail ballot, but many residents of the Navajo Nation do not have street addresses and have to receive their mail at a post office. In some instances, the distance between their home and their post office might be several hundred miles, so getting their mail in a timely fashion is extremely difficult, and many of the elderly do not read or write English. If Navajo citizens wanted to vote in person, many had to travel a four-hundred-mile round trip to do so (Lakusiak et al. 2016). On Election Day in 2016, malfunctioning voting machines and lack of paper ballots made it difficult for many individuals to vote.

While it was known that the Democratic National Committee's e-mail server had been hacked and WikiLeaks had been releasing embarrassing e-mails throughout the campaign, it was confirmed in January 2017 that the Russian government and its president, Vladimir Putin, were behind the hacking. Their intent was to help Donald Trump and to damage Hillary Clinton. This was the first time that a foreign entity had meddled in the United States elections. Whether Russia's interference affected the outcome is something that we will never know. Bipartisan committees in both the House and the Senate will be investigating the hacking, as well as the charges that some of the Trump campaign officials were in contact with the Russian government during the campaign. We have yet to grasp the full magnitude of and fallout from these events, but they have cast a cloud over the 2016 election and its results.

Despite the racial and racist nature of the 2016 presidential campaign, racial and ethnic minorities made progress in other elected offices. Latinos gained five more members in the House of Representatives, and the number of Latinos in the 115th Congress rose from twenty-nine to thirty-four members. Catherine Cortez Masto (Democrat) was elected to the vacated seat of former Senate Minority Leader Harry Reid and became the first Latina woman elected to the US Senate. California elected Kamala Harris, a black and South Indian American, as US senator, making her the second black women to be elected to the US Senate. She won in a race that saw two Democratic women of color, Harris and former House member Loretta Sánchez, compete for the office. There are forty-nine blacks in the US Senate and House of Representatives, up from forty-six in the previous Congress. Florida elected the first Vietnamese American woman, Stephanie Murphy, to the House. Washington State elected the first South Indian American woman,

Pramila Jayapal, to the House. Tammy Duckworth, Democrat from Illinois, is the first Thai American to be elected to the US Senate. The 115th Congress will be the most racially diverse in history.

INTEREST GROUP ACTIVITIES

As we mentioned at the beginning of this chapter, one of the principal components of pluralist theory is competition among interest groups. Although this theory presents some problems for the study of racial minority group politics, interest groups that focus on issues of importance to blacks, Latinos, Asians, and American Indians have been essential to the progress made toward the incorporation of these groups into the American political system. In this section, we will highlight several of the major groups—particularly those that have used litigation as a tactic—along with those that are the best known for each of the minority groups under consideration.

Racial and ethnic minority groups have frequently turned to the courts in an attempt to improve their positions because victories in the courts are more likely to be determined by an appeal to what is right than merely to what is politically popular. For African Americans—and, indeed, as a model for all other racial and ethnic groups—the **NAACP Legal Defense and Educational Fund (LDF)**, founded in 1939 by a group of attorneys dedicated to affirming and expanding the rights of blacks, has been the pathbreaking group. The LDF's strategy was to "secure decisions, rulings, and public opinion on the broad principle instead of being devoted to mere miscellaneous cases" (founder Charles Houston, quoted in Vose 1959:23). The LDF, using test cases and class action suits, became known as the group through which to attack segregation. Its most famous victory came in *Brown v. Board of Education of Topeka* (1954 and 1955; this case is discussed further in Chapter 4), which overturned *Plessy v. Ferguson* (1896), the case that had established the separate but equal doctrine.

The LDF and its litigation approach to removing the barriers to full participation in the political process by blacks have served as a model for Latinos. With the guidance of LDF attorneys and funding from the Ford Foundation, the **Mexican American Legal Defense and Education Fund (MALDEF)** was established in 1968. MALDEF functions for Mexican Americans in much the same way the LDF has historically functioned for African Americans. In 1972, the **Puerto Rican Legal Defense and Education Fund (PRLDEF)** was created in New York City to play a similar role for Puerto Ricans.

Additionally, as is characteristic of the diversity that exists within the Asian American community, there are various lawyers' interest groups—the Asian Law Caucus, based in San Francisco; the Asian American Legal Defense and Education Fund in New York; and the Asian Pacific American Legal Center, based in Los Angeles—loosely united under the aegis of the National Asian Pacific American Legal Consortium. The Asian Pacific American Legal Consortium was incorporated in 1991. It coordinates litigation on civil rights issues important to the Asian American community. It educates the public, files amicus curiae briefs, and provides legal counsel on a host of issues, including hate crimes, immigration, affirmative action, language rights, and census methods. Additionally, through its Community Partners Network, it disseminates successful strategies that Asian American communities around the country can use to achieve policy objectives (National Asian Pacific American Legal Consortium n.d.).

The Native American Rights Fund (NARF), located in Boulder, Colorado, was founded in 1970 with the help of the Ford Foundation. It was the first national program to provide legal aid to Indians. Although NARF was officially organized in 1970, it actually began as an outgrowth of California Rural Legal Assistance (CRLA). It soon became clear that Indians had unique legal problems that required special expertise; thus, the Indian Services Division of CRLA was organized. The division became a separate organization, California Indian Legal Services (CILS), in 1968, and CILS received a grant from the Ford Foundation in 1970 with which to establish NARF (James 1973). Most of NARF's attorneys and staff are Indians, although non-Indians are present in a number of positions, and its board of directors is composed of Indian leaders from across the country.

NARF has five priority areas: (1) the preservation of tribal existence; (2) the protection of tribal natural resources; (3) the promotion of human rights; (4) the accountability of governments to Native Americans; and (5) the development of Indian law (Native American Rights Fund 1993). NARF has been involved in a number of legal cases challenging barriers to Indian rights and political participation and challenging states and the federal government to honor treaties with Indian nations and peoples.

NARF has either filed or submitted amicus curiae briefs in numerous cases and has been successful in more than two hundred cases. NARF's litigation on behalf of the Catawba Tribe of South Carolina (*Catawba Indian Tribe of South Carolina v. United States* 1993) was settled when President Clinton signed Public Law No. 103-116, the Catawba Indian Land Claim Settlement Act of 1993. In another action, NARF won a suit against the Bureau of Indian Affairs on behalf of the Cheyenne-Arapaho Tribes of Oklahoma (*Cheyenne-Arapaho Tribes of Oklahoma v. United States* 1992) for failing to protect Indian interests in the pricing of minerals removed from Indian lands. NARF has also protected voting rights of Indians in several states, including South Dakota, New York, and Alaska.

In the area of nonlitigation-oriented interest groups, there is a plethora of African American interest groups, the longest lasting of which are the NAACP, founded in 1909 and the parent of the LDF; the National Urban League, founded in 1910; and the Southern Christian Leadership Conference (SCLC), organized in 1957. Others, such as the Student Nonviolent Coordinating Committee (SNCC) and the Congress of Racial Equality, were extremely important during the civil rights movement of the 1960s but are either diminished in their activity or are moribund today.

Some of the more prominent Latino interest groups are the **League of United Latin American Citizens (LULAC)**, a group of vocal, middle-class Mexican American citizens formed in 1929 in south Texas, and the National Council of La Raza (NCLR). LULAC was established to fight discrimination against Mexican Americans in Texas. From its inception through the 1960s, LULAC was actively engaged in protest and litigation for equal and civil rights for Mexican Americans. It has grown from a small organization in several south Texas cities to a national organization "with active councils in twenty-eight states, a national headquarters in Washington, DC, and a professional staff" (Márquez 1989:355–56).

NCLR, previously the Southwest Council of La Raza (founded in 1968), was initially oriented toward community organization and mobilization, but over the years it has developed into an umbrella organization for numerous local Latino organizations. It has voter education and registration programs and a research office that conducts studies and disseminates information on issues of concern to the broader Latino community. NCLR has recently focused its efforts on economic development and small-business investment (Hero 1992:77).

Asian American and American Indian interest groups have also been active. The Japanese American Citizens League (JACL), founded in 1930, is the best-established and largest national Asian American organization. JACL was instrumental in bringing the issue of reparations for Japanese interned during World War II to the political agenda and, in 1988, in pushing Congress to pass legislation providing for an apology and a payment of $20,000 to each of the survivors of the internment camps. When President Reagan signed the legislation, he admitted that the United States had committed "a grave wrong" (Takaki 1993:401).

Chinese Americans formed the Chinese American Citizens' Alliance (then known as the Native Sons of the Golden State) in 1895 in California. Still going strong after more than a hundred years, the alliance works to increase Asian American representation on college campuses, to increase voter registration in the Asian American community, and to ensure that Asian Americans have opportunities to learn English (Hong 1995). The Organization of Chinese Americans was founded in 1973 to promote Chinese American participation in local and national affairs and to ensure the equal and fair treatment of Chinese Americans. Its policy concerns include addressing and preventing hate crimes through prosecution and legislation (Organization of Chinese Americans 1997). The 1992 riots in Los Angeles precipitated the founding in 1994 of the National Association of Korean Americans. Its goals are to protect the civil rights of Korean Americans, to build bridges of understanding between Korean Americans and other racial groups, to promote Korean culture, and to promote the unification of North and South Korea (National Association of Korean Americans n.d.). Leadership Education for Asian Pacifics (LEAP) was founded in 1982 by members of various Asian American ethnic groups. Its goal is to increase Asian American participation in leadership positions throughout the country and to ensure the equitable treatment of Asian Americans. To achieve this goal, LEAP has sponsored four initiatives: the Leadership Management Institute, the Asian American Public Policy Institute, the Community Development Institute, and Community Forums (Leadership Education for Asian Pacifics 1996).

Other Asian American interest groups include the National Association for Asian and Pacific American Education, founded in 1977. Its primary objective is to give a voice to the needs of Asian American students. It advances Asian American educational needs and concerns, argues for the inclusion of Asian American history in school curricula, and lobbies for bilingual education and special educational opportunities for Asian Americans and for greater inclusion of Asian American students as subjects of educational research (National Association for Asian and Pacific American Education n.d.). The Asian Pacific American Labor Alliance is an Asian AFL-CIO affiliate founded in 1992 to organize Asian American workers and to enable them to address their concerns. It primarily seeks to eliminate barriers to promotion and unfair labor practices aimed at Asian Americans, but its policy initiatives toward these goals are varied. It has lobbied for reparations for Japanese Americans interned during World War II, for the prosecution of hate crimes directed at Asians and other minorities, for health care and fair wages, against employer discrimination, and for equal economic rights for women (Asian Pacific American Labor Alliance n.d.).

Indians organize along tribal lines when action involves members of one tribe in pursuit of tribal goals. But when the issue is of concern to more than one tribe, Indians organize along pan-tribal lines. Therefore, because many American Indian tribes enjoy some level of autonomy, they can and do act as interest groups. Many have lobbied the government and have brought cases to the federal courts, seeking to vindicate rights. Moreover, tribes hold the primary responsibility for Indian community development. There are also formal government agencies, such as the BIA and the National Council on Indian Opportunity (created by Lyndon Johnson), that are designed to look after the interest of Indians but do not usually follow through on their mandates. Over the decades, there has been sustained and increasingly vocal opposition to the BIA by both reservation Indians and urban Indians (Nagel 1982).

An example of a pan-tribal organization is the Alaska Federation of Natives, formed in 1966, which successfully filed land claims against the state amounting to 360 million acres, or a little more than the state's entire land area. Other pan-tribal Indian interest groups include the National Indian Youth Council (founded in 1961), the National Tribal Chairman's Association (circa 1960), the National Congress of American Indians (1944)—the largest intertribal interest group in the country—the Institute for the Development of Indian Law (1971), and the Native American Rights Fund (1970).

CONCLUSION

James Madison's assumption that conflict would prevail over consensus has proven to be well founded. Blacks, Latinos, Asians, and American Indians share some similar political attitudes and participation dimensions, but they differ dramatically on others. Clearly, racial minorities do not all think alike. This chapter highlights the fact that in the political game, each of the racial and ethnic minorities has been at a disadvantage, despite its efforts to be active in the polity. Still, some successes are noted. In Chapter 4 we explore the way these groups have been treated by the political system, a revisiting of the first dilemma.

- -

DISCUSSION QUESTIONS

1. Why is there a conflict within the scholarly literature over the utility of the pluralist framework for explaining the political behaviors of and outcomes for racial minorities in American politics?

2. Which of the approaches to the study of racial and ethnic politics do you find most useful? Why?

3. What are the elements of group cohesion? And why is group cohesion important to the political participation of racial minorities?

4. How would you characterize the ideological orientations of African Americans, Latinos, American Indians, and Asian Americans? Do you feel the terms *liberal* and *conservative* are appropriate labels for racial minority ideological and political orientations? Why or why not?

5. What is the history of partisan identification for the various minority groups? How strongly attached to the two major parties are the various racial minority groups?

6. What factors and strategies were responsible for President Obama's reelection in 2012? How important were the votes of racial and ethnic minorities to his reelection?

7. Why do you think Secretary Clinton was not able to hold the Obama coalition together to elect her as the first female president of the United States?

8. Given the racist and misogynistic tones of the 2016 presidential campaign, what are the prospects for the continued forward movement of racial and ethnic minorities?

- -

NOTES

1 Ralph J. Bunche, the first African American to receive a PhD in political science from Harvard (in 1934), was the founder of the Department of Political Science at Howard University. Bunche later worked for the United Nations and in 1950 received the Nobel Peace Prize for his negotiations with Israelis and Arabs in the Middle East. Mary McLeod Bethune, founder and president of Bethune-Cookman College, in Daytona Beach, Florida, was the director of the Division of Negro Affairs of the National Youth Administration. Robert C. Weaver served in the Department of the Interior under Franklin Roosevelt and later became secretary of labor under President Lyndon Johnson. Rayford W. Logan, a pioneer in the development of the study of what he preferred to call "Negro history," served as a consultant to the State Department, particularly on issues related to the Caribbean Basin and to Africa.

2 Earl Warren was a former Republican governor of California, and Eisenhower, who was pursuing a Southern white strategy, assumed—incorrectly—that Warren would hold the line on civil rights issues. After the 1954 *Brown* decision, when it became clear that the Warren Court was moving forward to dismantle segregation, Eisenhower was quoted as saying that his appointment of Earl Warren as chief justice "was the biggest damn fool mistake I ever made" (Rodell 1968:12).

▶ **CHAPTER 4**

America's Racial Minorities and the Policymaking Process

Jake Anantha, an Indian American eighteen-year-old college student from Charlotte, North Carolina, is an avid supporter of Donald Trump. Jake was removed from the Trump rally in Charlotte by police. Jake, a registered Republican intending to cast his first vote for the US presidency for Trump, arrived one hour early to the event and positioned himself close to the stage. He stated that, "I'm a huge Trump supporter—I was. I would never protest" (Anantha 2016; Helms 2016).

Jake wrote an op-ed in the *Washington Post,* reflecting on the situation. "I still don't know why I was asked to leave. But I think it has something to do with my race. My mother is white and my father is Indian. . . . I wonder whether he assumed that I couldn't possibly support Trump because of how I look" (Anantha 2016).

At the same rally in Charlotte, Rose Hamid, a fifty-six-year-old flight attendant and Muslim American woman who wears the headscarf, was also asked to leave the protest. Rose had been handing out pens to individuals who were entering the rally. This was not the first time that Rose was ejected from a Trump rally; her first ejection made national headlines in January 2016. She was forcibly removed for staging a silent protest, where she wore a T-shirt to the Trump rally stating, "Salaam, I come in peace" (Diamond 2016; Howell 2016; Siner 2016a; 2016b).

On October 29, 2016, C. J. Cary, a black Donald Trump supporter, was called a thug at a Trump rally. He is a Marine veteran and volunteered for the Trump campaign. He arrived at the rally in Kinston, North Carolina, to give Trump a letter. Trump saw him at the rally and stated, "We have a protester. . . . By the way, were you paid $1,500 to be a thug?" He was asked to leave the rally as well.

—CHARLOTTE, NORTH CAROLINA, AUGUST 18, 2016,
AND KINSTON, NORTH CAROLINA, OCTOBER 28, 2016

Public policies are what governments choose to do or not to do. These policies do not just happen; they are the outputs of the political process and of government institutions. Political scientists and public policy scholars speak of public policymaking as a process that consists of five interrelated stages—agenda setting, formulation, adoption, implementation, and evaluation.

Agenda setting is the process by which issues are identified and by which conflicts and concerns gain prominence and exposure so they are brought to the public arena for debate and possible government action (Cobb and Elder 1983). This stage occurs both within and outside of government institutions. **Formulation** is the stage at which policy issues are translated into actual proposals from which an alternative may be chosen for adoption, usually by a legislative body. Given the bargaining process that occurs in legislative bodies, political feasibility and ideological stances may become more important considerations than problem solving. Ideology may produce agreed-on policies that ultimately do not work (Lindblom 1980:39).

Policy **adoption** involves choosing between proposed alternatives to address the problem. In collective policymaking bodies, such as legislatures and appellate courts, adoption requires building majority coalitions. After policy is adopted, it then moves to the **implementation** stage, the stage at which the policy is put into action. This activity is usually the domain of federal, state, or local government agencies. The implementation process is very fluid and is subject to numerous internal and external influences; therefore, the manner in which a policy is implemented or the shape the policy assumes may or may not resemble the intent of the individuals who formulated the policy. The final stage, **evaluation**, is the process of determining whether the policy had its intended effect and what unintended consequences, both positive and negative, may have occurred.

We begin with a discussion of what is probably the most important stage of the public policymaking process for racial and ethnic minorities—agenda setting. Historically minority group members have been excluded from policymaking bodies, and so minorities' interests have often not been voiced and therefore have not been considered when setting an agenda. The chapter then examines the contemporary situation in the major branches of government, highlighting the increased representation of members of racial and ethnic minority groups.

Next, we present a detailed explication of the effect of **federalism** on public policymaking. Federalism, which involves the division of powers among the various layers of government—national, state, county, municipal—presents opportunities for access to the public policy process but barriers to effective, efficient policymaking. Although most believe the action and power reside in national political activity and offices, the reality is that most of the decisions that affect the everyday lives of US citizens are made on the state and local levels. These various levels of government mean that racial minorities should direct their attention to a multiplicity of governmental units because, depending on the policy issue, a victory at one level can be undermined or overturned at another.

Finally, we discuss two specific policy areas: equal educational opportunity and **affirmative action** in employment. We will look at concrete examples of the linkages between structural aspects of American government and what the government has actually done in these important areas. This discussion also provides important substantive information about the current issues and the current status of law and policy in these vital civil rights policy areas.

AGENDA SETTING

If an issue is never considered, it is impossible for the government to act upon it. Those who control the government agenda control the debate, the types of policies that are formulated, and the structure of the implementation process. The models of agenda setting are, in brief: (1) outside initiative; (2) mobilization; and (3) inside access. In the **outside initiative model**, groups outside of government push for their issues to be heard by the decision makers, usually through mass mobilization, such as demonstrations. The general issue is then translated into more specific demands and is expanded to include a broader number of groups, thus gaining attention as part of the public agenda.

In the **mobilization model**, issues are placed on the agenda by individuals either inside the government or with direct access to government, but the issues must be expanded to the public to gain its support. With the **inside access model**, items are placed on the agenda by individuals inside the government and are expanded only to those groups that place pressure on decision makers to move the problem forward. Issues are not expanded to the public, either because the policymakers do not require legitimation of the idea or do not want the public to know about it.

All of these models are based on pluralist theory, and the limited research on racial minorities and agenda setting has found that minorities have little access to or influence on the policy agenda-setting process (McClain 1993b). The only model minorities have thus far been successful in using in their attempts to influence the agenda has been the outside initiative model, of which the modern civil rights movement is a prime example.

Recent research suggests that the agenda-setting process is characterized by long periods of stability and of domination by privileged elites but may be subject to rapid change in political outcomes. Despite the disadvantage that outside groups have in getting access to the policy process, and the influence of policy monopolies on controlling the agenda, new issues do obtain a hearing through the extraordinary efforts of interested individuals and groups (Baumgartner and Jones 1993).

As is clear from this brief discussion of the policy process and agenda setting, individuals within the structures of government have tremendous influence on the policy outputs from those structures. It becomes necessary, therefore, for groups to have a significant presence in these institutions if they are to affect the policy process. The major national institutions of government—the office of the president, the Supreme Court, Congress, and the bureaucracy—play prominent roles in acting on or not acting on the issues that affect racial minorities. Furthermore, the fact that each of the national institutions is duplicated in some form at the state and local levels has often meant that racial minority groups' citizens have been caught between different levels of the federal system. Policies of both the US and state governments have directly affected the ability of racial minorities to gain access to and participate in the political process.

MINORITY REPRESENTATION IN THE US GOVERNMENT

In January 2001, 9,101 African Americans held office at all levels of government; of that number, 35.4 percent (3,200) were black females, a dramatic increase since 1970, when only 160 black women were in office. The number of black women elected to office grew at a faster rate than that of black men, which actually declined slightly (Joint Center for Political and Economic Studies 2001). As of 2011, the most recent data that we were able to locate, the number of black elected officials had grown to 10,500 (Brown-Dean, et al. 2015). Before the passage of the Voting Rights Act (VRA in 1965), it was estimated that there were fewer than 500 black elected officials.

The VRA has also been important for the election of Latinos to national, state, and local offices. In 2016, there were 6,084 Latino elected officials (NALEO 2017). Between 1996 and 2010, the number of Latina elected officials grew faster than the number of male Latino officials; the number of Latinas increased by 105 percent, compared to 37 percent for male Latinos. As a result, the Latina share of all Latino elected officials grew from 24 percent in 1996 to 32 percent in 2010 (NALEO 2011). In 2015, 4,000 Asian Americans held national, state, and local elected and appointed offices (UCLA Asian American Studies Center 2015). With regard to American Indian elected officials, excluding tribal government officials, we have found several conflicting numbers. As of November 2008, one source suggested there were a total of 61 American Indians that either held or had been elected to offices at all levels of government (INDN's List 2008; Toensing 2008). Although the National Caucus of Native American State Legislators indicates that there are 72 American Indian state legislators, this includes Native Hawaiian state legislators, so subtracting the latter puts the number even lower, at 57. Another source indicated that in 2015 there were 73 American Indian state legislators (Trahant 2015). The bottom line is that we have no accurate count of the number of American Indians serving in elective office.

MINORITY REPRESENTATION IN THE PRESIDENCY

Barack Obama is the first member of a racial or ethnic minority to be elected as president of the United States. This is important because although the executive branch is only one of the three branches of government, the president has an extraordinary ability to shape public policy through executive powers, as well as from the "bully pulpit" of the office. Historically, presidents have used their executive powers and powers of persuasion both to include and to exclude racial minorities from the political process.

In 1830, President Andrew Jackson used his influence and authority to push his Indian Removal Bill through Congress. Jackson was successful in instituting a program of removing Indians from the southern states to provide land for expanded cotton production. Although a Supreme Court decision, *Worcester v. Georgia* (1832), ensured the sovereignty of the Cherokees, President Jackson refused to follow the decision and initiated what has been called the Trail of Tears. The Five Civilized Tribes—Cherokee, Chickasaw, Choctaw, Creek, and Seminole—were removed from the southeastern states and forced westward to Oklahoma, then the center of what was called Indian Territory.

In 1941, President Franklin D. Roosevelt issued Executive Order 8802, which banned discrimination in the defense industries and the federal government on the basis of race, creed, color, or national origin, after a threatened march on Washington by blacks to protest racial discrimination in the defense industry. The executive order also created a Committee on Fair Employment Practices. Yet in 1942, Roosevelt signed Executive Order 9066, which created zones in the United States in which the military had the power to exclude people. Under this order, more than 112,000 Japanese Americans who were residing in these zones were forcefully removed to "relocation" camps. Of note is the fact that German Americans and Italian Americans, whose ancestors also came from countries with which the United States was fighting in World War II, were not subjected to the same exclusion from these zones.

President Lyndon B. Johnson used his knowledge of Congress and his political skill to persuade Congress to pass the Civil Rights Act of 1964 and the Voting Rights Act of 1965. More recently, President Bill Clinton invited

PHOTO 4.1 *Members of the Mochida family awaiting evacuation bus in Hayward, California. Identification tags were used to aid in keeping the family unit intact during all phases of evacuation. Mochida operated a nursery and five greenhouses on a two-acre site in Eden Township. He raised snapdragons and sweet peas. Evacuees of Japanese ancestry would be housed in War Relocation Authority centers for the duration of the war.* (Courtesy of the National Archives, 537505)

representatives from the 565 federally recognized Indian tribes to meet at the White House to discuss Indian issues. (This number continually changes. As of January 2016, the number of federally recognized entities—Indian nations, tribes, bands, organized communities, pueblos, and Alaskan Native villages and corporations—had risen to 566 [Federal Register, January 29, 2016].) This was the first time since 1822 that Indians had been invited to meet officially with a US president to discuss issues of concern to them. This high-profile visit indicated a shift in the US government's approach to Indian affairs.

Presidential Appointments

Presidents also send signals about their commitment to particular constituencies through the appointments they make. Four of President Clinton's initial cabinet officers during his first term were African American—Ronald Brown,

PHOTO 4.2 *President Barack Obama wears a ceremonial blanket given to him at the 2016 White House Tribal Nations Conference. On stage with Obama are Mohegan Chief Lynn Malerba, left, and Brian Cladoosby, center, President of the National Congress of American Indians.* (AP Photo/Pablo Martinez Monsivais; ID: 529194482737)

secretary of commerce; Hazel O'Leary, secretary of energy; Jesse Brown, secretary for veteran's affairs; and Michael Espy, secretary of agriculture. (Although his was not officially a cabinet-level office, the director of the Office of Drug Policy, Lee Brown, was another African American whom President Clinton informally recognized as a cabinet-level official.) This was the largest number of blacks to serve in cabinet posts in any administration to date. President Clinton also had two Latinos as cabinet officers—Henry Cisneros, former mayor of San Antonio, Texas, served as secretary of housing and urban development; and Federico Peña, former mayor of Denver, Colorado, was secretary of transportation. As with African Americans, this was at the time the largest number of Latinos ever to serve in the cabinet.

In his second term, President Clinton named three Latinos and four African Americans to serve in the cabinet or in cabinet-level positions. The Latino appointees were Transportation Secretary Federico Peña, who became secretary of energy, replacing Hazel O'Leary; New Mexico representative Bill Richardson, who became ambassador to the United Nations; and Aida Alvarez, director of the Small Business Administration. Peña resigned his post in mid-1998 and was replaced by Ambassador Bill Richardson. The African American appointees were Alexis Herman, secretary of labor; Rodney Slater, a Clinton friend and Arkansas highway secretary, who became secretary of transportation; Jesse Brown, who remained for a time as secretary of veterans' affairs, although he later resigned and was replaced by former secretary of the army Togo West; and Franklin Raines, director of the Office of Management and Budget, who resigned in April 1998. Clinton named the first Asian American, Norman Mineta, former representative from California, to a cabinet position as secretary of commerce. Clinton also named Bill Lann Lee, a Chinese American lawyer from Los Angeles who has worked for the NAACP Legal Defense and Educational Fund, to the position of assistant attorney general for civil rights. Lee is the first Asian American to hold this important (although not cabinet-level) post. As with Clinton's earlier nominee to this post during his first term, Lani Guinier, Lee was opposed by conservative Republicans, who refused his confirmation ostensibly because of his views on affirmative action and busing to achieve school integration. This Republican action outraged large segments of the Asian American electorate, who, as discussed in Chapter 3, have the highest proportion of independent voters. This action made it more difficult for the Republicans to appeal to Asian American voters. President Clinton made Lee acting assistant attorney general for civil rights. He served until the end of Clinton's presidency.

Clinton's appointments to the lifetime positions on the federal courts marked a "revolutionary" increase in minority group representation among a group of policymakers that prior to 1961 had included only one black male and one male who had a Mexican father (as well as the appointment of two white females). During his first term, a majority of Clinton's appointments to the federal judiciary were white women and male and female racial minorities. He appointed twenty-nine black men and eight black women, increasing the black proportion of the federal judiciary from 5.4 (at the time of his election) to 8.5 percent. The Latino proportion increased from 4 to 4.4 percent with the appointment of twelve Latinos and two Latinas. Although Clinton appointed three Asian American men, Asian representation dipped slightly from 0.6 percent to 0.5 percent (Goldman and Slotnick 1997). He also appointed fifty white women to the federal judiciary and appointed the first American Indian federal judge, Billy Michael Burrage of Oklahoma (Goldman and Saranson 1994).

Although he was of a different political party, President George W. Bush made initial cabinet appointments that were similar in racial and ethnic diversity to those of President Clinton. He appointed Colin Powell as the first black secretary of state; Rod Paige, a black former Houston superintendent, as secretary of education; Elaine Chao, an Asian American, as secretary of labor; and Mel Martinez, a Cuban American from Florida, as secretary of housing and urban development; Norman Mineta, an Asian American Democrat who served as President Clinton's secretary of commerce, was retained by Bush in the cabinet as secretary of transportation. Although national security adviser is not a cabinet-level post, Bush appointed Condoleezza Rice as the first female and second black to serve in that capacity. Bush continued the practice of diversity among his cabinet members in his second term. Condoleezza Rice replaced Colin Powell as secretary of state, and Alberto Gonzales, former White House counsel, was confirmed as the first Latino attorney general of the United States. Gonzales eventually resigned surrounded by controversy and questions about his veracity in testimony before Congress. Elaine Chao stayed on as secretary of labor; Norman Mineta was retained as secretary of transportation, although he died while in office; and Alphonso Jackson replaced Mel Martinez as secretary of housing and urban development. Bush's record of judicial nominations is more mixed. Of his two hundred judicial appointments, only fifteen were African American—four on circuit courts and eleven on district courts (Ruffin 2004). Despite this weak record, it should be noted that he appointed two blacks to the Fourth Circuit Court of Appeals, which has jurisdiction over states with high black populations—Maryland, North Carolina, South Carolina, Virginia, and West Virginia. Roger Gregory of Virginia, who was originally nominated by President Clinton but the Republican-controlled Senate refused to act on the nomination, and Allyson Duncan, a black Republican from North Carolina, were both confirmed. Gregory was nominated by Clinton but then confirmed (along with Duncan) during the Bush administration. Bush did marginally better with Latino judges, with seventeen being appointed, excluding territorial district courts.

President Obama's cabinet and cabinet-level appointments during his first term were even more diverse than either Clinton's or Bush's. He appointed four blacks to cabinet or cabinet-level positions—Eric Holder, attorney general of the United States, the first black to hold the office; Susan Rice, UN ambassador; Lisa Jackson, administrator of the Environmental Protection Agency; and former Dallas mayor Ron Kirk as US trade representative. Two Latinos held cabinet posts—former representative Hilda Solis served as secretary of labor; and former Colorado senator Ken Salazar served as secretary of the interior. In a first, there were three Asian Americans in the cabinet—Nobel Laureate Steven Chu as secretary of energy, retired general Eric K. Shinseki as secretary of veteran's affairs, and former Washington State governor Gary Locke as secretary of commerce. (Locke was later appointed ambassador to China.) In keeping with his campaign promise, President Obama appointed Wizipan Garriott, of the Rosebud Sioux tribe of South Dakota, as First Americans public liaison and named six American Indians to his transition team. Larry Echo Hawk, an enrolled member of the Pawnee Nation of Oklahoma, served as assistant secretary for Indian Affairs in the Department of Interior for three years and was replaced in October 2012 by Kevin K. Washburn, an enrolled member of the Chickasaw Nation in Oklahoma.

After his 2012 reelection, President Obama continued to appoint a diverse cabinet. According to the Pew Research Center, under the Obama administration, the number of blacks serving in cabinet positions consistently remained above 12 percent, exceeding the share of blacks in the US population (Brown and Atske 2016). Eric Holder stepped down in 2015 and Loretta Lynch, a black female former US attorney, was nominated and confirmed as his replacement as attorney general. In addition to Lynch, four other blacks served in Obama's second-term cabinet—John King, secretary of education, Jeh Johnson, secretary of homeland security, and Anthony Foxx, secretary of transportation, and Susan Rice who moved to national security advisor from her previous post as UN ambassador. Obama also appointed three Latinos: Julian Castro as secretary of housing and urban development, Thomas Perez as secretary of labor, and Ken Salazar as secretary of the interior (Salazar stepped down in 2013). Kevin Washburn stepped down as assistant secretary of Indian Affairs in 2015; he was replaced in an acting capacity by Michael Black, a member of the Oglala Sioux tribe, who was previously head of the Bureau of Indian Affairs (BIA). Weldon "Bruce" Loudermilk, a citizen of the Fort Peck Assiniboine and Sioux tribes of the Fort Peck Indian Reservation in Montana, replaced Black as head of the BIA.

Women also fared well during the eight years of President Obama's tenure. In the first term, former senator Hillary Rodham Clinton served as secretary of state, making her one of five women among his cabinet or cabinet-level appointments. Former Arizona governor Janet Napolitano served as secretary of homeland security, and former Kansas governor Kathleen Sebelius served as secretary of health and human services. The other women are Susan Rice, Hilda Solis, and Lisa Jackson. In his second term, women of all races were also present in more than a token fashion—Susan Rice; Sylvia Matthews Burwell, secretary of health and human services; Penny Pritzker, secretary of commerce; Loretta Lynch; and Sally Jewel, secretary of the interior.

Obama's judicial appointments were also diverse. Obama appointed two women to the Supreme Court, Justice Sonia Sotomayor (also the first Latina) and Justice Elena Kagan. He also appointed the first African American woman to sit on the Sixth US Circuit Court of Appeals in Cincinnati. Obama's appointments doubled the number of Asian Americans on the federal bench and added an Asian American to the Second US Circuit Court of Appeals. At the end of his eight years in office, President Obama had successfully seated a total of 329 federal judges during his two terms—all of them lifetime appointments. Forty-three percent of Obama's judges were women, shattering the old record of 29 percent under Bill Clinton, and 36 percent have been nonwhite, surpassing Clinton's record of 24 percent. Obama appointed eleven openly gay judges, when before him there was only one (Holland 2011).

President Trump's cabinet is the least diverse of any recent president. To date he has nominated one black, Dr. Ben Carson, former Republican presidential nominee, to be secretary of housing and urban development; two Asian American women, Elaine Chao, Taiwanese American, for transportation secretary and Nikki R. Haley, South Asian Indian, governor of South Carolina, for UN representative. There are also two white women—Betsy DeVos for secretary of education and Linda McMahon for administrator of the Small Business Administration. Besides these five, the remainder of his cabinet and subcabinet positions are filled by white males, most of whom are billionaires or millionaires like Trump. Initially, for the first time in twenty-nine years of both Republican and Democratic presidents there was no Latino in the president's cabinet. After his original labor secretary nominee withdrew, Trump nominated Alexander Acosta for labor secretary.

Black Presidential Candidacies

In the fourth edition of this book, we said that it was only a matter of time before a nonwhite candidate would make a serious attempt to gain the office. We did not anticipate, however, that this would happen as soon as it did. In this section, we examine those black candidates who paved the way for President Obama by running for president—the 1972 presidential campaign of Representative Shirley Chisholm, the 1984 and 1988 presidential candidacies of Jesse Jackson, and the 2004 campaigns of Carol Moseley Braun and Al Sharpton. Their candidacies are part of the second dilemma—what do racial minorities do to gain access to the political system?

Shirley Chisholm's Presidential Campaign: 1972. Most people think of Jesse Jackson's 1984 and 1988 presidential campaigns as the first by a "serious" black presidential contender—we tend to forget Shirley Chisholm's run in 1972. The late member of Congress Shirley Chisholm ran for president in 1972 on a Democratic Party ticket. She entered the race after no woman or black chose to run for the nomination. And although her goal was never to win but rather to show it was possible for an African American woman to make a good standing in a presidential run, she was serious about her bid and stayed in the race through the presidential primaries and into the Democratic Convention (McClain, Carter, and Brady 2005).

PHOTO 4.3 *Representative Shirley Chisholm, D-N.Y., pictured campaigning in Massachusetts on March 23, 1972, was the first of her sex to make a serious run for president of the United States. But that is not her only distinction. The Brooklyn-born Chisholm was the first black woman to be elected to Congress, and she was one of the most outspoken politicians of either sex on the national scene.* (AP Photo: 7203230193)

By building a coalition of African American and women voters, as well as concentrating her limited resources on more sympathetic states, she was able to make a good showing. Chisholm had a strong showing in Florida and Minnesota, despite the small number of blacks in both of these states, something she admits was "always so odd." It was the people in both of these states who raised $10,000 for her campaign and pushed her toward an actual run for the nomination. In fact, Chisholm received 430,000 votes before the Democratic National Convention began, and she became the first and only black woman to have her name placed into nomination at a national party convention.

Not all went well for Chisholm, however. She faced many obstacles in her bid for the presidential nomination. Many black males felt that her candidacy would divide the black voting bloc (Koplinski 2000). In fact, a number of black leaders claimed that "a vote for Shirley Chisholm is a vote for George Wallace" (one of the front-runner Democrats) (Koplinski 2000:100). Despite her attempt at coalition building, Chisholm faced criticism from the black community from those who felt that she was not representing the black point of view and was beholden to the women's rights movement. Ironically, many of the leading feminists would not endorse her because either they felt she never had a chance or they did not want to lose the favor of the eventual nominee. Thus, even though the strong base of her campaign was female and black voters, these groups at large were also unwilling to endorse what they perceived to be a doomed campaign, and so they threw their support to safer white male candidates. Nonetheless, she ran an impressive campaign considering her fairly late start and shoestring budget. In the end, she received 151 delegates on the first ballot of the roll-call vote.

Jesse Jackson's Presidential Campaigns: 1984 and 1988. Blacks represent the single largest voting bloc within the Democratic Party, and by the early 1980s they were well integrated into the affairs of the party. Despite their integration and their placement on committees of the Democratic National Committee, many—including Jesse Jackson—questioned the level of influence blacks had within the party. There was also the emergent feeling among the black electorate that the Democratic Party was not seriously committed to furthering the advancement of blacks. This feeling, combined with the Reagan administration's negative policies and attitudes toward blacks, and the perception that the Democratic Party had failed to oppose many of Reagan's initiatives, caused Jesse Jackson to seek the Democratic presidential nomination in 1984 (Tate 1993).

Jackson hoped to be the voice for those outside of the political system and to increase both his and, by inference, black influence on the policies and positions of the party. Jackson's 1984 candidacy was seen as a challenge to the Democratic Party and its leadership; it also represented a challenge and a problem to the black leadership establishment—that is, black elected officials and national civil rights leaders. His 1984 candidacy was opposed by most black elected officials—many of whom were already committed to other candidates at the point of Jackson's announcement—including most big-city black mayors and a majority of the **Congressional Black Caucus** (a group of black members of Congress who seek to exert influence and promote issues of interest to African Americans) as well as the leaders of the NAACP and the National Urban League. Jackson was also plagued by doubts regarding his ability to carry out a credible campaign, and there were fears that his candidacy would split the black vote and lead to the nomination of a conservative Democratic candidate (Smith 1990).

During the 1984 campaign, Jackson pushed a progressive agenda through the concept of a **Rainbow Coalition**—a joint effort of peoples of all colors—that he hoped might become the majority in the Democratic Party. This premise was based on the assumption that the black vote, which constituted 20 percent of the Democratic Party voter coalition, could be mobilized to form the base of the Rainbow Coalition and that enough nonblacks (whites, Latinos, Asians, and American Indians) would join in a coalition with blacks to form a multiethnic majority.

Jackson finished in third place, with 18 percent of the vote and 9 percent of the convention delegates, in the 1984 presidential primary and nominating process, and he received few concessions from the Democratic Party. All of his minority policy planks were defeated by the Walter Mondale forces at the national convention, and Mondale refused to meet or negotiate with Jackson until after the convention. "In 1984 Jackson's 'victories,' including his highly celebrated speech at the 1984 national convention, were largely symbolic" (Tate 1993:61).

Jackson's campaign for the presidency in 1988 contrasted sharply with the 1984 effort. Jackson gained the support of virtually the entire black leadership establishment: a majority of big-city black mayors, members of the Congressional Black Caucus, and leaders of the national civil rights organizations. "With the exception of Los Angeles Mayor Thomas Bradley and Atlanta's Andrew Young, who declared himself neutral (the latter ostensibly because of his role as convention city host); Detroit Mayor Coleman Young, who supported Mike Dukakis; and Missouri's Congressman Alan Wheat, who supported his home-state colleague, Richard Gephardt, it is difficult to think of a major national black leader that did not support Jackson's 1988 campaign" (Smith 1990).

In 1988, Jackson won the presidential primaries in the District of Columbia, Alabama, Georgia, Louisiana, Mississippi, and Virginia, and he won caucuses in Alaska, Delaware, Michigan, South Carolina, and Puerto Rico. By the time of the Democratic Convention, Jackson was second in a field of eight Democratic contenders; he garnered 29 percent of the primary vote compared to Dukakis's 43 percent and collected 1,105 delegates compared to Dukakis's 2,309 (Smith 1990:228). During the 1988 campaign, Jackson chose to focus on what political scientists call **valence issues**—issues that have universal appeal, such as anticrime and antipoverty issues—and he is credited by Democrats as well as Republicans with being the campaign's most effective advocate on the issues of drug use and teens' personal responsibility regarding sex and pregnancy.

Jackson's two presidential campaigns were historic, and they marked a change in the public role blacks were ready to play in presidential politics. First, they demonstrated that black voters were prepared to support and mobilize behind one of their own, as evidenced by significantly increased black voter registration and participation in both 1984 and 1988. Second, despite the inability of Jackson's delegates to play a balance-of-power role in the choice of the party nominee in either 1984 or 1988, Jackson's two campaigns were successful in inserting progressive ideas and policy initiatives into the campaign debates on domestic and foreign policy issues—a perspective that may not have been articulated without his presence.

Carol Moseley Braun and Al Sharpton: 2004. In 2003, Carol Moseley Braun and Al Sharpton were two blacks among the nine Democrats running in the Democratic presidential primary. Unlike Chisholm, who recognized the impossibility of her run for the presidency, Moseley Braun marketed herself as a realistic candidate, stating "that Americans are prepared to think outside the box and elect a person who is female and African-American, a person who does not fit the mold that we have resorted to for the last 200 years" (Younge 2003:3). Although Moseley Braun had little name recognition outside of the African American community, she represented an important demographic within the Democratic Party and the anti–Iraq War movement. She claimed to be "a budget hawk and a peace dove" (Younge 2003:1). With only 44 percent of African Americans in favor of the Iraq War and 51 percent of women in general, Moseley Braun fulfilled a much-needed voice (Younge 2003). Although she lost her bid for reelection to the Senate in 1998, Moseley Braun viewed her race for the Democratic nomination as a serious effort.

Al Sharpton was a Pentecostal minister, ordained at age nine, and is known more for his work as an activist than as a politician. He is founder and president of the National Action Network and was a candidate for the US Senate in 1992 and 1994 and for mayor of New York City in 1997.

Moseley Braun participated in only one presidential primary before she formally withdrew from the race on January 15, 2004. Sharpton, like Chisholm, stayed in the race through the presidential primaries and did well at several contests; for example, he was second in his home state of New York, pulling 34 percent of the vote to John Kerry's 54 percent.

Despite dropping out of the race early, Moseley Braun raised $627,869 as of December 31, 2004, which does not include federal matching funds because her campaign failed to file for them. She also had expenses and debts totaling $885,267. Interestingly, Moseley Braun raised more money than did

Al Sharpton, who raised $611,757, which included $100,000 in federal matching funds. Moreover, Sharpton ended the race $556,550 in debt.

MINORITY REPRESENTATION IN CONGRESS

The US Senate and House of Representatives are the national legislative bodies. They are responsible not only for making laws but also for determining budget allocations to the entire federal government. Clearly, these bodies have significant influence over, and importance to, the issues of concern to racial minorities.

In 1971, black members of the House of Representatives and the one black in the Senate formed the Congressional Black Caucus in an attempt to increase the influence of blacks in the House, as well as to provide research and information support for members. The 1992 elections—the first following the reapportionment and redistricting occasioned by the 1990 census—resulted in a substantial increase in the group's membership. Carol Moseley Braun of Illinois was elected to the Senate, the first black woman (and the first black Democrat) to serve in that body. She was the first black in the Senate since the defeat of Edward Brooke, a Massachusetts Republican, in 1978. She lost her reelection bid in 1998. In 2004, Illinois elected a second black Democrat, Barack Obama, to the US Senate. A former state senator, Obama, a Columbia undergraduate and Harvard-educated lawyer, received 70 percent of the statewide vote and won all but a handful of counties.

After Senator Obama's election as president of the United States, Governor Rod Blagojevich appointed former Illinois comptroller Roland W. Burris, a black, to Obama's former seat. But Blagojevich's indictment on charges of trying to sell Obama's Senate seat and his subsequent impeachment by the Illinois House tainted the appointment. Initially, Senate Democrats said that they would not seat any person appointed by Governor Blagojevich. After much debate and legal challenges, however, the Democrats relented, and Roland Burris was sworn in as the junior senator from Illinois. (Blagojevich was eventually impeached, removed from office, and convicted of federal charges related to the appointment to the Senate seat and other actions, and is currently in federal prison.)

In the 2012 elections, forty-two blacks were elected to the House of Representatives—thirteen of whom are women. In addition, two black female Democrats were elected as nonvoting delegates from the District of Columbia and the US Virgin Islands. Shortly after the election, Representative Jesse Jackson Jr. of Chicago resigned his seat, and the only black Republican member of the House of Representatives, Tim Scott of South Carolina, was appointed to the US Senate when Republican senator Jim DeMint resigned. A second black,

William "Mo" Cowan (D-MA), was appointed to the Senate seat vacated when former senator John Kerry was confirmed as secretary of state.

In 2017, there are three blacks in the US Senate—Tim Scott, Republican of South Carolina, Cory Booker, Democrat from New Jersey; and Kamala Harris, Democrat from California; who is of both African American and South Asian descent. Additionally, there are forty-eight blacks in the US House of Representatives, including the nonvoting delegates from the District of Columbia and the US Virgin Islands. Blacks now make up 10.6 percent of the House of Representatives, excluding the nonvoting delegates, and women, excluding nonvoting delegates, are about 39.1 percent of the black representatives (listed in Table 4.1). The influence of black representatives was magnified when the House of Representatives returned to Democratic control in the 2006 midterm elections. Several black members became chairs of major House committees—in particular, John Conyers of Michigan, chair of the Judiciary Committee, and Charles Rangel of New York, chair of the powerful Ways and Means Committee—based on the seniority system that is calculated from the first year of their election to the US House of Representatives (see Table 4.1). But the Republican takeover of the House of Representatives in 2010 reduced significantly the influence of black members. Republicans retained control of the House of Representatives in 2016, impeding the ability of black representatives to move their preferred legislation through the House.

Currently, four Latinos serve in the US Senate, three Cuban Americans—Robert Menendez (D-NJ), Marco Rubio (R-FL), and Ted Cruz (R-TX)—and one Mexican American, Catherine Cortez Masto (D-NV). Rubio and Cruz are conservative and are affiliated with and supported by the Tea Party. The number of Latinos in the House stood at thirty-five, excluding the nonvoting delegate from Puerto Rico, after the 2016 elections (listed in Table 4.2). Eight of those members are Latinas, and seven are Republicans. Table 4.2 also shows the ethnic origin of the Hispanic members of Congress. Twenty-two of the thirty-five are Mexican Americans, with five Cubans, five Puerto Ricans, and one each of Portuguese, Guatemalan, and Dominican ancestry. There is also a nonvoting delegate from Puerto Rico. In 1977, Latino representatives established the Congressional Hispanic Caucus along lines similar to the Congressional Black Caucus (see glossary). Of the Latino members of the 115th Congress, all twenty-seven Democrats are members of the caucus, whereas none of the Republicans are. The Republicans are members of the Congregational Hispanic Conference, formed in 2003.

There are three Asian American senators—Mazie Hirono (D-HI) was elected in 2012; Tammy Duckworth (D-IL), a former representative and military helicopter pilot that lost her legs in Iraq, was elected in 2016; and Kamala

TABLE 4.1 Black Members of the 115th Congress, January 3, 2017–January 3, 2019

SENATE	STATE	PARTY	FIRST ELECTED
Tim Scott	South Carolina	Republican	2012 (appointed; elected 2014)
Cory Booker	New Jersey	Democrat	2012
Kamala Harris	California	Democrat	2016
HOUSE OF REPRESENTATIVES	STATE	PARTY	FIRST ELECTED
John Conyers Jr.	Michigan	Democrat	1964
John Lewis	Georgia	Democrat	1986
Maxine Waters	California	Democrat	1990
Sanford D. Bishop Jr.	Georgia	Democrat	1992
James E. Clyburn	South Carolina	Democrat	1992
Alcee L. Hastings	Florida	Democrat	1992
Eddie Bernice Johnson	Texas	Democrat	1992
Bobby L. Rush	Illinois	Democrat	1992
Robert C. Scott	Virginia	Democrat	1992
Bennie G. Thompson	Mississippi	Democrat	1993
Sheila Jackson Lee	Texas	Democrat	1994
Elijah E. Cummings	Maryland	Democrat	1996
Danny K. Davis	Illinois	Democrat	1996
Barbara Lee	California	Democrat	1998
Gregory W. Meeks	New York	Democrat	1998
William Lacy Clay, III	Missouri	Democrat	2000
David Scott	Georgia	Democrat	2002
George K. Butterfield	North Carolina	Democrat	2004
Emanuel Cleaver II	Missouri	Democrat	2004
Al Green	Texas	Democrat	2004
Gwen Moore	Wisconsin	Democrat	2004
Yvette D. Clarke	New York	Democrat	2006
Keith Ellison	Minnesota	Democrat	2006
Hank Johnson	Georgia	Democrat	2006

TABLE 4.1 Black Members of the 115th Congress, January 3, 2017–
January 3, 2019

HOUSE OF REPRESENTATIVES (*Cont.*)	STATE	PARTY	FIRST ELECTED
Andre Carson	Indiana	Democrat	2008
Marcia L. Fudge	Ohio	Democrat	2008
Karen Bass	California	Democrat	2010
Cedric Richmond	Louisiana	Democrat	2010
Terri Sewell	Alabama	Democrat	2010
Frederica Wilson	Florida	Democrat	2010
Alma Adams	North Carolina	Democrat	2012
Joyce Beatty	Ohio	Democrat	2012
Hakeem Jeffries	New York	Democrat	2012
Robin Kelly	Illinois	Democrat	2012
Donald Payne, Jr.	New Jersey	Democrat	2012
Marc Veasey	Texas	Democrat	2012
Will Hurd	Texas	Republican	2014
Brenda Lawrence	Michigan	Democrat	2014
Mia Love	Utah	Republican	2014
Bonnie Watson Coleman	New Jersey	Democrat	2014
Anthony G. Brown	Maryland	Democrat	2016
Val Demings	Florida	Democrat	2016
Dwight Evans	Pennsylvania	Democrat	2016
Al Lawson	Florida	Democrat	2016
Donald McEachin	Virginia	Democrat	2016
Lisa Blunt Rochester	Delaware	Democrat	2016
NONVOTING DELEGATE IN THE HOUSE	STATE	PARTY	FIRST ELECTED
Eleanor Holmes Norton	District of Columbia	Democrat	1990
Stacey Plaskett	US Virgin Islands	Democrat	2016

TABLE 4.2 Latino Members of the 115th Congress, January 3, 2017–
January 3, 2019

SENATE	ETHNIC ORIGIN	STATE	PARTY	FIRST ELECTED
Robert Menendez	Cuban	New Jersey	Democrat	2006
Marco Rubio	Cuban	Florida	Republican	2010
Ted Cruz	Cuban	Texas	Republican	2012
Catherine Cortez Masto	Mexican	Nevada	Democrat	2016
HOUSE OF REPRESENTATIVES	ETHNIC ORIGIN	STATE	PARTY	FIRST ELECTED
Ileana Ros-Lehtinen	Cuban	Florida	Republican	1989
José E. Serrano	Puerto Rican	New York	Democrat	1990
Xavier Becerra	Mexican	California	Democrat	1992
Luis V. Gutiérrez	Puerto Rican	Illinois	Democrat	1992
Lucille Roybal-Allard	Mexican	California	Democrat	1992
Nydia M. Velázquez	Puerto Rican	New York	Democrat	1992
Grace F. Napolitano	Mexican	California	Democrat	1998
Henry Cuellar	Mexican	Texas	Democrat	2002
Mario Díaz-Balart Romero	Cuban	Florida	Republican	2002
Raul Grijalva	Mexican	Arizona	Democrat	2002
Linda Sánchez	Mexican	California	Democrat	2002
Jim Costa	Portuguese	California	Democrat	2004
Albio Sires	Cuban	New Jersey	Democrat	2006
Ben R. Luján	Mexican	New Mexico	Democrat	2008
Bill Flores	Mexican	Texas	Republican	2010
Jaime Herrera Beutler	Mexican	Washington	Republican	2010
Raúl Labrador	Puerto Rican	Idaho	Republican	2010
Tony Cárdenas	Mexican	California	Democrat	2012
Joaquín Castro	Mexican	Texas	Democrat	2012
Michelle Luján Grisham	Mexican	New Mexico	Democrat	2012
Juan Vargas	Mexican	California	Democrat	2012
Filemón Vela, Jr.	Mexican	Texas	Democrat	2012
Raúl Ruiz	Mexican	California	Democrat	2012
Pete Aguilar	Mexican	California	Democrat	2014
Carlos Curbelo	Cuban	Florida	Republican	2014
Ruben Gallego	Mexican/ Colombian	Arizona	Democrat	2014

TABLE 4.2 Latino Members of the 115th Congress, January 3, 2017–
January 3, 2019

HOUSE OF REPRESENTATIVES (*Cont.*)	ETHNIC ORIGIN	STATE	PARTY	FIRST ELECTED
Alex Mooney	Cuban	West Virginia	Republican	2014
Norma Torres	Guatemalan	California	Democrat	2014
Salud Carbajal	Mexican	California	Democrat	2016
Lou Correa	Mexican	California	Democrat	2016
Nanette Diaz Barragán	Mexican	California	Democrat	2016
Adriano Espaillat	Dominican	New York	Democrat	2016
Vicente González	Mexican	Texas	Democrat	2016
Ruben Kihuen	Mexican	Nevada	Democrat	2016
Darren Soto	Puerto Rican	Florida	Democrat	2016
NONVOTING DELEGATE IN THE HOUSE	ETHNIC ORIGIN	STATE	PARTY	FIRST ELECTED
Jenniffer González Colón	Puerto Rican	Puerto Rico	PNP/ Democrat	2016

Harris (D-CA). There are twelve Asian American members of the House of Representatives, all Democrats, plus two nonvoting Democratic delegates, one each from American Samoa and the Northern Mariana Islands (see Table 4.3). Representative Bobby Scott, who is of black and Filipino ancestry, is counted as an Asian American, as well as counted among the black members of Congress. Six of the members are women. The nonvoting delegate from Puerto Rico is also female. In May 1994, the Congressional Asian Pacific American Caucus was formed. The late representative Patsy T. Mink (D-HI) was quoted as saying that the Caucus was formed because the Asian Pacific members of Congress have felt that "we have not been consulted on important steps taken by this [Clinton] administration and ones in the past" (*Washington Post* 1994:A10).

Although the number of all of the minorities in Congress is small, none is smaller than the number (two) of American Indians serving—Republican Tom Cole (Chickasaw), elected to the House of Representatives from Oklahoma in 2002, and Republican Markwayne Mullin (Cherokee) elected from Oklahoma in 2012. (See Table 4.4 for a historical listing of American Indians who have served in the US Senate and House of Representatives.)

TABLE 4.3 Asian–Pacific Islander Members of the 115th Congress, January 3, 2017–January 3, 2019

SENATE	ETHNIC ORIGIN	STATE	PARTY	FIRST ELECTED
Mazie Keiko Hirono	Japanese	Hawaii	Democrat	2012
Tammy Duckworth	Thai	Illinois	Democrat	2016
Kamala Harris	Black/Indian	California	Democrat	2016
HOUSE OF REPRESENTATIVES	**ETHNIC ORIGIN**	**STATE**	**PARTY**	**FIRST ELECTED**
Robert C. Scott	Black/Filipino	Virginia	Democrat	1992
Doris Matsui	Japanese	California	Democrat	2005
Judy Chu	Chinese	California	Democrat	2009
Ami Bera	Indian	California	Democrat	2012
Tulsi Gabbard	Samoan	Hawaii	Democrat	2012
Grace Meng	Taiwanese	New York	Democrat	2012
Mark Takano	Japanese	California	Democrat	2012
Ted Lieu	Taiwanese	California	Democrat	2014
Pramila Jayal	Indian	Washington	Democrat	2016
Ro Khanna	Indian	California	Democrat	2016
Raja Krishnamoorth	Indian	Illinois	Democrat	2016
Stephanie Murphy	Vietnamese	Florida	Democrat	2016
NONVOTING DELEGATE IN THE HOUSE	**ETHNIC ORIGIN**	**STATE**	**PARTY**	**FIRST ELECTED**
Gregorie K. C. Sablan	Chamorro	Northern Mariana Islands	Democrat	2009
Amata Coleman Radewagen	Samoan	American Samoa	Republican	2014

MINORITY REPRESENTATION ON THE SUPREME COURT

The Supreme Court is often viewed as merely the final authority on constitutional issues, determining whether previous and current lower court judicial decisions, executive decisions, and legislative acts are constitutional. The court, however, plays a much greater role because in many instances its decisions may establish new public policy. We can, therefore, view the Supreme Court as a participant in the policymaking process. For racial minority groups, the

TABLE 4.4 American Indians Who Have Served in the US Senate and House of Representatives

SENATE	TRIBE	STATE	SERVICE YEARS
Hiram Rhodes Revels[†]	Lumbee	Mississippi	1870–1871
Matthew Stanley Quay	Abenaki or Delaware	Pennsylvania	1887–1899, 1901–1904
Charles Curtis*	Kaw-Osage	Kansas	1907–1913, 1915–1929
Robert L. Owen	Cherokee	Oklahoma	1907–1925
Ben Nighthorse Campbell	Northern Cheyenne	Colorado	1992–2004
HOUSE OF REPRESENTATIVES	TRIBE	STATE	SERVICE YEARS
Charles Curtis	Kaw-Osage	Kansas	1893–1907
Charles D. Carter	Choctaw	Oklahoma	1907–1927
W. W. Hastings	Cherokee	Oklahoma	1915–1921, 1923–1935
Will Rogers Jr.[††]	Cherokee	California	1942–1944
William G. Stigler	Choctaw	Oklahoma	1944–1952
Benjamin Reifel	Rosebud Sioux	South Dakota	1961–1971
Clem Rogers McSpadden[†]	Cherokee	Oklahoma	1972–1975
Ben Nighthorse Campbell	Northern Cheyenne	Colorado	1987–1992
Brad Cannon	Cherokee	Oklahoma	2000–2004
Tom Cole	Chickasaw	Oklahoma	2002–
Markwayne Mullin	Cherokee	Oklahoma	2013–

*Curtis served as Herbert Hoover's vice president, 1929–1933, and thus he served as president of the Senate during that time.

† From Jerry D. Stubben, *Native Americans and Political Participation: A Reference Handbook* (Santa Barbara, CA: ABC-CLIO, 2006).

†† From "List of Native Americans in the United States Congress," *Wikipedia,* https://en.wikipedia.org/wiki/List_of_Native_Americans_in_the_United_States_Congress, accessed August 2, 2016, and "Obituaries: Will Rogers Jr., Humorist's Son, Soldier, Politician and Actor, 81." *New York Times,* July 11, 1993, http://www.nytimes.com/1993/07/11/obituaries/will-rogers-jr-humorist-s-son-soldier-politician-and-actor-81.html, accessed August 2, 2016.

Source: The information in this table was drawn from a table developed by Gerald Wilkinson, National Indian Youth Council, provided to the authors by the Office of Senator Ben Nighthorse Campbell, and data from the Congressional Research Service. Information on the 2012 elections was drawn from *Indian Country Today.* This table is correct to the best of our knowledge. The Congressional Research Service indicates that the American Indian background of Quay is rumored, but has not been verified.

Supreme Court has been extremely important in their abilities to gain equal rights and constitutional protections. The court is a particularly important access point for racial and ethnic minorities because victories can be won by appealing to policymakers to do what is consistent with the Constitution rather than merely what the majority wants.

The Supreme Court has been especially important in establishing the legal framework within which racial minorities in the United States have had to exist. Although many of the most significant decisions—both favorable and unfavorable to minority litigants—have been made in cases involving African Americans, several decisions have also been made in cases brought by other groups. It should be understood that regardless of the minority group that brings the suit, the decision often has implications for the other groups as well.

Racial diversity on the court has been and continues to be a significant political issue each time a seat becomes available. The first black to serve on the court was the appeals court judge, former US solicitor general, and director/counsel of the NAACP-LDF Thurgood Marshall, who was nominated by President Johnson in 1967. Marshall's confirmation hearings were held up by Southern senators, particularly Strom Thurmond of South Carolina, who adamantly opposed the appointment of a black to the court. Marshall was a liberal member of the court led by Chief Justice Earl Warren, which issued many of the decisions that opened up the political process for racial minorities.

Marshall retired from the court in 1991, at which time President George H. W. Bush nominated the far-right black conservative Clarence Thomas to fill the vacancy. Thomas's nomination and the subsequent opposition by a sizable segment of black Americans highlight the fact that the race of a nominee does not ensure the support of other members of the racial group. Policy positions and attitudes may be even more important to racial minorities than similarities in color. Clarence Thomas's positions on a variety of issues—for example, equal protection, privacy rights, equal employment opportunity, and access to education—run counter to what many perceive to be the best interests of black America. Thus, whereas Anita Hill's accusations of sexual harassment and the televising of the second set of confirmation hearings drew attention to Thomas's nomination, many blacks, organized groups, and individuals testified in opposition to his nomination during the first set of hearings.

President Obama nominated the first Latino—also the first Latina—to the court in 2009, when he nominated Sonia Sotomayor. Sotomayor's nomination was opposed by a number of Republicans, and the phrase she used to describe herself—"a wise Latina"—was used by conservatives and the far right to suggest that she was a racist. Despite the attempt to derail her nomination, Sotomayor was confirmed by the Senate and assumed her position on the highest court in the United States. Marshall, Thomas, and Sotomayor are the only three racial minorities to have served on the court to date. (In addition, two white females, Ruth Bader Ginsberg and Elena Kagan, currently serve on the court.)

MINORITY REPRESENTATION IN THE BUREAUCRACY

Although the bureaucracy is technically part of the executive branch, any president quickly learns that he or she does not control it. People working within agencies cannot be strictly supervised; therefore, even when the law is very specific, bureaucrats must necessarily exercise discretion. For example, within US urban areas, the maximum speed limit is 55 miles per hour. Yet each of us has witnessed people breaking that law, and at times such transgressions are observed by law enforcement officers. If these local bureaucrats (police officers work within a bureaucracy and thus are bureaucrats) can affect the implementation of a specific policy such as speed limits, imagine the possibilities when they are charged with regulating in the public interest, detecting and prohibiting discrimination, or evaluating the work performance of subordinates—tasks assigned routinely to federal bureaucrats.

Because bureaucrats are appointed rather than elected, many people who are concerned about the representativeness of such bodies as Congress, or even with more visible nonelected bodies such as the Supreme Court, pay little attention to the composition of the bureaucracy. However, the representativeness of the bureaucracy can be important for a variety of reasons. First, such representativeness is a symbol of the openness of government. People may believe a government is legitimate if it employs people who are similar to them. Second, to the extent that people's attitudes are shaped by their socialization, a bureaucracy composed of a cross section of the nation's population will help to ensure that a full range of viewpoints will be articulated somewhere within the government. Third, to the extent that attitudes affect behavior, a more **representative bureaucracy**—one in which the demographic characteristics of the personnel mirror those of the population—may produce a more responsive bureaucracy. For example, there is evidence that black and Hispanic schoolchildren fare better when a greater number of black and Hispanic teachers, respectively, are present in their school systems (Meier, Stewart, and England 1989; Meier and Stewart 1991). Finally, citizens may be more willing to participate in government programs if the service providers are similar to them. For instance, there is evidence that HIV-infected patients, people desperately in need of bureaucratic services, clearly prefer to be served by people who share their race, gender, and sexual orientation (Thielemann and Stewart 1995).

Of course, the correspondence between the characteristics of the bureaucracy and those of the general population is not perfect. Studies from around the world, including the United States, consistently show that the middle class is overrepresented in the bureaucracy. This should not be surprising because members of the lower class generally lack the skills to perform bureaucratic tasks, and members of the upper class would not commonly engage in such activities. Further, these studies show that compared to other countries, on a variety of dimensions the United States has the world's most representative bureaucracy. To make another comparison, the federal bureaucracy much more closely mirrors the characteristics of the general population than does the "representative" legislative branch.

Beyond these generalizations, what specifically can be said about the representation of the nation's racial and ethnic minorities in the federal bureaucracy? Table 4.5 shows racial and ethnic group representation in federal civilian employment vis-à-vis that in the civilian labor force. Beyond the specifics, three points should be made. First, when compared to the general population proportions reported in Tables 2.1 and 2.2 (see pp. 29-30), blacks, American Indians, and Asian Americans are actually overrepresented in the federal bureaucracy. Second, the other groups fare poorly, using the same standard. Latinos are underrepresented in the federal bureaucracy. Third, blacks, Asian Americans, and American Indians are better represented among those employed in the public sector than among those who work in the private sector. Latinos are better represented in the civilian workforce than in the federal bureaucracy.

Even minority groups that are relatively well represented may not be distributed equitably within the federal bureaucracy. Table 4.6 shows the distribution of each minority racial and ethnic group across the federal pay grades. Blacks and American Indians are overrepresented at the lowest pay categories presented and underrepresented in the highest categories. They are also heavily concentrated in blue-collar jobs. In the $40,001 to $60,000 pay category, racial and ethnic minorities appear to be present in substantial numbers. But at the highest pay category ($160,001 plus), blacks, Latinos, and American Indians barely register. Only Asian Americans are represented similarly to their proportion in the national population.

It appears that the federal bureaucracy—despite its problems—is more open to minority employment than is the private sector, which bodes well for an improvement in the way minorities are treated by the government. In addition, the trends appear to be positive for minorities moving into higher levels of the bureaucracy, which is one of the most viable avenues available for upward mobility. But we must remember that effective public policymaking also requires action in the states.

TABLE 4.5 Representation of Racial/National Origin Groups in Federal Civilian Workforce and Civilian Labor Force, Fiscal Year 2014

	FEDERAL CIVILIAN WORKFORCE (%)	CIVILIAN LABOR FORCE (%)
Black	18.1	10.4
Latino	8.4	14.6
Asian/Pacific Islander	5.6	4.0
American Indian/ Alaskan Native	1.7	0.3
White	64.7	67.5
Non-Hispanic Multi-racial	1.2	1.5
Totals[a]	99.7	98.3

[a]Figures do not total to 100.

Source: US Office of Personnel Management, *Federal Equal Opportunity Recruitment Program (FEORP) Report to Congress, Fiscal Year 2014,* Washington, DC: Employment Service, Office of Diversity, February 2016, https://www.opm.gov/policy-data-oversight/diversity-and-inclusion/reports/feorp-2014.pdf, accessed August 2, 2016.

FEDERALISM

A structural feature of American government that has had a major impact on racial and ethnic minorities is the division of powers between the national and state governments—federalism. Although the two levels share some powers—concurrent powers—it is in the areas in which the powers do not overlap that minorities have been most affected. Multiple levels of government create multiple access points, which are both good and bad. People who want change have ample opportunity to petition the government; so, too, do people who oppose change. The result is that the outcome of policy disputes depends as much on the locus of decisions—jurisdictional issues—as it does on the merits of policy proposals.

Much of the struggle over policies that affects racial and ethnic minorities in the United States hinges on the federal structure. As was seen in the earlier discussions of the Constitution and voting rights, the fact that policy decisions have been made in the states assured that those engaged in discrimination would be judging themselves. The Supreme Court, in a series of decisions, permitted this situation to exist. In the *Slaughterhouse Cases* (1873) the court ruled that US citizens had dual citizenship, national and local, and that the Fourteenth Amendment defended citizens' rights only against laws adopted by

TABLE 4.6 Distribution of Racial/National Origin Groups in Federal Civilian Workforce by General Schedule and Related Pay Plans, Fiscal Year 2014

FEDERAL PAY PLANS[a]	BLACKS (%)	LATINOS (%)	ASIAN AMERICANS (%)	AMERICAN INDIANS (%)	NON-LATINO MULTI-RACIAL INDIANS (%)
Up to $20,000	0.0	0.0	0.0	0.0	0.0
$20,001 to $40,000	11.2	10.6	5.7	17.1	11.7
$40,001 to $60,000	25.7	22.5	14.1	28.0	21.1
$60,001 to $80,000	20.4	25.0	16.5	18.6	22.5
$80,001 to $100,000	16.1	17.8	21.3	11.9	18.5
$100,001 to $120,000	9.2	8.4	15.7	6.1	9.2
$120,001 to $140,000	4.5	3.7	8.6	2.8	4.2
$140,001 to $160,000	2.0	1.9	4.4	1.5	2.1
$160,001 and Greater	1.0	1.5	5.9	1.7	1.2
Unspecified	0.0	0.1	0.0	0.1	0.1
Blue Collar	9.8	8.5	7.8	12.2	9.3
Total[b] (Raw Total)	99.9 (343,663)	100.0 (159,540)	100.0 (106,111)	100.0 (31,409)	99.9 (22,752)

[a]In 2011, the Federal Equal Opportunity Recruitment Program (FEORP) altered its method of reporting salaries earned by the federal workforce. FEORP now reports salary ranges for federal employees in white-collar positions. This table includes aggregated salary range data for white-collar professional, administrative, technical, clerical, and other occupational positions.
[b]Some totals do not equal 100 due to rounding.

Sources: US Office of Personnel Management, *Federal Equal Opportunity Recruitment Program (FEORP) Report to Congress: Fiscal Year 2014,* Washington, DC: Employment Service, Office of Diversity, February 2016, https://www.opm.gov/policy-data-oversight/diversity-and-inclusion /reports/feorp-2014.pdf, accessed September 5, 2016.

the national government and not against state governments' incursions. The decision in *United States v. Reese* (1876) interpreted the Fifteenth Amendment as allowing states to impose various criteria, including literacy tests, on prospective voters. In the *Civil Rights Cases* (1883) the court voided the 1875 Civil Rights Act, ruling that the national government could not interfere with the private actions of individuals within states. And in *United States v. Harris* (1883) the court struck down the Ku Klux Klan Act because it applied to the "private activities" of individuals. Taken together, these decisions allowed states to infringe on the civil rights of citizens, especially minority citizens.

It was not until the 1960s that states' rights arguments against minority civil rights were apparently overridden. Basing its authority on the commerce clause of the Constitution, the Civil Rights Act of 1964 asserted authority over what had previously been thought to be part of the "private" sector, access to "public" accommodations—buses, waiting rooms, restaurants, and hotels. Furthermore, as detailed later, increased reliance of local educational systems on federal funding gave the national government heretofore unknown leverage in achieving school desegregation in the states that had maintained de jure discrimination.

The post-1964 era was qualitatively different in terms of civil rights policy than the decades that preceded it. Richard Nixon represents an important break point because he showed that one could win the presidency by not being overtly racist but by allowing civil rights opponents to believe he agreed with them. The trend that started with Nixon reached its fruition with the Reagan and first Bush administrations, during which enforcement responsibilities were left to the states. Who are the state policymakers?

STATE ELECTIVE OFFICE

At the state level, as of 2002 (these are the latest figures available from the US Bureau of the Census), the largest numbers of black elected officials were found in ten states—Mississippi (950), Alabama (757), Louisiana (739), Illinois (619), Georgia (640), South Carolina (547), Arkansas (535), North Carolina (523), Texas (466), and Michigan (353) (US Census Bureau 2010). With the exception of Texas, Illinois, Arkansas, and Michigan, these states are covered, at least in part, by the Voting Rights Act. Currently, there are no black governors; Nikki Haley (R-SC) was recently confirmed as the UN ambassador, so there are no Asian Indian governors, but there are two Latino governors, Susana Martinez (R-NM) and Brian Sandoval (R-NV) (see Table 4.7). As of the elections of 2016, excluding judicial and university governing board positions, five blacks hold statewide office—Denise L. Nappier (D), Connecticut state treasurer; Jesse C. White Jr. (D), Illinois secretary of state; Boyd Rutherford

(R), Maryland lieutenant governor; Jean Hampton (R), Kentucky lieutenant governor; and Sandra Kennedy, Arizona corporation commissioner. Other blacks who have held statewide office include Deval Patrick, governor of Massachusetts; L. Douglas Wilder, governor of Virginia; former lieutenant governors Jennifer Carroll (Florida), Merv Dymally (California), George Brown (Colorado), Joe Rogers (Colorado), and Michael Steele (Maryland); Roland Burris, former comptroller and state attorney general of Illinois; Ken Blackwell, former state treasurer and secretary of state of Ohio; the late Vikki Buckley, Colorado secretary of state; former state auditor of North Carolina Ralph H. Campbell Jr.; former New Jersey state attorney general Peter Harvey; Thurbert E. Baker, former Georgia state attorney general; Michael Thurmond, former Georgia labor commissioner; Michael L. Williams, chair, Texas Railroad Commission; Randolph Brock, Vermont state auditor; Kamala Harris, attorney general of California; Ed Brooke, former Republican senator from Massachusetts; Carol Moseley Braun, former Democratic senator from Illinois; and Barack Obama, former Democratic senator from Illinois.

Latinos also have had success in electing individuals to statewide offices. As of 2014, there were 6,053 Latino elected officials, including 2,090 women (34.5 percent) (NALEO 2016). In 2010, the largest numbers of Latino elected officials were found in nine states—Texas (2,459), California (1,311), New Mexico (714), Arizona (362), Colorado (167), Florida (158), New Jersey (113), Illinois (113), and New York (73). Latinas have also played a very active role in New Mexico state politics. Two women who are especially worthy of note are Nina Otero Warren and Soledad Chacon. Warren began her career in politics in 1917 when she was appointed school superintendent of Santa Fe (Vigil 1996). She later went on to become chair of the Women's Division of the Republican State Committee for Women and ran for US Congress, albeit unsuccessfully, in 1922. Also in 1922, Chacon ran for New Mexico secretary of state and won. She is most remembered for the fact that she served as acting governor in 1924, becoming the first Latina to serve in this capacity. Latinos have served as full-term, elected governors of New Mexico (Democrats Ezequiel Cabeza de Baca, 1917; Tony Anaya, 1983–1987; Jerry Apodaca, 1975–1979; Bill Richardson, 2003–2009; Republican Susana Martinez, 2011 to present; and Democrat-turned-Republican Octaviano Ambrosio Larrazolo, 1919–1921); Arizona (Democrat Raul Castro, 1975–1977); and Florida (Republican Robert Martinez, 1987–1991). Former Texas state attorney general Dan Morales was also Latino, as is former New Mexico attorney general Patricia Madrid and former New Mexico secretaries of state Rebecca Vigil-Giron and Dianna Duran. Currently Republican John Sanchez is lieutenant governor, Democrat Hector Balderas is attorney general and Democrat Valerie

TABLE 4.7 Black, Latino, and Asian Governors in the United States

CURRENT GOVERNOR	STATE	ETHNIC ORIGIN	PARTY	DATES IN OFFICE
David Ige	Hawaii	Japanese American	Democrat	2014–present
Susana Martinez	New Mexico	Mexican American	Republican	2011–present
Brian Sandoval	Nevada	Mexican American	Republican	2011–present
PREVIOUS GOVERNOR	**STATE**	**ETHNIC ORIGIN**	**PARTY**	**DATES IN OFFICE**
Nikki Haley	South Carolina	Indian American	Republican	2011–2017
Bobby Jindal	Louisiana	Indian American	Republican	2008–2016
David Paterson	New York	Black	Democrat	2008–2010
Deval Patrick	Massachusetts	Black	Democrat	2007–2015
Bill Richardson	New Mexico	Mexican American	Democrat	2003–2011
Gary Locke	Washington	Chinese American	Democrat	1997–2005
Ben Cayetano	Hawaii	Filipino American	Democrat	1994–2002
Douglas Wilder	Virginia	Black	Democrat	1990–1994
Robert Martinez	Florida	Cuban	Republican	1987–1991
John D. Waihee III	Hawaii	Native Hawaiian	Democrat	1986–1994
Toney Anaya	New Mexico	Mexican American	Democrat	1983–1987
Jerry Apodaca	New Mexico	Mexican American	Democrat	1975–1979
Raúl Castro	Arizona	Mexican American	Democrat	1975–1977
George Ariyoshi	Hawaii	Japanese American	Democrat	1974–1986
Octaviano Ambrosio Larrazolo	New Mexico	Mexican American	Democrat	1919–1921
Ezequiel Cabeza de Baca	New Mexico	Mexican American	Democrat	1917
Miguel Otero	New Mexico Territory	Mexican	Republican	1897–1906
Romualdo Pacheco	California	Mexican American	Republican	1875
P. B. S. Pinchback	Louisiana	Black	Republican	(Acting 36 days 1872–1873)
Donaciano Vigil	New Mexico (under US military rule)	Mexican	–	1847–1848

Espinoza is a public regulation commissioner in New Mexico. In addition, Latinos have made inroads into the judicial branch in New Mexico. A majority of the justices of the New Mexico Supreme Court are Latino—Patricio Serna, Petra Jimenez Maes, and Edward Chavez. New Mexico is the only state in which Latino political representation is at least equal to the state's Latino population proportion (Brischetto 1996).

Latinos have had success in statewide elective office in other states as well. Alex Padilla (D) is California's secretary of state, and Nellie Gorbea (D) is Rhode Island's secretary of state. Lieutenant governors include Carlos López-Cantera (R) of Florida and Evelyn Sanguinetti (R) of Illinois. George P. Bush (R) is Texas commissioner of the General Land Office, and Sean Reyes (R) is Utah's attorney general. In the 2016 election, Trinidad Navarro (D) was elected Delaware's insurance commissioner, and Susana Mendoza (D) was elected Illinois's comptroller.

Asian Pacific Americans have served as governor of Hawaii, lieutenant governors of Delaware and Hawaii, secretary of state and state treasurer in California, and in fifty-four state legislative seats in Hawaii. In a historic election in 1996, Democrat Gary Locke, former King County executive and second-generation Washingtonian, was elected governor of Washington State, the first Asian American governor outside of Hawaii. Locke is also the first Chinese American governor. To date, Asian electoral successes have been regional rather than national (Nakanishi 1991). Locke's election was a major breakthrough in Asian electoral outcomes. Locke is a second-generation Chinese American: His grandfather came to the United States around the turn of the century and worked as a houseboy in Olympia, Washington. He returned to China at some point to marry but came back to the United States around 1930, when Locke's father was thirteen years old. Locke's father served in the US Army during World War II and later owned a restaurant and grocery store in Seattle. Locke, born in 1950, was one of five children growing up in a public housing project in Seattle. Through part-time jobs, financial aid, and scholarships, Locke received a BA from Yale University and a law degree from Boston University. He worked as a King County deputy prosecutor for several years and also worked for US West. In 1982, he was elected to the Washington State House of Representatives, and he served in that body for eleven years. In 1993, he was elected chief executive of King County, running for governor in 1996. Many consider Locke to be a liberal Democrat. Locke was reelected handily to a second term in 2000, but he declined to run for a third term in 2004.

Bobby Jindal, an Asian Indian conservative Republican, was the governor of Louisiana. He was born in Baton Rouge, Louisiana, on June 10, 1971, and graduated from Baton Rouge High School at the age of sixteen. He later attended Brown University, where he graduated with honors in both biology and public policy. He then attended Oxford University as a Rhodes Scholar and received his graduate degree in 1994. In 1996, he was appointed secretary of the Louisiana Department of Health and Hospitals (DHH), relinquishing admissions to Harvard and Yale University medical and law schools. In 1998, Jindal was appointed executive director of the National Bipartisan Commission on the Future of Medicare, whose recommendations continue to be the driving force behind much of the ongoing debate on how to strengthen and improve Medicare. He returned to Louisiana State government in 1999, when he became president of the University of Louisiana system—the sixteenth largest higher-education system in the country, which oversees the education of around eighty thousand students a year. In March 2001, he was nominated by President George W. Bush, and later unanimously confirmed by a bipartisan vote of the US Senate, as the assistant secretary for planning and evaluation for the US Department of Health and Human Services. He was elected to Congress in 2004 and reelected to a second term in November 2006. He was elected governor of Louisiana on October 20, 2007, with 54 percent of the vote in the primary, winning sixty of sixty-four parishes, and was reelected in 2011. In 2015, he ran for the 2016 Republican presidential nomination, but his candidacy never took off.

Republican Nikki Randhawa Haley was the first female governor of South Carolina, and the second Asian Indian elected to governorship after Bobby Jindal. She was also the youngest governor in the United States (Liptak 2013). She was elected to her current position in 2010 with backing from the Tea Party and endorsements from former Massachusetts governor Mitt Romney and former Alaska governor Sarah Palin (Kraushaar 2010; *Huffington Post* 2011). Haley was born Nimrata Nikki Randhawa in Bamberg, South Carolina, in 1972 to an immigrant Sikh family. Her parents, Dr. Ajit Sing Randhawa and Raj Kaur Randhawa, are originally from the Amritsar District, Punjab, India. She graduated from Clemson University with a BS in accounting. Prior to serving as governor, she represented the Eighty-seventh District in Lexington County in the South Carolina House of Representatives from 2005 to 2010. Haley, who is one of the strongest fiscal conservatives in state government, won the seat by beating the longest-serving state legislator in a Republican primary, although she was a virtually unknown politician at the time. Haley's political career has been "marked by conservative leadership and an unwavering commitment to the taxpayers' bottom line" (State of South Carolina 2011). Haley consistently voted for bills that restrict abortion. As part of her campaign efforts in 2010, Haley pledged to bring South Carolina a law,

PHOTO 4.4 *Nikki Haley, US Ambassador to the United Nations, delivers remarks to the Security Council on Ukraine, February 2, 2017.* (REUTERS/Mike Segar; RTS10TJI)

similar to the one adopted in Arizona, to crack down on illegal immigration (Fausset 2012).

Haley took a strong stand for the removal of the Confederate flag from the capital grounds after Dylann Roof shot and killed nine members of Emmanuel African Methodist Episcopal Church during bible study on June 17, 2015. Among the victims was State Senator Clementa Pinckney, who was also the pastor of the church. Roof is a white supremacist and told police that he had to shoot black people because he wanted to start a race war and that someone had to do what he did. He was convicted on all thirty-three federal hate crime charges in December 2016 and sentenced to death.

American Indian successes at the statewide level have been even rarer than those of Asians. Byron Mallott (Tlingit Alaskan Native) is the current Democratic lieutenant governor of Alaska, one of the few American Indians to win statewide office. Democrat Larry Echo Hawk, a Pawnee Indian, has served in the Idaho state legislature and as attorney general but failed in his 1994 run for governor of that state. Democrat Bill Yellowtail, a Crow Indian, lost his bid in 1996 for Montana's only congressional seat. In 2010, Democrat Christopher Deschene, a Navajo, ran for Arizona secretary of state. In 2002, Republican Sharon Clahchischilliage, a Navajo, ran for New Mexico secretary of state and lost; then in 2012 she ran for the New Mexico House of Representatives and won. In the 2012 primaries in Arizona, Democrat Wenona Benally Baldene-gro, a Harvard-educated Navajo, ran in the state's first congressional district (Trahant 2012 Elections 2012: An Arizona Mystery—Will Native Voters Show Up?), but lost to former representative Ann Kirkpatrick, who went on to win the seat. Democrat Denise Juneau, a member of the Mandan and Hidatsa tribes, was elected Montana state superintendent of public instruction in 2008 and reelected in 2012. In 2016 Juneau ran against Representative Ryan Zinke for Montana's lone congressional seat. Zinke won and is now President Trump's secretary of interior.

American Indians serve in the state legislatures of New Mexico (5 in the House, 2 in the Senate), Arizona (3 in the House, 1 in the Senate), Oklahoma (8 in the House, 4 in the Senate), South Dakota (2 in the House), Montana (8 in the House, 2 in the Senate), North Dakota (1 in the House, 1 in the Senate), Alaska (6 in the House, 2 in the Senate), Colorado (1 in the Senate), Washington (2 in the House), Hawaii (5 in the House), Idaho (1 in the House), Kansas (1 in the House), Kentucky (1 in the House), Minnesota (5 in the House), Maryland (1 in the House), North Carolina (1 in the House), Utah (1 in the House), and Wyoming (1 in the House). As mentioned earlier, American Indian voters were central to the reelection of Senator Jon Tester in the 2012 election, although it appears that they lost two seats in the Montana House of Representatives.

Table 4.8 shows the state distribution, tribal and party affiliations, and first year in office of American Indian and Alaskan Native state legislators. Although we lacked the data in Chapter 3 decisively to categorize American Indians as either Democrats or Republicans, such is not the case for those elected to state legislative offices, an overwhelming majority of whom are Democrats. This also appears to be the pattern in the partisan affiliation of state legislators, even in Oklahoma, where in the past Republicans slightly outnumbered Democrats. The tribe with the largest number of representatives is the Cherokee, but this may be a function of the large number of Oklahoma elected officials who are enrolled members of the Cherokee nation.

How does this representation work within the federal system to produce public policy? We now turn to two examples: equal opportunity in education and affirmative action in employment.

EQUAL EDUCATIONAL OPPORTUNITY FOR MINORITIES

The struggle over equal educational opportunity provides a good example of the way the policymaking process within the federal system produces and thwarts policy change. Denial of such opportunity has been and continues to

TABLE 4.8 Native American State Legislators, 2017

STATE	BODY	NAME	TRIBE	PARTY	FIRST YEAR IN OFFICE
Alaska	House	Bryce Edgmon	–	Democrat	2007
		Neal Foster	Inupiaq	Democrat	2009
		Benjamin Nageak	Inupiaq	Democrat	2013
		Sam Kito III	Tlingit	Democrat	2014
		Charisse Millett	Inupiaq	Republican	2009
		Dean Westlake	Inupiaq	Democrat	2017
	Senate	Lyman Hoffman	Yup'ik	Democrat	1991
		Donny Olson	Inupiaq	Democrat	2001
Arizona	House	Sally Ann Gonzalez	Pascua Yaqui	Democrat	2011
		Wenona Jennifer Benally	Navajo	Democrat	2015
		Eric Descheenie	Navajo	Democrat	2017
	Senate	Jamescita Peshlakai	Navajo	Democrat	2017
Colorado	House	Joseph Salazar	–	Democrat	2013
Hawaii	House	James Tokioka	Native Hawaiian	Democrat	2007
		Ty Cullen	Native Hawaiian	Democrat	2011
		Andria Tupola	Native Hawaiian	Republican	2014
		Jarrett Keohoakalole	Native Hawaiian	Democrat	2014
		Lynn DeCoite	Native Hawaiian	Democrat	2015
Idaho	House	Paulette Jordan	Coeur d'Alene	Democrat	2014
Kansas	House	Ponke-We Victors	Ponca	Democrat	2010
Kentucky	House	Reginald Meeks	Cherokee	Democrat	2001
Minnesota	House	Susan Allen	Rosebud Sioux	Democrat	2012
		Peggy Flanagan	White Earth	Democrat	2015
		Susan Allen	Rosebud	Democrat	2017
		Jamie Becker-Finn	Ojibwe	Democrat	2017
		Mary Kunesh-Podein	Standing Rock	Democrat	2017

TABLE 4.8 Native American State Legislators, 2017

STATE	BODY	NAME	TRIBE	PARTY	FIRST YEAR IN OFFICE
Montana	House	Rae Peppers	Cheyenne	Democrat	2013
		George G. Kipp III	–	Democrat	2015
		Gilbert Bruce Meyers	Chippewa Cree	Republican	2015
		Susan Webber	Blackfeet	Democrat	2015
		Garrett Lankford	Little Shell	Democrat	2017
		Shane Morigeau	CSKT	Democrat	2017
		Sharon Stewart-Peregoy	Crow	Democrat	2017
		Jonathan Windy Boy	Chippewa Cree	Democrat	2017
	Senate	Frank Smith	Assiniboine-Sioux	Democrat	2017
		Jason Small	Northern Cheyenne	Democrat	2017
New Mexico	House	Nick Salazar	Ohkay Wingeh	Democrat	1973
		Georgene Louis	Acoma	Democrat	2013
		Patricia Roybal Caballero	Piro-Manso-Tiwa	Democrat	2013
		Sharon Clahchischilliage	Navajo	Republican	2015
		Doreen Wonda Johnson	Navajo	Democrat	2015
	Senate	John Pinto	Navajo	Democrat	1977
		Benny Shendo	Jemez	Democrat	2013
North Carolina	House	Charles Graham	Lumbee	Democrat	2011
North Dakota	House	Wayne Trottier	Sioux	Republican	2010
	Senate	Richard Marcellais	Chippewa	Democrat	2007

(Continues)

TABLE 4.8 Native American State Legislators, 2017 (*Continued*)

STATE	BODY	NAME	TRIBE	PARTY	FIRST YEAR IN OFFICE
Oklahoma	*House*	Chuck Hoskins	Cherokee	Democrat	2007
		Seneca Scott	Choctaw	Democrat	2008
		Cory Williams	Muscogee	Democrat	2008
		Dan Kirby	Creek	Republican	2009
		William Fourkiller	Cherokee	Democrat	2010
		Mark McBride	Potawatomi	Republican	2012
		Markwayne Mullin	Cherokee	Republican	2013
		Scott Fetgatter	Choctaw	Republican	2017
	Senate	John Sparks	Cherokee	Democrat	2006
		Brian Bingman	Muscogee	Republican	2007
		Anastasia Pittman (Freedman Member)	Seminole	Democrat	2007
		Anastasia Pittman (Freedman Member)	Seminole	Democrat	2007
South Dakota	*Senate*	Troy Heinert	Rosebud Sioux	Democrat	2015
		Kevin Killer	Oglala Lakota	Democrat	2017
Utah	*House*	Angela Romero	–	Democrat	2013
Washington	*House*	Jeff Morris	Tsimshian	Democrat	1996
		Jay Rodne	Bad River	Republican	2004
Wyoming	*Senate*	Affie Ellis	–	Republican	2017

Sources: "Home Page," *Ballotpedia,* https://ballotpedia.org/Main_Page, accessed November 18, 2016; "Less Representation, Not More, but a Few Important Wins Too," *Indian Country Today,* November 9, 2016, http://indiancountrytodaymedianetwork.com/print/2016/11/09/less-representation-not-more-few-important-wins-too-166393, accessed November 18, 2016; "Membership List," National Caucus of Native American State Legislators, 2016 (not published online); National Caucus of Native American State Legislators website, http://www.nativeamericanlegislators.org/Public%20Documents/Caucus%20Membership.aspx, accessed November 18, 2016; "List of Native American Politicians," *Wikipedia,* https://en.wikipedia.org/wiki/List_of_Native_American_politicians#State_offices, accessed August 10, 2016.

be a serious problem for members of the nation's racial and ethnic minority groups because it has important implications for one's chances for social mobility. The "American dream" of hard work being rewarded with higher income—which allows one access to better-quality housing, health care, and recreational opportunities—has always been, and is now even more, predicated on training or education. The way this works is not a mystery. Access to many jobs and to the professions, positions with greater responsibility and higher pay, is limited to those with higher levels of educational attainment. Unfortunately, education systems do not have a strong record of providing effective education for racial and ethnic minorities. Schools serve as "sorting machines" (Spring 1989), separating students into different categories based on a number of criteria—including race and ethnicity—and providing different groups of students with educations of different quality.

Blacks

When the US Supreme Court accepted the "separate but equal" interpretation of the equal protection clause of the Constitution (*Plessy v. Ferguson* 1896) and then soon made a decision that ignored the "but equal" part of the phrase in public education (*Cumming v. County Board of Education* 1899), racially segregated schools were legitimized. What followed was a long war, waged in courtrooms primarily by the legal arm of the NAACP, the NAACP Legal Defense and Educational Fund—the "Ink Fund"—in an attempt to overturn this momentous decision.

The Ink Fund, operating in an environment of uncertainty about how far courts were willing to go in reinterpreting the law and functioning with limited resources, adopted an incremental strategy. Litigation was seen as a means of minimizing costs while pursuing a benefit—education—that would improve the economic position of blacks, sometimes immediately and, at the least, in the long run. Litigation was also viewed as a way of testing and shaping public opinion that could facilitate policy change, of increasing the costs of maintaining segregation, and of mobilizing the black community. Any positive decision could be declared a victory in an attempt to assist in the mobilization effort (Tushnet 1987:2–14, 33–69).

Strategically, the Ink Fund focused on three types of cases—desegregation of public graduate and professional schools, salary equalization suits, and facility equalization suits. Attorneys won Supreme Court declarations that a black applicant to the University of Missouri Law School had the same right to an opportunity for legal education as did whites within the state (*Missouri ex rel. Gaines v. Canada* 1938) and that the pay differential between black and white teachers in the Norfolk public school system violated even *Plessy* (*Alston v.*

School Board of Norfolk 1940); yet, in spite of these victories, separate but equal remained the law. The Ink Fund continued to use courts as alternatives to legislatures in the pursuit of policy change (Tushnet 1987:32–42, 59–81).

But the limited types of cases pursued by the Ink Fund meant that at some point the organization would have to change strategies. With case law in these areas having been developed as extensively as possible, unless the organization established and pursued new goals, the basic problem—*Plessy*—would remain. Realization of this fact led to the adoption of a direct challenge to segregation that resulted in the Supreme Court's reversal of the *Plessy* decision in *Brown v. Board of Education of Topeka* (1954, 1955). In this case, the court consolidated appeals from Kansas, South Carolina, and Virginia; accelerated an appeal from Delaware; and declared unanimously that separate schools, segregated by race, were "inherently unequal." The Ink Fund and the US Supreme Court had combined to construct a new definition of equality and to make that new definition public policy (Tushnet 1987:142–161).

At that point, policymaking in the area of equal educational opportunity shifted from a focus on overturning a loathsome judicial precedent to implementing a favorable one. Initial euphoria led to overly optimistic predictions about the speed with which segregated school systems could be dismantled. Thurgood Marshall, the victorious attorney in the *Brown* case, thought it might take "up to five years" for segregation to be eradicated, but he was sure that by the "100th Anniversary of the Emancipation Proclamation [in 1963] . . . segregation in all its forms [will have been] eliminated" (quoted in Cruse 1987:25–26).

Reality, of course, was quite different. Encouraged by an implementation decree that called for desegregation **"with all deliberate speed"** and "at the earliest possible date," opponents of the court's order expended massive amounts of energy deliberating and virtually no time moving quickly. Many could not envision a possible implementation date. Furthermore, the vast majority of deliberations focused on ways to evade the intent of the *Brown* decision rather than on ways to comply with that intent.

In the face of this resistance, implementation efforts were inconsistent. In federal district courts, the scenes of most of the desegregation battles, results varied. For example, whereas Judge Frank Johnson (Alabama) sought to implement *Brown* conscientiously, refusing to let the court's "authority and dignity . . . be bent and swayed by . . . politically generated whirlwinds" (*In re Wallace* 1959:121), that same year Judge T. Whitfield Davidson (Texas) lectured black plaintiffs from the bench, saying that "the white man has a right to maintain his racial integrity and it can't be done so easily in integrated schools" (quoted in Peltason 1971:119). When the Fifth Circuit Court of Appeals, which heard most of the desegregation cases, remanded cases to these lower courts, the judges often found ways to further subvert the intent of *Brown*. By March 1961, for instance, district judges' opinions in the Dallas school desegregation case had already been reversed six times. Clearly, the appellate courts had difficulty establishing uniform standards at the trial court level.

Nor was support from the executive and legislative branches immediately forthcoming. President Eisenhower declared that he would not presume "that the judicial branch of government is incapable of implementing the Supreme Court's decision" (quoted in Peltason 1971:50); when he sent troops to Little Rock to help desegregate the schools there, his action was more unusual than it was typical. Presidential actions are generally explicable in terms of electoral rationality: "When presidential candidates faced an electoral imperative to seek blacks' votes, blacks finally began to gain allies in their struggle against a segregated second-class citizenship enforced by the laws of many states" (Robertson and Judd 1989:168).

Congress was even less supportive than the executive branch. Nearly all of the Southern members, fearful of electoral repercussions should the *Brown* decision be implemented, signed the infamous **Southern Manifesto**, a declaration decrying the decision (Lewis 1965:39). Only when its typical inertia was outweighed by a combination of shifting public opinion—prompted at least in part by media coverage of the civil rights movement—the assassination of President Kennedy; the strong leadership of a Southern-born president, Lyndon Johnson; and an influx of new members swept into office in the 1964 elections, did Congress overcome its usual timidity and enact significant legislation (Sundquist 1968).

This legislation took the form of the 1964 Civil Rights Act (see Orfield 1969). With this legislation, some of the responsibility for desegregation efforts shifted to the bureaucracy, to what was then the Department of Health, Education, and Welfare (HEW), which provided the department with a little-noticed but powerful tool—the power to cut off federal funds to school districts that practiced discrimination. That power, in conjunction with increased federal funds flowing to local school districts following the passage of the Elementary and Secondary Education Act of 1965, gave HEW the leverage it needed to begin to make significant changes. The Office for Civil Rights (OCR), the agency within HEW charged with enforcement responsibilities, and the federal courts gradually tightened the ratchet on school districts so that by fall 1970, school districts in the South were more desegregated than those in any other part of the country. This massive change occurred because of bureaucratic and judicial pressure, and it happened in spite of President Nixon's electoral "Southern" strategy (*Green v. New Kent County School Board* 1968; *Alexander v. Holmes* 1969; *United States v. Georgia* 1969; Panetta and Gall 1971).

In our federal system, because the national government does not actually operate an education system, the ultimate responsibility for providing equal educational opportunity lies with local school officials. For elected local officials, the calculus in the desegregation process was similar to that for other elected officials. For example, elected school superintendents in Georgia resisted desegregation more vigorously than did their appointed counterparts, for fear they would lose their positions (Rodgers and Bullock 1976:64–65).

Latinos

In the Latino community, equal educational opportunity issues generally paralleled those of black Americans but were resolved much later. As relatively late arrivals in the United States, Puerto Ricans and Cubans were not the path breakers in Hispanic equal educational opportunity battles. That role was played by Mexican Americans.

Mexican Americans, although not subject to separate but equal laws in quite the same way as blacks, were routinely denied access to education or received only an inferior segregated education. "Mexican-only" schools, established by local school boards, were present in Texas at the advent of the twentieth century (Rangel and Alcala 1972). In California, segregated Mexican schools were established as soon as a locale had enough students to hold classes.

As the twentieth century progressed, the policy of limited education evolved into one of Americanization—of transforming Mexican Americans into "Americans." Although these assimilationist pressures came from the state level, local officials often took actions that were at odds with these forces. Compulsory school attendance laws were often ignored if Mexican American children were involved. These children were counted in the school census that was used to obtain funds from the state of Texas, but local school districts did not need to spend money on truant children. Even if Mexican American children did attend schools, funds were not apportioned on an even remotely equitable basis. The provision of unequal education was possible because most school districts established separate classes for Mexican Americans within Anglo-dominated schools. Such segregation was based on local school board policies rather than on constitutional or statutory grounds, as was the case with blacks (San Miguel 1987:33–37, 47–55).

In some areas that had few Mexican American students, segregating students was too expensive and awkward. Even in districts with officially segregated schools, segregation was not total (Wollenberg 1978:111–17). Integration might be allowed on the basis of "apparent prosperity, cleanliness, the aggressiveness of parents, and the quota of Mexican-Americans already in the mixed school" (Tuck 1946:185–86). Segregation was less common at the secondary school level because (1) the Americanization rationale no longer held (if students were to be Americanized, the process should have occurred in the elementary grades); (2) many school districts could not afford two secondary schools; and (3) the Mexican American dropout rate was so high that few Hispanic students stayed in school that long (Wollenberg 1978:117–18).

Even in the 1950s, many Mexican American students were offered a segregated education, either through separate schools or within formally desegregated schools. Postwar protests by Mexican Americans and the 1947 repeal of the California statute that made it legal to segregate an ethnic group had no impact on segregation (although Mexican Americans were not specifically mentioned in the code [Cooke 1971]; see *Romero v. Weakley* 1955:836). Intraschool segregation was taken to such lengths, for example, that Mexican American and Anglo junior high school graduates sometimes held ceremonies on separate days (Weinberg 1977:286).

For Hispanics, the litigation campaign challenging segregated schools was spearheaded by the League of United Latin American Citizens (LULAC). LULAC's initial challenge against segregation was a class action suit brought against the Del Rio, Texas, Independent School District, alleging that Mexican American students were being denied equal protection under the law as stated in the US Constitution by being placed in segregated facilities (*Independent School District v. Salvatierra* 1930). For the first time in history "the courts were asked . . . to determine the constitutionality of the actions of a local school district with respect to the education of Mexican Americans" (San Miguel 1987:78). The court agreed that Mexican Americans could not be segregated simply because of their ethnicity but found that the school board was not engaged in this practice. The school board could continue to segregate Mexican Americans on the grounds of irregular attendance and, more important, language, which the court found permissible on educational grounds. Thus, its first foray into the courts was unsuccessful, and LULAC resolved to emphasize other tactics (San Miguel 1987:81).

Litigation was not used again until 1945, when LULAC came to the aid of several Mexican Americans who were challenging the segregation of Spanish-speaking pupils in Orange County, California. LULAC alleged denial of equal protection; a favorable ruling was obtained and upheld in the Circuit Court of Appeals (*Mendez v. Westminster School District* 1946, 1947). For the first time in history a federal court found segregation of Mexican Americans in public schools to be a violation of state law and a denial of the equal protection clause of the US Constitution. This latter finding meant the decision was relevant to Mexican Americans elsewhere. Thus, the attorney general of Texas issued an opinion banning segregation of Mexican American students except in cases of "language deficiencies and other individual needs and aptitudes demonstrated by examination or properly conducted tests . . . through the first three grades" (quoted in San Miguel 1987:120). The amount of actual change, however, varied. In Texas, with the absence of implementation guidelines, segregation continued. In California, many school systems desegregated, but de facto segregation in large urban areas led one observer to suggest that Mexican American students in California were more segregated in 1973 than they had been prior to *Mendez* in 1947 (Wollenberg 1978:132–34).

The legal battle shifted back to Texas in 1948. LULAC, in conjunction with a newly organized group of Hispanic World War II veterans, the American GI Forum, supported a lawsuit by several Mexican American parents charging officials in several central Texas school districts with unconstitutional segregation. The decision in this case, *Delgado et al. v. Bastrop Independent School District of Bastrop County et al.* (1948), enjoined local school officials from segregating Mexican American students. The decision in *Delgado* went beyond the one in *Mendez* to clarify that segregation of Mexican American students, even in the absence of articulated regulations or policies, was not permissible. The decision also held state school officials responsible for "condoning or aiding" the segregation of Mexican Americans. Unlike the aftermath of *Mendez,* implementation guidelines were issued by the state superintendent of public instruction,[1] but the results were much the same—massive noncompliance. When pressure from the Mexican American community convinced the state superintendent to withdraw the accreditation of the noncompliant Del Rio school district, the state legislature abolished that position and appointed another person to the newly created position of commissioner of education. It should be no surprise that the new commissioner was less than energetic about dismantling the dual schools for Mexican Americans and Anglos; in fact, his first decision was to reverse the disaccreditation of the Del Rio schools (San Miguel 1987:125–30).[2]

Throughout the 1950s—particularly after the *Brown* decision struck down segregation of blacks—cases were brought before the judiciary, occasionally resulting in a favorable decision or settlement. In *Hernandez v. Driscoll Consolidated Independent School District* (1957), the court found that Hispanics had been unconstitutionally assigned to separate classes on the basis of ancestry, but it allowed them to be assigned to such classes if they lacked English language skills.[3] The actual dismantling of dual schools for Anglos and Mexican Americans was rare, and litigation was again temporarily abandoned as a tactic by Hispanic interest groups because of its perceived futility (Rangel and Alcala 1972:345).

Litigation was revived as a major tactic in support of equal educational opportunity for Mexican Americans with the formation of the Mexican American Legal Defense and Education Fund (MALDEF) in 1968 (O'Connor and Epstein 1984). MALDEF participated in litigation that covered a wide range of issues, but education was an important focus.

The type of education litigation most frequently undertaken sought to eliminate segregated schools. Segregation was a necessary focus for MALDEF because OCR, the federal government's school desegregation enforcement agency, had originally treated Hispanics as whites for desegregation purposes; thus, they could remain segregated without arousing federal interest. In addition, local school districts could send both black and Hispanics students to the same schools to achieve some "desegregation," leaving other schools all Anglo (Rangel and Alcala 1972:365–72).

This policy changed formally in 1970, when Stanley Pottinger of OCR announced that the agency would henceforth be concerned with discrimination on the basis of national origin. As this applied to school districts, the memo stated, "Where inability to speak and understand the English language excludes national origin minority group children from effective participation in the educational program offered by a school district, the district must take affirmative steps to rectify the language deficiency in order to open its instructional program to these students" (quoted in Weinberg 1977:287).

A second weapon MALDEF needed in the fight against segregation was provided by the courts in *Cisneros v. Corpus Christi Independent School District* (1970). In this case, which was not filed by MALDEF, the plaintiffs asked the court to apply the principles of *Brown* to Mexican Americans. Such a finding would require that Mexican Americans be recognized by the courts as a separate class. The US District Court obliged, and for the first time in history, Mexican Americans were declared to be an identifiable group within public school systems and were protected by the Fourteenth Amendment.

The thrill of victory was short-lived, however, because that same month the Fifth Circuit Court of Appeals handed down a decision in the Houston desegregation case that allowed local authorities to treat Mexican Americans as whites for desegregation purposes, leaving Anglos unaffected by the process (*Ross v. Eckels* 1970). Another decision allowed school officials in Miami to consider Cubans as whites for desegregation purposes (Orfield 1978:203). Thus, the task facing MALDEF was to obtain higher court acceptance of the *Cisneros* decision. In pursuit of this goal, MALDEF filed amicus curiae briefs in a number of Mexican American school desegregation cases pending before the Fifth Circuit. MALDEF's position was basically that "we want to know where we stand" (quoted in San Miguel 1987:180).

The Fifth Circuit, in appeals from Corpus Christi and Austin cases, found that Mexican Americans were an identifiable group and that they had been denied their constitutional rights in these instances (*Cisneros v. Corpus Christi Independent School District* 1971; *United States v. Texas Education Agency* 1972). MALDEF obtained a victory, but the waters were still muddy. An intracircuit difference of opinion existed that had to be resolved.

The resolution came in *Keyes v. School District No. 1,* the Denver desegregation case decided in 1973. The decision in this case, which had been filed by blacks, required that the court take a position on the status of Mexican Americans. Denver had significant populations of blacks, Anglos, and Hispanics, so the court had either to lump Hispanics with Anglos or to recognize Hispanics as a separate group. The latter choice would have led to the conclusion that Hispanics also had been illegally segregated and would have required a plan to desegregate them as well. The US Supreme Court decided that Mexican Americans were an identifiable minority group and that they were constitutionally entitled to recognition as such for desegregation purposes (*Keyes v. School District No. 1, Denver, Colorado* 1973). School officials in systems found to be unconstitutionally segregated could not treat Hispanics as whites for the purpose of desegregation. Subsequent decisions extended the logic of *Keyes* to Puerto Ricans in New York and Boston (*Hart v. Community School Board of Brooklyn District #2* 1974:733; *Morgan v. Hennigan* 1974:415).

The *Keyes* case did not spawn an abundance of Hispanic desegregation. Even though Hispanics as a whole were more segregated than blacks in the mid-1970s (National Institute of Education 1977; Orfield 1978:205–6), MALDEF turned its attention from desegregation to other methods of achieving equal educational opportunities. The remedy MALDEF stressed in its fight was **bilingual education**—the idea that non-English-speaking students should be taught in their native language or should be taught English. But the legal groundwork for movement in bilingual education was laid not by Hispanics but by Asians.

Asians

The situation of Asians in US education systems has generally been one of discrimination. For example, in *Tape v. Hurley* (66 Cal. 473 [1885]) the parents of Mamie Tape, a seven-year-old US-born Chinese American, sued the San Francisco School Board because Mamie was denied entrance to Spring Valley public school because of her race. The California Supreme Court ruled that it was unconstitutional to deny "a child of Chinese parents entrance to public schools" based on the Fourteenth Amendment, but it stayed silent on "separate but equal." The San Francisco School Board responded by building a separate school for Asians, a so-called Oriental school. In a later case, the US Supreme Court, in *Gong Lum v. Rice* (1927), upheld Mississippi's exclusion of Asian Americans from white schools. School segregation did not exist only to separate blacks from whites but to separate Asians from whites as well.

Given the population concentrations of Asians, their situation can best be exemplified by the history of Chinese Americans in San Francisco schools. As soon as there was a significant number of Chinese taxpayers in San Francisco, the Chinese community pressed local authorities to fund public education for their children. Only when the number of Chinese youths increased to one that could not be ignored did the local school board respond, and then it provided a segregated education. Even under these conditions, Americanization was remarkably successful. But obtaining access for Chinese children to the education system required a constant struggle with state and local legislative and education agencies from the mid-nineteenth century onward (Low 1982).

More dramatic than legislation or administrative action in its impact on policy was a case filed on behalf of Chinese students in San Francisco. In *Lau v. Nichols* (1974), the US Supreme Court required that school districts "take affirmative steps to rectify the language deficiency [of national origin minority students] . . . to open [their] instructional program[s] to these students." The court found that the failure of school districts to provide non-English-speaking students—in this case 2,800 Chinese students—with instruction they could understand denied them their right to an equal educational opportunity. The court required that the school district take action but stopped short of mandating bilingual education.

American Indians

US educational policy toward American Indians since the nineteenth century had been to create separate boarding schools, removing children from their home areas to see that they received a "proper" education. Although approximately seventy of these schools still exist, policy has changed considerably. In 1969, a Special Senate Subcommittee on Indian Education found that "national policies for educating American Indians are a failure of major proportions. They have not offered Indian children—either in years past or today—an educational opportunity anywhere near equal to that offered the great bulk of American children" (US Senate 1969:163). Although nothing was done immediately to address this situation, the Indian Education Act of 1972 increased funding for Indian education, and the Indian Self-Determination and Education Assistance Act of 1975 and the Education Amendments Act of 1978 sought to promote "Indian control of Indian affairs in all matters relating to education" (25 US Code § 2010). Today, approximately 80 percent of American Indian schoolchildren attend public schools in the communities in which they live.

American Indian children are also covered by the *Lau* decision. Rather than attempting to eliminate the use of tribal languages, in seventeen states, bilingual education programs are offered to American Indian children who speak only their tribal language. Even where full-fledged bilingual/bicultural programs have not been required, tutors have been provided for such children (*Guadalupe Organization, Inc. v. Tempe Elementary School District* 1978).

Continuing Issues

With the provision of equal educational opportunity left in the hands of the same local officials who had operated dual school systems, we should not be surprised that discrimination continues. Three issues—bilingual education, re-segregation, and second-generation discrimination—demand attention.

Bilingual Education. In the United States, bilingual education refers to pedagogical approaches in the classroom that involve using the native languages of English language learners (ELLs) for instruction, although teaching English is one of the main goals of every bilingual program (National Association for Bilingual Education 2016). The US Department of Education's Office of English Language Acquisition (OELA) defines bilingual education programs as programs that "feature instruction in both English and a partner language" and cater to students with limited English proficiency (US Department of Education 2015: viii, 77). Even though bilingualism was given its impetus by litigation involving Chinese students, Hispanics are clearly the largest group of potential beneficiaries. In the late 1970s, data from the National Center for Education Statistics indicated that 70 percent of the estimated 3.6 million children in the United States with limited English proficiency were Latino (National Center for Education Statistics 1978).

Problems with implementing bilingual education programs quickly became apparent soon after these programs were implemented. MALDEF's plan for a bilingual/bicultural educational program in a desegregated Denver school system was rejected as working at cross-purposes with desegregation: "Bilingual education . . . is not a *substitute* for desegregation" (*Keyes v. School District No. 1, Denver, Colorado* 1973:480; emphasis in the original). Although bilingual programs could be part of a remedy for unconstitutional segregation, the court did not believe they could be a remedy in and of themselves (Fernández and Guskin 1981:113). Thereafter, court decisions generally chose between desegregation—that is, dispersing students throughout a school system—and bilingual programs, which seemed to promote segregation based on language or national origin (for an example of the latter, see *Serna v. Portales Municipal Schools* 1974), although in some cases the court did adopt a bilingual education plan as part of a remedy for segregation (see *Bradley v. Milliken* 1975:1144).

Although MALDEF remained nominally committed to both desegregation and bilingualism (Orfield 1978:211–14), it emphasized the establishment of bilingual classes. Hispanic students boycotting East Los Angeles high schools in 1968 asked for bilingual programs rather than desegregation (Wollenberg 1978:134–35). And when OCR struck at discrimination against Hispanics, bilingualism was often the preferred remedy, even if segregation remained (Orfield 1978:207).

In recent years, a numbers of states have passed legislation that did not support bilingual education. In 1998 California passed Proposition 227 eliminating bilingual education; Arizona passed Proposition 203 in 2000 eliminating instruction of students in any language besides English; the Colorado English for the Children Initiative was passed in 2001, similar to Proposition 227 in California and Proposition 203 in Arizona; and in 2002 over two-thirds of Massachusetts voters supported the Massachusetts English Language Education in Public Schools Initiative (also known as Question 2 on the November 2002 ballot) which replaced bilingual programs with a yearlong English immersion program (University of Michigan 2005; *Ballotpedia* 2016).

In 2009, the US Supreme Court issued a ruling in *Horne v. Flores* on Arizona's state funding of programs serving English language learners. The majority opinion in this case concluded that "research on ELL instruction and findings by the State Department of Education support the view that [structured English immersion] SEI is significantly more effective than bilingual education" (*Horne v. Flores* 2009).

According to the National Center for Education Statistics (2016), between 2013 and 2014 an estimated 4.5 million public school students were English language learners; this number translates to about 9.3 percent of public school attendees. The ten most commonly reported home languages of English language learner students were Spanish/Castilian, Arabic, Chinese, English, Vietnamese, Hmong, Haitian/Haitian Creole, Somali, Russian, and Korean. Students from Spanish-speaking homes make up the largest percent of ELL students by far. Nearly 3.8 million students who are English language learners have Spanish as their home language, representing 76.5 percent of all ELL students and approximately 7.7 percent of all public K–12 students (National Center for Education Statistics 2016).

The Puerto Rican Legal Defense and Education Fund (PRLDEF), a relative latecomer to Hispanics' civil rights struggle, never argued for desegregation. Perhaps because language and culture are more salient for Puerto Ricans, and perhaps because Puerto Ricans are concentrated in urban areas where desegregation is impractical because of the scarcity of Anglos, bilingualism was the organization's primary goal from the beginning. PRLDEF sued or intervened in cases in New York City; New Jersey; Boston; Wilmington, Delaware; Buffalo; Philadelphia; and Waterbury, Connecticut. It negotiated an out-of-court settlement to establish the nation's largest bilingual education program in the New York City school system (Orfield 1978:211–17). The general thrust of legal intervention had become even more specific by the late 1970s. When Hispanic legal organizations took action, they usually intervened in cases at the remedy stage for or in defense of bilingual programs.

In the wake of *Lau,* OCR used its regulatory authority to require that school districts test non-English-speaking students and place them in bilingual education programs. Despite provisions designed to prevent the "existence of racially/ethnically identifiable classes" within such programs (Teitelbaum and Hiller 1977:160), segregation remains common. Segregated bilingual programs are prevalent because

1. affected students normally attend schools that have considerable segregation.

2. although OCR has brought heavy enforcement pressure on school systems to provide bilingualism, it has done virtually nothing about desegregation.

3. the regulations in the various programs are filled with loopholes that are so large they make a mockery of the policy statements about segregation. The regulations permit segregating groups defined by linguistic ability when local school officials say doing so is educationally necessary.

As Orfield (1978) notes: "In practice there has been almost routine segregation at the local level and no federal enforcement of integration policies."

Resegregation. Blatant segregation remained the policy in some "desegregated" school systems—within classrooms (sometimes reinforced by room dividers), on buses, in lunchrooms, and in extracurricular activities (American Friends Service Committee et al. 1970). But these overt practices gradually stopped as a result of litigation or simply because of the inconvenience of maintaining such awkward policies.

More recent evidence, however, suggests that resegregation is occurring. Southern schools were the most fully desegregated schools in the nation by fall 1970, and the level of integration remained fairly stable until 1988. But after that date, racial segregation began to increase once again. The segregation of Latino students is also on the rise. During the 1991–1992 school year, almost two-thirds (66 percent) of black students and almost three-fourths (73.4 percent) of Latino students attended predominately minority schools. Slightly more than one-third of both groups (33.9 percent of blacks, 34 percent of Latinos) attended schools with a greater than 90 percent minority enrollment. Put another way, the typical black student attended a school with a 34.4 percent white enrollment; the typical Latino student attended a school with a 31.2 percent white enrollment (Orfield et al. 1993).

In 2016, data released by the Government Accountability Office (GAO) indicated that schools in the United States were resegregating, further isolating minority students from affluent white students. Moreover, the number of high-poverty schools serving black and Hispanic children more than doubled between 2001 and 2014 (Brown 2016). The GAO found that the percentage of all K–12 public schools that had high percentages (between 75 to 100 percent) of poor black and Hispanic students increased from 9 percent during the 2000–2001 school year to 16 percent during the 2013–2014 academic year (GAO 2016).

Second-Generation Discrimination. Even if schools are desegregated, such desegregation is not necessarily synonymous with the provision of equal educational opportunity. The "quality of desegregation varies as much as [the] quantity" (Hochschild 1984:33). More invidious has been the rise of more subtle means of minimizing interracial contact, which we refer to collectively as **second-generation discrimination**. Often in conjunction with desegregation, school systems have adopted or expanded the scope of ability grouping of students and have concentrated minority students in lower-level academic groups (Meier, Stewart, and England 1989). Such racial concentration might be justified as remedial action for the provision of inferior education in segregated schools, but the evidence from education research shows that "minority students are highly overrepresented in a situation that perpetuates their disadvantage. . . . [They] are resegregated, provided with an inferior educational experience compared to that of their peers, stigmatized by staff and other students—in short, placed in learning environments that do little to close the gap in minority-majority achievement levels" (Simmons and Brady 1981:132).

Noguera (2007) suggests that, in some ways, educational practices connected to second-generation discrimination are a by-product of the *Brown v. Board of Education* Supreme Court decision. These educational practices include tracking (which can limit minority students from enrolling in more academically rigorous classes), labeling and sorting through testing, as well as inequitable disciplinary practices where school districts tend to subject minority students to disproportionate amounts of punishment (Noguera 2007: 2–3).

Disciplinary practices can be used for purposes other than maintaining order and authority. Such practices are sometimes "a mere pretense for punishing a child for other reasons," including being black, Hispanic, or poor (Children's Defense Fund 1974:130, also 1975). "Black students are punished for offenses allowed white students or given heavier penalties for similar offenses" (Eyler, Cook, and Ward 1983:144).

AFFIRMATIVE ACTION IN EMPLOYMENT

Affirmative action is one of the most controversial subjects in American politics today. In many ways, this controversy arises from the distinction between individual and institutional racism. Equal opportunity is a concept that treats individuals only as individuals, assumes that if one is discriminated against it is out of prejudice, and assumes that victims of discrimination will act on their own behalf in reaction to this discrimination. Affirmative action, "the expenditure of energy or resources by an organization in the quest for equality among individuals from different discernible groups" (Crosby 2004:5), considers individuals as representatives of demographic groups, allows for the possibility that discrimination may be an effect of nonintentional or unconscious practices, and promotes a proactive stance against discrimination (Crosby 2004).

The laws and regulations that concern affirmative action at the federal level—between 150 and 200 in number (Dale 1995)—can be traced back to the 1960s. Presidents Kennedy and Johnson used the term in executive orders forbidding discrimination in federally financed construction and on work sites of federal contractors, but its exact meaning was unclear. When Congress weighed in with legislation to establish a federal presence as an antidiscrimination regulator in the private labor market with the inclusion of Title VII of the 1964 Civil Rights Act, it specifically rejected "preferential treatment to any individual or group on account of an imbalance which may exist with respect to the total number or percentage of persons of any race . . . employed by any employer . . . in comparison with the total number or percentage of persons of such race . . . in any . . . or in the available workforce in any community." The specification of *what* was required was left to an agency, the Office of Federal Contract Compliance Programs (OFCCP), which issued guidelines stating:

> A prerequisite to the development of a satisfactory affirmative action program is the identification and analysis of problem areas inherent in minority employment and an evaluation of opportunities for utilization of

minority group personnel. The program shall provide in detail for specific steps to guarantee equal employment opportunities keyed to the problems and needs of members of minority groups, including, when there are deficiencies, the development of specific goals and timetables for the prompt achievement of full and equal employment opportunities. (US Commission on Civil Rights 1971:173)

The move toward increased reliance upon statistical evidence and mandatory goals and timetables received a push from—of all sources—Republican President Richard Nixon. Seeking short-term political advantage, Nixon championed the "Philadelphia Plan" for desegregating that city's trade unions as a model for affirmative action. The plan, which required numerical evidence of minority representation, appealed to Nixon as a way of driving a wedge between two of the Democratic Party's prime constituencies: organized labor and members of minority groups. Thus, over the opposition of both conservative Republicans and Southern Democrats, Nixon successfully lobbied for a plan that included racial job quotas (Graham 1990:301–21; Belz 1991:32; Skrentny 1996:182).

The US Supreme Court added to the mix by issuing an opinion in 1971 in *Griggs v. Duke Power Co.* In this case, the plaintiffs, black employees, challenged the company's use of tests that disproportionately screened out blacks for hiring and promotion but that had no demonstrable relationship to job performance. A unanimous court ruled that if a test or qualification requirement disproportionately disqualified minorities, the employer could be compelled to defend it as a bona fide occupational qualification. This allowed plaintiffs to prevail in employment discrimination cases without proving intent. An easy way for an employer to reduce the possibility of a suit was to make sure that minority group members were not disproportionately underrepresented.

Public Reaction to Affirmative Action

Public acceptance of the idea of affirmative action, as expressed in public opinion polls, has been erratic, often depending upon the wording of the question. Only when respondents are assured that affirmative action does not mean "rigid quotas" do we find support exceeding 50 percent for affirmative action in the job market (Steeh and Krysan 1996). At least part of the opposition to affirmative action arises from the tendency of whites to believe that even if blacks have been discriminated against in the past, they no longer face such impediments. Thus, preferences are viewed as fundamentally unfair (Kluegel and Smith 1986:185).

Incrementalism and Affirmative Action

Despite partisan changes in presidential administrations, the basic infrastructure for applying affirmative action has remained intact. Perhaps the most likely source for nonincremental change, interestingly enough, is from the branch of government thought to be most insulated from popular opinion—the courts. The US Supreme Court, in 1989, issued two opinions that seemed to undermine affirmative action policy as it had developed. In *Ward's Cove Packing v. Atonio* the court ruled that it was insufficient for plaintiffs in job discrimination cases to demonstrate a statistical disparity in minority employment. They must also link the disparity to a specific employment practice or practices alleged to cause the disparity. In the second case, *Richmond v. Croson,* the court said that before a city could designate a certain amount of its contract work to be "set aside" for minority-owned firms, it must show that the program was narrowly tailored, temporary, and linked to established prior discrimination. These decisions threatened to place a greater burden of proof on plaintiffs in affirmative action litigation. Congress, however, reacted with the Civil Rights Act of 1991, a clear effort to counteract the *Ward's Cove* decision. Still, the sentiment against quotas is strong enough to include language in the act forbidding its interpretation to "require, encourage, or permit an employer to adopt hiring or promotion quotas on the basis of race, color, religion, sex, or national origin, and the use of such quotas shall be deemed to be an unlawful employment practice" (*Congressional Quarterly* 1991:255).

The Continuing Saga of Affirmative Action

Change seldom occurs in civil rights policy without presidential or judicial involvement, and President Clinton offered at least rhetorical support for affirmative action. Furthermore, a report commissioned by that president set out the parameters of what is to be considered a fair affirmative action program:

1. The avoidance of quotas;
2. An effort to remedy problems first with race-neutral options;
3. Flexibility in the use of race-conscious measures;
4. A program lasting only as long as needed; and
5. Demonstration that the effect on nonminorities is "sufficiently small and diffuse so as not to unduly burden their opportunities" (White House 1995).

There have been a number of lawsuits and complaints related to affirmative action policies in the United States in recent years. The Supreme Court, in 2003, handed down two highly publicized affirmative action decisions, *Gratz v. Bollinger* and *Grutter v. Bollinger,* both related to higher education. In the former, dealing with undergraduate admissions to the University of Michigan, the court ruled that by awarding an automatic 20 points (out of 150) to applicants who attended a predominantly minority high school or who were minority group members themselves, the university had committed impermissible racial or ethnic discrimination. On the other hand, in the *Grutter* case, the court upheld the holistic approach of the University of Michigan Law School in considering all aspects of an individual applicant and stressed the importance of having a critical mass of minority students as important to creating an environment that promotes free expression and ends racial stereotypes.

In 2006, Jian Li, a Chinese American student at Yale University, filed a civil rights complaint with the US Department of Education's Office for Civil Rights after not gaining admission to Princeton University and other Ivy League institutions, despite graduating at the top 1 percent of his class and having perfect SAT scores (de Vise 2012).

A nonprofit group called Students for Fair Admissions filed a lawsuit against Harvard University in 2014, alleging that the university discriminates against Asian American applicants because of admissions policies that seek to maintain racial quotas (Dixon 2016). A similar suit was filed against the University of North Carolina in the US District Court for the Middle District of North Carolina (Stancill 2015). Again, in May 2015, a coalition of Asian American organizations filed a federal complaint with the US Department of Education's Office for Civil Rights against Harvard University, contending that the institution discriminated against Asian American students in its admission process (Marcin 2015).

In a landmark case in June 2016, the Supreme Court handed down a 4–3 decision in *Fisher v. the University of Texas* (*Fisher II*), rejecting a challenge to the constitutionality of the race-conscious admissions program at the University of Texas at Austin (SCOTUSblog 2016). The case concerned whether the Court of Appeals for the Fifth Circuit had correctly applied strict scrutiny to the University of Texas at Austin's undergraduate admissions policy, in accordance with *Fisher v. University of Texas* (2013) in terms of the constitutionality of the university's admissions program, and included a warning to other universities regarding the ability of their race-sensitive admissions programs to actually pass constitutional muster (Liptak 2016). President Obama commended the court on its decision to uphold "the basic notion that diversity is an important value in [the United States]," and Harvard Law professor Lawrence H. Tribe noted: "No decision since *Brown v. Board of Education* has been as important as *Fisher* will prove to be in the long history of racial inclusion and educational diversity" (Liptak 2016).

The Fisher case had first gone before the Supreme Court three years prior to the 2016 ruling (*Fisher v. University of Texas*, 570 US 2013), and the Supreme Court voided a ruling by the US Court of Appeals for the Fifth Circuit in favor of the university on the basis that the lower appellate court had not applied strict scrutiny in its admissions program. The case concerned petitioner Abigail Fisher, who was denied admission to the university under Texas's Top Ten Percent Law. This plan gives automatic admission to students who finish in the top 10 percent of their high school class. Fisher, who is white, was not in the top 10 percent of her high school graduating class, and was denied admission, but argued that the university's admission plan discriminated against her because of her race, that it was inconsistent with *Grutter v. Bollinger*, and that the court should overturn its previous decision.

Supporters of affirmative action have hailed the *Fisher* decision as a landmark case promoting diversity, while some opponents decry the Supreme Court's ruling, suggesting that students admitted under diversity quotas are more likely to fail tests and tend to drop out of school (Liptak 2016; Barone 2016). In his dissent, Justice Clarence Thomas, who opposes affirmative action policies, wrote that "a State's use of race in higher education admission decisions is categorically prohibited by the Equal Protection Clause" (*Fisher v. University of Texas at Austin* 2016).

It is clear that the issue will not disappear from the national political agenda. President Bush, although indicating his opposition to affirmative action but his support for what he refers to as "affirmative access," adopted the concept in his signature education legislation—the No Child Left Behind Act of 2001. Section 441, b(2)(G) of the law calls for including "information [in reports on the effectiveness of the legislation] on special groups, including whenever feasible information collected, cross tabulated, compared, and reported by race, ethnicity, socioeconomic status, gender, disability, and limited English proficiency." President Obama's administration filed an amicus curiae brief on behalf of the University of Texas. As long as affirmative action programs are associated in the popular mind with quotas, they will serve valuable political functions, but the concept is not foreign to public policymaking.

CONCLUSION

This chapter provides a glimpse of the different stages of the public policymaking process and the interaction of the various institutional actors, operating within a federal system, in that process. The crucial hurdle for racial and ethnic minority groups has been getting issues placed on the agenda of a government institution, and the presence of minority group representatives within an institution can facilitate that step. Some progress has been made in increasing minority group representation across institutions at all levels of government. We do not know if this progress will continue under the Trump administration and its view of the federal bureaucracy.

The case study of equal educational opportunity policy reveals the evolution of the policy problem. The problem was originally defined as constituting the legally mandated racial segregation of black and white students in Southern schools. It was presumed that once black and white students entered the same school buildings, the equal educational opportunity problem would be solved. Yet it was discovered that students of other racial and ethnic groups were also denied this opportunity.

The complexity of the American public policymaking system is also illustrated here. The courts, prodded by interest groups, took the lead in defining the problem and articulating a policy, but they found themselves so far ahead of the executive and legislative branches that their decisions could not be implemented. The courts provided a forum in which the pro–civil rights coalition could appeal to "right" rather than to political power. And the conflict could be overt because the US legal system is adversarial yet muted because the format of the conflict is stylized.

Changes external to the policy subsystem were definitely of major importance in the outcome of the conflict. If E. E. Schattschneider is correct that "the *audience* determines the outcome of a fight" (1960:2; emphasis in the original), then the mass media served to change immensely the size and composition of that audience. The expansion of the availability and use of mass media meant the audience for the conflict was no longer strictly local and that it was more independently informed than had been the case when similar issues had previously been decided.

Local officials, who had to implement the policy change within the federal system, were able to thwart a momentous Supreme Court decision. Only when the legislature finally adopted a supportive policy, thus empowering the bureaucracy to participate in implementation, did significant policy change occur.

The accomplishments of those who fought the battles are monumental. Yet by defining the policy problem in terms of segregation, a solution was also defined: When schools were desegregated, success would be achieved. Subsequent experience has shown dramatically that segregated schools were only the symptom, not the disease. But in the minds of many, when schools in which de jure discrimination had existed were desegregated, it was time to focus on other policy problems. The results of this evolution of the policy process include an inertia and a lack of consensus about whether equal educational opportunity is being provided in this country and how one would recognize such opportunity if one saw it.

The consideration of affirmative action likewise shows the importance of framing an issue and the proposed solutions. Very different levels of public support for affirmative action can be attained by changing how one defines the term or the program. Thus, the contest between proponents and opponents of affirmative action is a struggle over presentation, which affects the legitimacy of the policy adopted. Change in civil rights policy has been erratic and time consuming and will continue to be so.

- -

DISCUSSION QUESTIONS

1. By what process is public policy made, and what potential and what pitfalls does this process have for members of racial and ethnic minority groups?

2. Why is access to the policy process important for the continued incorporation of racial groups into the political system?

3. Because we are all affected by public policy, we are all "targets" of public policymaking. Why might being such a target be of greater concern to a member of a racial or an ethnic minority group than to a member of a majority group?

4. Which of the major political institutions do you think has the greatest impact on public policies that affect minority group members? Defend your position.

5. What has been the effect of Shirley Chisholm's 1972 presidential bid, Jesse Jackson's two presidential campaigns, and Carol Moseley Braun's and Al Sharpton's forays into the 2004 presidential primaries on the presidential selection process? Did these campaigns lay the groundwork for the election of President Barack Obama? On the access of racial minorities to the political system? Or has there been little or no change as a result of these campaigns? Give examples for your position.

6. Why should anyone be concerned about whether members of racial and ethnic minority groups are represented in the executive, legislative, and judicial branches of government?

7. What are the advantages and disadvantages of the federal system of government for members of racial and ethnic minority groups?

8. Fierce political battles have been fought in attempts to attain equal educational opportunity. Why is this goal considered to be so important? What has been achieved? What is left to be accomplished?

9. List the various definitions of affirmative action and discuss the implications of each definition for policymaking and public support.

- -

NOTES

1 These regulations clearly noted that segregation was still mandated for "members of the Negro race or persons of Negro ancestry" but not for "members of any other race" (quoted in San Miguel 1987:126).

2 In Arizona, a similar case banned the segregation of Mexican American students in 1951 (see *Gonzales v. Sheely*).

3 The plaintiffs in this case challenged the local school board's practice of segregating Mexican American students for the first two grades and requiring these students to spend four years in these grades regardless of their academic achievement. Thus, Mexican American youngsters could not enter the third grade until their fifth year of school. The school board countersued, asking that the parents of the children involved in the suit be enjoined from speaking any language other than English in the presence of school-age children and that they keep their children from associating with anyone who did not speak English. The federal judge dismissed the defendants' counterclaim in a terse footnote.

► CHAPTER 5

Intersectional Identity in Racial and Ethnic Politics

On a Delta Air Lines flight from Detroit, Michigan, to Chicago, Illinois, on October 9, 2016, a man became unresponsive and the flight crew indicated to passengers that they needed assistance from physicians or nurses. A young black female physician sitting two rows back stood up to help. She later reported that the flight attendant denied her attempts to provide medical assistance, saying "Oh, no, sweetie, put your hand down, we are looking for actual physicians or nurses or some type of medical personnel. We don't have time to talk to you." The flight attendant eventually asked for the black female physician's credentials, but as the doctor was explaining her experience, a white man came forward, also claiming to be a doctor. The black female physician reported that the flight attendant then told her, "Thanks for your help but he can help us, and he has his credentials," although it appeared he did not produce any documentation, which physicians rarely carry outside of a medical setting. Initially Delta Air Lines issued a statement largely defending the actions of the flight attendant and claiming their policy was to require medical credentials. After numerous responses from physicians of color indicating that this sort of disbelief that they are doctors occurs frequently, Delta Air Lines altered its policy so as to no longer require credentialing while in flight (Johnson 2016).

—CHICAGO, ILLINOIS, OCTOBER–DECEMBER 2016

In Chapter 3, we noted that group identity is an important aspect of political attitude formation and political participation, and we examined this in the context of race and ethnicity. The development of race as a salient identity is connected to the concept of white superiority. This concept of superiority developed based on the need to create a social hierarchy that would provide stability to the US socioeconomic/class-based system, given the purported American ideals of equality of "mankind," as well as "liberty and justice for all." By developing a racialized system of social hierarchy, the elites largely eliminated the ability of multiracial coalitions of people at lower levels of the socioeconomic scale to form. This effectively maintained an elite ruling class that would withstand democratic demands regarding the interests of lower classes, given that their potential numbers were diminished by the decreased ability to interact and cooperate across racial lines. Separating people on the basis of appearance and family lineage (the latter specifically in the case of African slaves) became an economic, political, and social imperative. In order to maintain this separation, American society developed lasting narratives of biological inferiority to explain how nonwhite people are all essentially the same, and not capable of or deserving of the same opportunities for advancement and success available to all white Americans. This narrative of "sameness," and the codification of prohibiting minorities from moving out of marginalized positions in society, has allowed for the stripping of humanity and individuality from members of these groups both in terms of public perceptions and political realities.

The societal perception and treatment of members of minority groups, especially African Americans, as all the same, and innately different from the broader white American society, has resulted in the negative effect of separating these groups from one of the nation's most important core values: individualism (Kinder and Mendelberg 2000). It has also led to the notion that these minority groups do not believe in engaging in their own hard work as individuals, which would then determine their life outcomes, thus creating a justification for a significant race-based inequality gap.[1] This flawed viewpoint, which is necessary for the maintenance of the US racial hierarchy, is one that must be challenged and deconstructed in order to provide a clearer understanding of how race and ethnicity operate within the American political system. One important way to do this is to examine identity and its link to politics through an *intersectional* lens.

This chapter will delve more deeply into the intricacies of sociopolitical topics concerning racial and ethnic minority groups by working to broaden the traditionally accepted, unidimensional approach to the examination of identity politics. Central to this chapter is the concept of **intersectional identity**, the idea that salient identity dimensions—race, ethnicity, gender, physical ability, sexuality, class, and religion—are inextricably linked. The existence of multiple, linked salient identities leads to the development of distinctive identity groups that have their own unique experiences, perspectives, and ideologies, which influence how members of those groups connect to and work both within and outside of the American political system. Given the sheer volume of topics that can be examined in the area of intersectional identity and racial/ethnic minority politics, only a few can be examined herein, in order to illustrate the concept and how it operates within the American political system. Consequently, this examination is focused and illustrative, rather than exhaustive; this is a call for the continual development of nuanced and intersectional investigations into how the political system influences racial and ethnic minorities, as well as how these groups approach the system. Given the salience of race/ethnicity and gender as dimensions of identity in the United States, much of the focus of this chapter is on nonwhite women.

INTERSECTIONALITY: IDENTITY ALONG MULTIPLE DIMENSIONS

People who are racial and ethnic minorities cannot and should not be viewed as universally the same solely based on racial and/or ethnic identity. Treating racial and ethnic groups as monolithic is inadequate for developing a clear understanding of how American society views and treats these groups individually, collectively, and systemically. Further, this approach continues the tradition of overly simplified categorization and essentialization of people in a way that strips them of humanity and individuality. A more useful approach, which we engage throughout this book, is to view racial and ethnic identity as intersectional, meaning that an individual's or group's identity comprise multiple salient dimensions of identity that come together to produce a unique set of circumstances for people within any one identity group (Gay and Tate 1998; Simien and Clawson 2004; Smooth 2006; Simien 2007; Jordan-Zachery 2007; Philpot and Walton 2007; N. Brown 2014).

McClain et al. define **racial group identification** as "an individual's awareness of belonging to a certain group and having a psychological attachment to that group based on a perception of shared beliefs, feelings, interests, and ideas with other group members" (2009: 474). This definition moves beyond mere societal categories and into incorporating the degree to which people internalize and feel attached to those categories. Much of this identification is tied to common experiences with other group members. Racial group identification in the United States is especially salient given the common ways in which race exists as a means for sociopolitical and socioeconomic hierarchy. Perceptions and realities of oppression have necessitated the development of group cohesion, and more specifically, the development of a belief that one's fate is linked to the well-being and life outcomes of the group (Dawson 1994). In turn, this feeling of linked fate can act as a basis for increasing levels of group consciousness. This is especially the case for people who find themselves at the intersection of multiple marginalized identity groups (Hochschild and Weaver 2007; Keating 2009; Moraga and Anzaldúa 2015; Capers and Smith 2016).

A person's life experiences are never solely influenced by one dimension of identity at a time. Nevertheless, we frequently discuss identity in terms of one category at a time—"she is Asian," "I am a woman," "they are rich," and so forth. When identity is examined in this way, a mental picture is formulated based upon the prototypical image of an identity group, which generally corresponds with the most privileged hierarchical identities in other dimensions (and/or those identities that fit most closely with stereotypes about the group in question) (Schneider 2005). For example, the prototypical image for "black" is a heterosexual, cisgendered[2] black male, while the prototypical image for "woman" is a heterosexual, cisgendered white woman. Consequently, the way in which society thinks about various racial and ethnic groups is generally in terms of one nonprivileged identity at a time, such as race, gender, sexuality, or class. This effectively renders people with multiple marginalized identities as invisible and less important to society because they are less frequently considered (King 1988; Crenshaw 1989, 1991; Giddings 1996; Cohen 2003; Hancock 2007; Collins 2008; Purdie-Vaughns and Eibach 2008; Alexander-Floyd 2012; Yamada 2015). Importantly, it is necessary to recognize that these prototypes of unidimensional identity groups are actually *intersectional* in nature—they comprise various salient identities.

The acknowledgment of identity as intersectional is the beginning of how we can turn away from the essentialization of race. Understanding that many different people within any race or ethnic group have a wide variety of experiences and ideologies aids in refuting the idea that race is innate and biological, while simultaneously exposing the social construction of race and ethnicity. This more detailed analysis of race and ethnicity illuminates how these identities have been used to maintain power hierarchies in the United States, both across racial and ethnic groups and within them. The idea that hierarchies exist *within* racial and ethnic groups can be seen in terms of how increased value is placed on lighter skin or more European features across many groups, homosexuality and transgender identity is often denigrated and at times violently policed, individuals at the lower end of the socioeconomic scale are viewed negatively, and women are not as highly valued as men in terms of their social position and political interests. Sexism, classism, ableism, and colorism, among other forms of discrimination, exist within racial and ethnic minority communities, and members of those minority groups suffer the weight of that discrimination at a broader societal level, as well as within their closer identity circles.

Our various salient identities are inextricably linked, and they operate together to form hierarchies that create systems of domination and marginalization (Zinn and Dill 1993).

Much of the foundational academic literature on racial and ethnic groups recognizes the diversity of the individuals within the groups but does not examine directly the differences in experiences, interests, and forms of political engagement by way of an intersectional lens. Rather, it has focused more on the average experiences, ideologies, opinions, and strategies of the most visible sections of these racial and ethnic groups. However, scholars are increasingly utilizing intersectional methods to develop a more nuanced and complete picture of how racial and ethnic minority politics operate. Intersectional identity research concerning race and politics has developed into a robust and diverse body of literature, particularly over the past two decades. Not only are scholars examining the influence of multiple marginalized identities on how people view themselves and how they interact with the political world, but they are also utilizing a multidimensional identity approach as a dynamic analytical tool for examining all facets of racial and ethnic politics, like pinpointing the mechanisms that lead to barriers and advantages for nonwhite women in politics (Hawkesworth 2006; Dill and Zambrana 2009; Brown and Gershon 2016).

The importance of intersectional approaches to the examination of racial and ethnic minorities in the American political system becomes apparent when examining sociopolitical movements and advocacy. Often, the individuals residing at the intersection of multiple oppressed identities are on the frontlines of advocacy on issues that affect their identity- and place-based communities most directly—for example, criminal justice reform, environmental justice, education, health care, and so forth (Pinderhughes 1996; Naples 1998; Dill and Zambrana 2009; Rainey and Johnson 2009). People with multiple oppressed identities have fewer privileges in terms of social, economic, and political power, and so they are less able to rely on some other hierarchy that places them in an elevated status as compared to others within one of their oppressed identity groups. The type of "otherizing," isolation, and exclusion that occurs and the processes of identity formation that play out at these junctures of multiple identities significantly increase the likelihood that these individuals will develop a greater sense of community as well as a greater sense of interest in working to improve sociopolitical and socioeconomic conditions for themselves and those around them. This is based on higher levels of group consciousness connected to their intersectional identities (e.g., poor transgender Asian American women), as well as connected to the broader categories with which they identify (e.g., race, gender, class, and so forth). In order to illuminate how and why this occurs, the next section will examine three dimensions along which intersectional identity is salient for racial and ethnic minorities.[3]

SALIENT DIMENSIONS FOR RACIAL AND ETHNIC INTERSECTIONAL IDENTITIES
Sex/Gender

The Colored Women's Club movement in the late nineteenth and early twentieth centuries demonstrates that sociopolitical activity among women of color is a longstanding tradition (Lee 2008). Black women such as Ida B. Wells-Barnett, Mary Church Terrell, Anna Julia Cooper, and Mary McLeod Bethune, among many other middle-class and affluent organizers, worked to provide aid and education to less fortunate African American women and their children in an attempt to improve the status of blacks throughout the nation, both in terms of direct outcomes for those families and in terms of attempting to alter negative societal stereotyping regarding blacks (Mullane 1993; Robnett 1997). In spite of being prohibited from electoral participation, women of color have been civically engaged in grassroots mobilization and social welfare efforts to improve the status of their groups, which demonstrates a high level of group consciousness (McClain et al. 2009).[4]

On the whole, identity based upon sex allows women to occupy an odd position in society that serves simultaneously as a place of seeming protection combined with a reality of hierarchical domination. Traditionally, society views womanhood as an identity that must be protected and cared for; however, the means for doing so has been connected to the framework of female inferiority. This subordinated position of women as compared to men has placed significant social, economic, and political restrictions on women, and various social movements over the past two centuries have worked to dismantle these limitations. Nevertheless, gender must be understood intersectionally. Societal protections connected to white women have not been and continue to not be extended to racial and ethnic minorities to the same degree due to societal devaluation of these groups. For example, nonwhite women have been particularly vulnerable to sexual assault with no avenues to seek justice, particularly in the face of white male perpetrators. White femininity, especially when connected with middle and upper socioeconomic statuses, continues to be highly valued and to carry the privilege of societal protection. The devaluation of nonwhite women and girls continues to be seen in the area of missing persons and kidnapping cases. There is significant media coverage in cases of missing young white females, but the media rarely covers young black females who are missing, and their cases go largely unnoticed and unsolved (Jiwani and Young 2006; Liebler 2010).

Another example of this abuse, domination, and devaluation of black women comes in the case of Daniel Holtzclaw:

"In Oklahoma, officer Daniel Holtzclaw stopped a 57-year-old grand-mother on her way home from a game of dominoes with friends. He pub-licly strip-searched her, ostensibly looking for drugs, and then forced her to perform oral sex, prompting her to file a complaint. Further investigation uncovered allegations that he had raped and/or sexually assaulted at least 12 other Black women over a period of several years, often in the context of traffic stops. Holtzclaw generally preyed on women with criminal records or those who were caught with drug paraphernalia, which inhibited them from coming forward." (Crenshaw and Ritchie 2015)

Officer Holtzclaw, whose racial/ethnic background is white and Japanese American, specifically targeted vulnerable African American women in the low-income neighborhood he patrolled because he knew that they would have no one to go to in order to report his crimes. His arrest, trial, and conviction in 2015 and 2016 were of particular note because of how rarely this sort of justice actually comes to fruition, given the social and political pressures against these types of convictions. The jury found Holtzclaw guilty of the charges brought forward, and they sentenced him to 263 years in prison. As the pros-ecutor, Lori McConnell, noted in her closing arguments: "He didn't choose CEOs or soccer moms; he chose women he could count on not telling what he was doing. . . . He counted on the fact no one would believe them and no one would care" (Larimer 2016).

The intersection of the marginalized identity points for these women placed them at the mercy of an individual who was largely protected by politi-cal institutions. As noted earlier, these intersectional identities operate as a part of the power-based hierarchical system of inequality that influences racial and ethnic minorities in differing ways, based upon all salient aspects of their identities.

Sexuality and Gender Fluidity

Sexuality and gender fluidity remains a subject of great debate within the United States and continues to be a source of marginalization and hierarchy. While somewhat on the decline in terms of public opinion, heteronormativity remains deeply entrenched within society. Laws and policies both broadening and restricting civil rights and protections for the lesbian, gay, bisexual, transgender, and queer (LGBTQ) community are simultaneously being en-shrined at various levels of government throughout the nation. For example, in *Obergefell v. Hodges* (2015), the Supreme Court ruled that bans on same-sex marriage are unconstitutional; conversely, in 2016 the state legislature in North Carolina pushed through HB2, a law that forces transgender people to use the bathroom that corresponds to the sex on their birth certificate and protects businesses from charges of discrimination on the basis of sexuality. In line with the sentiment behind the latter type of policy, there remains a great deal of stigma and violence that negatively influence the lives of LGBTQ people. This is especially the case in terms of racial and ethnic minorities who are LGBTQ.

Many nonwhite communities traditionally have held high levels of stigma and discrimination against homosexuality and gender fluidity. One way this continues to be apparent is that many people legitimately fear revealing to family, friends, and employers that they are not heterosexual and/or cisgender, as there may be serious familial, economic, and social repercussions, some of which include the threat of violence. Asian American boys are the group that is most reticent to "come out" to their families, because they are apprehensive of backlash and stigmatization (Ahuja and Chlala 2013). This concern is highly justified: People who are LGBTQ are the most likely to be victims of hate crimes (Park and Mykhyalyshyn 2016). Nonwhite LGBTQ people are twice as likely as whites to encounter physical violence, and immigrants who are un-documented are four times more likely to be violently attacked (NCAVP 2016). Additionally, of the transgender murder victims killed on the basis of their identity between 2013 and 2015, an astounding 87 percent were racial and ethnic minorities (HRC and TPOCC 2016). The challenges transgender people encounter in terms of health care, housing, extreme poverty, unemploy-ment, and law enforcement make social, much less political, inclusion ex-tremely difficult (HRC and TPOCC 2016).[5] Nonwhite LGBTQ people also encounter police abuse and sexual assault that often goes unreported (Cren-shaw and Ritchie 2015). These data further demonstrate that individuals with multiple marginalized identities are far more vulnerable within society. Ignor-ing their experiences by way of using a one-dimensional lens to understand the effects of sexuality on sociopolitical outcomes obscures important realities that must be addressed.

The issue of violence against nonwhite LGBTQ people came to the atten-tion of the nation on June 12, 2016, in Orlando, Florida. At around 2 a.m., Omar Mateen, an Afghan American security guard, entered a gay nightclub called Pulse on "Latin Night" and shot and killed forty-nine people, injuring an additional fifty-three. This constituted the largest mass killing on US soil since the September 11, 2001, attacks and the largest mass shooting perpetrated by one individual in the history of the nation. While much attention was paid to his pledge of allegiance to the Islamic State and his claim that he was attacking the United States for its airstrikes in the Middle East, it appears quite likely that this attack was connected with his own struggles to come to terms with his own sexuality. Various individuals came forward to indicate that Mateen had used a gay dating app and had attended the Pulse nightclub on a few occasions (Hennessy-Fiske, Jarvie, and Wilber 2016). His father's negative comments on homosexuality seem to indicate that his coming out would not have been positively received within his family. While some media outlets focused on the terrorist aspects of this case and others focused on the sexuality aspects, few took a deep intersectional approach to examining this tragedy. Approximately 90 percent of the victims were nonwhite, most of whom were LGBTQ. The hatred felt by Mateen expanded beyond any single salient identity; it directly reflected society's devaluation of nonwhites at many different intersections of identity. This attack was not specific to any one group: It targeted LGBTQ people, nonwhites, and America all at once.

Class/Socioeconomic Status

As we discussed at the start of the chapter, elites needing to establish their own superior socioeconomic status (SES) worked to create and solidify the race-based hierarchy that has shaped practically every aspect of American politics throughout the nation's history. Today, SES continues to influence health outcomes, life expectancy, educational opportunities, housing, occupation, and much more (Dill and Zambrana 2009). It can also influence one's likelihood of being more heavily policed, and therefore more heavily penalized, for criminal activity that people across all SES groups engage in at equal proportions, such as drug offenses. Individuals at lower levels of the SES ladder have far fewer educational, occupational, and economic opportunities as compared to those in the middle- and upper-income ranges, thus belying the oft-touted belief of the ease of social mobility—the American Dream. The intersection of race/ethnicity and SES means that many of the aforementioned outcomes that are worsened by lower levels of SES lead to even greater disparities for racial and ethnic minority groups (Dill and Zambrana 2009; Barr 2014). For example, there is a greater wealth gap between racial and ethnic minorities as compared to whites (NWLC 2014; Oliver and Shapiro 2016).

Nonwhite women make up higher percentages of the low-wage workforce than their corresponding male counterparts and constitute nearly half of all women working in these low-wage positions (NWLC 2014). Further, while increasing attention is being paid to the fact that women earn 77 percent of what men in similar positions make, intersectional examination reveals that this figure is specific to white, non-Hispanic women. Black women and Latinas earn 64 percent and 56 percent of what white men earn, respectively (NWLC 2015). These low-wage positions perpetuate cycles of poverty, in that it becomes difficult for these women to work toward middle-class earnings and neighborhoods with strong secondary education systems, in order to provide their families with strong opportunities for the future.

SOCIOPOLITICAL EXPERIENCES WHEN MULTIPLE IDENTITIES INTERSECT
The Criminal Justice System

Racial and ethnic minorities, especially blacks and Latinos, have traditionally been (and continue to be) directly targeted by policy formation and law enforcement that work in concert to increase the perception of these groups as "criminal." In 2014, African American men and women were incarcerated at rates higher than any other racial or ethnic group, followed by Latinos (Carson 2015). Women are often overlooked as inmates, and little attention is paid to their experiences with the criminal justice system. In 2013, black women and Latinas accounted for 81 percent of all police stops of women in New York City (Crenshaw and Ritchie 2015). Interestingly, while proportions of black women and Latinas who are imprisoned remain high on average, they have declined for both groups since 2000, while the imprisonment rate for white women has increased (Mauer 2013). Nevertheless, nonwhite women still constitute 64 percent of women in jails throughout the nation, which means that they are significantly overrepresented as inmates as compared to their proportion of the US population (Swavola, Riley, and Subramanian 2016).

Higher rates of incarceration for any group should not be considered to demonstrate an increased propensity toward criminality but rather should be understood as a complicated reality that is closely connected to the ways in which race-based and class-based hierarchies influence the life trajectories of large groups of people. The rates of incarceration in the United States are based on structural, policy-based systems rather than merely on any individual's activity. Recent attention to the growing system of mass incarceration in the United States has led to greater recognition that the current system is closely connected to the sociopolitical structures surrounding slavery and Jim Crow laws (Alexander 2012). Once slavery was abolished by way of the Thirteenth Amendment, the criminalization of black Americans, particularly black men, through Jim Crow laws became an economic and social imperative in order to maintain the racial order in terms of class, social status, and cheap or free labor (Blackmon 2008). When the Civil Rights Act of 1964 rang the death knell for these laws, legislators turned to policies that made them appear "tough on crime," thus allowing them to build on this stereotypical narrative of black criminality in a way that targeted this group for increased policing, arrests, and sentencing for crimes that were occurring in similar proportions throughout the US population, regardless of race—as especially seen in the "War on Drugs" (Alexander 2012). In investigating the Ferguson, Missouri, police department beginning in 2014, the US Department of Justice (DOJ) found that the law enforcement and municipal court systems specifically focused their efforts on generating revenue from this lower-income area, largely comprising nonwhites. The DOJ report notes aggressive policing tactics, violations of civil liberties, significant racial bias, and harsh monetary penalties for people unable to pay fines and court fees associated with the aggressive policing in the area (DOJ 2015). The tactics used here reflect the ways in which communities of color, especially at lower SES levels, are targeted by law enforcement, thus intensifying financial difficulties, increasing perceptions of crime in these areas, and eroding public safety and trust in political institutions (DOJ 2015).

This racialized targeting of nonwhite communities that political institutions engage in is especially pronounced when understood in the context of class. Poor, nonwhite communities are far less likely to have employment and economic opportunities, thus creating a need for some members of them to turn to drug-based economies in order to provide for themselves and their families. In turn, this illegal activity is far more likely to be heavily monitored and penalized by law enforcement in these communities as compared to others (Alexander 2012). As a consequence, poor people of color are far more likely to be arrested for and convicted of felonies, often leading to the removal of various political and civic rights, such as the ability to vote, serve on a jury, obtain federal and state-based assistance, and so forth (Brown-Dean 2007; Alexander 2012).

These experiences with the criminal justice system are not singular to Latinos and African Americans. In areas with larger populations of Pacific Islanders and Southeast Asians, boys and young men within these groups are frequently stopped by police, under the assumption that they are involved in gang activity (Ahuja and Chlala 2013). In various localities in California, Laotian, Vietnamese, Samoan, Chinese, and Cambodian youth have among the highest arrest rates (Ahuja and Chlala 2013). Given the differences in average socioeconomic status for various Asian American groups, and given the greater likelihood of law enforcement patrols in neighborhoods with fewer economic resources, it is no surprise to find significant variations in arrest and incarceration rates among Asian Americans. Additionally, American Indian girls are approximately five times more likely to be sent to juvenile detention facilities as compared to their white counterparts (Wiltz 2016). American Indians are killed by law enforcement at higher rates than any other group (Males 2014). Further, American Indian men are four times more likely, and American Indian women six times more likely, to be incarcerated as compared to whites (Males 2014). These statistics and reports demonstrate the ways in which intersectional racial identity is closely linked with the American criminal justice system, to the social, economic, and political detriment of communities of color.

Immigration and Refugee Status

Another area of differentiation in terms of treatment and policy at the intersection of various identities for racial and ethnic minorities is undocumented immigration. One's experience with the US immigration system varies based on race, ethnicity, nationality, class, gender, age, and so forth. Nevertheless, in the American psyche, the dehumanizing and derogatory concept of "illegal immigrant" is inextricably tied to the image of "Latino." Americans implicitly and automatically associate Latinos with immigration, thus decreasing the degree to which immigration is viewed in a positive manner. These negative implicit attitudes regarding Latino immigration have developed due to negatively biased media framing that not only directly influences how people perceive Latino immigration, both legal and undocumented, but also how people negatively perceive immigration of other racial and ethnic groups (Pérez 2016). The effect of this is a highly racialized, negative, and inaccurate portrayal of immigration that has a direct effect on public opinion, political preferences, and policymaking (Pérez 2016). These implicit, negative associations render the fastest-growing population of immigrations, Asian Americans, invisible; consequently, perceptions regarding this pan-ethnic group are less influential on public opinion regarding immigration.

One of the ways stereotyping and implicit bias have affected policymaking relates to how refugees from Central American nations are treated. In 2014, many thousands of women and, sometimes unaccompanied, children fled severe drug cartel and gang-related crime and violence in nations such as Guatemala, El Salvador, and Honduras, and they attempted to take refuge in the United States. Rather than immediately working to grant them refugee status, the United States chose to attempt to "aggressively deter" further refugee migration. Many were, and continue to be, treated as undocumented migrants and are subjected to overcrowded detention centers for an indeterminate amount of time (Hiskey et al. 2016). The United States hired private prison companies to build more facilities in which to detain these asylum seekers (Harlan 2016). The prisonlike conditions within these centers are often inhumane and place women and children at risk of hunger, sickness, violence, and sexual assault (Hylton 2015). As noted in our earlier discussion of sex and gender, women and children of color are not valued and "protected" in the same ways as their white counterparts, which contributes to why there has been little media attention to and little societal outcry concerning the treatment of these asylum seekers.

Racial and ethnic immigrants in America by and large connect themselves in varying ways, and to varying degrees, to the American political system. Ramakrishnan (2005) notes that political mobilization, incorporation, and participation proceed "in a different manner for members of different racial and ethnic groups" (86). Consequently, it should not be assumed that all immigrants perceive and interact with the political system in the same way; an intersectional approach is of supreme importance when considering the topic of immigrants and the political system. Racial and ethnic minorities emigrate from a wide variety of nations that have a multitude of different political engagement levels and policies for their residents. Further, various immigrants have different levels of resources and varying sociopolitical and socioeconomic experiences within the United States which lead to differing levels of political engagement that expand across generations (Ramakrishnan 2005). Incorporation into the existing racial schema can also influence the ways in which racial and ethnic immigrants perceive themselves within the American context, as especially seen in the case of black immigrants from the Caribbean and Africa (C. Smith 2014).

Employment

As seen in Tables 2.1–2.3 (see pp. 29–31), unemployment rates among racial and ethnic minorities are generally higher than those of non-Hispanic whites. When viewed intersectionally in terms of gender, women of color are less likely to be unemployed than their male counterparts. Nevertheless, these women are more likely to be working low-wage jobs (National Women's Law Center 2015). In spite of policy-based efforts to ameliorate race-based and gender-based employment discrimination over the past fifty years, as seen with Title VII of the Civil Rights Act of 1964, the Equal Employment Opportunity Commission, and the Lily Ledbetter Act of 2009, a significant amount of employment discrimination continues to exist at a variety of levels, from hiring practices to evaluation and promotion. With regard to hiring practices, studies have demonstrated that job applicants with Anglo-sounding names receive at least 50 percent more callbacks than those with black-sounding names (Bertrand and Mullainathan 2004). The same has been found for men with Arab-sounding names (Widner and Chicoine 2011). Additionally, Muslim women wearing the hijab are less likely to receive interview callbacks and job offers and often perceive high levels of interpersonal discrimination when they are hired (Ghumman and Ryan 2013). In terms of the intersection of race and criminal convictions in employment decision making, white men with criminal records have more positive responses to their employment searches than black men without criminal records (Decker et al. 2014). These realities concerning hiring and employment practices demonstrate that racial and ethnic minorities with a variety of intersectional identities encounter significant barriers within the realm of employment, thus placing them in a position of lower stability in terms of socioeconomic status.

Individuals who are in the United States without the proper documentation are especially in danger of being terrorized by unscrupulous employers. Knowing that these workers are unable to seek the help of the proper authorities for fear of exposing their undocumented status (which is even more likely to be questioned if they are not white), unethical business owners and managers withhold wages, force longer working hours, and engage in sexual assault, largely with impunity (Harris 2013). Those workers who attempt to speak out about these abuses risk employers working to have them deported. These practices have direct and powerful negative effects on nonwhite individuals and their communities in terms of economic and personal life chances and outcomes, thus influencing the ways in which they can become incorporated into the political system. This involvement influences whether and the degree to which they can advocate for their political interests through various means of participation.

PARTICIPATING IN ELECTORAL POLITICS
Voting

Free and fair elections, in which all constituents can participate without regard to their identities, are the keystone of democratic governance. It is only within the past five decades that the United States has committed itself to ensuring that the voting rights of all citizens eligible to vote are protected by way of clear and enforceable laws. Currently, the nation's dedication to this concept is coming under question, specifically in that many states and localities are working to roll back these protections under the guise of guarding against voter fraud (Brennan Center 2016). By claiming voter fraud as a rampant problem, politicians have been able to create justifications for laws that have the effect of disenfranchising specific segments of voters, particularly racial and ethnic minorities. More specifically, stringent voter identification laws and restrictions on processes for voter registration inevitably most directly affect individuals at the intersection of traditionally marginalized identities, such as poor, elderly

African Americans. Further, Hajnal et al. (2017) find that strict electoral laws in which government-issued photo identification is required negatively influence voter turnout among African Africans, Latinos, and people who are multiracial, as well as Democrats.

After the US Supreme Court ruling in *Shelby County, AL v. Holder* (2013) which effectively gutted the preclearance mechanisms requiring the US Department of Justice to approve any electoral law changes proposed by states and localities that have previously engaged in voter suppression, states such as Texas, North Carolina, Alabama, Ohio, Wisconsin, and Arizona have implemented laws that effectively restrict voter access. While various federal courts have walked back some of these voter restrictions, it is still apparent that these laws purposefully target various intersectional groups connected with race and ethnicity.

Despite increased voter restriction efforts, the proportion of women of color in the eligible voter population has climbed at rates faster than those of the general population, as well as those of white women (Harris 2014). From 2000 to 2014, the number of nonwhite women who are voting-eligible increased by 55.1 percent, while the number of white women who are voting-eligible increased by only 5.8 percent (Harris 2014). Much of this change is attributable to Latinas and Asian American women. As we noted in Chapter 3, nonwhite women have both higher registration rates and higher registered turnout rates as compared to their male counterparts, and African American women had the highest registered turnout rate of all minority groups during the 2014 midterm elections. In the 2012 general election (a presidential election year), African American women had the highest registered turnout rate among all intersectional groups, at 91.9 percent. Voter turnout rates are often lower for midterm elections, but this is especially the case for racial and ethnic minorities. These increasing proportions of voting-eligible and registered nonwhite women demonstrate the increasing electoral power of these voting blocs. Given that Democratic Party victories are often tied to the electoral support of nonwhite women, as especially seen with both the 2008 and 2012 elections for President Obama, the increasing electoral power of these groups will necessitate increased partisan attention in terms of the interests and policy positions of these groups. Further, an intersectional approach to understanding electoral support and success demonstrates that nonwhite women are uniquely positioned to understand and advocate for the needs of their communities, thus allowing them to work toward having their interests, as they define them, recognized and represented.

As with previous presidential elections, the 2016 Democratic candidate, Secretary Hillary Clinton, won the majority of the female vote; however, an intersectional examination of this statistic demonstrates that this was only the case due to the overwhelming support of nonwhite women. In fact, 52 percent of white women voted for Donald Trump, while 94 percent of African American women supported Clinton (CNN 2016). This differential racial support along party lines plays out across all age groups as well. While this overwhelming support for the representative of the Democratic Party is not surprising given traditional partisanship among African Americans, this racial differentiation along gender lines calls into question some of the widely accepted beliefs and findings regarding women and political partisanship and ideology. It is necessary for any examination of the politics of gender to approach each aspect of politics with an intersectional lens in order to provide a more accurate report of how various identities influence political decision making.

Latinas and Asian American women also overwhelmingly supported Hillary Clinton's candidacy in the general election. The traditional exit polling data presented by mainstream news media outlets for these groups was, however, flawed, and underreported their electoral support; it provided an inaccurate sample of smaller populations and did not engage adequate samples from voting precincts where there are higher concentrations of Latinos and Asian Americans. In working to address this problem, political science scholars Taeku Lee, Matt Barreto, and Gary Segura developed more accurate polling methodologies to capture the electoral realities of these groups by way of separate, focused polling. As such, while the traditional exit polling sources reported that only 66 percent of Latinos and 65 percent of Asian Americans voted for Hillary Clinton, in actuality 79 percent of Latinos and 75 percent of Asian Americans voted for her (Asian American Decisions 2016; CNN 2016; Latino Decisions 2016). Further, 79 percent of Asian American women and 86 percent of Latinas voted for Hillary Clinton—much more in line with the realities of the race-based targeting and alienation of the Clinton and Trump campaigns (Asian American Decisions 2016; Latino Decisions 2016). As indicated earlier within this book, these pan-ethnic groups encompass a significant number of different ethnicities that cannot be viewed as monolithic. This is reflected in terms of partisan support within these data, in that not all groups voted for these candidates with the same proportions, with Japanese Americans and Cuban Americans giving the least electoral support to Clinton, though these still reached the level of being a majority for each group (Asian American Decisions 2016; Latino Decisions 2016).

Running for Office

Running for and serving in political office is an important aspect of political participation that can easily be overlooked. Office-holding is of particular importance because of the ways in which individuals in elective and appointed offices are able to create and/or shape policy that may pertain to communities of color.[6] Various scholars have found that descriptive representation—having political representatives who reflect salient ascriptive identity traits—is important for communities of color because these representatives are more likely to engage in agenda setting that focuses on race- and ethnicity-based interests, political efficacy, trust in government, and political knowledge (Bratton and Haynie 1999; Mansbridge 1999; Tate 2004; Hardy et al. 2006; Orey et al. 2006; Philpot and Walton 2007). Specifically, many studies have found that black women in state and national legislatures engaged in agenda setting geared toward both race-based and gender-based interests, thus demonstrating the importance of recognizing and understanding the effects of intersectional identity in politics (Bedolla et al. 2005; Bratton, Haynie, and Reingold 2006; Orey et al. 2006; N. Brown 2014; Brown and Banks 2014; Minta and Brown 2014). Nonwhite women are able to garner a good deal of positive support and evaluation among voters, though their race/ethnic and gender identities influence their electoral prospects (Prestage 1977; Gay and Tate 1998; Philpot and Walton 2007).

Nevertheless, there are a variety of barriers to increasing descriptive representation at the intersection of race/ethnicity and gender. One major barrier concerns stereotypes and perceptions. There are a variety of stereotypes that the broader public holds that are specific to women of color, which vary by racial/ethnic minority group. Scholars recognize the importance of examining these stereotypes at the intersection of race/ethnic group and gender and of examining their effects on candidate evaluation (Matland and King 2002; Gordon and Miller 2005; Banducci et al. 2008; Adams et al. 2011; Carew 2012; Carew 2016; Cargile 2016). Cargile (2016) notes the importance of unpacking the idea of "women of color," especially in the context of political candidates, as the perceptions concerning Latinas differ from those concerning Asian American women, and so forth. The evidence of this is borne out in the data, as Cargile (2016) finds that voters evaluate Latina candidates more positively than male candidates on issues such as assisting the poor, health care, education, and reproductive health, while Carew (2012) finds that black female candidates are more positively evaluated in terms of competency on issues such as welfare and civil rights. On the whole, these studies show that voters are more likely to view nonwhite women in politics as most competent on issues that are perceived to be connected to race/ethnicity-based and female/family-based interests. In turn, this means that electoral success for nonwhite women may hinge upon the degree to which voters find that those issues are pertinent and important to their vote choice.

Nevertheless, black women candidates are not viewed as more competent concerning issues of jobs, the economy, national security, and the military or national security (Carew 2012). Cargile (2016) finds that Latina candidates are perceived as more competent concerning matters of immigration, racial discrimination, education, health care, and assisting the poor as compared to male candidates and more competent on public safety and crime as compared to white candidates; however, Latina candidates are considered to be less competent on issues of foreign affairs than whites. Further, these perceptions of competency can influence electoral outcomes, thus demonstrating that intersectional stereotyping influences the composition of the electorally based governmental structures (Carew 2012). These findings concerning perceptions of nonwhite women running for political office demonstrate that a full picture of the effects of race and ethnicity on the electoral prospects of candidates cannot be gleaned from a one-dimensional examination, and consequently, it is essential to examine the ways in which intersectional identities influence electoral prospects and outcomes.

Skin tone also acts as a relevant and influential identity marker in the context of intersectional identity (Hill 2002; Hunter 2002; Wade, Romano, and Blue 2004; Gyimah-Brempong and Price 2006; Hochschild and Weaver 2007). Darker skin tones are frequently tied to more negative racial stereotyping of and class-based outcomes for racial and ethnic minorities, particularly as seen with African Americans (Hill 2002; Hunter 2002, 2007; Herring, Horton, and Keith 2004; Russell-Cole, Hall, and Wilson 2013). Research concerning gendered colorism in the political arena is still relatively new (Hochschild and Weaver 2007; Carew 2012; N. Brown 2014; Carew 2016). In the context of electoral prospects, African American women and men with darker complexions are more likely to be evaluated positively, as compared to their counterparts with lighter complexions, but the former are less likely to be electorally successful (Terkildsen 1993; Weaver 2012; Carew 2016). The findings tend to suggest that voters, when evaluating candidates in terms of stereotypes and areas of competency, are more prone to being aware that they are being asked about their beliefs concerning race when a candidate has a darker skin tone. Consequently, they are more likely to give answers that are more socially desirable in order to not appear to evaluate a candidate negatively solely due to his or her race. Nevertheless, especially given that skin tone and hair texture are more influential upon social, economic, and political outcomes for women of color, it is clear that they can play a subconscious role in the evaluation of political candidates (N. Brown 2014; Carew 2016).

An additional barrier to increased descriptive representation among nonwhite women is media framing of these candidates. It is widely recognized that the media can profoundly influence the outcomes of elections, from the amount of coverage to the specific messages relayed concerning candidates, as particularly evidenced in the 2016 presidential election. This influence of the media operates in the same way for nonwhite women seeking office. Media outlets choose whether and to what degree they will cover candidates, as well as how they will frame stories regarding their campaigns. Previous research demonstrates that candidates who are racial/ethnic minorities and those who are female receive less media coverage, and the coverage they receive is more negative in tone (Kahn 1996; Entman 1997; Reeves 1997; Bystrom 2006). In addition, the coverage they receive often has focused on "race" or "feminine" issues, respectively, thus potentially decreasing their appeal to broader sets of voters (Carroll and Schreiber 1997; Terkildsen and Damore 1999; Zilber and Niven 2000; Schaffner 2002; Banwart, Bystrom, and Robertson 2003). Gershon (2012) finds that, while the race/ethnicity and gender of political representatives on their own do not have an effect on media coverage, representatives who are minority women receive less media attention than their fellow representatives. In a study examining media coverage of racial and ethnic minority female representatives, Gershon (2013) finds that black female representatives receive a small amount of coverage, thus potentially limiting their ability to communicate with voters by way of the media, while Latina representatives receive both less coverage and more negative coverage that is likely to be geared toward topics concerning immigration, thus limiting their outreach to voters as well as their appeal. This study also found that white female representatives receive higher levels of media attention as compared to their black female and Latina colleagues, thus supporting their efforts to communicate their messages to constituents.

Minority Women in the 2016 US Senate Races

The number and proportion of minority women serving in elective offices throughout the United States has grown substantially over the past few decades. In 2016, nonwhite women constituted 32.4 percent of the women serving in the 114th US Congress, thus constituting 6.4 percent of the members of Congress (Center for American Women and Politics [CAWP] 2016). There were an additional three nonvoting congressional delegates to the House of Representatives who represented Washington, DC; the Virgin Islands; and American Samoa (CAWP 2016). Eighteen African American women, nine Latinas, and six Asian Pacific Islander women served as voting members in the US House of Representatives, and one Asian Pacific Islander woman served within the US Senate (CAWP 2016). Nine nonwhite women served in statewide elective executive offices, with two serving as Republican governors (Nikki Haley of South Carolina and Susana Martinez of New Mexico).

Nonwhite women also made up 5.4 percent of all state legislators, and there were two Latinas, one Asian Pacific Islander woman, and four African American women serving as mayors of one of the one hundred largest cities in the United States (CAWP 2016). While these data demonstrate an increase of representation by nonwhite women since the period in which they obtained the ability to successfully run for political office,[7] we still find that nonwhite women were underrepresented descriptively, given that they make up approximately 19.6 percent of the total US population (American Community Survey 2015).

The US Senate elections of 2016 marked what may prove to be a watershed moment in terms of an increase in descriptive representation for minority women, with three candidates winning their electoral bids, bringing the total number of female racial and ethnic minority senators in the 115th US Congress to four. As a Japanese American legislator from Hawaii (elected in 2012), Mazie Hirono was the only nonwhite woman serving as a senator in the 114th US Congress. The three new women of color who joined Hirono in 2017 are Kamala Harris, Tammy Duckworth, and Catherine Cortez Masto.

In January 2015, Senator Barbara Boxer (D-CA) announced that she would be retiring at the end of her current term in 2016, after twenty-four years in that office. Thirty-four candidates ran in the primary to determine who would replace the four-term senator. This election unfolded in a somewhat unconventional and nonpartisan fashion, given recent changes in California's electoral laws. In 2010, California Republican state senator Abel Maldonado proposed an amendment to the California Constitution that would create a single primary election for nonpresidential, state-level elections. All candidates would run on one ballot, with the top two candidates then moving on to the general election, regardless of party affiliation. Proposition 14 appeared on the June 2010 primary election ballots and passed with 53.8 percent of the popular vote.

In the 2016 California Senate primary, the two candidates received the largest number of votes in the primary election were California attorney general Kamala Harris (40.2 percent) and US Representative Loretta Sánchez (19.0 percent), both of whom ran as Democratic candidates. This marked the first ever Senate race in the United States in which all candidates running in the general election were women from racial and ethnic minority groups. Harris is of mixed-race heritage, as the daughter of immigrants; her mother is Indian American (Tamil), and her father is Jamaican American. Sánchez is the daughter of Mexican American immigrants from Sonora, Mexico. She also has made important political history in that she and her sister, Linda Sánchez, are the first pair of sisters to serve concurrently in the US House of Representatives.[8]

PHOTO 5.1 *Senator-elect Kamala Harris (D-CA) and Senator-elect Catherine Cortez Masto (D-NV), two of the four new women of color elected to the Senate in 2016., get together with Sen. Barbara Mikulski (D-MD), Sen. Kirsten Gillibrand (D-NY), Sen. Tammy Baldwin (D-WI), and Senator-elect Maggie Hassan (D-NH) for coffee on Capitol Hill in Washington shortly after the election.* (AP Photo/Susan Walsh; ID: 16320813814453)

Kamala Harris was heavily favored to win the Senate seat, and she received the endorsements of a wide variety of powerful political players: both sitting California senators, Dianne Feinstein and Barbara Boxer, as well as President Barack Obama, Vice President Joe Biden, and various US senators and representatives. While Sánchez did obtain a significant number of political office-holder endorsements, many of these came from her colleagues in the US House of Representatives. Both candidates had strong and well-established political backgrounds, which significantly strengthened their electoral viability as compared to the other candidates during their primary race. Sánchez touted her wealth of national security experience, which she developed over twenty years in Congress, while Harris emphasized her experience in the areas of civil rights and criminal justice reform. Both candidates worked to appeal to voters throughout the state on many important issues, such as foreign policy, the environment, education, and immigration; however, Harris's campaign raised more funds than did Sánchez's, and various gaffes by Sánchez placed her campaign in a defensive stance at various points throughout the race. In the end, Harris won the general election with 61.6 percent of the popular vote. Kamala

Harris is the first Indian American woman to serve in the US Senate and only the second African American woman within that legislative chamber (following Carol Moseley Braun [D-IL], whose term ended in 1999).

With her victory in the 2016 general election in Nevada, Catherine Cortez Masto (Democrat) became the first Latina[9] ever elected to the US Senate, as well as the first female senator from her state. After three decades in the US Senate, the Democratic Party leader, Harry Reid, announced in March 2015 that he would not seek reelection. The open seat was hotly contested—the Democratic and Republican Parties had several candidates running in the primary election for the Senate seat. Former Nevada attorney general Cortez Masto won the candidacy with 81 percent of the primary vote, and her Republican rival, US Representative Joe Heck, won his party's nomination with 65 percent of the primary vote. The general election campaign for this seat was especially contentious given that it provided an opportunity for the Republican Party to pick up an additional seat in the Senate. This led to large amounts of money coming into the state to influence the election on both sides. Senator Harry Reid threw his support and mobilization efforts behind Cortez Masto, helping to ensure her successful bid for the seat. Cortez Masto ran a campaign focused on education, renewable energy, and comprehensive immigration reform, and she skillfully mobilized the Latino voting population through a variety of forms of outreach, including Spanish-language ads focusing on family and her record of protecting many vulnerable groups as attorney general. While her opponent, Representative Heck, attacked her on issues relating to lack of legislative experience, he encountered his own difficulties with determining whether, and the degree to which, to support Donald Trump as the Republican candidate for president. Providing and withdrawing his support for Trump several times throughout the primary and general election cycles may have decreased some of the support from his Republican electoral base. In the end, Cortez Masto won the election with 47.1 percent of the vote, while Heck received 44.7 percent of the vote (Rindels 2016).

While Senators Harris and Cortez Masto won in open-seat elections in positions vacated by long-standing senators who supported their candidacies, Senator Tammy Duckworth won her 2016 electoral bid against incumbent Republican senator Mark Kirk. Winning against an incumbent is often a difficult feat, as there is a significant incumbency advantage in US congressional elections. Working in Duckworth's favor was the fact that this seat had a recent history of oscillating between Democratic and Republican senators and had previously been held by Barack Obama and Carol Moseley Braun. Tammy Duckworth was born in Thailand to a Thai-Chinese mother and American father whose family traced its ancestry and military service back to the American Revolutionary War. She joined the US Army in 1992 and served until 2014, despite losing both legs and suffering other severe injuries during a 2004 deployment in Iraq. At the time of the election, Duckworth was the US representative for the Eighth Congressional District in Illinois and was the first Asian American woman to be elected to the US Congress from her state. Both Duckworth and Kirk easily won their 2016 primary elections, and the general election between them for the Senate seat was highly competitive. In particular, sparring between the candidates in a debate on October 27, 2016, brought the issue of race to the forefront of the election. In responding to a debate moderator, Representative Duckworth said the following:

> My family has served this nation in uniform going back to the Revolution. I am a daughter of the American Revolution. I've bled for this nation. But I still want to be there in the Senate when the drums of war sound. Because people are quick to sound the drums of war, and I want to be there to say this is what it costs, this is what you're asking us to do. And if that's the case, I'll go. Families like mine are the ones that bleed first. But let's make sure the American people understand what we are engaging in, and let's hold our allies accountable because we can't do it all. (Hauser 2016)

This response indicated precisely what might be expected in terms of the ideology and policy positioning of a US veteran who is a woman of color from a nonwealthy family: encouragement to strongly evaluate decisions about the use of war powers, consideration of the fact that military families (disproportionately people of color and people with few monetary resources) directly bear the brunt of these policies, and dedication to the protection of the nation. As seen in Duckworth's case, the congruence of these subordinate identity points increases the likelihood of a unique set of experiences that can lead to a moderated yet firm position on military interventions. Notwithstanding her statement touching on these topics, Senator Mark Kirk's immediate and only response when given the opportunity for rebuttal was a highly racialized and not-too-subtle personal attack spoken directly as a challenge to Duckworth: "I had forgotten that your parents came all the way from Thailand to serve George Washington" (Kirk-Illinois US Senate Debate, October 27, 2016).

While Duckworth did not directly respond to Kirk, there was audible reaction of disbelief from audience members, and the moderator gave her the opportunity to respond (at which point she outlined her family ties to the

American Revolution and indicated her pride in the heritage on both sides of her family). Senator Kirk's comment was immediately denounced by many across party lines, and he issued an apology to Representative Duckworth by Twitter the following day. His attempt at a jab against her Asian ancestry reflected the well-established concept of "Asian" as foreign and non-American. It also clearly reflected what Claire Jean Kim (1999) calls the "racial triangulation of Asian Americans," in which this pan-ethnic group is viewed as superior to other racial minority groups, but is perpetually relegated to the position of "outsider"/"foreigner" in terms of the idea of belonging within America and American culture. The negative reaction to Senator Kirk's comment, in conjunction with Representative Duckworth's strong, policy-based campaign, helped to lead to her eventual victory. When the general election took place in November 2016, Duckworth garnered 54.9 percent of the vote, while Kirk gained only 39.8 percent.

These electoral victories are of particular importance given the ways in which descriptive representation can be important for nonwhite women, not only for people in the states that are represented by these individuals, but also more broadly in terms of the types of national policy for which these individuals can advocate. Senator-elect Cortez Masto indicated the importance of this sort of descriptive representation in her victory speech.

> It's not just about making history. It is about ensuring we have a seat at the table to get something done. Don't you think it is about time that we had diversity in the U.S. Senate? Don't you think it's about time that our government mirrors the people we serve every day, that it should mirror the population we represent? That's what this is about. (Hauser 2016)

As noted earlier in this chapter, the importance of descriptive representation comes in terms of the increased substantive representation that can flow from it, as well as the increased political efficacy and engagement that it can produce among those who are descriptively represented. This increased engagement, in conjunction with people fighting to place the interests of various groups on the legislative agenda, can lead to a far greater degree of strong and functional democratic processes that include the voices of highly marginalized groups at a variety of intersectional identities. The current political environment has made this sort of descriptive representation all the more important, as forces working to *decrease* democratic representation for all and *increase* the foothold of traditional racialized power bases gather strength at all levels of government, as seen especially with Donald Trump's 2016 presidential electoral success, as well as various state legislative actions.[10]

PHOTO 5.2   *Patrisse Cullors, Opal Tometti, and Alicia Garza, left to right, cofounders of the Black Lives Matter movement, were honored at* Glamour*'s Women of the Year 2016 awards.* (Frazer Harrison/Getty Images for *Glamour*; ID: 623253784)

SOCIAL ACTIVISM AND PROTEST
Black Lives Matter

When it comes to social activism and protest, it is nonwhite women who are the forefront, particularly those not in positions of privilege in terms of class and sexuality, often placing their lives and livelihoods on the line. As noted earlier, examinations of political and civic engagement through an intersectional lens have demonstrated that individuals whose identity resides at the intersection of multiple marginalized identities are often the people who are most directly involved in building sociopolitical movements in order to place pressure on the system to make necessary alterations. This is precisely what can be found in the work of the founders of the #BlackLivesMatter movement. Alicia Garza, Patrisse Cullors, and Opal Tometi cofounded Black Lives Matter following the 2013 acquittal of George Zimmerman for the murder of an unarmed black teenager, Trayvon Martin. Garza, Cullors, and Tometi used nontraditional (social media) and traditional (grassroots organizing) methods to develop a movement geared toward combatting antiblack racism within both governmental and societal systems.

Much of the emphasis of the Black Lives Matter movement has focused on police brutality, given the increased media attention specific to the shooting deaths of unarmed black people at the hands of police. These incidents do not indicate an increase in this negative behavior by political actors, but rather they reflect the ongoing realities of police brutality, often perpetrated against non-white, frequently lower socioeconomic status, communities. The increased attention to these violent arrests and brutal shootings is directly attributed to the advent of video recording technology in mobile telephone devices. These videos, which are widely shared across social media outlets, as well as traditional mainstream broadcast media, often provide seemingly incontrovertible evidence of unnecessary deadly force that is administered by state actors (i.e., police officers). While this phenomenon, in and of itself, is certainly enough to increase the likelihood of broad grassroots organizing based upon the clear violations of civil rights regularly occurring at the intersection of race and class, often the major spark that sets this kindling ablaze is the lack of justice found within the American judicial system for this sort of unwarranted brutality. Time and again, these extrajudicial killings have been implicitly or explicitly deemed justified, whether by a jury choosing to not convict an officer charged in the death of an unarmed black person, or even more frequently in the event that local prosecutors either choose not to attempt to present charges to a grand jury against an officer, or said prosecutors present the cases in a way that grand juries are encouraged not to indict an officer on charges for this violence.[11] It is particularly the lack of a criminal trial that leads to organizing and protest, given the apparent message that the laws of the nation that ought to be in place to protect all individuals residing within the United States are not, in practice, ensuring a fair trial for justice for the loss of life of these individuals.

Interestingly, it often appears that the point at which unprovoked killings of black men are most likely to lead to indictments of officers is when those officers are not white men, as was the case in the Akai Gurley and Philando Castile shootings in 2014 and 2016, respectively. Officer Jeronimo Yanez, who is Mexican American, allegedly shot and killed Philando Castile during a traffic stop on July 6, 2016, in Falcon Heights, Minnesota, the day after the highly publicized police shooting of Alton Sterling in Baton Rouge, Louisiana. Castile's unwarranted shooting occurred as soon as Castile advised the officer that he was legally carrying a concealed weapon. Diamond Reynolds and her four-year-old daughter were in the vehicle when Castile was killed, and Reynolds amazingly had the presence of mind to calmly speak with Officer Yanez and capture her conversation and the aftermath of the shooting by live-streaming video via the Facebook app on her smartphone (Chappell 2016). Reynolds's quick actions led to the video being viewed widely across the nation and provided evidence leading to Officer Yanez's indictment on charges of second-degree manslaughter and dangerous discharge of a firearm. Family members, friends, and community organizations such as Black Lives Matter and the NAACP engaged in prayer vigils and peaceful protests throughout the first week after Castile's death, much of which was led by African American women. The president of the Minneapolis NAACP, Nekima Levy-Pound, pushed for the case to be investigated by an independent body, thus further demonstrating the varying methods used by individuals at many different intersections of identity to place demands on the political system based upon the needs of the community. Given that video evidence has not always led to an indictment of an officer on criminal charges, particularly in the case of white officers (as seen in the Eric Garner chokehold case), the indictment of a Latino officer in the Castile case may suggest that the likelihood of "justice" by way of a trial increases when someone who is a nonwhite representative of the law enforcement system can be presented as a seeming sacrificial offering for the sins of systemic racism.

Another example that is touted as the scapegoating of officers who are not white males is the Akai Gurley case. On November 20, 2014, New York Police Department officer Peter Liang, who is the son of Chinese immigrants, was engaged in a vertical patrol in a darkened stairwell at a New York City Housing Authority home when he claims to have accidentally discharged his firearm. Akai Gurley, an unarmed black male resident in the building, was in the stairwell at the time and was struck and killed by the ricocheting bullet (Yee and Schweber 2015). A grand jury indicted Officer Liang on charges of second-degree manslaughter, official misconduct, reckless endangerment, and criminally negligent homicide, and a jury convicted him on the first two charges in February 2016. After Liang's grand jury indictment, several thousand Asian Americans, largely comprising Chinese Americans of all ages, organized protests in March and April 2015, and approximately fifteen thousand protested in February 2016 in favor of Peter Liang and against what they saw as his scapegoating for something that was an accident. Many protestors believed that Liang was only indicted and convicted due to racial bias and a desire to have someone to make an example of in the midst of Black Lives Matter pressure on police departments and city officials. They claimed that Liang was being used to demonstrate that officers are held accountable for unjustified killings, and that Liang would not have been charged if he had been white. Protestors held signs reading "One Tragedy, Two Victims," "No Scapegoat," and "No Selective Justice," thus suggesting that all officers should be equally prosecuted, or not, in these types of cases (Shyong et al. 2016). Various groups, including Black Lives Matter, held demonstrations in favor of Liang's indictment and conviction—these were attended by multiracial

PHOTO 5.3 *Protesters hold a rally in support of former NYPD officer Peter Liang in the Brooklyn borough of New York February 20, 2016. Liang was convicted of manslaughter and official misconduct on Thursday for fatally shooting an unarmed black man, Akai Gurley, in a darkened public housing stairwell in 2014.* (REUTERS/Brendan McDermid; RTX27UQ3)

populations, including Asian Americans, who tended to be young adults (Wang 2016).

As seen in this brief examination of highly publicized police brutality cases resulting in the deaths of African Americans, much of the media focus (and thus national attention) was drawn to black male victims. As is often the case when an intersectional approach is not used to examine sociopolitical realities, people at various intersectional identities and their experiences are rendered practically invisible. This is precisely what occurred in the reporting of these incidents, which led to the African American Policy Forum (AAPF) developing the #SayHerName campaign. Kimberlé Crenshaw, a foundational scholar in the area of intersectionality, and Luke Harris created the AAPF in 1996 in order to develop research and strategies for combatting structural inequalities connected to marginalized intersectional identities, particularly as connected to race, gender, and class (Crenshaw and Ritchie 2015). The hashtag and physical demonstration campaign #SayHerName was developed in order to call attention to the largely overlooked police brutality against African American women, particularly in terms of gender and sexuality (Crenshaw and Ritchie 2015). The cases of Natasha

McKenna, Sandra Bland, and Rekia Boyd had received a small degree of national attention prior to this campaign, but they largely went unnoticed. This intersectional approach of #SayHerName provided the basis for examining state-based police violence outside of the one-dimensional context of "race" in order to more clearly demonstrate that this sort of injustice exists on a broader scale than that which is reported in media narratives, and consequently it exists in a variety of forms that are rarely recognized or acknowledged. Major examples of these invisible abuses include sexual assault, transphobic and homophobic physical and sexual abuse, excessive force used on mothers and their children, and lack of attention to physical pain and medical problems (Crenshaw and Ritchie 2015). These abuses get lost in the "white officer shoots unarmed black man" narrative, and the lack of attention to these realities has resulted in the continued marginalization of and state-sponsored abuse against black women, nonblack racial and ethnic minorities, LGBTQ communities, and people who are poor, without policy-based attention to remedying these problems.

These sorts of injustices are often at the root of organizing and protest among nonwhite women, as seen in the development of the Black Lives Matter movement. Unfortunately, as cofounder Alicia Garza highlights, it is often the case that the work of queer black women in these processes gets coopted and erased from public view, often to the detriment of the original purpose of the organizing (Garza 2016). This is precisely what has occurred with the various movements attempting to remove the idea of "black" from Black Lives Matter in order to develop "inclusive" narratives with the purpose of shouting down the rationale of Black Lives Matter, or in order to develop separate movements with the purpose of placing the focus on other significant sources of hierarchical oppression. Garza identifies this as problematic because the entire purpose of focusing on and addressing antiblack ideologies and pathologies becomes lost, thus diminishing the possibilities for combatting destructive and oppressive hierarchies (2016).

Workers' Rights

Racial and ethnic minorities and immigrants, especially those without the necessary documentation, are among the most vulnerable groups in the realm of employment in the United States. The latter group is exceptionally vulnerable to exploitative employers that will subject employees to unsafe working conditions and long hours with little pay. These employers engage in this sort of behavior because they know that undocumented workers have no means for reporting these illegal employment practices, given their own status. While it is rare that people can stand up against these abuses, civic engagement and political participation can develop among the most vulnerable populations.

For many decades, community leaders and activists have organized workers' rights and labor movements in order to seek greater equality and justice, particularly in the realm of the treatment of workers. César Chávez and Dolores Huerta cofounded the National Farm Workers Association (now called United Farm Workers of America) in 1962, and their work in organizing pioneered the way for successful unionization, strikes, boycotts, and policy-based lobbying that helped to improve the conditions and lives of farmworkers, many of whom were racial and ethnic minorities. Various groups have been able to build upon the work of Huerta and Chávez, and particularly in the past decade, we have seen increasing organization around the interests of workers. This recent increase in organizing has been necessitated by increasing economic inequality and decreasing policy-based protection for vulnerable workers and their families.

A recent example of this sort of civic engagement and community organizing occurred on May 1, 2016, when thousands of people (most racial and ethnic minorities) came together under the organization of Voces de la Frontera in order to peacefully demonstrate and protest policies relating to immigration and workers' rights (Matz 2016). With a major theme of "We Are All Wisconsin," the demonstrators held signs calling for protection of immigrant families, raising the minimum wage to $15 per hour, and ending Islamophobia, among many other calls for social justice (Matz 2016). While largely organized by Latinos, the demonstration included participants of a wide variety of intersectional identities. Increasingly, it appears that there is more racial/ethnic minority intergroup interaction and coordination, which may suggest a future of greater minority intergroup cooperation. This sort of cross-group, intersectional ally support was also seen in terms of the Standing Rock Sioux tribe's attempts to stop the construction of the Dakota Access Pipeline.

Dakota Access Pipeline (DAPL)

> Most of all, we have to protect the water. And you know, water is female. And it's woman's right to protect the water, because through water we bring the children into this world. Through water we care for our families. And so water has always been female. —LaDonna Brave Bull Allard (CBC Radio interview, November 20, 2016)

In April of 2016, LaDonna Brave Bull Allard, of the Standing Rock Sioux tribe, founded the Sacred Stone Camp on her land by the Cannon Ball River, as a means of establishing a spirit camp in opposition to the Dakota Access Pipeline construction plans. The idea for starting a spirit camp, an area where people can congregate for prayer, education, and support in connection with a major issue, came from other successful movements that included spirit camps. For example, in 2014 and 2015, the Rosebud Sioux tribe founded spirit camps in opposition to the Keystone XL Pipeline, which is scheduled to run from Canada to Texas. This pipeline would have run around the Rosebud Sioux reservation land, and there are concerns that it will threaten the water supply for the tribe. These are the same concerns that led to significant opposition to the Dakota Access Pipeline (DAPL) by the Standing Rock Sioux tribe, and their concerns are well founded. According to the Pipeline and Hazardous Materials Safety Administration (PHMSA), which is an agency within the US Department of Transportation, there have been 11,208 pipeline incidents in the past twenty years, leading to 360 fatalities, 1,376 injuries, and a total cost of $6.86 billion (PHMSA 2016). In January 2015, in the midst of the opposition to the Keystone XL Pipeline, there was a spill of at least fifty thousand gallons of crude oil into the Yellowstone River in Montana that resulted in the pollution of water supply of the city of Glendive, Montana, which made it so that residents could not use their tap water for cooking or drinking (Lutey and Chiofi 2015).

Allard's DAPL activism started in 2014 when the tribe was informed of the planned route for the oil pipeline. The Standing Rock Sioux tribe indicated its opposition to the route of the pipeline, which was scheduled to cross beneath the Missouri River/Lake Oahe near the tribe's reservation land. In order for the pipeline to cross the river, the Dakota Access LLC needed to obtain federal permission, which it acquired through the US Army Corps of Engineers (USACE). Nevertheless, the federal government, by way of the USACE, is required to consult with federal-recognized tribes when projects such as these may influence their land. Allard met with the USACE in March 2016 and, in a walkthrough of the area, identified for them the locations of sacred ceremonial, cultural, and burial sites. In spite of the tribe's opposition, the USACE granted the easement to allow the DAPL to cross the river, leading the Standing Rock Sioux tribe to file a lawsuit against the USACE in July 2016 (*Standing Rock Sioux Tribe v. US Army Corps of Engineers* 2016). In July 2016, the DAPL began preparations at the construction site, and the protest movement grew, with a new spirit camp, the Oceti Sakowin ("Seven Council Fires") Camp, which, as of this writing, continues to grow in size just off of Standing Rock reservation land, near the easement grant.

The purpose of these spirit camps has been to provide a place for prayer over this matter of potential water contamination and desecration of sacred lands and to provide a staging position for people engaged in nonviolent action as water protectors (individuals attempting to halt the progress of the DAPL

PHOTO 5.4 *Native Americans march to the site of a sacred burial ground that was disturbed by bulldozers building the Dakota Access Pipeline (DAPL), near the encampment where hundreds of people have gathered to join the Standing Rock Sioux Tribe's protest of the oil pipeline slated to cross the nearby Missouri River, September 4, 2016, near Cannon Ball, North Dakota. Protestors were attacked by dogs and sprayed with an eye and respiratory irritant yesterday when they arrived at the site to protest after learning of the bulldozing work.* ROBYN BECK/AFP/Getty Images; ID: 599236808.

through peaceful means of civil disobedience). The individuals residing within the camps exemplify the ways in which intersectional identity can influence and work as a part of political participation, as people of many ages, genders, tribal affiliations, classes, races, and occupations come together in a highly organized system that begins to operate as its own community, which includes medical, legal, media, sustenance, and infrastructure resources (Oceti Sakowin Camp 2016). Indigenous peoples from across the globe, as well as individuals who see themselves as allies in a struggle against the DAPL's proximity to the Standing Rock reservation, have visited and participated in these camps to stand in solidarity. Unfortunately, as with many of the actions of civil disobedience in the 1950s and 1960s civil rights movements, the water protectors[12] have been met with violent reactions by DAPL security forces, law enforcement from various localities and states, and the National Guard.

Starting in August 2016, eyewitness news reports and videos began appearing on various social media outlets showing the DAPL forces allowing dogs to charge and bite the activists. Many of the water protectors are young indigenous women who have been key organizers for the effort of setting up prayer lines at the construction site, and these Standing Rock activists were frequently attacked and injured by a highly militarized response team that used rubber bullets, pepper spray, compression grenades, tear gas, and water cannons, the last of which were used in subfreezing temperatures on both the activists and their fires that were in place for keeping warm. UN human rights observers denounced the use of excessive force by US officials against the activists and indicated that the conditions of the detention centers where law enforcement kept several hundred protesters were "inhuman and degrading" (OHCHR 2016). Some of these detention centers were reported to have been dog kennels that included chain-link fencing and tarp and were places in which those that had been detained were not able to obtain medical attention.

In this setting, once again, intersectional identity and the powers and privileges that may be attached to various identities have had profound effects on political outcomes. When US veterans organized and worked to join the protests in order to act as a protective barrier for the water protectors in December 2016, the USACE denied the easement for the DAPL to cross Lake Oahe, essentially halting the completion of construction. It is unclear whether the presence of the veterans definitively influenced the government's decision; however, given that prior to the arrival of the veterans, the USACE announced that protestors would be evicted from their prayer camps, it appears that the presence of men and women of all racial and ethnic backgrounds with the additional identity of military/veteran very likely influenced the governmental decision making. The veterans chose to use the privileges they had earned through service as a means of protecting a vulnerable racialized population that has frequently been oppressed and marginalized by governmental actions, further demonstrating how intersecting identities can influence politics.

CONCLUSION

This chapter provides a brief overview of the importance of utilizing an intersectional lens to examine racial and ethnic minorities in the American political system. In order to do this, we have defined how to move away from one-dimensional conceptions of identity and have indicated that this approach should not be used merely to create "new" groups to study—for example, poor women of color—but rather should be used to better understand how varying circumstances and experiences create the political realities of the system. This chapter also identifies various sociopolitical problems and demonstrates the key role that racial and ethnic minorities at various intersections of identity have played in working to bring about positive political change for their communities and for the nation as a whole.

Intersectionality, as a discipline, allows for a focus on understanding race and ethnicity in American politics that provides a more positive view for the prospect of intergroup coalition versus competition. As different racial and ethnic groups find more points of commonality in terms of experiences and interests across their intersectional identities, the difficulties for cooperation may wane. In recent years, we have seen greater coalition across minority groups in the context of growing protest movements, many of which have people whose identities reside at the intersection of multiple marginalized identities. One example of this cross-sectional support is the fact that Black Lives Matter organizers, various Occupy movements, and many other individuals and groups worked to aid the Standing Rock protest and indigenous rights movement to prevent the completion of the Dakota Access Pipeline. It appears that the increased likelihood of intersectional approaches to this sort of political activism has, in some circumstances, led to greater opportunities for working together against common sources of structural inequality. The fact that one of the major sources of this inequality—namely beliefs regarding white supremacy—seems to currently be on the rise may act as a catalyst for intergroup coalition. This will greatly depend upon racial and ethnic minority groups being able to overcome the forces that promote competition.

- -

DISCUSSION QUESTIONS

1. Why is it important to examine race and ethnicity in politics from an intersectional perspective?

2. What is intersectional identity? Why has society not traditionally spoken of or examined identity along more than one dimension at a time?

3. Why are people within groups composed of multiple oppressed identities often more likely to engage in political activism?

4. In what ways do people with different intersectional identities have varying experiences with sociopolitical issues, such as the criminal justice system, employment, and immigration?

NOTES

1 This phenomenon of perceptions is what leads researchers to recognize the idea that people object to race-based policy due to adherence to American principles of individualism and equality rather than racist views is a flawed argument (Kinder and Mendelberg 2000). The "American value" of individualism is a racialized concept that largely is not applied to and does not benefit racial and ethnic minorities.

2 Cisgender is a term that refers to people whose gender identity matches the sex they were assigned when they were born.

3 These categories of intersectional racial identity are by no means the only salient identities. The three chosen here are showcased in order to illustrate how the combination of multiple centers of oppression influences the life experiences of, and consequently the political ideologies and forms of engagement of, various intersectional identity groups.

4 While this movement geared toward "Lifting While We Climb" was useful in terms of the concept of racial uplift, it included approaches connected with classism.

5 For example, "transgender Latina/os are seven times more likely than the general U.S. population, and more than five times more likely than the general Latina/o population to live in extreme poverty" (HRC and TPOCC 2016).

6 In Chapter 4, we examine the concept of minority representation. There we categorize and identify various levels of participation in office-holding among the major racial and ethnic minority groups.

7 The prohibition of voting rights for nonwhites and for women rendered office-holding by women of color virtually impossible. The Fifteenth and Nineteenth amendments to the US Constitution extended the franchise on the basis of race and gender, respectively. Nevertheless, it was not until the Voting Rights Act of 1965 that these voting rights were broadly protected for racial and ethnic minorities (and thus for women of color as well).

8 Linda Sánchez is also the first Latina and first woman of color to serve in a leadership position in the US Congress, as the vice chair of the House Democratic Conference.

9 Cortez Masto is of Mexican American and Italian American ancestry. Her paternal grandfather immigrated to the United States from Chihuahua, Mexico.

10 One major example includes the North Carolina legislative and gubernatorial partisan-based power overreaches in 2016.

11 Examples include the cases of Michael Brown, Walter Scott, and Keith Scott, among many others.

12 Given the purpose of the work they are engaging in, the activists prefer to be referred to and recognized as "water protectors" rather than "protestors," as their main focus is on ensuring the continued safety of the water supply and the earth.

CHAPTER 6

Coalition or Competition?
Patterns of Interminority
Group Relations

In the 2016 race for the California Senate position, there were two Democrats on the ballot. Kamala Harris is the highest-ranking black politician in the state of California. Loretta Sánchez is a Latina US Representative who has spent over twenty years working in Congress. The race between them became very competitive. When President Obama and his administration endorsed Harris for the Senate position, Sánchez was extremely displeased. "I don't know why the leadership of the party did not want a Latino; they did not speak with us," Sánchez said. "They chose [Harris] from the beginning" (Willon and Ulloa 2016). Sánchez insinuated that since President Obama, like Kamala Harris, is African American, that influenced the administration's endorsement decision (Mai-Duc 2016; Michaelson 2016; Willon and Ulloa 2016).

—CALIFORNIA, JULY 22, 2016

Manifest changes have occurred and continue to occur in the demographics of most major cities in the United States. Whereas we once referred to urban political dynamics in terms of whites versus blacks, today Latinos, increasing numbers of Asians, and—to a lesser extent—Indians have been added to the mix. These demographic changes not only have altered the political dynamics of urban politics, but also have created a new context for relationships among the various racial groups that may take the form of coalition, conflict, or mutual nonrecognition. The continuing second dilemma faced by racial minorities in American society is represented by the question posed by Rodney King at his first postverdict news conference in the wake of the 1992

PHOTO 6.1 *Rodney King makes a statement at a Los Angeles press conference, May 1, 1992, pleading for the end to the rioting and looting that has plagued the city following the verdicts in the trial against four Los Angeles Police officers accused of beating him.* (AP Photo/David Longstreath; ID: 92050101645)

Los Angeles riots—"Can we all get along?" What options within the American political system are available to members of minority groups, and what are the consequences of pursuing each of these options? Is it feasible for blacks, Latinos, Asians, and American Indians to form coalitions to attain political outcomes? Or is it more common for the goals and objectives of these groups to be in conflict? The debate over biracial coalition politics has been intense and enduring. The looming questions have always been, "Should minorities go it alone and bargain with the larger society, or do they need to form alliances to counter their minority status? And if they make alliances, with whom should they link their fate?" (Sonenshein 1993:3).

This chapter focuses on aspects of the second dilemma by examining (1) **coalition politics**—the aggregation of groups to pursue a specific political goal—of blacks, Latinos, and Asian Americans; and (2) the increasing tensions among blacks, Latinos, and Asians and between these groups and the white majority. (Although half of the American Indian population consists of "urban Indians," little research has been conducted on its participation in urban politics.) Additionally, we present three case studies—Durham,

North Carolina; Memphis, Tennessee; and Little Rock, Arkansas—that high-light the various patterns of interminority and majority group relations.

INTERMINORITY GROUP RELATIONS

When differences among groups are found with regard to political goals and outcomes, the potential for conflict exists. Political coalitions require that groups have similar goals, desire similar outcomes, and be willing to pursue their objectives in a collaborative and cooperative fashion. Coalitions may be loosely or tightly organized, and cooperation may be tacit or explicit. As with coalitions, the form of competition between groups with differing goals may also vary. Competition may be pursued on an "enemies always" basis or on a "not permanent enemies" stance (Eisinger 1976:17–18).

Group competition accounts for some aspects of the discrimination experienced by minorities. Individuals and groups accrue power and status in a variety of ways; thus, some power contests are understood as involving group against group. Competition exists, therefore, when two or more groups strive for the same finite objectives, whereby the success of one group may imply a reduced probability that another will attain its goals. We could view group competition in terms of power contests that exist when there is rivalry and when groups have roots in different cultures. Furthermore, the greatest per-ceived competition may occur among groups that are nearly equal in political power (Blalock 1967). This framework, although it is addressed to majority minority relations, is also useful in examining relationships among minority-groups if we recognize that not only status differences but also status similari-ties may become bases for conflict.

COALITION OR COMPETITION POLITICS?

The presence of multiple minority groups in major metropolitan cities has led to the assumption that shared racial minority group status generates the poten-tial for political coalitions among the various groups. One of the assumptions of coalition theory has been that the relationship among the various racial minority groups will be one of mutual respect and shared political goals and ideals. Another assumption of coalition theory, however, has been that black political assertiveness is incompatible with the existence of biracial political coalitions between blacks and whites (Sonenshein 1993). Although they were referring to African Americans, Stokely Carmichael and Charles V. Hamilton, in their definitive work, *Black Power* (1967:79–80), offer four bases on which viable biracial coalitions may be formed. These may also apply to coalitions among blacks, Latinos, Asians, and Indians.

1. Parties entering into a coalition must recognize their respective self-interests;

2. each party must believe it will benefit from a cooperative relationship with the other or others;

3. each party must have its own independent power base and also have control over its own decision-making; and

4. each party must recognize that the coalition is formed with specific and identifiable goals in mind.

Accordingly, *interests* rather than *ideology* provide the most substantial basis for the most productive biracial coalitions. Arguing that "politics results from a conflict of interests, not of conscience," Carmichael and Hamilton (1967:75) suggest that whites—liberal or otherwise—would desert blacks if their own interests were threatened.

Yet the argument of interests versus ideology is at the heart of the debate over a theory of biracial coalitions. One side of the argument sees interests as the ties that bind biracial coalitions together, coalitions that are, at best, short-lived tactical compromises among self-centered groups. Those who emphasize ideology argue that the essential element of biracial coalitions is common beliefs. This perspective of coalition theory holds that preexisting racial attitudes influence one's perception of racial issues and that these attitudes shape political actions. Thus, coalitions form not from objective self-interests but from shared ideology. The most likely coalition will be one between groups that are close in ideology even when another union would be more advantageous.

The interests-versus-ideology distinction for biracial coalitions is not as clear-cut and dichotomized as it may appear. When black and liberal white—primarily Jewish—interests came into conflict in New York City, liberal sentiments were insufficient to hold the coalition together (Sonenshein 1990). Nevertheless, although ideology alone may not hold coalitions together, without a shared ideology, biracial and interracial coalitions are unlikely to form in the first place (Sonenshein 1993).

There are numerous instances of coalitions between blacks and Latinos. Common concerns during the 1960s, such as poverty, formed the foundation for unions between blacks and Latinos, especially Mexican Americans (Estrada et al. 1981), and there is clear evidence of coalition building between blacks and Latinos (see, for example, Browning, Marshall, and Tabb 1984, 1990; Henry and Muñoz 1991; Sonenshein 1993). Since the early 1970s in Los Angeles, the mechanism for minority **political incorporation** has been a tightly knit coalition of African Americans and liberal whites, primarily Jews, with subsidiary support from Latinos and Asians (Sonenshein 1993).

The coalitions between blacks and Latinos, however, began to break apart when policies designed to promote equal access and equity for different groups were sometimes in conflict. For example, blacks were concerned that bilingual education would shift resources from the effort toward desegregation and thus were not supportive of it (Falcón 1988:178). Other policy issues of concern to Latinos that were not perceived as being supported by blacks included the English-only movement, employer sanctions, and the extension of coverage to Latinos in amendments to the Voting Rights Act (National Council of La Raza 1990). Furthermore, Latinos began to question whether affirmative action had benefited them as much as it had blacks because they felt blacks had secured more municipal jobs than had Latinos (Cohen 1982; Falcón 1988).

The coalition between blacks and liberal whites in Los Angeles was begin-ning to show signs of strain during the last years of Thomas Bradley's adminis-tration because of divergent economic interests among the primary partners and increasing demands on the part of Asians and Latinos for **incorpora-tion**—the extent to which a group is represented in dominant policymaking coalitions—into city politics (Sonenshein 1990). In Los Angeles, Asians and Latinos differ significantly from blacks and whites in terms of ideology and interests (Henry and Muñoz 1991:329). (These ideological differences among blacks, Latinos, and Asians are discussed in Chapter 3.) Although recogniz-ing—as we stressed—that standard labels of liberal, moderate, and conserva-tive are too simplistic to reflect the range of ideological orientations within racial minority groups, we can safely conclude that historically African Ameri-cans, Mexicans, and Puerto Ricans hold more liberal perspectives on a range of issues than do Cubans and Asians. Within the Asian group, Chinese Americans are far more conservative than are either Japanese or Koreans.

A 1993 *Los Angeles Times* survey of Southern California residents—whites, blacks, Asians, and Latinos—found that 65 percent of blacks identified whites as being the most prejudiced group, and 45 percent felt Asians were the next most prejudiced group, an increase from the 19 percent of blacks who ex-pressed this feeling in a similar 1989 survey. Moreover, blacks believed that Asians (39 percent), far more than whites (29 percent), were gaining economic power to an extent that was not good for Southern California (UCLA Asian American Studies Center 1993:5). When pressed to be specific about which group of Asians was perceived as causing problems, a quarter of both blacks and Latinos felt all Asians were doing so, although 19 percent of blacks identi-fied Koreans as the source of problems, and a similar percentage of Latinos mentioned Vietnamese. For the most part, blacks did not view Latinos as being prejudiced (11 percent) nor as gaining more economic power than was good for the area (16 percent). These results support the inference that blacks and

Latinos are the most likely coalition partners, followed by Asians and then Anglos (Henry and Muñoz 1991:330). Other analysis has found affinities between blacks and Latinos as compared to whites and Asians (Uhlaner 1991). Evidence such as this demonstrates the difficulties in forming coalitions of racial minorities (Sonenshein 1993:263).

Competition may also arise among the various groups when blacks, Latinos, and Asians each have different goals, when there is distrust or suspicion among the groups, or when the size of one group is such that it no longer needs to form coalitions with other minority groups to gain political success (Falcón 1988; McClain and Karnig 1990; Warren, Corbett, and Stack 1990; Meier and Stewart 1991; McClain 1993a). There is increasing evidence that in many communities, blacks, Latinos, and Asians compete for scarce jobs, adequate housing, and government services (MacManus and Cassell 1982; Welch, Karnig, and Eribes 1983; Oliver and Johnson 1984; Falcón 1988; Johnson and Oliver 1989; Mollenkopf 1990). Moreover, some survey data suggest that a growing hostility and distrust exist among the three groups (Oliver and Johnson 1984; Johnson and Oliver 1989), with a majority of Mexican Americans not in favor of building coalitions with blacks (see also Grebler, Moore, and Guzman 1970; Ambrecht and Pachon 1974; Henry 1980; Browning, Marshall, and Tabb 1984).

A study using data from the 1980s of all forty-nine US cities with more than twenty-five thousand people and whose populations were at least 10 percent black and 10 percent Latino found that analyses of socioeconomic data—income, education, employment, and percent not in poverty—revealed no harmful competition in general between blacks and Latinos. The results support a positive covariation relationship: When any group (black, Latino, or white) prospers with respect to education, income, and employment, the other groups do significantly better as well. Political outcome data—percent on the city council, proportionality of council representation, black or Latino mayor—present a somewhat different picture. When either blacks or Latinos made political gains, they did so at the expense of whites. Political competition between blacks and Latinos was evident only when controls for white political outcomes were introduced. This suggests that as black and Latino political successes increase, political competition between blacks and Latinos may be triggered, especially as fewer whites reside in minority-dominated cities (McClain and Karnig 1990; McClain 1993a).

Evidence also indicates that competition appears to occur as the size of the black population increases, with negative consequences for Latinos, particularly on several socioeconomic measures. However, increases in the Latino proportion of a city's population do not appear to be related to competition that is harmful to blacks. Moreover, in a small sample of cities in which blacks constitute a plurality or a majority, Latinos seem to fare less well socioeconomically and, in particular, politically (McClain and Karnig 1990).

In the area of municipal employment, black and Latino outcomes are negatively related to white employment outcomes, which indicates a degree of competition for municipal jobs (McClain 1993a). Blacks or Latinos gain at the expense of non-Latino whites. But evidence also indicates that competition in municipal employment appears to occur as the size of the black workforce increases, with consequences for Latinos. The most significant predictor of limits to Latino municipal employment opportunities is the black percentage of the workforce. As the black share increases, Latino opportunities decline. Latino workforce percentage, however, does not appear to have the same effect on black municipal opportunities. Furthermore, in a small sample of cities in which blacks constitute a plurality or a majority, Latinos seem to fare less well in municipal employment outcomes; in cities in which Latinos constitute a plurality or a majority, the consequences for black municipal employment are inconsistent. Clear evidence that blacks suffer deleterious effects in municipal employment outcomes exists in only one city, Miami.

In a follow-up study using 1990s data of the now ninety-six cities in the United States with more than twenty-five thousand people and whose populations were at least 10 percent black and 10 percent Latino, McClain and Tauber (2001) found that political competition between blacks and Latinos had increased somewhat—increasing size of the black population had negative consequences for Latino city council representation. Interestingly, the new source of political competition was between blacks and Asians in many urban centers. The increasing size of Asian populations in cities had significant negative consequences for black city council representation and the election of a black mayor. What these results suggest is that as Asian presence in cities intensifies, blacks may lose their political advantage and indeed see their political outcomes reduced. As the demographic changes continue in urban cities, we are likely to see more rather than less competition among blacks, Latinos, and Asians in the future.

Bobo and Hutchings (1996), examining attitudes in multiracial settings, found that the more that members of a racial group felt alienated or oppressed, the more likely they were to regard other racial groups as competitive threats to their own group's social position. They also found that blacks and Latinos were most likely to perceive their relations with other minority groups in zero-sum terms. Moreover, the greater the social distance that Asians and Latinos perceived between themselves and blacks, the more likely they were to see blacks as competitors.

Oliver and Wong (2003) also examined attitudes of racial groups in multi-racial settings, finding that, with the exception of Asians, people who lived in neighborhoods where their group dominated tended to harbor greater negative stereotypes toward other racial minority groups. In other words, racial stereotypes increase as the percentage of one's own group in the neighborhood increases—the greater the perceived percentage of ingroup members within the neighborhood, the greater the sense of zero-sum competition with minority outgroups and the greater the perception of threats from immigration. Blacks and Latinos, who are the most racially isolated, harbored the most negative views toward other groups, but this pattern was not as pronounced among blacks and Latinos residing in neighborhoods that were racially diverse.

Gay (2006), in examining black attitudes toward Latinos, finds that in urban areas with diverse populations, the relative economic status of blacks and Latinos in a neighborhood is an important influence on black attitudes toward Latinos. In neighborhoods where Latinos held an economic advantage over blacks, blacks had more negative stereotypes of Latinos, were reluctant to extend equal political benefits to Latinos, and were less likely to view blacks and Latino economic and political interests as compatible.

Whereas this brief summary of research on interminority group relations indicates increasing competition between blacks and Latinos in certain urban areas, we must recognize that both coalitional and competitive behaviors may occur in the same city but between different strata of each group. For example, elites may engage in political coalition building, whereas working-class and lower-class people may see their interaction with other racial groups as constituting competition for jobs, housing, and city services. Recent Latino immigration into urban areas, especially in the South, has introduced a new dynamic into interminority group relations. Memphis, Tennessee; Little Rock, Arkansas; and Durham, North Carolina, are illustrative of this changing dynamic.

RACIAL THREAT AND COMPETITION THEORIES: MEMPHIS, LITTLE ROCK, AND DURHAM[1]

Demographic changes in all regions of the United States have been occurring at a steady clip over the past several decades. Almost all of the changes are the result of immigration, especially Latino immigration, which soared between 1990 and 2000 and continued at high rates between 2000 and 2013. The region of the country most affected by immigration is the South, and especially the Southeast (Brown and Lopez 2013).[2] A number of Southern states—North Carolina, Alabama, Georgia, Arkansas, and Mississippi—reported substantial increases in their Latino populations from 2000 to 2011 (Brown and Lopez 2013). Many saw even greater growth between 2000 and 2011. Alabama, for

PHOTO 6.2 *Cesar Alamilla, program director of KTUV, a Spanish-language radio station, is seen in the studio in Little Rock, Arkansas. The state also has two television stations broadcasting Univision programming and a wide range of Spanish-language newspapers and magazines.* (AP Photo/Mike Wintroath; ID: 060613033376)

example, experienced a 185 percent increase in its Latino population from 75,152 in 2000 to 186,209 in 2011. South Carolina, for example, experienced a 154 percent increase in its Latino population from 94,652 in 2000 to 240,884 in 2011, and Arkansas saw a 123 percent increase from 85,303 in 2000 to 190,192 in 2011 (Brown and Lopez 2013). Moreover, eight of the top ten states with the largest growth in Latino population were in the South—Alabama, South Carolina, Tennessee, Kentucky, Arkansas, North Carolina, Mississippi, and Georgia (Brown and Lopez 2013). The South, in fact, has the second-largest concentration of Latinos, 36.1 percent, following close behind the West, at 40.8 percent (US Census Bureau 2011). It is conceivable that by the 2020 census, the South might be home to the largest concentration of Latinos in the country.

Most of the literature on political and economic threat focuses on the threat whites perceive from blacks, but the framework may be useful for examining relations among similarly situated racial minority groups. Blumer's (1955, 1958) group position model argues that feelings of competition and hostility emerge on the part of whites (ingroup) as whites begin to feel that blacks (outgroup) are encroaching upon their status and position. Central to this model are the subjective feelings where whites feel they stand vis-à-vis blacks, with negative feelings and beliefs toward blacks being central to whites' reactions.

In research on immigration attitudes using the group threat framework, Wilson (2001) finds that Americans' perceptions of threatened group interests were related to negative attitudes toward immigration policy. Among nonwhites, perceived threats to group interests were related to opposition to legal immigration and policies benefiting undocumented immigrants. Overall, group interest threats appeared to be related to negative attitudes toward immigrants for both whites and nonwhites. Stephan et al. (2005), in three different experiments using college students at one university, identified that perceiving threats from immigrants can lead to prejudice. Various factors contributed to the negative attitudes—realistic and symbolic threats, negative stereotypes, and high levels of intergroup anxiety. Racial differences among the respondents were not explored.

McClain et al. (2007) found that in general, blacks and whites in Durham, North Carolina, perceived a potential economic threat from continued Latino immigration, but blacks felt more threatened than did whites. Among blacks, those who held negative stereotypes of Latinos were significantly more likely than were blacks with fewer stereotypes to feel that continued immigration would lead to decreased economic opportunity for blacks. Blacks and whites both appeared to be concerned about the rapid growth in the Latino population, but the factors contributing to the concern appeared to be different for blacks and whites. The perception of economic threat was not the only significant factor in blacks' concerns over Latino immigration. Holding negative stereotypes of Latinos was also a prominent contributor. Blacks with negative stereotypes of Latinos were more likely than were blacks with fewer stereotypes to be concerned about the rapid growth in the Latino population.

The changes in the racial dynamic of the South raise many questions that need to be addressed. Research in the area of the effects of Latino immigration on intergroup relations in the South is very recent and not extensive (Marrow 2005; McClain et al. 2006, 2007). Research by McClain et al. (2011) on three Southern locations—Durham, North Carolina; Memphis, Tennessee; and Little Rock, Arkansas—provides a glimpse at the context in which racial intergroup relations are playing out. These locations represent different Southern environments—from a majority black city (Memphis) to one where blacks and whites are basically represented in equal proportions in the population (Durham) to one where blacks are a minority of the population (Little Rock).

Durham, North Carolina

The city of Durham, like many Southern locations, is undergoing demographic change. In 1990, Latinos were slightly more than 1 percent of the population, but by 2000, their percentage reached 8.6 percent. For decades, whites were the majority in Durham (51.6 percent in 1990), but the increasing Latino population, along with a smaller increase in the Asian population, reduced the white proportion to the point where in 2000 blacks and whites were almost equal percentages of the population, 45.5 percent for whites and 43.8 percent for blacks, respectively.[3] By 2008, both the white and black populations had declined as a proportion of the city's population, yet were still virtually equal in proportion, with whites declining to 40.9 percent and blacks declining to 39.6 percent. Latinos as a proportion of the population had risen from 8.6 percent in 2000 to 12.3 percent in 2008. In 2012, those numbers were 39.2 percent for whites, 39.7 percent for blacks, and 13 percent for Latinos (US Census Bureau 2012).

Despite a history of racial segregation extending back to the 1870s, Durham is a city that has historically had a very prosperous upper- and upper-middle-class black community. In fact, one of the great ironies of segregation was that it allowed many black businesses to flourish and prosper, as is the case in Durham. The largest black-owned insurance company in the United States, North Carolina Mutual, was founded in Durham and is still headquartered there. In addition, Durham supports a number of black banks, libraries, hospitals, educational institutions, and other businesses. Much of this black middle class is present and active in everyday Durham today. For example, the median black family income in Durham in 2012 was $48,580. (For comparison, the median family income for whites was $87,642.) Slightly more than four-fifths, 84.3 percent, of the Durham black population age twenty-five and over had finished high school. Despite these gains, black poverty was significant in Durham. Almost a quarter, 23.1 percent of the Durham black population lived below the poverty level (US Bureau of Census 2012).

Given the strength of this elite group, black political power in Durham was in the hands of highly educated, oftentimes very wealthy, black citizens, and they had been very successful in achieving their objectives, primarily through their political organization. Due to blacks' political success and access to the ballot, Durham County was not one of forty North Carolina counties covered by Section 5 of the Voting Rights Act of 1965.

PHOTO 6.3 *The Reverend William Barber, head of the North Carolina NAACP, announces that the group is filing a lawsuit against the recently passed voter ID bill during a press conference held in Durham, North Carolina on Tuesday August 13, 2013. Seated are plaintiffs Carolyn Q. Coleman, left, Mary Perry, second from right, and Rosanell Eaton, right. Lead attorneys Adam Stein, top left, and Penda Hair, second from top left, stand behind Barber.* (AP Photo/ *The News & Observer*, Chris Seward; ID: 571295316461)

While black elites were the face of civil rights in Durham, the movement would not have thrived without significant contributions from the black poor and working class (Davidson 2007). Though the exigencies of racism made the coalition between poor and wealthy blacks necessary, there were significant tensions between these communities (Davidson 2007). Despite this alliance, wealthier blacks were much more economically secure, primarily due to the strong business sector, than were poor blacks, many of whom risked being fired for their activism by white employers (Davidson 2007). Moreover, in many poor black communities, black elites owned and operated the services and housing, and poor blacks found that racial solidarity did not preclude wealthier blacks from exploiting them.

Durham's Latino population is from economically depressed countries, for example, Mexico and Central America, with the majority of immigrants coming from Mexico.[4] As such, many of the immigrants have low education levels, and they are mostly unskilled workers. In 2012, only 37.1 percent of Latinos age twenty-five and over in Durham had finished high school, and the median family income was $31,062 (US Census Bureau 2012). The low level of education and skills among Latino immigrants led them primarily to low-paying, unskilled jobs in Durham. As such, Latino immigrants were most likely to come into competition for jobs and social services with low-skilled blacks.[5] The lack of resources also led to these new immigrants settling in poor black neighborhoods with high vacancy rates and no amenities (Flippen and Parrado 2012).

Memphis, Tennessee

Memphis is a much larger city than the other two in the study, with a 2008 population of 643,329 people. Memphis is also a majority black city. In 2012, 63 percent of the population was black, 27.2 percent was white, and 6.6 percent was Latino. In 1990, there were only 4,455 Latinos in Memphis, but by 2008 that number had risen to 32,371, and the numbers continue to increase. Most of these Latino residents are of Mexican heritage. More specifically, interviews with local immigrants reveal that many of them are from the west-central Mexican states of Jalisco, Michoacan, Guanajuato, and San Luis Potosi (Burrell et al. 2001).[6] Despite being a majority black city, majority status has not translated into higher socioeconomic resources. In 2012, the white population had higher median incomes ($72,220), education level (91.9 percent high school graduates), and lower poverty levels (11.9 percent in 2012) than did the majority black population ($32,237 median income; 81.1 percent high school graduates; and 33.6 percent poverty level). The metrics for Latinos were even lower ($28,335 median income; 49.5 percent high school graduates; and 43.1 percent poverty level).

In some ways, Memphis is similar to Durham, in that, although Jim Crow dictated the parameters of black and white public interactions and blacks were often disenfranchised at the state and national level, blacks enjoyed the right to vote in municipal elections—a pattern that was incongruent with that of most other Southern cities at the time. This modicum of political muscle had its limitations, however. Black votes in Memphis city politics counted only to the extent that they were cast in favor of the Republican political machine spearheaded by Edward Crump, which dominated local politics from the early 1900s through the early 1950s (Dowdy 2006).

Political power did not come easily to black Memphians. The Crump machine refused to run black candidates. This extended exclusion from elective office made it extremely difficult for blacks to gain a foothold politically (Wright 2000). The Memphis civil rights movement, and events such as the assassination of Martin Luther King Jr. in 1968, substantially increased tensions between blacks and whites. The first black candidate for mayor ran in

1967, but blacks were not successful in electing a black mayor until 1991 in a racially divisive and polarizing campaign (Wright 2000:123–72).

Despite the racial tensions, segregation, and political polarization, black Memphis developed the full range of black class structures similar to that of Durham. Blacks owned businesses, newspapers, banks and savings and loans, an amusement park, and numerous other businesses (Wright 2000:35). Thus, it resembled Durham in class structure but differed in its level of cooperative race relations.

Little Rock, Arkansas

For most Americans of a certain age cohort, Little Rock is seared in their memory as the site of the integration of Central High School in 1957. It is a city with a tortured civil rights history, a history that still appears to affect the attitudes of its residents. Little Rock is a city where, in 2012, non-Latino whites were still the dominant portion of the population, 47 percent, although their proportion was not as great as it was in past years. Blacks represented about two-fifths of the population, 41.1 percent, while Latinos were 6.5 percent (American Community Survey 2012). In 2005, 67 percent of the Arkansas immigrant population came from Mexico as well as other Latin and Central American countries (Capps et al. 2007), but many Latinos in the state were also arriving from initial immigration destinations, including California, New Mexico, and Arizona (*Economist* 2007).

Latino immigrants began to put down roots in Arkansas beginning in the 1980s, although there have been transient communities of Latinos in the state due to seasonal agricultural work since the 1890s (Capps et al. 2007; Leidermann 2007). As the poultry industry in the northwestern and southeastern regions of Arkansas grew, demand for unskilled, cheap labor increased. These jobs were largely filled by Latino immigrants.

Little Rock has a history of both relative integration (from the 1870s to 1890s/1900s) and fierce segregation (particularly from the turn of the twentieth century on). Public schools were widely segregated almost immediately after the end of the Civil War, though there had been some peaceful integration before 1957, as seen with the state university, some medical and law schools, and some small colleges. Public transportation became segregated under Jim Crow laws, though the bus system was integrated before 1957. Some of the race relations problems in Little Rock came out of the relative independence of the city's black community. This independence allowed for some black economic mobility, which was not acceptable to many whites, especially lowerclass whites (Graves 1989).

PHOTO 6.4 *Elizabeth Eckford ignores the hostile screams and stares of fellow students on her first day of school. She was one of the nine African American students whose integration into Little Rock's Central High School was ordered by a federal court following legal action by NAACP.* (Bettmann/Contributor, ID: 517322800)

Black independence also created increased tensions between blacks and whites. These tensions came to a head with the forced integration of Central High School in September 1957. The struggle between Governor Orval Faubus and President Eisenhower over the use of federal troops created more tensions as the state National Guard was used to keep the nine black students out on one day and ordered to support and protect their integration the next. Although federal troops were eventually called in to enforce the integration, their failure to protect black students from attacks by some white students served to encourage more anti-integration behavior. Additionally, once the troops left, the black students faced even more violent and nonviolent backlash from white students, and the black students generally received harsher disciplinary action for the incidents they were involved in (Kirk 2002).

Concern About Continued Latino Immigration

Using data collected in the three cities in 2007, McClain et al. (2011) found that in Durham, blacks were the most concerned about the possible overall effects of continued Latino immigration. Whites were as well, but to a slightly lesser extent. Of particular interest is the fact that the majority of Latinos in Durham also appeared to be concerned about the growing Latino population. Unlike in Durham, whites in Memphis appeared to be more concerned about continued Latino immigration than did blacks. But the levels for both groups were not at the level of concern of blacks and whites in Durham. Again, McClain et al. (2011) found that the vast majority of Latinos in Memphis were also concerned about continued Latino immigration, a level that was greater than that of blacks and whites in Memphis. Whites in Little Rock appeared to be more like whites in Memphis, where a larger proportion of whites were concerned about continued Latino immigration than was the majority proportion of blacks. But, again, the levels for both groups were not as high as the level of concern of blacks and whites in Durham. The fact that Latino immigrants also appeared to be concerned about the growing Latino population in both Durham and Memphis seems counterintuitive, but it suggests that Latino immigrants might perceive increased immigration as not being in the best interests of immigrants already in the area.

Economic Effects of Continued Latino Immigration

In Durham, the group that felt it had the most to lose economically from continued Latino immigration was native-born blacks, while whites in Durham believed that their economic opportunities were not affected by continued Latino immigration. On the other hand, even though Latinos in Durham were concerned about increased Latino immigration, most felt that continued Latino immigration would lead to increased economic opportunity for them. A similar pattern was observed in Memphis. Despite being a majority black city, the group that felt it had the most to lose economically was native-born blacks, while whites in Memphis, for the most part, appeared not to perceive an economic threat from continued Latino immigration. A sizable proportion of Latinos in Memphis was concerned that continued Latino immigration would reduce economic opportunities for Latinos overall, suggesting that Latinos in Memphis were more concerned about the economic threat posed by continued immigration than were Latinos in Durham (McClain et al. 2011).

As was the case in Durham and Memphis, the group in Little Rock that felt it had the most to lose economically was native-born blacks. And similar to their findings in the aforementioned cities, McClain et al. (2011) found that a majority of whites in Little Rock believed that they would have no more or less economic opportunities as a result of continued Latino immigration. While an extremely large proportion of Latinos in Little Rock was concerned about continued Latino immigration, a level that was on par with those of blacks and whites in Little Rock, they did not feel that continued Latino immigration would reduce economic opportunities for Latinos. In fact, Latinos felt they might actually gain economically.

Political Effects of Continued Immigration

Whereas whites in Durham did not feel an economic threat from Latino immigration, they did perceive a political threat—that is, they felt they would have less political influence. Blacks also perceived a loss of political influence from continued Latino immigration. As such, blacks in Durham felt that Latino immigration threatened both their economic and political positions, while whites in Durham believed the threat was a political one only. As one would expect, Latino attitudes differed substantially from those of blacks and whites in Durham—Latinos perceived that they would gain in political influence from continued Latino immigration. Of course, Latino immigrants have to become US citizens in order to exert electoral power. Yet we are at a point in the latest immigration cycle where there are now second-generation US-born Latino citizens. The most recent voter registration figures indicate that the number of citizen Latinos is increasing in North Carolina. As of January 21, 2017, there were 163,744 Latino registered voters in North Carolina, which is about 2.4 percent of the states' registered voters. In Durham, Latinos are now 3.3 percent of the registered voters, suggesting that in tight elections they might be able to swing the result to one candidate or the other (North Carolina Board of Elections, 2017).

In Memphis, both whites and blacks were concerned about a loss of political influence as a result of continued Latino immigration. As was the case in Durham, the overwhelming majority of Latinos in Memphis believed that they would have more political influence with continued Latino immigration. Again, it appeared that blacks in Memphis perceived both an economic and political threat, while whites perceived more of a political threat from Latinos. Given that Memphis is a majority black city, whites might have perceived a threat on both fronts, both from Latinos and from blacks.

In a similarity to the patterns present in Durham and Memphis, whites in Little Rock were also concerned about a loss of political influence, as were blacks. Similarly, Latinos overwhelmingly believed that they would have more political influence with continued Latino immigration. Thus, it appeared that whites in Little Rock were not concerned about economic losses but were definitely concerned about a loss of political influence due to Latino immigration. Blacks, as in Durham and Memphis, were concerned about a loss of both.

Relations Between Blacks and Whites

In Durham, a majority of whites and blacks believed that relations between whites and blacks in general were positive, but blacks appeared to view their relations with whites more positively than whites viewed their relations with blacks. On the other hand, in Memphis a majority of whites felt that relations between blacks and whites were negative, while only a small proportion of blacks felt the same way. Maybe the fast of being a minority in the city created a dynamic among whites, where their perception of the nature of relations with blacks was markedly different from that of blacks, who are in the majority, perceptions. Despite a very tortured racial history, or maybe because of it, blacks and whites in Little Rock believed that relations between the two groups were positive.

Relations Between Whites and Latinos

On the other hand, when whites were asked about relations between whites and Latinos in general in Durham, a slightly different picture emerged. Whites were more conflicted about their relations with Latinos than they were about their relations with blacks. Less than half felt that relations between Latinos and whites were positive, but more than a fourth were not sure about the nature of the relationship between whites and Latinos. Latinos were more positive about their relations with whites than whites were about their relations with Latinos. On the other hand, in Memphis, both whites and Latinos believed that relations between the two groups were positive, in contrast to their view of their relations with blacks. In Little Rock, both whites and Latinos believed that relations between the two groups were positive.

Relations Between Blacks and Latinos

In Durham, Latinos perceived a more negative relation with blacks than blacks perceived of their relations with Latinos. This same divergence in opinion on the part of blacks and Latinos on the nature of their relations was also present in Memphis. Latinos felt that relations between themselves and blacks in Memphis were negative compared to only a small portion of blacks who perceived relations in this manner. Again, maybe it was the situation of being a small minority in a majority black city that created this perception. But it might also be that since blacks were in the majority in the city, they were not as aware of the nature of relations with whites and Latinos, who were minorities in the city. The same differences were also present in Little Rock. Blacks felt that relations between blacks and Latinos in Little Rock were positive, while a sizeable portion of Latinos felt that relations were negative. A pattern that emerges in all three cities is that blacks perceived more positive relations with Latinos than Latinos perceived with blacks.

McClain et al.'s (2011: 232–234)[7] objective was to see what effect Latino immigration into three Southern cities had on intergroup relations. Additionally, they wanted to see if city context made a difference on the perceptions of intergroup relations. What they found was that city context does make a difference, but in other instances concerns about the effects of Latino immigration were more generalized. In Durham, blacks and whites were similar proportions of the population, and both groups were the most concerned about the growing Latino population than were blacks and whites in other cities. While both blacks and whites in Durham were concerned about increases in Latino immigration, in Memphis, a majority black city, whites were more concerned about the growing Latino population than were blacks. This same situation existed in Little Rock, where whites were in the majority but were still more concerned about the increasing size of the Latino population than were blacks. Thus, at least on this issue, it might not matter if whites live in a city in equal proportion, minority proportion, or a majority proportion; concerns about Latino immigration might be more generalized among whites across Southern areas that are unaffected by the demographics of their specific cities. Moreover, regardless of city context, whites also did not feel threatened economically by Latino immigrants.

What was clear across all three cities was that blacks perceived that they had the most to lose—economically and politically—from the increasing Latino population in their cities. The fact that blacks in Memphis also felt this threat politically and economically from the increasing size of the Latino population might suggest that the blacks in Memphis, a majority black city, might perceive that their hold on political power is tenuous. Yet whites in Memphis also felt threatened politically by increased Latino immigration. This latter finding might suggest that while whites may have perceived their economic situation as being secure from Latino immigration, they viewed their political situation far more apprehensively. Thus, city population demographics appeared to matter for whites' views of their declining political influence as a result of Latino immigration.

What is different, however, is that whites in Memphis, a majority black city, overwhelmingly believed that race relations were negative, as opposed to blacks and Latinos, who were more positive in their assessment of race relations in general. But whites and Latinos converged on their perceptions of each groups' relations with blacks—both perceived them to be negative, while blacks believed that they had positive relations with both groups. The fact that both whites and Latinos were a minority of the population in Memphis might have accounted for their view that their relations with blacks were negative.

On the other hand, blacks and whites in Little Rock, where whites were the majority, believed that relations between the two groups were basically positive. Blacks were a numerical minority in Little Rock, and while they did not manifest the angst against whites that whites did against blacks in Memphis, they were concerned about a loss of political power from continued Latino immigration.

The question of whether coalition formation is possible in Southern locations, like what was seen in the early 1970s and later in Los Angeles, is an open question. Only time will tell if blacks and Latinos will find common ground on political issues or if that common ground will be found between Latinos and whites.

CONCLUSION

We used three cities—Durham, Memphis, and Little Rock—as case studies of the ways in which the second dilemma is manifested. These cases identify possible patterns of relations among blacks, Latinos, and whites in Southern locations. The piece that is missing from these cases is the role that Asians might play in what we are constructing as a three-way dynamic; it might, in reality, be a four-way dynamic. Elements of these patterns of interaction are found in other cities as well—as demonstrated by our brief discussion of Los Angeles and its pattern of racial minority group coalition or competition politics at the beginning of the chapter. Our three case studies are suggestive of different patterns based on city context. In cities in which political parties are strong and actively involved in city politics, a different dynamic of coalition politics may be present. The increasing tension in urban politics among blacks, Latinos, whites, and Asians, however, seems to be present in many cities regardless of government structure and partisan activities. Whereas the competition between whites and various racial minority groups in urban politics is still a reality in some cities, competition among blacks, Latinos, and Asians will continue to increase as the white presence in many urban centers diminishes. Thus, the second dilemma for America's racial minority groups—what options to choose in attempts to gain access to the political process—is continuing and very complex.

DISCUSSION QUESTIONS

1. Should minorities work alone and bargain with the larger society, or do they need to form alliances to counter their minority status?

2. Why is there a popular assumption that blacks, Latinos, Asians, and American Indians will form coalitions? Is this assumption accurate? Under what conditions are multiracial alliances feasible?

3. One pattern of interminority group relations is competition. What are the conditions under which racial minorities view themselves as competitors with other minorities?

4. The immigration of Latinos into the South is changing the racial dynamics and interminority group relations. Under what conditions do you think blacks and Latinos will form coalitions? Under what conditions will those coalitions be between Latinos and whites? What about coalitions between blacks and whites?

5. What role do you think that Latino registered voters in the South might play in state and local elections?

NOTES

1 The results reported in this section are drawn extensively from: Paula D. McClain, Gerald F. Lackey, Efrén O. Perez, Niambi M. Carter, Jessica Johnson Carew, Eugene Walton Jr., Candis Watts Smith, Monique L. Lyle, and Shayla C. Nunnally, "Intergroup Relations in Three Southern Cities," in *Just Neighbors? Research on African American and Latino Relations in the United States*, edited by Edward Telles, Mark Q. Sawyer, and Gaspar Rivera-Salgado (New York: Russell Sage Foundation, 2011).

2 According to Anna Brown (2014), the Latino population increased fastest in North Dakota, although New Mexico, California, and Texas still have the highest Latino populations overall.

3 Both of these groups gained in absolute numbers of people but lost as a proportion of the population from 1990 to 2000 and in the 2000 to 2006 time interval.

4 The *News and Observer* (Raleigh, North Carolina) identified that many of the Mexican immigrants into North Carolina come primarily from rural towns in the State of Puebla (November 29, 1998; November 30, 1998). For the most part, these immigrants are unskilled and poorly educated.

5 In a series of articles throughout 2002 chronicling the lives of area residents living in poverty, the *Herald Sun* (Durham) provided a picture of life for Latinos in Durham. Fully 26 percent of the more than sixteen thousand Latinos in Durham lived below the federal poverty level, and, in order to make a good living, it was necessary for them to work more than one job (Assis and Pecquet 2002:A12).

6 This is based on interviews by Burrell et al. (2001) with local immigrants. But anecdotal evidence comports with this more systematic evidence. For instance, several buses offer direct trips from Memphis to various cities in the aforementioned Mexican states.

7 The discussion in this last section is drawn with some paraphrasing, from our 2011 article.

CHAPTER 7

Will We "All Get Along"?

Members of the Standing Rock Sioux community have been camping out since April in order to protest the construction of the Dakota Access Pipeline, a $3.8 billion proposed oil project that would build a 1,172-mile pipeline and would pass under Lake Oahe in North Dakota. Lake Oahe is home to a burial site sacred to the Standing Rock Sioux. Moreover, it serves as a key source of drinking water for their community.

Members of the Standing Rock Sioux community say they were not properly consulted about the project. Thousands of protestors have since joined the community in solidarity, and representatives from more than one hundred tribes have come to the Standing Rock Sioux Reservation to support the community. More than three hundred tribal nations have now pledged their support for the Standing Rock Sioux tribe. In August 2016, protestors began entering construction site areas, and over four hundred protestors have been arrested as a result. Tensions between demonstrators and law enforcement have flared repeatedly. On October 31, over 1.4 million Facebook users "checked in" to the Standing Rock Sioux Reservation in solidarity with the protests and escalating tension with law enforcement.

On December 4, 2016, the US Army Corps of Engineers under the Obama administration denied the easement needed for crossing Lake Oahe for the completion of the pipeline, thus necessitating a halt of the construction. After being in office for less than a week, President Trump signed an executive order on January 24, 2017, allowing the government to move forward with reconsidering the pipeline, which will likely mean the construction will resume in the near future.

—NORTH DAKOTA AND WASHINGTON, DC,
APRIL 2016–JANUARY 2017

The epigraphs that begin each chapter in this book are real, although some names, to rephrase the ending of the old television series *Dragnet,* have been withheld to protect the guilty. For many residents of this country, incidents such as these—such as race-based mortgage denials and race-based attacks against political supporters as well as the president's daughter—are thought to be long past. Even when they do occur, most people think they are limited to "backward" rural areas and Southern states. In fact, many citizens argue vociferously that "some people" (that is, racial and ethnic minorities) today make far too much of race and ethnicity. They deny the existence of widespread differences in treatment or opportunities based on race or ethnicity as America moves through the twenty-first century. Sadly, these are only a small sample of recent interracial conflicts that have been documented in the United States. Indeed, for other individuals, the events depicted here constitute evidence of the continuing salience of race and ethnicity in the American political fabric and of the differential treatment accorded many US residents based solely on the color of their skin.

When the Rodney King incident and the subsequent verdict galvanized the nation, they simply made undeniable what any conscious human would find difficult to deny—the fact that racial and ethnic conflicts were common in the United States as we moved toward the beginning of the twenty-first century. Yet, particularly during the Reagan and two Bush administrations, it was popular to think of racism as something long past. Over the past couple of years, the nation has once again found itself in the midst of a sort of "Rodney King 2.0," in that a plethora of video evidence of (often fatal) police violence against black and brown bodies surfaces practically every week. This evidence is now ubiquitous due to the advances in technology that allow a large segment of the population to carry smartphones with video-recording capabilities with them at all times. Twenty-five years after the Rodney King incident, the broader American public has again become privy to the realities of state-sponsored violence and ultra-targeted law enforcement, which many racial and ethnic minority communities experience at far higher rates as compared to the general population. Unfortunately, various segments of the population do not view this as evidence of a need to understand and address the ways in which the American political system continues to be strongly influenced and guided by race and ethnicity. Instead, many continue to use racialized ideologies to create justifications for the evidence of the lack of equality and justice, which remains a critical part of the system.

This new period in which we find ourselves, an amplified mirroring of the time around the release of the King video, brings to the forefront once again this crucial question: Can we all get along? In order to be able to fully consider the possibilities for the cooperation and togetherness that this musing calls into question, it is necessary to consider who this "we" references. There are two options that should be examined: the people and the nation, as governed by institutions. With regard to "the people," it is crucial to examine the state of race relations and to see the hopes and challenges we face when it comes to cooperation and coalition. This must be considered not only in terms of non-white and white, but particularly in terms of interminority group relations. The picture the data paint is one of realistic limitations and cautious optimism. While racial and ethnic minority groups cannot be considered automatic coalition partners, or even groups that identify with one another, there is evidence of both community-based coalitions in various localities and nation-based coalitions in which people from many different racial and ethnic groups come together to support one another's interests and livelihoods, as seen in the cases of Black Lives Matter demonstrations and the Standing Rock pipeline demonstrations. There is also evidence of intergroup competition that cannot be ignored, particularly if organizers are to work toward finding ways to build coalition and consensus.

With regard to de jure "the nation, as governed by institutions," it is essential not to fall into the trap of believing that the removal of racial and ethnic segregation and discrimination automatically demonstrates the end of racism within the sociopolitical environment. While the nation has certainly moved in a positive direction by working to remove many forms of inequality from the laws, as noted throughout this book, it is abundantly clear that systemic and institutionalized racism are still alive and well within America. There has been some acknowledgment of the persistence of these institutional realities—Hillary Clinton identified this as a problem within a 2016 presidential debate, there has been bipartisan support in Congress to engage in criminal justice reform, and so forth. Nevertheless, there continue to be consistent denials of and efforts to increase the existence of systemic injustice, like Republican-controlled state legislatures implementing stringent, racially targeted voter ID laws, vice presidential candidate Mike Pence's debate comments denying police bias and institutional racism, and so forth. Whether we can all get along comes down to which of these viewpoints—recognition or denial—holds the majority of political power at each level of government.

Nonetheless, as it becomes increasingly apparent that institutionalized racism and its explicit and implicit supporters give a resounding "no" to the question of "Can we all get along?," various racial and ethnic minority groups may be able to find ways to respond "yes, we can" to this same question. The degree to which racial and ethnic minority groups work together will depend upon their ability to find a sense of commonality and common interests, as well as their ability to reject the negative racialized narratives that are advanced by society at large. The resurrection of explicit white supremacist and white nationalist sentiment may work as a catalyst for coalition, but it will take time to determine whether, as Martin Luther King Jr. asked, there would be movement toward "community or chaos."

Race has been, and still is, an enduring piece of the American political fabric. Although the overt signs of segregation and discrimination that persisted through the vast majority of the nation's history are less common today, racism continues and is still practiced. Further, the vitriolic and highly racist response to the first black president has stripped the cover off the racist beliefs that we, as a nation, worked hard to pretend had simply vanished with the Civil Rights Acts of the 1960s. Perhaps the most direct and strongest evidence for the fact that race and ethnicity continue to be salient in the American political system is the rise and election of Donald Trump to the office of the presidency. President Trump's campaign rhetoric was highly racialized and xenophobic, and many of his strongest and most vocal supporters were white supremacist and white nationalist leaders and groups.[1] Given the continued salience of race and ethnicity, it is essential that people gain an understanding of the politics of America's racial minority groups in order to understand the American political system in general. One cannot truly be a student of American politics without also being familiar with the politics of race and the political behaviors of America's racial minority groups.

THE DILEMMAS REVISITED

We began this book by identifying the two primary dilemmas racial minority groups have faced and continue to face as participants in the American political process. The first dilemma is the asymmetry of the US commitment to freedom and equality for all and the denial of these rights, first to African Americans and American Indians and then to Latinos and Asian Americans. This contradiction, identified early by Alexis de Tocqueville, has been addressed in part, but problems still exist. African Americans, American Indians, Latinos, and Asian Americans are citizens, and no one questions the concept that the protections and privileges embodied in the Constitution apply to all citizens. Also, the right to vote is an accepted principle, and denial of the right to vote on the basis of color is prohibited—at least in theory.

Yet the issue of citizenship is still of grave importance for the Latino and Asian American communities. Because of new immigration into the United States of foreign-born Latinos and Asians, some segments of the American electorate see all members of these groups as immigrants. This perception of "immigrant status" has resulted in discrimination against and denial of rights of American citizens of Latino and Asian descent. For example, in November 1997, the Republican attorney general of Arizona issued a report detailing how in July of the same year police from the city of Chandler, with no interference and perhaps even with some assistance from the Border Patrol, detained people on the basis of their skin color and charged them with being illegal immigrants if they did not speak English well or if they could not produce a birth certificate. Whereas the action netted 432 illegal immigrants, it also netted hundreds of US-born Latinos and legal immigrants, including schoolchildren, threatening them with deportation to Mexico (where they had never been). Given the anti-Latino rhetoric of the 2016 Trump presidential campaign and his purported policy position of using a deportation force to remove eleven million undocumented immigrants in his first term, there is reason for concern that similar detentions and possible deportations of American citizens and immigrants with legal status could occur in the near future (and, in fact, is happening). Further, given the current appalling and dangerous status of detention centers, it is reasonable to predict that an administration that uses dehumanizing language and policy positions will extend and worsen the current human rights and due process abuses.

American-born Latinos have also encountered other significant and costly forms of government-enforced discrimination. Recently, Mexican Americans born with the assistance of midwives in the Southwest have been routinely denied passports by the US Department of State. In September 2008, nine Latino American citizens who were denied passports sued the US Department of State for racial discrimination. The lawsuit charges that the Department of State categorically questions the citizenship status of virtually all midwife-delivered Mexican Americans born in Southern border states (*Castelano et al. v. Rice et al.*). One plaintiff, David Hernandez, was born in San Benito, Texas, lived and attended school in the Rio Grande Valley, and served honorably in the US Army. Another plaintiff, Juan Aranda, was born in Weslaco, Texas, and has lived and worked in the United States all of his life. Hernandez and Aranda each submitted their birth certificate with their passport application, but the Department of State requested that they submit more documentation to prove their citizenship. Hernandez even had a letter from the Mexican Civil Registry stating that there was no record of his being born in Mexico, but to no avail. Despite his military service, Hernandez, along with Aranda and seven other Mexican Americans, were denied US passports. Both of the authors only had to submit their birth certificates with their passport applications, as is the case with most US citizens. In 2009, President Obama's Department of State settled the class action suit and agreed to implement new procedures designed to ensure that US passport applications by Mexican Americans whose births in

Texas were attended by a midwife would be processed promptly and that no eligible applicant would be denied a passport.

Many Asian Americans have been victims of similar injustices. As a result of the hearings on foreign campaign contributions to the 1996 election that focused on contributions from Asian foreigners, Asian Americans visiting the White House had their citizenship on official entry documents changed from "United States" to "foreign" based on their Asian surnames by a Secret Service security guard. In 1998, Matt Fong, a fourth-generation American and Republican California state treasurer, was asked by a reporter whether his loyalty was divided between the United States and China. In 2001, US representative David Wu (D-OR) and an Asian American colleague were detained at the US Department of Energy and were asked by a guard three times whether they were US citizens. Ironically, Wu was at the Department of Energy to address a group of employees, including some Asian American employees, who had concerns about racial discrimination and bias in that department (*Oregonian* 2001).

More recently, passage in 2010 in Arizona of the strict anti-immigration law, SB 1070, which, among other provisions, required Latino immigrants to carry their immigration papers to show to law enforcement that they were in the country legally, raised the question of how law enforcement would be able to tell the difference between a Latino American citizen and a Latino immigrant. (Various courts issued injunctions against the enforcement of this and other provisions of the law.) Clearly, as "foreign-looking" individuals, Latinos and Asian Americans may find themselves called upon at any moment to prove their citizenship. Few American citizens, except for Latinos, Asian Americans, and Muslim Americans, are confronted with this aspect of the first dilemma in the twenty-first century, although many Americans who change jobs are discovering that they have to prove their identity and employment eligibility to the satisfaction of the Immigration and Custom Enforcement (ICE), the agency that replaced the Immigration and Naturalization Service (INS).

A second part of the first dilemma, the right to vote, is still very much at issue. The debate is no longer about whether everyone has the right to vote— although there are still instances of localities blatantly attempting to deny or to interfere with the voting rights of racial minorities—but is now about the mechanisms used to protect the right to vote or the dilution of the vote of racial minorities. The issue is complex.

Chapter 2 discussed the Voting Rights Act of 1965 and its subsequent amendments. Debates over the intent, scope, and enforcement of the act continue. On June 25, 2013, the Supreme Court released its decision on the *Shelby County, Alabama v. Holder* case, and this proved to be a watershed decision for

Section 5 of the Voting Rights Act of 1965. The Supreme Court found Section 4(b), which provides the formula for determining which jurisdictions are covered, unconstitutional; consequently, this ruling made Section 5 (preclearance) inoperable without new legislation from Congress creating a new formula. The result of this ruling was an immediate onslaught of redistricting and changes in voting procedures and processes aimed toward diluting racial and ethnic voting strength and making it difficult for these groups to cast their votes. Attempts to dilute racial and ethnic minority voting strength occurred even before the Supreme Court heard the case.[2] The first among the blitz of new state and local laws came just a few hours after the Supreme Court's ruling, when the Texas State legislature enacted a strict Voter ID law that had previously been blocked by a federal court, given the disproportionate, negative effects it would have had on minority constituents. The Supreme Court eventually struck down the Texas law under Section 2 of the Voting Rights Act because it discriminated against Latino and black voters. Further, according to the Brennan Center for Justice, ten of the fifteen states that were completely or partially covered under Section 4(b) of the Voting Rights Act put forward legislation that aimed to restrict the voting rights and access of racial and ethnic minority voters in 2013 and 2014.

The second dilemma, what racial minorities should do to increase their access to the political process, is ongoing. As we live through the twenty-first century, what do we, the authors, see as the future for racial minorities in American politics? Do we envision more coalitions among racial minority groups, or do we anticipate increased tensions? As the numbers of the various minority groups increase in urban centers and, concomitantly, as the size of the white population decreases, interracial and interethnic tensions are bound to increase. As we have seen throughout this book, African Americans, Latinos, Asian Americans, and American Indians can differ in ideology, partisan identification, and policy preferences. Clearly, the old stereotype that "all minorities think alike," a variant of the racist stereotype "they all look alike," has been shown to be totally false. The groups may have some issues in common, but there are just as many issues on which they may disagree. Nevertheless, given the increasing outward manifestations of racial animus against all racial/ethnic minority groups throughout the Obama presidency, in conjunction with rising levels of white racial identification and group consciousness (Jardina 2014; Dentice and Bugg 2016), it is quite possible that racial and ethnic minority groups will begin to coalesce around common antidiscrimination, equal access, and due process interests.

Complicating this issue of the possibility of coalition are interminority group attitudes and beliefs. We must remember that racial minorities, having been socialized in a society that sees them as inferior to whites, are equally likely to believe in the inferiority of members of racial groups other than their own. Thus, blacks are likely to have stereotypical attitudes toward Asians and Latinos, Asians toward blacks and Latinos, and Latinos toward Asians and blacks. Moreover, immigrants coming to this country have formed their images of African Americans and American Indians from exported Hollywood films and US television. As a result of all of these factors, tensions among the groups will continue to increase and, unless elite members of the communities intervene, will only become worse.

Chapter 6 explored the effects of Latino immigration into the South and the potential effects this might have on the nature of intergroup relations— black and white and Latino and the various combinations. The findings of the studies discussed in the chapter do not bode well for relations between black Americans and Latino immigrants in the South. As Latino immigration continues at such high rates, this might suggest that Southern blacks will have to be concerned with racism and its consequences not only among whites but also among new Latino immigrants as well.

Another direction in which racial minority group politics may move is toward the formation of voting coalitions with other racial minorities. This clearly was the case nationally with the reelection of President Obama. Such movement, however, depends upon the political context within which these groups interact. In cities in which the various groups are numerical minorities and competition for representation appears to be between minorities and whites, the desire to increase the minority share of favorable political outcomes may represent the basis for coalitions. The opposite may be true, however, in cities where a racial minority has become a numerical majority. In those instances, the majority minority no longer needs to form coalitions with others to maintain electoral domination; thus, coalitions may be formed between other racial minorities and whites. At no time should we presume that the extant white power structure will not act in an attempt to maintain its hegemony. We are not sure what is going to happen in the South, but at the moment it looks as if coalitions between blacks and Latinos in the South might be rather difficult. Nevertheless, as many scholars are careful to note, minority group coalition and competition are highly contingent upon context: The history of those groups within a locality; the current social, economic, and political strength of those groups in local structures; and the proportions of the population held by those groups are all highly influential. These many different factors influence how groups will interact; as seen in Chapter 6, various cities in the South have differing levels of competition and coalition. In examining the issue of competition, Baretto, Gonzalez, and Sánchez (2013) find that in various places in California, where Latino and black populations are well established, Latinos may be less likely to see blacks as competitors, while perceiving higher levels of competition with other Latinos, which may suggest greater opportunities for interracial and multiethnic coalitions. They also find that Latino immigrants in California, as compared to Latinos who have been in the United States for more generations, perceive less competition with blacks. These findings are particularly important in that they bring forward the essential fact that minority groups, particularly pan-ethnic groups, are not monolithic. This diversity of histories, interests, and views shapes the political realities and outcomes people experience. Consequently, this brings us back to the points made in Chapter 5 concerning the necessity of utilizing intersectional approaches in order to develop accurate, nuanced, and contextual examinations of political environments.

An arena in which access for racial minorities is crucial and to which attention will also be directed in the future is the policy process. Only in recent years have a sufficient number of minority policymakers appeared to allow us to begin to gauge their influence. Obviously, much work remains. Although the number of minority elected officials contrasts starkly with the small numbers prior to the Voting Rights Act of 1965, the number is still a fraction of what it should be. As more racial minorities are elected to public office—particularly at the state and local level—appointed to significant government decision-making positions, and hired in larger numbers as professionals within the public sector, racial minorities' access to the policy process will improve, which will allow the mobilization and inside access models of agenda setting to be used. However, until the time when racial minorities have greater input into the policymaking process, they are likely to remain targets, rather than initiators, of public policy.

TARGETING RACIAL AND ETHNIC MINORITIES

Racial and ethnic minorities find themselves the targets of various negative policies. California passed an initiative curtailing public services to illegal immigrants (Proposition 187) in 1994 and an initiative terminating race- and gender-based affirmative action programs (Proposition 209) in 1996. Analysis of voting on Proposition 187 shows that counties with the largest Latino populations were strongest in their support of the proposition, despite the fact that statewide, Latinos voted against it 77 percent to 23 percent (Hero and Tolbert 1996:866). The implementation of Proposition 187 was blocked by an appeal, and in November 1997, a federal district court declared all provisions denying services to illegal immigrants in education, health care, social services, and law enforcement unconstitutional.

Overwhelming majorities of blacks (74 percent), Latinos (76 percent), and Asians (61 percent) voted against Proposition 209.

It was appealed to the Supreme Court after the Ninth Circuit Court of Appeals in San Francisco found it constitutional. In November 1997, the Supreme Court refused to hear the appeal, thereby setting the stage for Proposition 209 to go into effect.

In November 2004, Arizona voters overwhelmingly (56 percent) approved Proposition 200, a scaled-down version of California's Proposition 187. Proposition 200 requires individuals applying for public benefits to provide proof of citizenship. Additionally, it requires state workers to report to federal officials illegal immigrants applying for benefits; if they do not, they could be jailed. Support for the initiative was strongest among whites, but exit polls suggest 47 percent of Latinos in Arizona also supported the measure (Marosi 2004). In late November, the Mexican American Legal Defense and Education Fund (MALDEF) filed suit to block implementation of Proposition 200 and received a temporary restraining order against the state, keeping the measure from going into effect. In late December, however, a federal judge lifted the restraining order and ruled that the measure should be implemented. The measure was opposed by politicians from both political parties—Democratic governor Janet Napolitano and Republican senator John McCain. In 2006, Arizona voters passed Proposition 300, which stated that only US citizens, legal residents, or persons legally in the country would be eligible to participate in adult education classes offered by the Arizona Department of Education. Arizona voters also passed Proposition 102, which prohibits a person who wins a civil lawsuit from receiving punitive damages if the person is in the United States illegally. Concerns with illegal immigration and the determination of the constitutionality of Proposition 200 have generated efforts in other states; for example, in 2006, Colorado passed Referendum K, which directs the Colorado attorney general to initiate, or join other states in, a lawsuit against the US attorney general to demand that the federal government enforce existing federal immigration laws. In the 2008 elections, Colorado became the first state to turn back an anti–affirmative action initiative, but Nebraska passed an amendment to its state constitution prohibiting the use of affirmative action criteria in any agency of state government, including public universities.

As we mentioned earlier, in 2010 Arizona passed SB 1070, the broadest and strictest immigration law in the country at the time. The bill required immigrants to carry at all times documents indicating that they were in the country legally, made failure to carry them a state crime, and gave police broad power to stop and detain anyone suspected of being in the country illegally. It also made it a crime to apply for and hold a job without immigration papers.

The law, which became known as "Show Me Your Papers," was viewed as leading to racial profiling of Latino Americans, who would not have "papers" because they are US citizens, but could be detained because they could not prove their citizenship. To say the law was controversial would be an understatement. It was criticized by President Obama and former Arizona governor Janet Napolitano, then secretary of homeland security, as well as elected officials around the country and civil rights and immigrant rights groups. Protests were held in the state in opposition to the law in Arizona, and the issue of immigration and this law were part of the 2012 presidential campaign. The United States sued Arizona (*Arizona v. the United States*) to keep the law from going into effect. The US Supreme Court declared three of the four major provisions unconstitutional, leaving only the provision to be able to go into effect that police can check the immigration status of people they arrest before releasing them. This was a major victory for the federal government.

As the nation moves forward into the era under the Trump administration, it is likely that the targeting of racial and ethnic minorities will only increase. In the period since September 11, 2001, there has been a significant amount of targeting of Arab and Muslim Americans. The PATRIOT Act has made this far easier, in that it has given the federal government, particularly the FBI, the ability to encroach upon the civil liberties of Muslim Americans, especially in the areas of search and seizure and the questioning of "suspects" (Musabji and Abraham 2007). In his presidential campaign, Donald Trump indicated support for banning Muslim immigration into the country and for creating a registry of Muslim Americans. He also made it very clear that he planned to engage in mass deportation of at least eleven million undocumented people in the United States. In his first week as president, Trump signed executive orders to move forward on the Keystone XL and Dakota Access pipelines, which are directly targeted against American Indian populations. Additionally, throughout the Trump campaign, as well as directly within presidential debates, he painted himself as a "law and order" candidate; this particular rhetoric is directly connected with the movement toward policies supporting the targeting of black populations for mass incarceration.

VRA: LOOKING TO THE FUTURE

We foresee the nature of partisan politics and racial minority group voting undergoing changes, mainly in that parties will be forced to engage in policy-based outreach in order to obtain the support necessary for electoral victories. Blacks are not likely to shift dramatically from the Democratic Party to the Republican Party, primarily because the Republican Party is moving further away from issues of importance to the national black community. Moreover, the intolerance of differences that is seen among some Republicans, which was cultivated during the Reagan and first Bush administrations and exhibited at their 1992 national convention in Houston and in Pat Buchanan's presidential race in 1996, makes it even more unlikely that blacks will find the Republican Party a welcome alternative. Initially, the Republican Party during the first four years of the George W. Bush administration appeared to be reaching out to blacks, but that initiative fell by the wayside. Some of the actions by the Republican Party during the 2008 and 2012 presidential elections aimed at President Barack Obama were seen as racist, many of which we discussed in Chapter 3. In 2011, Marilyn Davenport, a Southern California Tea Party activist and member of the Central Committee of the Orange County Republican Party, circulated a racist cartoon that depicted three chimpanzees, labeled as a portrait of President Obama's family. The caption over the picture was, "Now you know why no birth certificate." Such events are not pulling blacks to the Republican Party. The election of President Obama might reverse the weak attachment to the Democratic Party that we have seen over the years. As you will recall from our discussion of the 2008 and 2012 elections, Democrats did not take black votes for granted and actively worked to increase registration and turnout. Blacks constitute an important voting bloc for the Democrats, and any significant weakening of party attachment is likely to create electoral problems in certain regions of the country. While Hillary Clinton maintained a great deal of African American electoral support, and this group was by far the demographic that gave her the strongest support, her campaign was not as successful at appealing to and mobilizing black voters in 2016 as the Obama campaigns had been in 2008 and 2012. In spite of Donald Trump's claims that 95 percent of the African American population will support him in 2020, as well as his parading of several black celebrities in front of video cameras, his race-baiting and antiblack policy positions will likely further solidify this partisan divide.

We also expect that Mexican Americans and Puerto Ricans will essentially remain within the Democratic Party fold, but that in some instances and some regions of the country—for example, parts of the Southwest—they will adopt an independent stance or see the outreach by the Republican Party as inviting. In 2005, members of the Congressional Hispanic Caucus were withholding their Democratic Party membership dues until House Democratic Party leaders assured them that the party would make concerted efforts to mobilize Latino voters and to address more actively the policy needs of Latino communities. But the anti-immigrant rhetoric of the Republicans might have curtailed what once appeared to be an opening. We also predict that Cubans' primary attachment to the Republican Party will continue to wane. Cracks are beginning to appear in the solid Cuban American Republican leanings. The exiled Cuban community appears to consist of three groups—those born in Cuba and who came to the United States before 1980, by far the largest group, who are solidly Republican; those who fled the island since 1980, have closer ties to Cuba, and are slightly more Democratic than Republican in their leanings, a small group; and those who are American-born decendants of Cubans with no ties to Cuba and who are more heavily Democratic than the other two groups, an ever-growing group. In the future, the latter two groups will begin to outnumber the first group, and we may begin to see a more pronounced shift to the Democrats among Cubans. We were cautious in our acceptance of the Pew 2008 National Survey of Latinos' finding that a majority of Cubans identified with the Democratic Party, but this might in fact be indicative of a trend in Cuban partisanship. This is further supported by the Latino Decisions 2016 National Election Eve Poll, which found that a majority of Cuban voters supported Hillary Clinton, as well as the Democratic candidate running for the House of Representatives within their districts, in the 2016 general election.

The groups most susceptible to being recruited by the political parties in the future are Asian Americans and American Indians. The group with the highest proportion identifying themselves as political independents is Asian Americans. Yet voting patterns in the 1996, 2000, 2004, 2008, 2012, and 2016 presidential elections suggest that they are moving toward the Democratic Party. The allegiance and voting patterns of American Indians appear to depend on the policy positions taken by the parties on issues of concern to the various subgroups. The defection of US senator Ben Nighthorse Campbell from the Democratic to the Republican Party in 1995 did not significantly move American Indians in the Republican direction.

Lest one think the politics and political behaviors of racial minorities are unimportant components of the American political process, estimates are that by the year 2060, Latinos will constitute 28.6 percent of the population. African Americans will be second, with 14.3 percent of the populace, with Asian Americans third at 9.3 percent. American Indians, although fourth, will also experience an increase to 1.3 percent of the population (Colby and Ortman 2015). In some regions of the country—for example, California—whites, according to the 2010 census, are already in the minority because the combination of racial minority groups constitutes a majority of the population. Hence, California has become the first nonwhite majority state in the continental United States. (The majority of Hawaii's population is Asian American and Pacific Islander.) Thus, despite barriers—past and present—to effective participation of these groups in American politics, racial minority groups will become more, rather than less, important to the American political system. And the increase in the numbers and geographic concentration of specific populations will make these minorities more potent political forces—forces with which both Democrats and Republicans will have to contend.

CONCLUSION

As we end this book, the answer to Rodney King's plea, "Can we all get along?" remains uncertain. Issues of race were at the heart of the beginnings of this nation, and they remain central to the American political system in the twenty-first century. Barriers to the full participation of racial minorities in that system remain. Many school districts are still effectively segregated, and second-generation discrimination issues are moving to the forefront. Racial prejudice does not appear to be waning and in fact is on the rise in the context of overt prejudicial statements and policy positions. Thus, one should not be so smug as to suggest, as some do, that "all that stuff happened in the past and has nothing to do with the situation today." History has a causal effect on the future, and historical effects linger for several generations and, in some instances, perpetuate themselves.

In spite of these ongoing concerns, progress has clearly been made. The authors are both black women: One was raised in the West and North, the other was raised in the South; one was born in 1950 into a society that was highly segregated, the other was born in 1982 into a society that was simultaneously relatively integrated and socially segregated. In our lifetimes, we have seen a major transformation in the social, educational, and political opportunities of various racial groups. One of us has seen grandsons and granddaughters of slaves registering to vote for the first time, the signs that designated "colored" water fountains and restrooms removed, and the election of the first big-city black mayors. We have both seen the election of the first black governor in the state that was at the heart of the Old Confederacy, integrated churches and police forces in the rural Deep South, and most importantly the election of the first black president of the United States. Progress has been made, although not equitably or swiftly.

We also have seen David Duke, a past and perhaps current Ku Klux Klansman, make a serious run for governor of Louisiana and providing his endorsement for Donald Trump's candidacy without electoral repercussions for the latter; three highly publicized cases of individuals—Charles Stuart in Boston, Susan Smith in South Carolina, and Jesse Anderson (the man who was killed at the same time and in the same prison as Jeffrey Dahmer)—who allegedly murder family members but initially blamed the crime on an unknown black assailant; a high school principal in Wedowee, Alabama, cancel (then reinstate) a high school prom to prevent interracial couples from attending; teachers label a bored black elementary school student as mentally retarded when he would not (not *could* not) read a passage he had been assigned; members of the US military at Fort Bragg, North Carolina, murder a black couple as an initiation rite into a neo-Nazi group; black churches burned, many for racial hatred reasons; a major oil company's executives tape recording of racially disparaging remarks about black employees; a black female university professor in Maryland rent a bungalow on her property to a white couple who subsequently terrorized her with racial epithets and threats of physical violence; New York City police officers brutalize an innocent black man with a toilet plunger in a precinct bathroom; black students receive death threats at Pennsylvania State University, necessitating police protection at graduation; a black professor let go after he complained that a white professor hung a portrait of a Klansman on a classroom wall, left a Confederate license plate in the professor's office, and gave him a film showing a runaway slave being hacked to death; a football coach of Marshall University calling the members of the Ohio State University football team "a bunch of Mandingos"; three crosses, reminiscent of the terror tactics of the Ku Klux Klan, burned in Durham, North Carolina; two white supremacists arrested for plotting to kill President Obama shortly before the 2008 elections; four white North Carolina State University students who wrote racist graffiti, including the phrases, "Shoot Obama," "Kill the Nigger," and "Let's shoot that nigger in the head," on a school wall after the election of President Obama; a University of Texas backup center on the football team who wrote on his Facebook page, "All the hunters gather up, we have a Nigger in the White House"; the chief US district judge in Montana, who was appointed by George W. Bush in 2001, use his government e-mail account to forward a racist e-mail message about President Obama to friends; the execution-style killings of three young Muslim Americans in North Carolina and of an imam and his assistant in New York City; someone setting fire to a Muslim woman's hijab in a crowded street in Manhattan; numerous unarmed black men killed by white male police officers who were subsequently either not indicted, or once indicted not convicted in spite of clear video evidence of wrongdoing; and, in a throwback to times we thought were long gone, three white teenagers in Mississippi pleading guilty to killing a black man because of his race and admitting to previously driving into Jackson to assault blacks. Unfortunately, this list is not remotely exhaustive. Obviously, many issues still need to be resolved, and such resolutions will only come with a great deal of conflict. Given the potential political influence of minority groups, we try to remain hopeful that progress will continue.

DISCUSSION QUESTION

1. What do you see as the future of racial minority group politics?

NOTES

1 In addition to endorsements from groups such as the Ku Klux Klan, various groups that supported Donald Trump had rebranded themselves as "Alternative Right"/"Alt-Right." This is a repackaging of white supremacist and neo-Nazi ideologies.

2 The Virginia State Senate was split at twenty Democrats and twenty Republicans after the 2012 elections. One senior Democrat, Henry Marsh III, a civil rights leader, attended President Obama's second inauguration. Taking advantage of his absence, Republicans introduced a surprise bill to redistrict the 2011 districts to ensure that Republicans would regain the state Senate in the elections of 2015, because they had one more vote than the Democrats did on that day. This stunt did not work as the Republican governor refused to support the effort, but if it had been signed into law, it would have to be precleared by the Justice Department under Section 5 because critics argue that the new map dilutes black voting strength. Given the Supreme Court's ruling, if the governor had not stopped this legislation, there would have been no mechanism for stopping this maneuver.

Glossary

Adoption is the stage in the public policymaking process in which decisions are made among proposed alternatives for dealing with a problem. This activity is most often conducted by the legislative branch of government.

Affirmative action programs operate on the premise that equal protection of the laws cannot be achieved simply by stopping discrimination but requires positive action to make sure that equality is realized.

Agenda setting is the phase in the policymaking process in which the particular issues gain exposure that is significant enough to cause policymakers either to choose to act or to feel compelled to act on them. The policy output is often determined by which actors are involved in the agenda-setting process. See also **inside access model**, **mobilization model**, and **outside initiative model**.

Antimiscegenation laws, which existed in more than half the states, banned interracial marriages. Most antimiscegenation laws addressed black and white marriages, although many states included prohibitions on white and Asian marriages and white and Hispanic marriages. Antimiscegenation laws were declared unconstitutional by the Supreme Court's 1967 ruling in *Loving v. Virginia*.

Bilingual education is the concept that purports that non-English-speaking students should be taught in their native language or should be taught to speak English. For Latino activists, **MALDEF** in particular, this issue has surpassed desegregation in importance and, in fact, can conflict with it.

Black and Tan Republicans constituted the wing of the Republican Party that favored Reconstruction and strong enforcement of civil rights laws. The Republican nomination of Barry Goldwater in the 1964 presidential election signaled the final demise of this faction.

Citizenship is the status of enjoying to the fullest extent the privileges and immunities granted by a sovereign state. At present the Constitution provides citizenship to all those born or **naturalized** in the United States. In the pre–Civil War United States, citizenship was determined by the state in which one resided, and as a means of furthering racial discrimination virtually every state refused to confer citizenship upon nonwhites. The Fourteenth Amendment (1868), at least on paper, mandated that states could not deny citizenship on the basis of race; however, it took more than a century and countless legislative acts and executive orders before all eligible racial minorities were granted full citizenship.

Classical liberalism is the political and economic theory—normally associated with John Locke and John Stuart Mill, among others—that posits that the individual possesses a sphere of rights free from interference by the state. These rights are both civil and economic in nature. Classical liberalism is the primary political theory underlying the US Constitution. Although it has conferred civil rights on the populace, it was also the justification for perpetuating slavery. The government was not allowed to regulate slavery because the slaves were viewed as their owners' property.

Coalition politics constitutes the way in which a collection of disparate groups come together to fight for a specific political purpose that is shared to some degree by all of the groups. In minority politics, coalitions form among the various racial groups, and controversy exists over how well the groups cooperate versus how much they are in competition with one another.

Congressional Black Caucus is a group of black senators and representatives that was formed in 1971 as a means of concentrating black power in Congress. The purpose of the group is to combine forces to promote issues of special concern to African Americans, and it has been influential on certain minority issues.

Congressional Hispanic Caucus. Latinos followed their black counterparts in 1977 with the formation of the Congressional Hispanic Caucus, and in 1994 Asians in Congress formed the Congressional Asian Pacific American Caucus.

Cumulative voting is a technique in which each voter can register an intensity of preference. Voters are not required to vote for only one candidate per open seat; they may apply all of their votes to one candidate or choose any other distribution up to the maximum number of positions to be filled. For example, a cumulative voting scheme for a six-person governing body would assign six votes to each voter. A voter, therefore, could vote for six separate candidates, place all six votes for one candidate, apply two votes to one candidate and four votes to another, or any other combination adding up to six. Cumulative voting is important because it allows minority groups—whether racial, religious, or partisan in nature—to concentrate their votes and, thus, to increase their chances for representation. Although controversial, cumulative voting schemes were used by Illinois to elect its state representatives for almost a century, and they have been present in several local jurisdictions throughout the United States.

Dominated groups are those groups that have been excluded from participation in the decision-making process by which society's resources are distributed. Racial minorities, among others, qualify as dominated groups.

Ethnicity subsumes a set of learned characteristics often, but not always, associated with nationality. These characteristics, such as language and religion, have frequently been the basis for discrimination against groups.

Evaluation is the final step of the policymaking process in which it is determined whether or not the policy had the intended effect. The methods employed to assess a particular policy are extremely crucial in the final evaluation.

Federalism constitutes the division of powers between the national government and the state governments. Each level exercises some powers exclusively while sharing others.

Formulation is the stage in the policymaking process at which issues on the agenda are converted to actual proposals to be considered for adoption into policy. The formulation stage is characterized by a number of alternatives to be chosen from in reaching a particular policy goal; therefore, a crucial element of the formulation stage is the composition of the institution(s) making the policy choices.

Grandfather clause was a device used by Southern states in the late nineteenth and early twentieth centuries to prevent black suffrage. By denying the right to vote to those whose grandfathers were slaves, the South effectively denied suffrage to virtually all Southern blacks. The grandfather clause is one of many examples of how the South circumvented Reconstruction. In 1915 the Supreme Court, in *Guinn v. United States,* declared that the grandfather clause was unconstitutional.

Group identity or cohesion, in terms of racial politics, refers to the extent of the solidarity expressed by members of a racial minority. Cohesion can be measured by the proportion of minorities who believe that their group experiences discrimination and by feelings of closeness to other members of the group. Cohesion is important because it is a strong predictor of how effectively a minority group can be mobilized for political action.

Group political consciousness is a measure of how individuals in a racial minority view themselves within that minority group—in particular, what they prefer to be called. It is an important gauge of group cohesion.

Implementation involves putting a policy into action after it has been formulated and adopted. As with the other stages of the policymaking process, implementation is subject to numerous influences that are both internal and external to the implementing agency or agencies; consequently, following implementation a policy may or may not resemble the form in which it was actually developed.

Incorporation is the degree to which groups are represented in the dominant policymaking coalitions within a city. Racial and ethnic minority groups have rarely been incorporated.

Inside access (initiative) model is a type of agenda-setting process in which issues arise within the sphere of government and are not extended to the mass public. Until racial minorities' presence within the policymaking elite is increased, this model is the least applicable to setting the civil rights agenda.

Interest group activities are the actions of organized associations of individuals who share the same views on a particular issue or set of connected issues and attempt to influence related government policies. Racial minorities can be classified as interest groups when they solicit the government on racial policies.

Intersectional identity is identity based on multiple salient dimensions—race, ethnicity, gender, physical ability, sexuality, class, and religion—given the recognition that these dimensions are inextricably linked.

League of United Latin American Citizens (LULAC) is an organization formed by middle-class activists to advance the goals of Latinos. The group has been instrumental in fighting segregation of Latinos in education.

Lily White Republicans represent a wing of the Republican Party that did not favor a strong Reconstruction or a civil rights platform. By 1964, the Lily White wing had emerged as the leader of the party.

MALDEF. See **National Association for the Advancement of Colored People Legal Defense and Educational Fund**.

Mobilization model is a model of agenda setting that considers issues that are initiated by the policymaking elite, yet for interest in the issue to be sustained, policymakers must extend it to the public at large. As with the **inside initiative model**, the mobilization model's applicability to the civil rights agenda is largely dependent upon the presence of minorities within the policymaking elite.

National Association for the Advancement of Colored People Legal Defense and Educational Fund (NAACP LDF) is a group of attorneys whose primary goal is to advance the cause of African Americans by using the legal system. Once fused with the NAACP, the LDF, or Ink Fund, is now an independent organization that has won many significant cases involving African Americans—most notably the *Brown v. Board of Education of Topeka* (1954, 1955) case, which outlawed segregation in public schools. Today, in addition to fighting racial discrimination, the LDF works on behalf of death-row inmates and the economically disadvantaged. Other minorities have followed the litigation-oriented model of the LDF, particularly the Mexican American Legal Defense and Education Fund (**MALDEF**) and the Puerto Rican Legal Defense and Education Fund (**PRLDEF**).

Naturalization is the process by which nonnative-born people can become citizens of the United States. In the past, restrictive naturalization procedures have been used to keep racial minorities—particularly Asians, American Indians, and Latinos—from becoming citizens.

Outside initiative model is an agenda-setting model that considers the process by which issues are brought to the agenda through the nongovernmental ranks. The issue is initiated by a particular group, then moves to the public at large, and, finally, reaches the relevant policymakers. This model of agenda setting is the most applicable to the efforts by racial minorities, who have not been present within the policymaking elite, to bring civil rights issues to the agenda.

Partisan identification is the attachment a group or an individual feels to a particular political party. It measures direction toward a particular party and intensity of support. Party identification is a useful indicator in predicting voting behavior. Blacks,

Chicanos, and Puerto Ricans are strong Democratic identifiers; Cuban Americans generally identify with the Republican Party; and Asians identify less strongly with either party.

Pluralism is a theory of government that contends that power is group based. Moreover, pluralism claims that because there are multiple points of access within American government, each group possesses an equality of opportunity when competing with other groups for power and resources. In minority politics, pluralism views each minority group as having the ability to compete adequately for power and resources; however, many scholars criticize pluralism for not taking into account systematic racial discrimination that exists within the system.

Political ideology constitutes the underlying beliefs, intentions, and attitudes of a particular social or political group, which in turn shape the group's actions and opinions on political issues. Ideology is traditionally conceived in terms of liberal, moderate, and conservative; however, numerous scholars find that classification scheme to be unsatisfactory. Furthermore, in relation to minority group politics, scholars have experienced difficulty in attributing a particular ideology to each racial group.

Political incorporation constitutes the extent to which a particular racial minority is able to exert influence within a political system. Incorporation goes beyond mere representation; rather, it is based on quality of leadership and coalition building with other racial groups.

PRLDEF. See **National Association for the Advancement of Colored People Legal Defense and Educational Fund**.

Public policies are the result of a purposive course of action by government officials attempting to deal with a problem. They represent what government does, as opposed to what it says it is going to do, about public problems.

Racial Group Identification is an individual's awareness of belonging to a certain group and having a psychological attachment to that group based on a perception of shared beliefs, feelings, interests, and ideas with other group members.

Racism is the belief that race is the chief determinant of human characteristics and capabilities and that differences among the races provide for the superiority of one race. Racism is the primary condition that leads to discrimination against one race by another.

Rainbow Coalition is a concept advanced by then presidential candidate Jesse Jackson in the hopes of forging a majority within the Democratic Party. Jackson sought to build a coalition of blacks, Latinos, Asians, American Indians, poor whites, and liberal whites as a means of pushing the party in a leftward direction. In 1984 the Rainbow Coalition met with limited success in influencing the Democratic Party platform; in 1988, following a more professionally managed campaign, Jackson was able to transform the Rainbow Coalition into a slightly more influential force.

Representative bureaucracy is a concept concerned with the degree to which the public workforce shares the demographic characteristics of the population at large. The presumption is that shared characteristics yield shared attitudes. If this is true, a representative bureaucracy should be a responsive bureaucracy.

Second-generation discrimination refers to a subtle form of discrimination against minority students in public education. Many schools group minority students together under the guise of remedial education, yet evidence indicates that this is in reality a form of resegregation—that is, schools are merely finding ways to keep minority groups separate and to provide them with an inferior education.

Separate but equal doctrine constitutes the interpretation of the equal protection clause of the Fourteenth Amendment, articulated in *Plessy v. Ferguson* (1896), which allows for racially segregated facilities as long as they are of equal quality. In reality, however, the facilities for blacks have been inferior to those for whites.

Social movements are efforts by disadvantaged groups to empower themselves. Prerequisites to the formation of social movements include an existing structure of social organizations, a leadership pool, the ability to tap outside resources, and skillful planning.

Socioeconomic status (SES) is a measure used in the social sciences that gauges the social and economic condition of a particular group or individual. Some of the indicators include educational attainment, income, unemployment rate, and poverty. For racial minority groups, socioeconomic status is a good predictor of political activity and of the ability of the group to overcome discrimination.

Southern Manifesto was the statement issued by most white Southern politicians immediately following the *Brown v. Board of Education of Topeka* (1954, 1955) decision, which outlawed segregation. The statement decried the decision and indicated that the South would be willing to fight its implementation. The Southern Manifesto was one of the first indications that the South would resist integration regardless of national policy.

Suffrage is, simply, the right to vote. Traditionally, the jurisdiction conferring the right to vote, or the franchise, has been the individual state. The states have used their ability to determine suffrage as a means of discriminating against women and racial minorities. Constitutional amendments (Fifteen, Nineteen, Twenty-four, and Twenty-six) and federal legislation (e.g., the Voting Rights Act of 1965) have been enacted to ensure universal suffrage for all citizens over age eighteen regardless of race, gender, or financial status.

Three-fifths compromise was the settlement reached at the Constitutional Convention maintaining that slaves would be counted as three-fifths of a person for ascertaining the population to determine representation in the US House of Representatives. This aspect of the Constitution, rendered void by the Thirteenth and Fourteenth Amendments, demonstrates the fact that slaves were not considered citizens by the framers of the Constitution. At the time of its adoption, the compromise was viewed as a means of cooperation between the North and the South; yet, as the history of the nineteenth century reveals, this harmony between the two regions was short-lived.

Valence issues are the issues on which political candidates compete by claiming to stand for the same universally desired values without specifically explaining how they will achieve those values. For example, many candidates campaign as being antipoverty. Valence issues can have a critical impact on elections by influencing voter support for the candidate who most effectively articulates those values.

Vote dilution impedes the ability of minority voters to translate votes into the election of candidates of their choice. Devices such as at-large elections and racial gerrymandering have been used for this purpose.

Voting behavior is the way people vote in elections and the forces that influence those votes. Contrary to some perceptions, voting behavior varies both among and within minority groups.

Voting Rights Act (VRA) of 1965 is the federal legislation that was passed at least partially in response to the black civil rights movement to protect the rights initially of blacks, and later, Latinos and American Indians.

White primary was a device used by Southern states by which the Democratic Party would claim that as a private organization it could prohibit African Americans and other minorities from participating in primary elections to select its nominees. The South was a one-party region; thus, the primary election almost always determined the eventual winner. As a result of the white primary, blacks and other minorities were effectively disenfranchised. In 1944 the Supreme Court, in *Smith v. Allwright,* ruled that the Democratic Party was a public institution and that, therefore, the white primary violated the Fifteenth Amendment.

With all deliberate speed was a concept formed by the Supreme Court in the 1955 case *Brown v. Board of Education of Topeka* (*Brown II*). The court ruled that desegregation must be implemented as quickly as possible, although not immediately. The vagueness of this doctrine allowed Southern communities to resist desegregation for almost two decades.

Time Lines

TIME LINE OF AFRICAN AMERICAN POLITICAL HISTORY

1619 The first twenty indentured servants arrive in Jamestown, Virginia, from Africa.

1641 Slavery is first officially recognized by American colonial law when Massachusetts incorporates slavery into its body of laws.

1776 The Declaration of Independence is issued; Southern states force Thomas Jefferson to eliminate antislavery rhetoric from the document.

1777 Vermont becomes the first American territory to abolish slavery.

1780 Seven black residents of Massachusetts petition for the right to vote, arguing "no taxation without representation," and have their claim upheld by a state court.

1781 The Articles of Confederation are ratified, extending citizenship to all free inhabitants. An effort by Southern states to limit citizenship to all free whites is defeated; however, the states soon find ways to circumvent this edict.

1787 The US Constitution is drafted. It considers a slave to be three-fifths of a person for apportionment purposes; it leaves citizenship requirements to the states; Article I, Section 9, forbids Congress to outlaw international slave trade prior to 1808 (after ratification, Delaware was the only state to forbid the importation of slaves).

1787 The Northwest Ordinances ban slavery in the Northwest Territory, which later includes Illinois, Indiana, Michigan, Ohio, and Wisconsin.

1793 The Fugitive Slave Law is passed (and is later upheld by the Supreme Court in 1842). It requires that the federal government assist in returning runaway slaves.

1804 Ohio passes a series of laws restricting the rights of freed blacks.

1807 Congress bans the importation of slaves. This action results in an increase in the number of domestic slave laws and in a stepped-up illegal international slave trade.

1820 The Missouri Compromise is passed, representing a settlement between slave owners and abolitionists. The act strikes a balance between the admission of slave states and free states to the union; it later turns out to be a failure.

1829 David Walker, a free black, begins publishing *Walker's Appeal,* calling for slaves and free blacks to rise up against slavery, using violence if necessary.

1831 The first National Negro Convention convenes in Philadelphia. It marks the first time that African Americans from all over the country meet to advance the plight of all blacks (free and slaves) living in the United States.

1836 Alexander Twilight is elected to the Vermont legislature, becoming the first black man elected to a state legislature.

1848 The Massachusetts Supreme Court, in *Sarah C. Roberts v. City of Boston,* upholds the practice of segregation. The language "separate but equal" appears in common law for the first time.

1850 The Compromise of 1850 allows California to be admitted as a free state and halts slavery in the District of Columbia but requires stricter enforcement of the Fugitive Slave Law. Alabama, Georgia, Mississippi, and South Carolina are disgruntled with the compromise and begin talk of secession.

1854 The Kansas-Nebraska Act rescinds the Missouri Compromise, allowing each state to decide for itself whether to be a free state or a slave state. For many states this decision ultimately leads to violence between the two factions.

1857 The Supreme Court decides *Dred Scott v. Sanford.* The decision, written by Chief Justice Roger Taney, declares that the Constitution recognizes the slave owners' "property" rights regarding slaves above the citizenship rights of blacks; it also declares that any attempt by Congress to regulate slavery in the territories is unconstitutional.

1861 The Confederate States of America commence the Civil War with an attack on Fort Sumter in South Carolina.

1861 The Federal Confiscation Acts call for freeing the slaves; however, they make exceptions in the border states, where the Fugitive Slave Law continues to be enforced.

1863 The Emancipation Proclamation frees all but the eight hundred thousand slaves in the loyal border states.

1865 The Civil War ends, and the Thirteenth Amendment abolishing slavery is ratified.

1868 The Fourteenth Amendment is ratified, requiring states to grant full citizenship to all citizens regardless of race; this includes forbidding states to deny "equal protection of the law" and "due process of law." Section 5 grants Congress broad discretion in enforcing the amendment.

1870 The Fifteenth Amendment, barring states from denying any man the right to vote because of race, is ratified; the Southern states easily circumvent the spirit of this amendment with poll taxes, literacy tests, and even violence.

1870 Hiram Revels of Mississippi becomes the first black to serve in Congress when he takes his seat in the Senate on February 25, 1870.

1870 Joseph Rainey of South Carolina becomes the first black member of the House of Representatives on December 12, 1870.

1875 The Civil Rights Act outlaws racial segregation in public accommodations and in the military; however, in the 1883 *Civil Rights Cases,* the US Supreme Court declares the act to be unconstitutional.

1876 When the presidential race is thrown into the House of Representatives, Republican Rutherford B. Hayes bargains with Southern Democrats, exchanging their support for ending Reconstruction. Upon assuming office in 1877, Hayes removes the military from the Southern states, leaving blacks unprotected in the process.

1880 In *Strauder v. West Virginia,* the US Supreme Court finds West Virginia's statute mandating all-white juries to be in violation of the equal protection clause of the Fourteenth Amendment.

1881 Tennessee passes a railroad segregation law. Similar laws are passed in other states: Florida (1887); Mississippi (1888); Texas (1889); Louisiana (1890); Alabama, Arkansas, Georgia, and Kentucky (1891); South Carolina (1898); North Carolina (1899); Virginia (1900); Maryland (1904); and Oklahoma (1907).

1883 In the *Civil Rights Cases,* the Supreme Court declares the Civil Rights Act of 1875 to be unconstitutional.

1884 In *Ex Parte Yarborough,* the US Supreme Court affirms the power of the federal government to enforce the Fifteenth Amendment. This case and several others, such as *Strauder,* demonstrate that the court was willing to enforce the Fourteenth and Fifteenth Amendments; however, this willingness was short-lived.

1895 Booker T. Washington delivers his Atlanta Exposition address, expounding the philosophy of his Tuskegee Institute, which purported that blacks should master labor skills and achieve economic independence before attempting to obtain political equality.

1896 In *Plessy v. Ferguson,* the US Supreme Court upholds Louisiana's practice of racial discrimination, declaring that separation of the races is allowable as long as the facilities are equal. This is known as the separate but equal doctrine.

1900 In reaction to the Supreme Court's sanctioning of segregation, Southern states begin to officially sanction segregated facilities. Some African Americans combat this unequal treatment with organized boycotts.

1901 George H. White, representative from North Carolina, the last remaining black in the Congress, leaves the US House of Representatives after being defeated when the Southern states rewrite their state constitutions to disenfranchise blacks.

1905 W. E. B. DuBois and other black leaders organize the Niagara Movement, a crucial national political convention for the development of the civil rights movement.

1909 Developing out of the Niagara Movement, the NAACP is founded as the lobby organization for black rights. W. E. B. DuBois is the editor of *The Crisis,* the NAACP's official publication.

1915 The Grandfather Clause, a device used by Southern states to deny the franchise to those whose grandparents were slaves—thereby effectively circumventing the Fifteenth Amendment—is declared unconstitutional by the US Supreme Court in *Guinn v. United States;* the NAACP is instrumental in sponsoring this litigation.

1919 The Nineteenth Amendment is ratified, giving women the right to vote.

1924 Mary Montgomery Booze is the first woman elected to the Republican National Committee.

1925 The Brotherhood of Sleeping Car Porters and Maids is founded by A. Philip Randolph; this is the first major black labor union, made necessary by the discriminatory practices of the white unions.

1927 Minnie Buckingham Harper assumes her husband's unexpired term in the West Virginia legislature, thus becoming the first African American female to serve in any legislative body in the country.

1932 In *Nixon v. Condon,* the Supreme Court rules that the Democratic Party in Texas is part of the state government; therefore, its white primary violates the equal protection clause of the Fourteenth Amendment.

1938 Crystal Bird Fauset becomes the first female African American state legislator when she is elected to the Pennsylvania House of Representatives.

1941 A. Philip Randolph threatens a large-scale march on Washington as a means to protest racial discrimination. He calls off the march after the government creates the Fair Employment Practices Commission, which can investigate instances of discrimination only in the government's war industries.

1944 In *Smith v. Allwright,* the US Supreme Court completely invalidates the Texas white primary as violating the Fifteenth Amendment.

1944 Adam Clayton Powell Jr. is elected as the first black US representative from New York.

1945 The Supreme Court, in *Screws v. United States,* rules that a Georgia sheriff did not violate a black man's Fourteenth Amendment rights by beating him to death "without the due process of law" for stealing a tire.

1946 The Supreme Court rules in *Morgan v. Virginia* that states cannot compel segregation on interstate buses.

1948 The Democratic Party and Harry Truman begin to extend themselves to African Americans by desegregating the military, creating a Commission on Civil Rights, and adopting a pro–civil rights platform at the party's nominating convention. The latter move causes many Southern state delegations to abandon the Democratic Party and form the States Rights Party, headed by South Carolina governor Strom Thurmond.

1948 Racially restrictive covenants in housing contracts are declared unenforceable by the Supreme Court in *Shelly v. Kraemer.*

1952 Charlotta Bass is the first African American female to be nominated for the US vice presidency by a major political party (the Progressive Party).

1954 The Supreme Court issues its unanimous landmark ruling *Brown v. Board of Education of Topeka,* declaring that in education, separate facilities are inherently unequal, thereby overturning the precedent set in *Plessy v. Ferguson.* This ruling renders segregated schools unconstitutional.

1955 The Supreme Court issues *Brown II,* which outlines the way the ruling in *Brown I* should be implemented. The court's standard of "all deliberate speed" is sufficiently vague to allow the Southern states to stall in desegregating their schools.

1955 The Reverend Martin Luther King Jr., Rosa Parks, and other civil rights leaders organize the Montgomery bus boycott, which ultimately results in ending discrimination on Montgomery, Alabama, buses.

1957 The first Civil Rights Act since 1875 passes.

1957 President Dwight Eisenhower, who initially opposes the Supreme Court's *Brown v. Board of Education of Topeka* ruling, dispatches federal troops to Little Rock, Arkansas, to enforce a court order to desegregate its schools.

1960 The Civil Rights Act of 1960 is passed.

1963 The Reverend Martin Luther King Jr. organizes the historic march on Washington, which more than two hundred thousand people of all races attend to protest racial discrimination; it is here where Reverend King gives his immortal "I Have a Dream" speech. The march on Washington is arguably one of the largest nonviolent protests in US history up to then.

1964 The Twenty-Fourth Amendment to the Constitution bans poll taxes in all federal elections.

1964 As a result of intensive lobbying by civil rights leaders and the keen political skill of President Lyndon Johnson, Congress passes a comprehensive Civil Rights Act; this legislation gives the federal government enormous power in compelling states to end their practices of racial discrimination.

1964 Constance Baker Motley is the first African American female elected to the New York State Senate.

1965 Again as the result of intensive lobbying by civil rights activists and the political know-how of Lyndon Johnson, Congress passes the Voting Rights Act; to ensure fair voting practices, this act places the voting practices of states that lag in ending voting-booth discrimination under the jurisdiction of the federal government.

1966 The US Supreme Court invalidates poll taxes in state elections in *Harper v. Virginia Board of Elections;* this case opens broad access to the polls to many previously disenfranchised African Americans.

1966 Edward W. Brooke, a Republican from Massachusetts, is the first black man elected to the Senate.

1967 Lyndon Johnson appoints appeals court judge and former US solicitor general and director counsel of the NAACP LDF Thurgood Marshall to the Supreme Court; he is the first nonwhite to sit on the court. The first big-city black mayors are elected—Carl Stokes in Cleveland, Ohio, and Richard Hatcher in Gary, Indiana.

1968   Dr. Martin Luther King Jr., arguably the most important civil rights leader in African American history, is assassinated in Memphis, Tennessee.

1968   Shirley Chisholm, from New York's Twelfth District, becomes the first African American female elected to the US House of Representatives.

1972   Representative Shirley Chisholm runs for president, becoming the first African American to launch a serious campaign for the US presidency.

1973   Thomas Bradley is elected mayor of Los Angeles. Lelia K. Smith Foley is elected mayor of Taft, Oklahoma; she is the first African American woman mayor in the continental United States.

1976   Barbara Jordan becomes the first African American to deliver a keynote speech at a major political party convention when she does so at the Democratic National Convention. Yvonne Brathwaite Burke, a representative from California, is the first woman to chair the Congressional Black Caucus. Unita Blackwell is elected the mayor of Mayersville, Mississippi, becoming the first African American mayor in that state.

1978   The Supreme Court issues its complicated affirmative action decision in *Bakke v. California*. The court rules that states may not use quotas as a means to ensure racial diversity; however, the court does allow states to use race as a "plus" for admissions qualifications to universities and professional schools.

1981   Ronald Reagan takes office as president of the United States; he instantly scales back the federal government's role in protecting the rights of minorities in the name of the "New Federalism."

1981   Liz Byrd is elected to the Wyoming House of Representatives; she is the first African American to be elected to the Wyoming State House.

1984   The Reverend Jesse Jackson becomes the first African American candidate to run for president within one of the two major political parties when he enters the Democratic primary. Although his campaign suffers from logistical problems, he still finishes third behind Gary Hart and the eventual nominee, Walter Mondale. At the Democratic National Convention, Jackson contends that his level of influence does not match the proportion of votes he garnered.

1987   Lottie Shackelford is elected mayor of Little Rock, Arkansas, becoming the first black woman elected as mayor in the United States.

1988   As a result of the liberalized primary process and better organization, Jesse Jackson runs a more successful presidential campaign; he finishes second behind eventual nominee Michael Dukakis. At the Democratic Convention, Jackson delivers his "Quilt Speech." In the general election, Republican nominee George H. W. Bush employs the racially charged Willie Horton commercial.

1989   L. Douglas Wilder, the grandson of slaves, becomes the first African American to be elected governor of a state, when he ekes out a victory over Marshall Coleman in Virginia. In the same month, David Dinkins is the first African American elected mayor of New York City.

1989 *Wards Cove Packing, Inc. v. Atonio* and a series of other cases are decided. The Supreme Court rules that when employees file discrimination suits, the burden of proof is on the employee to show the existence of discrimination; statistics are no longer considered evidence of racial discrimination in the workplace.

1989 General Colin Powell is appointed the twelfth chair of the Joint Chiefs of Staff, the first black to hold that position.

1990 In response to the *Ward's Cove* decision, Congress passes the Civil Rights Act of 1990, which allows for more statistical evidence to be used in employee discrimination suits. The act is vetoed by President Bush, and Congress is unable to override the veto.

1990 Sharon Pratt Dixon (Kelly) becomes the first woman and the first Washington, DC, native to be elected mayor of the nation's capital, as well as the first African American woman to be elected mayor of any major US city.

1991 Thurgood Marshall retires from the Supreme Court, and President Bush appoints black conservative Clarence Thomas as his replacement. Thomas's nomination faces problems because of his judicial ideology and charges of sexually harassing his employees. His nomination becomes a public show trial, pitting him against his African American accuser, Anita Hill.

1991 Congress passes another Civil Rights Act, virtually identical to the one passed in 1990. President Bush, whose popularity is waning, signs the bill.

1992 Four white Los Angeles police officers are tried for use of excessive force against black motorist Rodney King. The beating was captured on videotape; however, the officers are acquitted by an all-white, all-suburban jury. As a result of the verdict, Los Angeles erupts with racial violence and rioting; the physical, economic, and psychological damage is enormous.

1992 Arkansas governor Bill Clinton defeats incumbent George Bush as president of the United States; he promises to seek a new racial diversity.

1992 Carol Moseley Braun from Illinois is elected to the US Senate. She is the first African American female and the first African American Democrat elected to the Senate.

1992 Robert C. "Bobby" Scott is the first African American representative since Reconstruction, and the second African American ever to be elected to the US Congress, from the commonwealth of Virginia. He is of African American, white, and Filipino descent.

1993 The US government pursues a federal civil rights case against the four Los Angeles police officers accused of beating Rodney King, resulting in convictions and prison terms for two of the officers. The city is peaceful following the verdicts.

1996 Representative Gary Franks, Connecticut Republican, loses his bid for reelection. Franks was first elected in 1990.

1996 Members of Congress Cynthia McKinney (D-GA), Sanford Bishop (D-GA), and Corrine Brown (D-FL) all survive reelection in their redrawn districts. Their districts were declared unconstitutional and redrawn in *Miller v. Johnson* (1995) and *Johnson et al. v. Mortham* (1996).

1998 Carol Moseley Braun of Illinois loses her bid for reelection to the US Senate; President Clinton appoints her ambassador to New Zealand and the Independent State of Samoa.

1998 President Clinton is impeached by the House of Representatives; black Americans provide him the highest level of support of any group in the United States.

1999 President Clinton is acquitted by the Senate on impeachment charges.

2000 A contested presidential election occurs amid charges of black disenfranchisement in Florida and other states. The Supreme Court instates George W. Bush.

2001 President George W. Bush appoints Colin Powell as the first black secretary of state; Condoleezza Rice is appointed the first female and second black national security adviser. Bush also appoints John Ashcroft as attorney general of the United States, causing outrage from black politicians, civil rights groups, and the black public in general.

2003 The Supreme Court upholds affirmative action in undergraduate admissions at the University of Michigan but strikes down the procedure at the law school.

2003 The Reverend Al Sharpton and Carol Moseley Braun both decide to run for president.

2004 Condoleezza Rice becomes the first African American female to be nominated as secretary of state.

2004 Barack Obama is elected to serve in the US Senate over another black candidate, Alan Keyes.

2004 Texas A&M University abolishes its "Legacy Policy" after political and civil rights leaders pointed out the university allowed preferential admissions policies to children of alumni but refused to consider race in admissions.

2004 Bill Cosby lambastes poor blacks at an NAACP event recognizing the 50th anniversary of *Brown v. Board of Education* for "not holding their end in this deal."

2004 George W. Bush wins the black evangelic vote to be reelected. He captures 15 to 20 percent—about ninety thousand—of the African American vote in Ohio.

2004 Gwen Moore becomes the first African American elected to Congress from Wisconsin.

2005 Black civil rights activists press Mexican president Vicente Fox for an apology after Fox stated that Mexicans take US jobs that "not even blacks want."

2005 Judge John Roberts becomes chief justice of the Supreme Court. African American leaders express concern because he has a record of limiting federal courts to desegregating schools.

2005   Hurricane Katrina hits the Gulf Coast. Media images of mostly black victims and looters lead Americans to question the role that race played in the slow federal response.

2006   President George W. Bush addresses the NAACP after refusing to do so for the previous five years—the first president since Warren G. Harding to refuse to address the organization.

2006   The Voting Rights Act is extended for twenty-five years.

2006   Democrats control the US House and Senate. Black congressional leaders chair major House committees for the first time.

2006   Keith Ellison becomes the first black representative from Minnesota to be elected to the US House of Representatives. He is also the first Muslim in Congress.

2006   Mayor Ray Nagin of New Orleans wins a second term with the help of black absentee voters and white crossover votes.

2006   Deval Patrick wins the Massachusetts governor race; he is the first black governor of the state and the second elected nationally since Reconstruction.

2007   The Jena Six, the name given to a group of six black teenagers charged with the beating of a white teenager, sparks protests of between fifteen thousand and twenty-thousand people who believe that the charges held against them, including attempted murder, are excessive and racially discriminatory.

2008   Barack Obama becomes the first African American major party presidential candidate in American history.

2008   Cynthia McKinney becomes the Green Party nominee for the president of the United States, naming Rosa Clemente as her running mate.

2008   Barack Obama becomes the first African American elected president of the United States.

2008   David Paterson, former lieutenant governor of New York, becomes the first African American governor of New York State. Paterson is only the fourth black governor of any state, and is also the first legally blind American governor.

2008   President-elect Barack Obama nominates several African Americans to his cabinet, including Eric Holder Jr., Susan Rice, Lisa P. Jackson, and Ron Kirk.

2009   Barack Obama is inaugurated as the forty-fourth president of the United States on January 20.

2009   Eric Holder Jr. is installed as attorney general of the United States.

2009   Dr. Susan Rice becomes the first African American woman to serve as the US ambassador to the United Nations.

2009   Ronald "Ron" Kirk is appointed as the US trade representative to the United Nations.

2009 Lisa Perez Jackson becomes the first African American administrator of the Environmental Protection Agency (EPA).

2009 Michael Steele, former lieutenant governor of Maryland, becomes the first African American chair of the Republican National Committee, and thus effectively heads the Republican Party.

2009 The US Postal Service (USPS) issues a stamp set, consisting of six different stamps, in commemoration of twelve civil rights pioneers.

2009 President Barack Obama is awarded the Nobel Peace Prize on October 9.

2009 The Department of Education reports that over 2.2 million African Americans are enrolled in institutions of higher education. This is the highest number of blacks enrolled in higher education in US history.

2010 Shirley Sherrod is forced to resign from her appointed position as Georgia State director of rural development for the US Department of Agriculture but immediately receives an apology after being wrongly accused of expressing racist sentiments toward white Americans during a March 2010 NAACP event.

2011 Michael Steele, the first African American chair of the Republican National Committee, loses his bid for reelection to Reince Priebus.

2011 Herman Cain, a Republican Party member and Tea Party activist, unsuccessfully seeks the Republican presidential nomination for the 2012 election.

2012 Barack Obama is reelected as president of the United States.

2012 The Obama administration launches an initiative on Educational Excellence for African Americans in July.

2013 According to a US Census Bureau report released in May 2013, a higher percentage of African Americans than whites voted in the 2012 presidential election, meaning that blacks outvoted whites for the first time on record.

2013 Tim Scott, a member of the Republican Party, is sworn in as senator of South Carolina on January 3, becoming the first African American senator since the retirement of Illinois senator Roland Burris. Senator Tim Scott is also the first black Southern senator since Reconstruction.

2013 President Barack Obama's second inauguration takes place on January 21, 2013, marking the official beginning of his second term in office.

2013 On January 30, William Maurice "Mo" Cowan is sworn in as interim senator of Massachusetts to fill the vacancy left by John Kerry. Cowan, a Democrat, declines to run in the 2013 special election.

2013 Cory Anthony Booker, former mayor of Newark, is sworn in as senator from New Jersey on October 31, 2013.

2013 The Black Lives Matter (BLM) movement is established after the fatal shooting of Trayvon Martin, an African American teenager. Black Lives Matter is an activist movement that began with the use of the #BlackLivesMatter hashtag on social media. Participants in the movement organize protests and demonstrations to highlight issues connected to antiblack racism, particularly in terms of problems of police brutality and extrajudicial violence against African Americans.

2014 In November 2014, protests erupt in Ferguson, Missouri, and other cities around the country, including New York, Boston, Los Angeles, and Chicago, following a grand jury decision not to indict Darren Wilson, a white police officer in Ferguson, on civil rights violations for the fatal shooting of Michael Brown on August 9. Michael Brown, an eighteen-year old black man, was unarmed when he was shot.

2014 In December 2014, protests that began in Ferguson, Missouri, in November spread throughout the country after a grand jury in Staten Island does not indict the police officer who was involved in the chokehold death of Eric Garner in July 2014.

2015 Ludmya Bourdeau "Mia" Love assumes office on January 3, becoming the first black female Republican in Congress. She is also the first black to be elected to Congress from Utah. Love is the US representative from Utah's fourth congressional district.

2015 Vincent R. Stewart becomes the twentieth director of the Defense Intelligence Agency of the United States on January 23. Stewart is the first African American to hold this position.

2015 The 114th Congress includes two black senators and forty-six black members of the House of Representatives.

2015 Boyd Rutherford, a member of the Republican Party, assumes office as the ninth lieutenant governor of Maryland.

2015 Loretta Lynch is sworn in as attorney general of the United States on April 27. She is the first black woman to serve as attorney general.

2015 On May 3, Ben Carson announces his candidacy for president of the United States.

2015 Jenean Hampton, a member of the Republican Party, assumes office as the fifty-seventh lieutenant governor of Kentucky on December 8.

2016 HR 4238 passes unanimously in the House of Representatives and the Senate. The bill updates the language that the US federal government will use when describing members of minority groups. The new measure requires the federal government to use the terms African American, Asian American, Native American, and Hispanic, instead of Negro, Oriental, American Indian, and "Spanish speaking individual of Spanish descent."

2016 Kamala Harris, a Democrat representing California, is the second black woman elected to the US Senate. Harris, who is of mixed ethnicity, is also the first Indian American woman to serve in the US Senate.

2016 Ilhan Omar, a former refugee, is elected to the Minnesota State legislature, making her the first Somali American Muslim female legislator.

TIME LINE OF AMERICAN INDIAN PEOPLES,
ALL TRIBES AND ALL REGIONS

1000   This is the approximate date of the formation of the Iroquois League, the oldest political alliance in North America.

1638   The first reservation is established in Connecticut; remaining members of the Quinnipiac tribe are placed on this reservation.

1775   American colonists declare war against England. The colonies' provisional government—the Continental Congress—establishes three Indian commissions (northern, middle, and southern); each commission is charged with preserving amiable relations with indigenous tribes and keeping them out of the violence. However, many Indians ally themselves with the British, and many join forces with the American colonists.

1777   The Articles of Confederation organize the new government of the United States. The articles assume authority over Indian affairs except when the "legislative right of any State within its own limits [is] infringed or violated."

1778   The United States signs its first Indian treaty with the Delaware Nation; in exchange for access to that nation's land by US troops, the United States promises to defend and admit the Delaware Nation as a state.

1789   The US Constitution is adopted. Article I, Section 8, grants Congress power to regulate commerce among foreign nations and Indian tribes.

1789   Congress places Indian affairs under the War Department.

1802   Congress appropriates more than $10,000 for the "civilization" of Indians.

1803   As part of the Louisiana Purchase, the United States acquires lands on which numerous Indian tribes reside.

1815   The United States begins the process of removing Indians to western lands.

1816   Congress restricts licenses for trade with Indians to American citizens.

1824   The Bureau of Indian Affairs (BIA) is created within the War Department.

1827   John Ross is elected president of the Cherokee Nation; he is the first president since the adoption of the nation's new constitution that year in New Echota, Georgia.

1830   President Andrew Jackson successfully pushes his Indian Removal Act through Congress.

1831   The US Supreme Court, in *Cherokee Nation v. Georgia,* holds that Indian tribes are domestic dependent nations, not foreign nations.

1832   In *Worcester v. Georgia,* the US Supreme Court, in an opinion written by Chief Justice John Marshall, ensures the sovereignty of the Cherokees; however, President Andrew Jackson refuses to follow the decision and initiates the westward removal of the Five Civilized Tribes (Cherokee, Chickasaw, Choctaw, Creek, and Seminole). The term *Five Civilized Tribes* originated because these five tribes modeled their governments after American and state institutions and had been assimilated into the white culture.

1835   The Treaty of New Echota is signed. Cherokees agree to westward removal.

1838   The Trail of Tears begins. Cherokee Indians are forced to travel almost thirteen hundred miles without sufficient food, water, and medicine; almost one-quarter of the Cherokees do not survive the journey. The Potawatomis in Indiana experience similar hardships on their Trail of Death.

1847   Pueblos in Taos, New Mexico, ally with Latinos to overthrow the newly established US rule.

1848   The Treaty of Guadalupe Hidalgo (see Mexican American time line) is signed, bringing the Mexican War to an end. As a result of the vast amount of land ceded to the United States, many new Indian tribes fall under US jurisdiction.

1849   The Department of the Interior is created, and the Bureau of Indian Affairs (BIA) is shuffled from the War Department to the Interior Department.

1853   The Gaddsen Purchase (see Mexican American time line) is completed. More tribes come under the jurisdiction of the United States.

1854   Several southeastern US tribes (Cherokee, Chickasaw, Choctaw, Muskogee, and Seminole) form an alliance.

1861   The Civil War begins. Various Indian tribes fight on both sides. Stand Watie, a Cherokee, becomes the only Indian brigadier general in the Confederate Army; he leads two Cherokee regiments in the Southwest.

1864   Approximately eight thousand Navajos are forcibly marched to Fort Sumner, New Mexico, on the Navajo Long Walk; after three years of harsh imprisonment, the survivors are released.

1865   Confederate General Robert E. Lee surrenders to Union General Ulysses S. Grant at Appomattox; at General Grant's side is Colonel Ely S. Parker, a full-blooded Seneca.

1867   The Indian Peace Commission finalizes treaty making between the United States and Indian tribes.

1869   President Ulysses S. Grant appoints Brigadier General Ely S. Parker to head the Bureau of Indian Affairs (BIA); he is the first Indian to fill this position.

1871   Congress passes legislation that ends treaty making with Indian tribes.

1884   In *Elk v. Wilkins,* the US Supreme Court holds that the Fourteenth Amendment's guarantee of citizenship to all persons born in the United States does not apply to Indians, even those born within the geographic confines of the United States.

1901   Congress passes the Citizenship Act of 1901, which formally grants US citizenship to members of the Five Civilized Tribes.

1921   Congress passes the Snyder Act, which appropriates money for Indians regardless of their amount of Indian blood or their residence.

1924   Congress passes the Indian Citizenship Act, conferring citizenship on all American Indians.

1934   Congress passes the Indian Reorganization Act, which allows for tribal self-government, and begins the Indian Credit Program; concurrently, the Johnson-O'Malley Act provides for general assistance to Indians.

1939   Chief Henry Standing Bear and other Sioux leaders appeal to Korczak Ziolkowski, who worked on the presidential sculptures at Mount Rushmore in ex-Sioux territory, to create a similar monument to Chief Crazy Horse. Ziolkowski began work in 1947; in 1998, his son Casimir continued to work on the monument.

1944   In Denver, Colorado, the National Congress of American Indians is founded.

1948   Through judicial means, Indians in Arizona and New Mexico win the right to vote in state elections.

1949   The Hoover Commission recommends "termination," which would mandate that Congress no longer recognize Indian sovereignty, thus eliminating all special rights and benefits.

1953   Congress passes a law—introduced by Wyoming Representative William Henry Harrison—that gives California, Minnesota, Nebraska, Oregon, and Wisconsin legal jurisdiction over Indian reservations, thus initiating the termination process.

1958   Secretary of the Interior Fred Seaton begins to retract the termination policy.

1961   More than 210 tribes meet at the American Indian Chicago Conference, where the Declaration of Indian Purpose is drafted for presentation to the US Congress.

1968   Congress passes the American Indian Civil Rights Act, giving individual Indians constitutional protection against their tribal governments. This protection is the same as the protection the US Constitution provides against state and local governments.

1968   The American Indian Movement (AIM) is founded; it is a protest movement based on the model of the black civil rights protest groups.

1969   Indian activists occupy Alcatraz Island near San Francisco in addition to staging sit-ins at the Bureau of Indian Affairs (BIA).

1960s   From the late 1960s to early 1970s, tribes begin to create tribal colleges to ease the transition from reservation life to mainstream schools. Twenty-seven such colleges are created.

1971   The Alaskan Native Claims Settlement Act is passed; it eliminates 90 percent of Alaskan Natives' land claims in exchange for a guarantee of 44 million acres and almost $1 billion.

1972   In protest of a history of broken promises to Indian tribes, two hundred Indians participate in the Trail of Broken Treaties march, ultimately occupying the Washington, DC, office of the Bureau of Indian Affairs.

1973   AIM organizes an occupation of Wounded Knee on the Pine Ridge Reservation in South Dakota, near the Nebraska border; the occupation ends with an armed confrontation with the FBI. AIM member Leonard Peltier is still (as of

2017) held in federal prison for the murder of two FBI agents, despite evidence that his trial was unconstitutional and unfair.

1975 The Indian Self-Determination and Education Act is passed, returing to Indian tribal governments more control over their tribal affairs and appropriating more money for education assistance.

1979 The US Supreme Court awards the Lakota Nation $122.5 million in compensation for the US government's illegal appropriation of the Black Hills in South Dakota.

1980 The Penobscots and Passamaquoddies accept monetary compensation from the US government for their lands (the Massachusetts Colony—now the state of Maine), which the government took illegally in 1790.

1986 Congress amends the Indian Civil Rights Act and grants tribal courts the power to impose criminal penalties.

1988 The Alaskan Native Claims Settlement Act is amended, giving corporations the option to sell their stock after 1991.

1988 Congress officially repeals the thirty-five-year-old termination policy.

1992 Representative Ben Nighthorse Campbell, a Cheyenne from Colorado, is elected to the US Senate.

1993 Ada Deer is appointed assistant secretary for Indian affairs by President Bill Clinton. She is the first Indian woman to hold the position.

1994 Three hundred representatives from the 545 federally recognized Indian tribes meet with President Clinton, the first time since 1822 that Indians have been invited to meet officially with a US president to discuss issues of concern to Indian peoples.

1994 President Clinton signs a law that provides Indians with federal protection in the use of peyote in religious ceremonies.

1996 Laguna Pueblo faces a legal challenge regarding its long-standing tradition of allowing only men on the ballot for tribal office.

1996 The University of Arizona creates the first PhD program in American Indian studies.

1996 Congress passes the Native American Housing and Self Determination Act (NAHASDA). The legislation is designed to provide federal assistance for Indian tribes in a manner that recognizes the right of tribal self-governance.

1997 For the first time in history, American Indians are included in the presidential inaugural festivities as special and individual participants. American Indians are in the parade and have an American Indian ball.

1997 Alaskan Natives take a case to the Supreme Court regarding their right to tax others on their land (44 million acres in Alaska). The question posed: Does "Indian country" exist in Alaska as a result of the 1971 Alaskan Native Claims Settlement Act?

1997   Tribal constitutional problems in the Cherokee Nation in Oklahoma lead to intervention by federal officials. Tribal Justice Dwight Birdwell calls upon the United States to intervene and reinstate the Constitution of the Cherokee Nation.

1998   Four thousand Alaskan Natives march in Anchorage in protest of Alaska legislative and legal attacks on tribal governments and native hunting and fishing traditions.

1998   In a unanimous decision, the Supreme Court rules that, in the absence of a reservation, the Venetie Tribe of Alaska does not have the right to tax others on land conveyed under the 1971 Alaskan Native Claims Settlement Act. In essence, the court decrees that "Indian country" does not exist in Alaska.

1999   President Clinton visits the Pine Ridge Indian Reservation.

2000   The US Supreme Court declines to review a religious freedom case centering around the use of Devil's Tower in Wyoming, a sacred site to several Indian nations. This decision upholds a federal court ruling that supported the religious rights of Indians against challenges from recreational rock climbers.

2000   In *Rice v. Caetano,* the US Supreme Court strikes down a restriction that had allowed only persons with Native Hawaiian blood to vote for the trustees of the Office of Hawaiian Affairs.

2000   Assistant Secretary of the Interior Kevin Gover (a Pawnee) issues a startling apology to American Indians on behalf of the Bureau of Indian Affairs (BIA), decrying the poor treatment Indians have experienced from his agency.

2001   Census data show that the self-identified population of American Indians has increased from 1 million to more than 2.4 million, a 26 percent increase. An additional 4 million Americans claim at least part Indian ancestry.

2001   President George W. Bush nominates Neal McCaleb, a Chickasaw, to be the assistant secretary for Indian affairs.

2001   Loyal Shawnees gain federal recognition.

2001   A federal appeals court rules that tribal trust funds had been mismanaged by the government.

2002   Senator John McCain introduces legislation to reform the trust fund process.

2002   President Bush declares support for tribal colleges and universities.

2002   Interior Secretary Gale Norton and Assistant Secretary for Indian Affairs Neal McCaleb are placed in contempt of court for continued issues with trust fund reform.

2003   In a major appellate court decision on Native American sovereignty, the court rules that the Oneida Nation is exempt from having to pay New York State taxes.

2004   The National Museum for the Native American opens.

2004 The Bureau of Indian Affairs (BIA) rescinds both the Connecticut Schaghti-coke and the Eastern Pequot Tribal Nation's federal status. It is the first time the BIA repealed a federal acknowledgment.

2005 The Oneida Nation independently pledges $1 million to efforts to help survivors of the Indian Ocean tsunami and earthquake.

2005 Judge John Roberts becomes chief justice of the Supreme Court. Indian leaders are concerned because Roberts decided a number of cases that put limits on Indian country sovereignty.

2005 The Supreme Court, in *City of Sherrill, New York v. Oneida Indian Nation of New York,* rules that the Oneida Indians cannot reestablish sovereignty over land within their historic reservation that had been purchased in open-market transactions.

2005 The National Collegiate Athletic Association (NCAA) bans the use of "hostile and abusive" American Indian mascots from postseason tournaments.

2006 The Cherokee Nation's highest court, the Judicial Appeals Tribunal, rules that freedmen are full citizens of the Cherokee Nation; the court declares that Cherokee freedmen retain citizenship and voting rights, among other privileges.

2007 Cherokee tribes amend the Cherokee Nation Constitution, removing 2,800 freedmen descendants from tribal roles.

2007 The Mashpee Wampanoag tribe receives federal acknowledgment; this group spent thirty-two years in the Bureau of Indian Affairs (BIA) queue.

2007 Diane J. Humetewa of the Hopi tribe becomes the first American Indian woman to serve as a US attorney in Arizona.

2007 The UN General Assembly adopts the Declaration on the Rights of Indigenous Peoples. The United States, along with Canada, Australia, and New Zealand, vote against the adoption.

2008 The Wabanaki Council of Chiefs passes a resolution calling on UN nongovernmental organizations, the Human Rights Council, and the Organisation of American States to intercede on the tribes' behalf against incursions on tribal sovereignty by states and courts. This is directed toward the US failure to adopt the declaration.

2008 The *Cobell v. Kempthorne* (previously *Cobell v. Norton* and *Cobell v. Babbit*) class-action lawsuit filed in 1996 is closed. The suit was aimed at forcing the federal government to account for billions of dollars belonging to approximately five hundred thousand American Indians and their heirs and held in trust since the late nineteenth century. The trust is supposedly valued at over $100 billion, but US District Judge James Robertson mentions that any awarded restitution may range between $100 million and $9.9 billion.

2008 Steve Burrage, a member of the Choctaw Nation, is appointed state auditor and inspector of the state of Oklahoma.

2008   John Tyler Hammons, a member of the Cherokee Nation, is elected as mayor of Muskogee, Oklahoma. Hammons, a nineteen-year-old student, is one of the youngest mayors in US history.

2009   America's Affordable Health Choices Act of 2009 (HR3200 Healthcare Bill) promises to provide better health care for the American Indian population, with an approximate 13 percent increase in funding going directly to the Indian Health Service.

2010   John Tyler Hammons is reelected as mayor of Muskogee, Oklahoma.

2010   The Obama administration reaches a $760 million settlement with American Indian farmers and ranchers in the *Keepseagle* case, which alleged discrimination by the Department of Agriculture (USDA) in loan programs.

2010   President Obama signs the Tribal Law and Order Act (TLOA) into law in July. The TLOA "gives tribes greater sentencing authority; improves defendants' rights; establishes new guidelines and training for officers handling domestic violence and sex crimes; strengthens services to victims; helps combat alcohol and drug abuse; helps at-risk youth; and expands recruitment and retention of Bureau of Indian Affairs and tribal officers and gives them better access to criminal databases."

2011   Brad Carson, an enrolled tribal member of the Cherokee Nation and former member of Congress, is nominated by President Barack Obama, and confirmed by unanimous consent, to serve as the general counsel of the US Department of the Army.

2011   The American Bar Association passes a resolution recommending that all law schools around the nation require additional information or evidence of tribal affiliation from all individuals who indicate on their applications that they are American Indian.

2012   The US Department of Justice announces a pilot plan to establish a joint federal-tribal response to counter sex crimes on reservations.

2012   On October 12, the Department of Justice announces a policy that allows members of federally recognized Indian tribes to possess or use eagle feathers. In line with the policy, tribal members will not be prosecuted for possessing or using eagle feathers and other protected bird parts for tribal, cultural, and religious purposes.

2013   Carlyle Begay, a member of the Navajo Nation, assumes office as senator from Arizona. On November 23, Begay announces that he has switched from the Democratic to the Republican Party, describing the GOP as the "Party of Progress."

2013   Members of Congress take part in a ceremony on November 20 to bestow the Congressional Medal to honor code talkers from thirty-three American Indian tribes for their contributions during World War I and World War II.

2014   President Obama appoints Diane Humetewa as judge of the US District Court for the district of Arizona on May 16.

2014 Keith M. Harper assumes office as the US ambassador to the UN Human Rights Council on June 5, 2014. Harper becomes the first American Indian to receive the rank of US ambassador.

2014 On November 13, the US Government Accountability Office (US GAO) releases a report outlining recommendations for the Bureau of Indian Education that will enable the organization to improve its oversight of school spending.

2015 On December 7, the US Supreme Court hears oral arguments in *Dollar General Corporation v. Mississippi Band of Choctaw Indians*. The case considers whether American Indian tribal courts have jurisdiction to arbitrate civil tort claims against nonmembers, including situations where the sexual conduct of nonmembers is an issue. The case arose over the claim that the manager of a Dollar General store on tribal land had molested a thirteen-year-old Indian boy.

2016 A judge in Albuquerque, New Mexico, approves a $940 million settlement in a class-action lawsuit against the Obama administration by nearly seven hundred American Indian tribes and tribal agencies that have claimed the government underfunded contracts to manage education, law enforcement, and other federal services.

2016 In May, the US House of Representatives and the Senate unanimously pass a new law, HR 4238, that requires the federal government to use the terms African American, Asian American, Native American, and Hispanic, instead of Negro, Oriental, American Indian, and "Spanish speaking individual of Spanish descent."

TIME LINE OF MEXICAN AMERICANS

1540 Explorers from Mexico first enter the Southwest.

1821 The Republic of Mexico gains its independence from Spain.

1829 The Republic of Mexico outlaws slavery, thereby creating a conflict with many Anglo immigrants who were invited to settle in northern Mexico (now Texas) to fill a capital void and who wanted to retain the practice of slavery.

1836 Anglos and dissident Mexicans in Texas revolt and secede from Mexico, creating the Republic of Texas, where slavery is legal. The United States instantly recognizes Texas, whereas Mexico does not.

1845 The Republic of Texas officially becomes a US state.

1846 After almost a decade of hostility, the United States declares war on the Republic of Mexico. Many Americans believe Mexico is weak and can be easily conquered.

1848 The Treaty of Guadalupe Hidalgo officially ends the hostilities between the United States and Mexico. Mexico cedes a tremendous amount of territory to the United States. The United States increases its territories by 33 percent, acquiring most of the present states of Arizona, New Mexico, California, Colorado, Texas, Nevada, Utah, Kansas, Oklahoma, and Wyoming. Mexican citizens living in the ceded territories are given the option to go to Mexico or to remain and live under US rule. The United States grants Mexican citizens who elect to stay all guarantees of citizenship and freedom of religion; these guarantees, however, are not fully enjoyed.

1850 The California Foreign Miners Tax Law is passed, barring Mexicans from mining occupations. The hardships of the law are exacerbated by anti-Mexican violence.

1851 All native Mexicans are excluded from the California State Senate, and California passes the California Land Law, which strips most native Mexicans of their land. The Mexican American population in California is divided into the rich Chicanos, called Californios, and the poor masses, the Cholos.

1853 The United States dispatches James Gaddsen to Mexico to purchase land. Mexico is financially strapped and, therefore, is willing to sell the territory of what are now the southern portions of New Mexico and Arizona (the Gaddsen Purchase). The United States wants the land for a rail line to California.

1853 Antonio Francisco Coronel is elected mayor of Los Angeles, California.

1855 California passes a statute prohibiting vagrancy that is referred to colloquially as "the Greaser Law." The Bureau of Public Instruction in California requires that all schools use English exclusively.

1859 In Texas, Mexican Americans revolt against Anglo leaders; this is known as the Juan Cortinas revolt.

1879 Romualdo Pachecho, a Californio politician, is elected to Congress. Pachecho is the first Hispanic representative to Congress with full voting privileges.

1884 Juan Patrón is murdered in the territory of New Mexico. Educated at Notre Dame University, Patrón had been elected speaker of the New Mexico House at age twenty-four. He is best known, however, for his support of Alex McSween in his battle against Judge Warren Bristol and District Attorney William Rynerson in the Lincoln County, New Mexico, wars, which begin as a property feud and end with a violent shoot-out; other notable participants include Billy the Kid.

1889 In New Mexico, Chicano resistance efforts begin. The two predominant groups directing the revolt are the Gorras Blancas and the Manos Negros.

1890 The political party for the Gorras Blancas, the United People's Party, has several candidates in local elections in New Mexico.

1894 One of the first *mutualistas* (community-based support organizations) is formed in Tucson, Arizona. The Alianza Hispano Americano provides insurance and funeral services for Mexican Americans; it soon expands its activities to include political action and publishing.

1902 The United States passes the Reclamation Act, which significantly increases agricultural efforts in the Southwest and thus expands the demand for agricultural labor, which is satisfied by Chicanos.

1903 Two thousand Mexican American laborers march through Clifton-Morenci, Arizona, while striking against the arduous conditions they face in the Clifton-Morenci copper mines.

1907   Ricardo and Enrique Magon found El Partido Liberal Mexicano (PLM); the PLM organizes workers in Southern California and, at times, is regarded as militant. The PLM and followers of the Magon brothers spread throughout the United States, organizing Chicano workers.

1912   New Mexico and Arizona are admitted as states into the United States. In Arizona, Anglos control both politics and industry, whereas Chicanos control little of either. In New Mexico, Anglos control industry, but Chicanos are better represented in state government.

1915   The first Latino to serve in the US House of Representatives, Benigno "B. C." Hernandez from New Mexico, takes office; he serves from 1915 to 1916 and from 1919 to 1920.

1916   Ezequiel Cabeza de Baca becomes the first Hispanic governor in the United States when he is elected governor of New Mexico.

1917   The Immigration Act of 1917 places a tax on Mexican employees and requires literacy tests. Industrialists and agriculturalists in the Southwest, who rely on this cheap source of labor, eventually pressure the government into repealing the law. Ezequiel Cabeza de Baca is inaugurated as governor of New Mexico after serving as lieutenant governor (1912–1916) but dies after six weeks in office.

1928   The League of United Latin American Citizens (LULAC) is founded in Texas, composed primarily of relatively wealthy Chicanos. LULAC's main function is to compel all Chicanos to learn English as a means of getting ahead in the United States. LULAC is considered assimilationist in focus.

1929   The first Latino US senator, Octaviano A. Larrazola, a Republican from New Mexico, is elected to fill the unexpired term of a New Mexico senator who died in office. Larrazola serves only one year.

1930   Fedelina Lucero Gallegos, a Democrat, and Porfiria Hidalgo Saiz, a Republican, are elected to the New Mexico State legislature, becoming the first Latina women elected to a state legislature.

1935   Democratic member of Congress Dennis Chavez is appointed to fill one of New Mexico's Senate seats, which became vacant when the incumbent was killed in a plane crash; Chavez is reelected five times and dies in office in 1962.

1940   Unity leagues begin to arise in California; their primary objective is to combat segregation and discrimination directed at Chicanos.

1942   The federal government establishes the Bracero Program (Public Law 45) in response to the labor shortages caused by World War II; the program calls for Mexico to send workers to the United States to fill the void, with wages determined by both countries. This program increases the number of Chicanos in the Southwest, and the workers are given legal immigrant status. Chicano labor leaders oppose the program.

1944   The Comite Mexicano Contra el Racismo is founded to provide Chicanos with the necessary legal aid to fight discrimination and racism; its chief publication is *Fraternidad.*

1946   In what is later dubbed "the Lemon Grove Incident," California judge Paul J. McCormick holds that segregation of Chicano schoolchildren violates both California law and the US Constitution (*Mendez v. Westminster School District*).

1948   The American GI Forum is founded by Hector Garcia and other Mexican American veterans in response to a Three Rivers, Texas, funeral home's denial to bury a Mexican American killed in the Pacific during World War II. The forum works to advance political and social causes of Mexican Americans.

1949   Edward Roybal becomes the first Latino to be elected to the Los Angeles City Council since 1881; his victory is in part a result of the Community Service Organization's (CSO) work in registering Chicano voters.

1950   Operation Wetback commences. Since the end of World War II, there has been less need for agricultural labor; thus, many Mexicans are indiscriminately apprehended and deported to Mexico.

1951   The Bracero Program is renewed; many Chicano labor leaders view the Braceros as major hindrances in their unionization efforts.

1954   The Supreme Court acknowledges in *Hernández v. Texas* that Latinos are not being treated as "white" and recognizes them as a separate class of people suffering extreme discrimination. It is also the first US Supreme Court case argued and briefed by Mexican American attorneys.

1960   Chicanos who support John F. Kennedy's candidacy for the presidency form Viva Kennedy clubs. The activity of these clubs significantly aids the Kennedy-Johnson results in California and Texas.

1961   Reynaldo Garza, a native of Brownsville, becomes the first Latino to be appointed to a federal judgeship in Texas by President John F. Kennedy.

1962   Edward Roybal becomes the first Latino from California to be elected to the US House of Representatives when he defeats a white Republican incumbent in the Thirtieth District in Los Angeles.

1962   César Chávez leaves the CSO to form the National Farmworkers Association (NFWA) to unite all farmworkers.

1964   The Bracero Program is ended. Joseph Montoya from New Mexico is elected to the US Senate to the seat previously held by Dennis Chavez, serving until 1976, when he is defeated in his run for reelection.

1965   The NFWA supports the Filipinos in the Agricultural Workers Organizing Committee in their labor dispute with grape growers in Delano, California. This incident helps launch César Chávez to a position of national prominence.

1966   César Chávez negotiates contracts between his NFWA and the Schenley Corporation, Gallo, Christian Brothers, Paul Masson, Almaden, Franzia Brothers, and Novitiate.

1967   Reies Lopez Tijerina enters a courthouse in Tierra Amarilla, New Mexico, and attempts to place the district attorney under citizen's arrest. A shoot-out erupts, and Tijerina escapes. After a long manhunt, he is apprehended but is later acquitted of all charges.

1967   David Sanchez establishes the Brown Berets, a paramilitary group interested in defending Chicano communities.

1967   Elizar Rico, Joe Raza, and Raul Ruiz found *La Raza,* a magazine that serves as a primary chronicler of the Chicano movement.

1968   Chicano students walk out of five Los Angeles high schools, demanding more Chicano administrators and teachers, courses in Mexican American history, and a cessation of discrimination against Chicano students. The walkouts receive national attention. The leaders of the walkouts are indicted by a Los Angeles grand jury, but the indictments are soon dismissed as unconstitutional.

1969   Chicano university students form El Movimiento Estudiantil Chicano de Aztlan; the organization leads the Chicano movement throughout the Southwest.

1969   The Ford Foundation funds the Mexican American Legal Defense and Education Fund (MALDEF) as a legal aid group to fight for the rights of Chicanos.

1970   La Raza Unida Party (LRUP) chapters are formed to place candidates in races for office. LRUP's presence is felt in Colorado, Texas, California, Arizona, and New Mexico.

1970   Mexican American Ricardo Romo runs for governor of California on the Peace and Freedom Party ticket.

1971   In Crystal City, Texas (more than 80 percent Chicano), LRUP candidates dominate the elections for the board of education and city council.

1971   The First Chicana Conference is organized. The conference examines the role of women in the Chicano movement.

1972   Brown Berets occupy Santa Catalina Island for twenty-four days to protest illegal land seizure violating the Treaty of Guadalupe Hidalgo.

1972   The Dixon-Arnett Law is passed by the state of California; it provides that any employer who knowingly hires undocumented workers will be fined. The Supreme Court of California deems the law unconstitutional.

1972   Chicano lawyer Ramsey Muniz runs for governor of Texas on the LRUP ticket.

1973   In *San Antonio v. Rodriguez,* the US Supreme Court upholds the Texas school financing system despite claims that its inequities unconstitutionally deprive Mexican American students of their fundamental right to education. The court reasons that the Mexican American students are not absolutely deprived of education and that education is not a fundamental constitutional right.

1974   Raul Castro is elected the first Chicano governor of Arizona. LRUP does relatively well in California, Texas, and Colorado.

1977   The Congressional Hispanic Caucus is established to monitor legislation and "other governmental activity that affects Hispanics" and to "develop programs and other activities that would increase opportunities for Hispanics to participate in and contribute to the American political system."

1981 Henry Cisneros is elected mayor of San Antonio, Texas, which is 55 percent Chicano; he is reelected in 1983, 1985, 1987, and 1989 and steps down as mayor in 1991.

1983 Federico Peña is elected mayor of Denver, Colorado; he is reelected in 1987.

1986 The Immigration Reform and Control Act, which is a major effort to reduce illegal immigration, is passed. The act increases border patrol activities and provides for harsh sanctions against employers who knowingly hire undocumented workers; additionally, the law provides for legalization of all people who have resided illegally in the United States since January 1, 1982.

1989 President George H. W. Bush appoints conservative former New Mexico representative Manuel Lujan as secretary of the interior.

1989 Ileana Ros-Lehtinen becomes the first Cuban American elected to the US Congress, as well as the first Republican woman elected from Florida.

1993 President Bill Clinton appoints Federico Peña as secretary of transportation and Henry Cisneros as secretary of housing and urban development.

1996 Hector Garcia, founder of the American GI Forum, dies. Garcia's GI Forum is a veterans' organization that works to break down discrimination against Mexican Americans.

1996 Bob Dole receives a smaller proportion of the Latino vote (21 percent) than did any Republican candidate in twenty-five years. (Reagan won almost 40 percent in 1984.)

1997 President Clinton appoints Federico Peña secretary of energy; Bill Richardson, ambassador to the United Nations; and Aida Alvarez, director of the Small Business Administration.

1998 Cruz Bustamante is elected lieutenant governor of California; Antonio Villaraigosa succeeds him as the second Latino Speaker of the California Assembly.

2000 Latinos pick up four seats in the California Assembly, bringing the total to twenty, the largest in California history. Latinos have seven seats in the state Senate.

2000 Heather Fargo is elected mayor of Sacramento, becoming the first Latina mayor of a US city.

2001 The 2000 US Census indicates that Latinos are tied with blacks as the largest racial minority group in the United States and will surpass them and become the largest minority by the 2010 census.

2001 President George W. Bush appoints Alberto Gonzales as the White House counsel.

2001 Antonio Villaraigosa loses the mayoral election of Los Angeles to James Hahn.

2002 Loretta and Linda Sánchez are the first pair of sisters to serve simultaneously in the US Congress.

2003 Cruz Bustamante is the lead Democratic gubernatorial candidate in the California recall election but loses to Republican candidate Arnold Schwarzenegger with only 31.6 percent of the vote.

2004 Alberto Gonzales is the first Mexican American nominated as US attorney general.

2005 Antonio Villaraigosa is elected mayor of Los Angeles, the first Mexican American mayor in 133 years.

2007 Bill Richardson, governor of New Mexico, runs for Democratic nominee for president of the United States.

2008 The UN Court of Justice calls for a stay in the case of five Mexican nationals awaiting execution in Texas. The court argues that the five men may have been denied access to the Mexican Consulate, as required by the Vienna Convention on Consular Relations.

2009 Hilda Solis, former member of Congress from California, is confirmed as secretary of labor in President Obama's administration.

2009 Ken Salazar, former senator from Colorado, is confirmed as secretary of the interior in President Obama's administration.

2009 Univision, the most-watched Spanish language broadcast television network in the United States, is sold for a reported $13.7 billion to a consortium of broadcasting partners, including Saban Capital Group, Providence Equity Partners, Madison Dearborn Partners, Texas Pacific Group Capital LP, and Thomas H. Lee Partners.

2010 The state of Arizona passes a law known as the Support Our Law Enforcement and Safe Neighborhoods Act (introduced as Arizona Senate Bill 1070 and thus often referred to simply as Arizona SB 1070). This law requires immigrants to carry registration documents with them at all times. The law also requires police officers to question all individuals who they suspect may be in the country illegally.

2010 The US Department of Justice files a lawsuit against Arizona asking that Arizona SB 1070 be declared invalid because of the way that the state law interfers with immigration regulations that are federal affairs.

2010 Brian Edward Sandoval is elected governor of Nevada.

2011 The US Court of Appeals for the Ninth Circuit rules against the state of Arizona, blocking the most controversial elements of Arizona SB 1070, Arizona's immigration law, from going into effect.

2011 Susana Martinez becomes the first female governor of New Mexico, and the first female Hispanic governor in the United States.

2012 President Barack Obama indicates his willingness to visit Mexico in 2013 for the North American Leaders Summit.

2012 In January, a state administrative law judge rules that a Mexican American studies program violates Arizona law.

2013 Joaquín Castro assumes office as a member of the US House of Representatives for Texas's Twentieth District on January 3.

2013 Susana Martinez is reelected governor of New Mexico with 57 percent of the vote.

2013 President Obama makes an official visit to Mexico in May 2013, as part of a government effort to reinforce cultural, economic, and political ties between Mexico and the United States.

2014 On July 28, Julian Castro, a member of the Democratic Party, assumes office as the sixteenth US secretary of housing and urban development. Julian Castro is the identical twin brother of US Representative Joaquín Castro.

2014 The Ninth US Circuit Court of Appeals hears oral arguments on January 12 in a lawsuit against Arizona officials who eliminated a Mexican American studies program from public schools in Tucson, Arizona.

2014 MALDEF files a lawsuit in July against the City of Bellflower, California. The lawsuit is on behalf of three plaintiffs who contend that the city is violating their rights under the California Voting Rights Act of 2001.

2015 The Texas legislature passes a resolution declaring May 1 Mexican American Studies Day. The resolution, which is introduced by Democratic senators José Rodríguez and Sylvia Garcia, seeks to encourage people to learn about the value of educational programs with Mexican American curricula.

2016 Catherine Cortez Masto, a Democrat, is elected the first Latina senator from Nevada.

TIME LINE OF PUERTO RICANS

1493 Christopher Columbus lands on present-day Puerto Rico; he claims it as the Spanish island of Boriquén. Columbus calls the island San Juan Bautista. Approximately thirty thousand Taíno Indians are living on the island.

1508 Ponce de León is appointed governor of the island and founds the first settlement, known as Puerto Rico; he conscripts the Indians to mine for gold. The first school in Puerto Rico is established in Caparra.

1775 The population of Puerto Rico is 70,250, 6,467 of whom are black slaves. The Indian population has been completely wiped out.

1873 Slavery is abolished on Puerto Rico.

1897 Spain grants autonomy to Puerto Rico; as a result of immigration, the population approaches nine hundred thousand.

1898 The Spanish-American War begins. By July, American forces land on the island.

1899 The Treaty of Paris is ratified, ending the Spanish-American War. The United States annexes the island of Puerto Rico.

1900 The Foraker Act is passed, making Puerto Rico an "unincorporated" US territory. President William McKinley appoints a governor to administer the territory. The first fifty-six Puerto Ricans arrive in Hawaii.

1901 Luis Muñoz publishes the first bilingual Spanish-English newspaper in New York City.

1917 The Jones Act grants US citizenship to all Puerto Ricans.

1937 Oscar Garcia Rivera becomes the first Puerto Rican to be elected to the New York State legislature.

1942 Hiram C. Bithorn becomes the first Puerto Rican Major League baseball player (with the Chicago Cubs).

1946 The first Puerto Rican governor, Jesús T. Piñero, is appointed by President Woodrow Wilson.

1947 Felisa Rincón de Gautier is elected as the first female mayor of San Juan, Puerto Rico. She is the first female mayor of a major city in any of the Americas.

1950 Public Law 600 gives Puerto Rico a chance to draft its own constitution.

1950 Nationalists attack the governor's mansion, killing seventy-seven and wounding ninety. In Washington, DC, Nationalists attempt to assassinate President Harry Truman, killing a White House police officer. Pedro Albizu Campos and other Nationalist leaders are given lengthy prison sentences.

1952 The commonwealth of Puerto Rico ratifies its new Commonwealth Constitution. In the first election, the Popular Democratic Party wins the most votes, and the Independence Party finishes second.

1953 The United Nations directs the United States to discontinue classifying Puerto Rico as a non-self-governing territory.

1954 Four Puerto Rican Nationalists begin shooting in the US House of Representatives; five members of Congress are wounded.

1958 Tony Mendez becomes the first Puerto Rican to be appointed Democratic Party district leader in El Barrio, New York.

1966 Herman Badillo becomes the first Puerto Rican to be elected Bronx borough president, New York City.

1970 The 1970 census reveals that 2.8 million people live on the island of Puerto Rico and that 1.5 million Puerto Ricans live in the mainland United States. Herman Badillo becomes the first Puerto Rican member of Congress from the mainland.

1973 Maurice Ferré, a Puerto Rican, is elected the first Latino mayor of Miami. He serves six terms before he is defeated in 1985.

1974 A consent decree is signed between the New York City school system and Puerto Rican plaintiffs represented by PRLDEF, mandating bilingual programs in New York City schools.

1978   Olga Mendez becomes the first Puerto Rican woman elected to a major post in the United States, the New York State Senate.

1979   Luis Roviera is appointed Colorado State Supreme Court justice.

1990   José Serrano assumes office in the US House of Representatives.

1992   Luis Gutierrez (D-IL) is the first Latino to be elected to Congress from the Midwest.

1993   Nydia Velázquez (D-NY) becomes the first Puerto Rican woman to be elected to the US Congress.

1994   Carmen E. Arroyo is the first Puerto Rican woman elected to the New York State Assembly and the first Puerto Rican woman elected to any state assembly in the United States.

1997   A federal district court declares the majority Latino Twelfth District (Nydia Velázquez's congressional district) unconstitutional.

1997   Evelyn Mantilla becomes a member of the Connecticut House of Representatives.

1997   Gloria Tristani becomes the first Latina member of the Federal Communications Commission.

2000   Puerto Rico elects its first female governor, Sila María Calderón.

2001   Three Puerto Rican politicians are sentenced to jail for protesting the US Navy's bombing of Vieques Island in Puerto Rico.

2001   Eddie Perez becomes the first Latino mayor of Hartford, Connecticut.

2002   In an effort to increase political influence in the mainland United States, more than three hundred thousand Puerto Ricans living in strategic areas are registered to vote prior to the 2002 election.

2004   Anibal Acevedo Vila wins an extremely close race for governor of Puerto Rico over a strong showing from the pro-statehood party.

2004   George Pabey becomes the first Latino mayor of East Chicago, Indiana.

2008   Hillary Rodham Clinton wins the Democratic primary in Puerto Rico.

2008   Military widows and veterans in Puerto Rico are found to receive fewer health benefits than those in the United States, even though Puerto Ricans are US citizens.

2009   President Barack Obama nominates Sonia Sotomayor to the US Supreme Court on May 26. Sotomayor becomes only the second jurist to be nominated to three different judicial positions by three different presidents.

2009   Sonia Maria Sotomayor, who is of Puerto Rican descent, is sworn as a US Supreme Court justice on August 8.

2010   Antonia Coello Novello, MD, a Puerto Rican physician and public health administrator who served as the first woman and first Hispanic surgeon general of the United States from 1990 to 1993, is indicted on charges of fraud and theft.

2011   President Barack Obama makes an official visit to Puerto Rico on June 14.

2012   A referendum on the political statehood of Puerto Rico is held on November 6. Fifty-four percent vote to reject Puerto Rico's current classification as a US territory, and 61 percent favor statehood as an alternative.

2012   The Obama administration calls on Congress to look into the issue of statehood for Puerto Rico.

2013   José E. Serrano assumes office as US representative for New York's Fifteenth District on January 3.

2013   The Puerto Rico Status Resolution Act in introduced in Congress by Pedro Pierluisi, Puerto Rico's only nonvoting representative. The proposed legislation, which has thirty bipartisan cosponsors, would allow Puerto Rico to be admitted as the fifty-first state in the United States if voters supported the measure.

2014   A Pew Research report released is August reveals that the Puerto Rican population in the United States has surpassed the number of people living on the island.

2014   Jose Torres is elected mayor of Paterson, New Jersey.

2015   The Obama administration draws up a proposal to help Puerto Rico out of a $72 billion debt crisis.

2016   In June, the US Supreme Court strikes down a Puerto Rico Debt-Restructuring Law, effectively rejecting any effort in Puerto Rico that will allow public utilities in the country to restructure $20 billion in debt.

TIME LINE OF CUBAN AMERICANS

1801   Spain allows Cuba to engage in open commerce; although the Spanish government withdraws this privilege in 1809, many Cubans still engage in free trade.

1823   The United States adopts the Monroe Doctrine, thus indicating US willingness to become involved in Spain's dealings with Cuba.

1885   Vicente Martínez Ybor, who migrated to Cuba from Spain to avoid compulsory military service, purchases a plot of land immediately northeast of Tampa, Florida. On his land, he develops a cigar manufacturing operation, which grows at a phenomenal rate. Ybor's development eventually becomes Ybor City, and the Cuban American population in Tampa mainly resides there. Cubans migrate to Ybor City to work on the tobacco farms and in the cigar factories.

1886   Slavery is abolished in Cuba.

1894   José Martí, a Cuban exile living in Florida, and others unsuccessfully attempt to raid Cuba from Jacksonville; the expedition is funded by donations from Cuban tobacco-field workers in Key West and Tampa.

1895   With the support of the US government, Cuba launches a war of independence against Spain.

1898   The US battleship *Maine* is sunk in Havana Harbor, Cuba, which begins the Spanish-American War. The United States ultimately wins the war, thus achieving Cuba's independence from Spain. Cuba, however, remains under US military rule.

1901   Congress approves the Platt Amendment, granting Cuba conditional independence; the United States reserves the right to intervene on Cuba's behalf.

1959   Fidel Castro successfully overthrows General Fulgencio Batista y Zaldívar as president of Cuba. Castro soon becomes prime minister of Cuba, declaring that free elections will be held in four years, after problems are solved. Upper-income and professional Cubans, with financial help from the United States, begin to arrive in Florida.

1961   In the infamous Bay of Pigs operation, 1,500 Cuban American exiles, supported by the US government, attempt to invade Cuba. The invaders are handily defeated, as almost 1,200 (80 percent) of the exiles are captured and imprisoned in Cuba.

1962   US intelligence services spot Soviet missiles in Cuba; President John F. Kennedy blockades the island with air and naval forces. The United States and the Soviet Union are pushed to the brink of nuclear war over the issue. Soviet premier Nikita Khrushchev admits that missiles are present and promises to withdraw them.

1966   The Cuban Adjustment Act allows any native or citizen of Cuba who has been inspected and admitted into the United States after January 1, 1959, and has been present in the United States for at least one year to become a permanent resident.

1973   The "freedom flight," which brought more than 250,000 anti-Castro Cubans to the United States, ceases operations.

1980   President Jimmy Carter publicly announces that the United States will accept 3,500 Cuban refugees from the port of Mariel, thus beginning an immense wave of Cuban immigration to the United States. The United States is deluged with Cuban immigrants, many of whom are not political prisoners but ordinary criminals. The United States detains the new immigrants for an indefinite period.

1980   President Carter declares a state of emergency in Florida and authorizes $10 million for refugee assistance. He also calls up nine hundred Coast Guard reservists to help administer aid to Cuban refugees.

1980   Cuba halts the 159-day Mariel boat lift.

1980   A group of politically conservative, anti-Castro Cuban Americans in Miami, Florida, form the Cuban American National Foundation, which functions as a trade association and political lobbying organization; Miami construction mogul and Cuban American community leader Jorge Mas Canosa is elected the foundation's first president.

1982   With the support of the Cuban American National Foundation and the Reagan administration, Congress authorizes the Voice of America to initiate Radio Martí, an anti-Castro, anti-Communist radio broadcast transmitted to Cuba.

Radio Martí angers Fidel Castro, who suspends agreements and dialogue with the United States.

1984 African American city manager Howard Gray, of Miami, Florida, who is extremely unpopular with the Cuban community, is fired. This incident demonstrates the emerging political power of Miami's Cuban American community.

1985 Nonideological technocrat Xavier Suarez becomes the first Cuban-born mayor of Miami, Florida (although it is important to note that the first Latino mayor of Miami was Maurice Ferré, a Puerto Rican). Suarez defeats Democratic incumbent Ferré and Raul Masvidal, a Reagan supporter and a member of the Cuban American National Foundation.

1986 The former mayor of Tampa, Republican Bob Martinez, is elected governor of Florida; Martinez, a Cuban American, is the first Latino governor of the state.

1990 Martinez, who is extremely unpopular, is defeated by former US senator Lawton Chiles, a Democrat, in his bid for reelection.

1995 President Bill Clinton signs a revision of the Cuban Adjustment Act of 1966; the new policy is known as the "Wet-Foot, Dry-Foot Policy." The revision ceases admitting people found at sea (sending them back to Cuba or to a third country) and only allows expedited "legal permanent resident" status and US citizenship to those who make it to shore.

1996 Florida Cuban Republicans support a Cuban Democrat against a black Republican for mayor of Dade County.

1996 Florida Cubans give half of their votes to Bill Clinton, putting the state's electoral votes in his column. Bob Dole and the Republicans alienate a significant portion of the Cuban vote with anti-immigrant rhetoric during their campaign.

2000 The Elián Gonzalez case further strains relations between Cuban Americans and the Clinton administration. It also increases tensions between Cuban Americans and blacks and non-Cuban Latinos.

2000 Despite anger at the Clinton administration for the removal of Elián Gonzalez, close to half of Florida's Cuban American population votes for the Democratic candidate, Al Gore.

2001 President George W. Bush appoints Mel Martinez of Florida as secretary of housing and urban development.

2001 In April, the first US cargo shipment in forty years leaves for Cuba, although it fails to dock a few weeks later. This first commercial food shipment since 1963 arrives in December.

2002 Mario Diaz-Balart is elected, and his brother Lincoln is reelected, to serve in the 108th Congress.

2002 Former president Jimmy Carter's visit to Cuba marks the first time a US president, current or former, is in the country since the 1959 revolution.

2003 The United States Commission for Assistance to a Free Cuba is formed.

2003 Eduardo Aguirre Jr. becomes the first director of US Citizenship and Immigration Services.

2004 President Bush tightens US restrictions on travel to Cuba.

2004 Mel Martinez is elected to the US Senate; he is the first Cuban American to serve.

2005 Carlos Gutierrez becomes the thirty-fifth US secretary of commerce.

2006 It is revealed that at least ten Florida journalists received regular payments from the US government to undermine the Cuban government through radio and television media.

2006 Marco Rubio becomes speaker of the Florida House of Representatives.

2008 Raul Castro becomes president of Cuba.

2008 In the 2008 general election, Democrat Barack Obama receives 47 percent of the Cuban American vote in Florida.

2010 Marco Antonio Rubio, a member of the Republican Party, is elected and represents Florida as a junior US senator.

2010 David Mauricio Rivera, a Republican from Florida, is elected to the US House of Representatives. (Rivera loses the 2012 election to Joe Garcia.)

2010 Mario Rafael Diaz-Balart Caballero is elected to the US House of Representatives. Caballero's aunt, Mirta Diaz-Balart, was the first wife of Fidel Castro.

2012 Cuban Americans vote for Barack Obama in record numbers, signifying a shift in this constituency's views on US policies in Cuba. President Obama captures 48 percent of the Cuban American vote in Florida, a record high for a Democratic candidate.

2012 Anitere Flores is elected to the Florida Senate, representing the 114th District.

2013 Albio Sires, a member of the Democratic Party, assumes office as the US representative for New Jersey's Eighth District.

2013 Mario Díaz-Balart, a Republican US representative from Florida, assumes office on January 3. Díaz-Balart represents Florida's Twenty-Fifth District.

2013 Ileana Ros-Lehtinen assumes office as the US representative from Florida's Twenty-Seventh District on January 3. She previously served as the US representative from Florida's Eighteenth District from 1989 to 2013. She is the most senior representative in Florida's congressional delegation.

2014 Carlos López-Cantera, a member of the Republican Party, assumes office as lieutenant governor of Florida on February 3.

2015 Evelyn Sanguinetti, a member of the Republican Party, assumes office as the forty-seventh lieutenant governor of Illinois. Sanguinetti is the first female Hispanic lieutenant governor in the United States, as well as the first Hispanic to be elected to the office of lieutenant governor of Illinois.

2015 On January 3, Carlos Curbelo assumes office as the US representative from Florida's Twenty-Sixth District.

2015   On April 13, Marco Rubio, US Republican senator from Florida, announces his decision to run for president of the United States.

2015   In December, the United States and Cuba reach an agreement to reestablish regular direct flights between Cuba and the United States for the first time in over fifty years.

2016   In March, the US Department of the Treasury authorizes Americans to travel to Cuba, provided that travelers "engage in a full-time schedule of educational exchange activities that result in meaningful interaction with individuals in Cuba." President Obama makes a historic trip to Cuba in that same month, becoming the first sitting president to visit the country since Calvin Coolidge in 1928.

TIME LINE OF ASIAN AMERICANS: CHINESE, JAPANESE, KOREANS, FILIPINOS, EAST INDIANS, SOUTHEAST ASIANS

1785   Three Chinese sailors land in Baltimore, Maryland.

1790   The first known native of India is reported in the United States in Salem, Massachusetts.

1790   The Naturalization Act of 1790 grants the right of US citizenship to all "free white persons."

1834   The first Chinese woman in the United States, Afong Moy, is put on display in a New York theater.

1843   The first known Japanese immigrants arrive in the United States.

1848   The *Eagle* docks in the San Francisco Harbor, bringing the first reported Chinese immigrants.

1850   Following an influx of Chinese immigration to California as a result of the discovery of gold, the Foreign Miners Tax is imposed on the Chinese to impede further immigration.

1852   Sugar plantation owners in Hawaii bring in 180 Chinese indentured servants.

1868   The first Japanese contract workers are brought to sugar plantations in Hawaii.

1869   The first transcontinental railroad is built with the labor of Chinese immigrants; two thousand Chinese railroad workers go on strike for better working conditions.

1870   The anti-Chinese movement is initiated. Many communities single out Chinese immigrants through discriminatory laws and violence.

1875   The Page Law prohibits prostitution and "coolie" labor in the United States.

1880   The California Civil Code forbids marriage between a white person and a "Negro, Mulatto, or Mongolian."

1882   The Chinese Exclusion Act is passed and signed into law; it bars the immigration of Chinese laborers and prohibits Chinese from becoming naturalized citizens.

1885 The Japanese government allows its workers to go to Hawaii as contract laborers; in the ensuing decade, more than thirty thousand workers migrate.

1885 In *Tape v. Hurley* (66 Cal. 473 [1885]), the parents of Mamie Tape, a seven-year-old US-born Chinese American, sue the San Francisco School Board because she has been denied entrance to Spring Valley public school because of her race. The California Supreme Court rules that it is unconstitutional to deny "a child of Chinese parents entrance to public schools" based on the Fourteenth Amendment, but it stays silent on "separate but equal." The San Francisco School Board responds by building a separate school for Asians, a so-called Oriental School.

1898 The United States officially annexes Hawaii.

1898 The Spanish-American War ends with the signing of the Treaty of Paris. The Philippine Islands are given to the United States. Filipinos are viewed as "wards" of the United States and thus do not need visas to travel here. Filipino women who marry American veterans are allowed to migrate to the United States as war brides.

1898 The Supreme Court rules in *United States v. Wong Kim Ark* that children of Chinese immigrants born in the United States are US citizens despite the Chinese Exclusion Act of 1882.

1902 The US Congress passes the Cooper Act; this law makes it illegal for Filipinos to own property, vote, hold public office, or become a citizen.

1905 The Asiatic Exclusion League is formed; it lobbies to prevent the immigration of Asians.

1913 The California Land Act is passed; it bars aliens from owning land. Many Japanese farmers are adversely affected.

1917 The 1917 Immigration Act prohibits immigration of labor from all parts of Asia except Japan.

1918 The Act of May 9 allows all people who served in the US armed forces in World War I, regardless of race, to become naturalized citizens.

1922 The Cable Act rescinds the citizenship of women who marry aliens who are ineligible for citizenship (which includes all Asians except Hawaiians and Filipinos).

1923 The Supreme Court rules in *United States v. Thind* that Asian Indian immigrants are not eligible for US citizenship.

1924 The Immigration Quota Act excludes all aliens who are ineligible for citizenship. It allows the entry of alien wives of Chinese merchants but not of alien wives of US citizens.

1929 Anti-Filipino riots break out in Watsonville, California, after Americans are replaced by Filipinos to work for lower wages; other riots follow when Filipino men are accused of dating white women.

1931 Filipinos who served in the US armed forces are eligible for US citizenship.

1934   The ruling in *Morrison v. California* mandates that Filipinos are not eligible for citizenship.

1934   The Tydings-McDuffle Act limits Filipino immigration via a quota system, allowing only fifty immigrants per year.

1935   A reparations bill is passed by Congress encouraging Filipinos to return to the Philippines; only two thousand leave.

1942   President Franklin D. Roosevelt signs Executive Order 9066, which creates zones from which the military has the power to exclude people; consequently, more than 112,000 Japanese residing in these zones are forcefully removed to ten "relocation" camps.

1943   Congress repeals the Chinese Exclusion Acts; however, Congress establishes an annual quota of 105 Chinese immigrants.

1946   Wing F. Ong, the first Asian American to be elected to state office outside of Hawaii, is elected to the Arizona State House of Representatives.

1952   The McCarran-Walter Act upholds the national origin quotas for Asian Americans based on the figures from the 1924 Immigration Quota Act. Aliens previously ineligible for citizenship are subsequently allowed naturalization rights.

1955   Peter Aduja is elected to the Hawaii State House of Representatives, becoming the first Filipino to be elected to office.

1956   The first Asian American—Californian Dalip S. Saund—is elected to the US House of Representatives.

1958   Hiram Fong of Hawaii is the first Asian American to be elected to the US Senate.

1962   Patsy T. Mink is the first Asian American woman elected to a state legislature. Mink, a member of the Democratic Party, is a third-generation Japanese American.

1963   Daniel Ken Inouye is elected as Hawaii's first representative after it becomes a state. He is also the first Japanese American to serve in the US House of Representatives.

1964   The Civil Rights Act is passed, outlawing all racial discrimination.

1964   Hiram Fong becomes the first Asian American to run for the Republican Party's nomination for the president of the United States; he receives the votes of the Hawaii and Alaska delegations.

1965   The Voting Rights Act is passed, forbidding outright electoral discrimination on account of race.

1965   The Immigration and Naturalization Act eliminates national origin quotas; hemisphere-based quotas are used instead. The Eastern Hemisphere's quota is set at 170,000, limited to 20,000 immigrants per country.

1965   Patsy Mink, a Japanese American, is the first Asian American woman elected to Congress.

1971 The provisions of the McCarran-Walter Act providing for detention camps are repealed.

1971 Herbert Choy becomes the first Asian American federal judge.

1971 Norman Y. Mineta is elected mayor of San Jose, California. Mineta is the first Japanese American mayor of a major US city.

1972 Patsy Mink is the first Asian American to run for the Democratic Party's nomination for the president of the United States.

1974 Eduardo Malapit is elected in Kauai, Hawaii, as the first Filipino American mayor in the United States.

1974 *Lau v. Nichols* rules that school districts must provide special education for students who speak little or no English.

1974 George Ariyoshi is the first Asian American man to be elected governor in the United States. Ariyoshi is the third governor of Hawaii.

1975 Congress establishes the Indochinese Refugee Assistance Program (Public Law 94-23); this act resettles approximately 130,000 Southeast Asians (mostly Vietnamese and Cambodians) to the United States.

1976 *Wong v. Hampton* allows resident aliens to be eligible for federal jobs.

1976 After thirty-four years in existence, Executive Order 9066 is repealed by President Gerald Ford.

1982 Following a racially motivated argument in a Detroit, Michigan, bar, twenty-seven-year-old Vincent Chin is clubbed to death with a baseball bat; the two white assailants receive light sentences. In response, Chinese Americans (with the assistance of other Asian American groups) form the Citizens for Justice. A federal grand jury investigates, and one of the assailants is given a twenty-five-year prison sentence. His conviction is later overturned by the Sixth Circuit Court of Appeals.

1982 A Southeast Asian immigration quota of ten thousand is set by President Ronald Reagan.

1983 With the assistance of the Japanese American Citizens League, the National Committee for Japanese American Redress initiates federal litigation seeking monetary compensation for the more than one hundred thousand Japanese Americans who were interned during World War II. Meanwhile, the convictions of Fred Korematsu, Minoru Yasui, and Gordon Hirabayashi, who were convicted of curfew violations during World War II, are reversed.

1985 Michael Woo is elected to the Los Angeles City Council; he is the first Chinese American to serve in that position.

1986 California passes an initiative declaring English as the official state language.

1988 The US Congress, with the reluctant agreement of President Reagan, publicly apologizes for interning Japanese Americans during World War II and authorizes payment of $20,000 to each former internee.

1990 The Immigration Reform Act of 1990 grants citizenship to Filipino World War II veterans.

1992 President George H. W. Bush signs into law the Civil Liberties Act Amendments of 1992, which appropriates $400 million to the remaining victims of Japanese internment camps; he also issues a formal apology on behalf of the US government.

1992 Jay Kim is elected, becoming the first Korean American to serve in Congress.

1992 Tony Lâm, defeating Jimmy Ton Nguyen, is elected to the Westminster City Council in California. He is the first Vietnam-born person to be elected to a political office in the United States.

1993 Michael Woo loses his race for mayor of Los Angeles to Richard Riordan.

1994 The Congressional Asian Pacific American Caucus is founded.

1994 Benjamin J. Cayetano becomes the first Filipino American to serve as a state governor; he is elected in Hawaii.

1996 Asian Americans donate $10 million legally to the Clinton campaign. (Money also is donated illegally by foreign Asians.)

1997 The US Senate holds hearings on illegal foreign Asian contributions. Asian Americans feel that the hearings are creating a backlash against Asian Americans.

1997 Asian American government officials and several visitors have their nationality changed from "United States" to "foreign" on official entrance documents by White House security guards and the Secret Service. The reason later given by embarrassed US officials is that their last names "sounded foreign."

1997 A complaint is filed with the US Commission on Civil Rights by the National Asian Pacific American Legal Consortium, the Organization of Chinese Americans, and other groups alleging that as a result of the campaign finance scandal, public officials, the Democratic and Republican Parties, and the media had evidenced a pattern of bias against Asian Americans based on their race and national origin.

1997 Gary Locke, governor of Washington, becomes the first Chinese American governor in US history.

1998 David Wu is elected from Oregon to the US House of Representatives; he is the first Taiwanese American to serve.

1999 President Clinton appoints Norman Mineta, former representative from California, as secretary of commerce, making him the first Asian American to hold a cabinet post.

2000 Asian Americans, for the first time, give a majority of their votes to a Democratic presidential candidate, Al Gore.

2000 Asian Americans in the California State Assembly form the Asian Pacific Islander Legislative Caucus (APILC), the first in California history.

2000 Norman Bay becomes the first Chinese American US attorney.

2001 Viet D. Dinh, born in South Vietnam, begins his service as the assistant attorney general of the United States and authors the USA PATRIOT Act.

2001 Elaine Chao is confirmed as secretary of labor and is the first female Chinese American to serve in the cabinet.

2002 Washington governor Gary Locke signs legislation that bans the use of the word *Oriental* in official government documents.

2004 Van Thai Tran is the first Vietnamese American to serve in a state legislature; he serves in California.

2004 Hubert Vo, one month behind Tran, becomes the second Vietnamese American to serve in a state legislature; he is the first and only Vietnamese to be elected to the Texas legislature.

2004 UCLA becomes the first major US research institution with an Asian American Studies Department.

2005 Doris Matsui decides to run in the race to fill her late husband's seat in the US House of Representatives and wins.

2006 Hong Thi Tran is a candidate in the Washington Democratic primary for US Senate.

2006 The first monument dedicated to Filipino World War II soldiers is revealed in Los Angeles, California.

2008 Anh "Joseph" Quang Cao wins a special election for a seat in the US House of Representatives, representing New Orleans, Louisiana. He is the first Vietnamese American to serve in Congress. Cao is defeated in 2010 when he runs for reelection.

2008 Piyush "Bobby" Jindal, a member of the Republican Party, becomes the first Indian American governor of an American state. Jindal is governor of Louisiana.

2009 Nobel Laureate Steven Chu is confirmed as secretary of energy and retired general Eric K. Shinseki is confirmed as secretary of veterans affairs in President Obama's administration. Former Washington State governor Gary Locke is confirmed secretary of commerce.

2009 President Barack Obama signs an executive order that restores the White House Initiative and President's Advisory Commission on Asian Americans and Pacific Islanders to address issues concerning the Asian American and Pacific Islander (AAPI) community.

2010 Peter M. Rouse is appointed interim chief of staff for President Barack Obama, becoming the first Asian American to fill this position. Rouse's mother is Japanese.

2010 Daniel Ken "Dan" Inouye is sworn in as president pro tempore of the US Senate, making him the highest-ranked Asian American politician in US history. Inouye is also chair of the US Senate Committee on Appropriations and a Medal of Honor winner for his heroics in World War II.

2010 Charles Kong Djou becomes the first Thai American (his mother is Thai American) and the first Chinese American (his father is Chinese American) Republican to serve in the US House of Representatives. Djou leaves Congress in 2011.

2010 Two US cities, San Francisco and Oakland, California, elect Asian American mayors. Edward Lee and Jean Quan, respectively.

2010 Nikki R. Haley becomes the first Asian American woman elected governor in the United States, when she becomes governor of South Carolina. Haley is the second Indian American governor in the United States.

2011 Hansen H. Clarke becomes the first Bangladeshi American to serve in the US Congress. Clarke is the US Representative for Michigan's Thirteenth Congressional District.

2011 Jean Quan is the first Asian American woman to become mayor in the United States. Quan, a Democrat, is also the first female mayor of Oakland, California.

2011 Gary Locke becomes US ambassador to China.

2012 During the 2012 general election, Barack Obama receive overwhelming support from the Asian American community, with Asian Americans backing the president nearly three to one.

2012 Ladda Tammy Duckworth, who was born in Thailand, becomes the first female Thai American to serve in the US Congress.

2012 Mazie Hirono is elected US senator from Hawaii.

2012 Senator Daniel Inouye dies December 17, 2012.

2012 Shan Tsutsui, a Democrat, is appointed the twelfth lieutenant governor of Hawaii.

2013 Tulsi Gabbard assumes office as the US representative for Hawaii's Second District on January 3, 2013. Gabbard is the first American Samoan and Hindu member of the US Congress.

2013 Ami Bera, an Indian American physician, assumes office as the US representative for California's Seventh District. Bera, a member of the Democratic Party, is currently the only Indian American serving in the US Congress.

2013 Grace Meng becomes the first Asian American to represent part of New York in Congress when she assumes office as the US representative for New York's Sixth District on January 3.

2013 Mark Takano begins his term as the US representative for California's Forty-First District on January 3.

2014 Hyeok Kim becomes the first Asian American female deputy mayor of Seattle.

2014 Ronald Falconi becomes the first Filipino American mayor in Ohio when he is elected mayor of Brunswick, Ohio.

2014   Secretary of Veterans Affairs Eric Shinseki resigns following a scandal over health care for veterans.

2014   David Ige is elected governor of Hawaii and assumes office on December 1.

2014   The UCLA Asian American Studies Center releases the fifteenth edition of the *National Asian Pacific American Political Almanac*, which lists more than four thousand Asian Americans who hold public office at the state and federal level.

2015   On January 3, Ted Lieu assumes congressional office, representing California's Thirty-Third District.

2015   Mark Takai begins his term as the US representative for Hawaii's First District on January 3.

2015   A Pew Research Center report released in September projects that Asians will become the largest immigrant group in the United States by 2065.

2016   In May, the US House of Representatives and the Senate unanimously pass a new law, HR 4238, which updates the terminology that the federal government uses when referencing minorities. Among the changes is the elimination of the term *Oriental* to describe Americans of Asian descent.

2016   Kamala Harris, a Democrat representing California, is the first Indian American woman (and second black woman) elected to the US Senate.

2016   Stephanie Murphy (D-Florida) is the first Vietnamese American woman elected to the US House of Representatives.

2016   Pramila Jayapal (D-Washington) is the first Indian American woman to be elected to the US House of Representatives.

2016   Tammy Duckworth, a Democrat representing Illinois, is the second Asian American woman in the US Senate.

References

ABC News/USA Today/Columbia University. 2008. "Blacks, Politics, and Society." Poll, September 23, 2008.

Adams, James, Samuel Merrill III, and Elizabeth N. Simas. 2011. "When Candidates Value Good Character: A Spatial Model with Applications to Congressional Elections." *Journal of Politics* 73, no. 1:17–30.

Ah Nee-Benham, Maenette K.P and Ronald H. Heck. 1998. *Culture and Educational Policy in Hawaii: The Silencing of Native Voices*. Oxford: Taylor & Francis.

Ahuja, Sarita, and Robert Chlala. 2013. "Widening the Lens on Boys and Men of Color: California AAPI and AMEMSA Perspectives." Asian Americans/Pacific Islanders in Philanthropy (AAPIP). http://www.aapip.org.

Alexander, Michelle. 2012. *The New Jim Crow: Mass Incarceration in the Age of Colorblindness*. New York: New Press.

Alexander v. Holmes. 1969. 396 US 19.

Alexander-Floyd, Nikol G. 2012. "Disappearing Acts: Reclaiming Intersectionality in the Social Sciences in a Post–Black Feminist Era." *Feminist Formations* 24 no. 1:1–25.

Alston v. School Board of Norfolk. 1940. 112 F.2d 992.

Ambrecht, Beliana C., and Harry P. Pachon. 1974. "Ethnic Political Mobilization in a Mexican American Community: An Exploratory Study of East Los Angeles, 1965–1972." *Western Political Quarterly* 27:500–19.

American Community Survey (ACS). 2012. US Census Bureau. http://www.factfinder.census.gov.

American Community Survey (ACS). 2015. US Census Bureau. http://www.factfinder.census.gov.

American Friends Service Committee et al. 1970. *The Status of School Desegregation in the South, 1970*. American Friends Service Committee, Delta Ministry of the National Council of Churches, Lawyers Committee for Civil Rights Under Law, Lawyers Constitutional Defense Committee, NAACP Legal Defense and Educational Fund, and Washington Research Project.

Anantha, Jake. 2016. "I Was a Donald Trump Supporter. Then I Got Booted from His Rally." *Washington Post,* August 22. https://www.washingtonpost.com/posteverything/wp/2016/08/22/i-was-a-donald-trump-supporter-then-i-got-booted-from-his-rally/?utm_term=.0636cc88aeb9.

Anaya, S. James, "The Native Hawaiian People and International Human Rights Law: Toward a Remedy for Past and Continuing Wrongs," 28 *Georgia Law Review* 309 (1993–1994).

Apuzzo, Matt, Michael S. Schmidt, and Adam Goldman. 2016. "Emails Warrant No New Action Against Hillary Clinton, FBI Director Says." *New York Times,* November 6. http://www.nytimes.com/2016/11/07/us/politics/hillary-clinton-male-voters-donald-trump.html.

Asian American Decisions. 2016. "2016 Asian American Election Eve Poll." http://asianamericandecisions.com/wp-content/uploads/2016/11/2016-Asian-American-Election-Eve-Poll-Infographic.pdf.

Asian Pacific American Labor Alliance, AFL-CIO. n.d. Membership brochure.

Assis, Claudia and Julian Pecquet. 2002. "Hispanics Search for a Better Life Pushes Durham into Poverty." *Herald Sun*, September 25, A12.

Associated Press. 2016. "Judge: North Carolina Counties Must Restore Voters Removed in 'In-sane' Process." *Chicago Tribune,* November 4. http://www.chicagotribune.com/news/nation-world/ct-north-carolina-voter-purge-ruling-20161104-story.html.

Babington, Charles. 2006. "Voting Rights Act Extension Passes in Senate 98–0." *Washington Post,* July 21, A01.

Ballotpedia. 2016. "Massachusetts English in Public Schools Initiative, Question 2 (2002)." https://ballotpedia.org/Massachusetts_English_in_Public_Schools_Initiative,_Question_2_(2002).

Banducci, Susan, Jeffrey Karp, and Michael Thrasher. 2008. "Ballot Photographs as Cues in Low-Information Elections." *Political Psychology* 29, no. 6:903–917.

Banwart, Mary Christine, Dianne G. Bystrom, and Terry Robertson. 2003. "From the Primary to the General Election: A Comparative Analysis of Candidate Media Coverage in Mixed-Gender 2000 Races for Governor and U.S. Senate." *American Behavioral Scientist* 46, no. 5:658–76.

Barboza, Tony. 2008. "Irvine Voters Embrace Diversity in Mayoral Election." *Los Angeles Times,* November 9.

Barnes, Robert. 2016. "Supreme Court Won't Let North Carolina Use Strict Voting Law." *Washington Post,* August 31. https://www.washingtonpost.com/politics/courts_law/supreme-court-wont-let-north-carolina-use-strict-voting-law/2016/08/31/b5187080-6ed6-11e6-8533-6b0b0ded0253_story.html.

Barnes, Robert, and Ann E. Marimow. 2016. "Appeals Court Strikes Down North Carolina's Voter-ID Law." *Washington Post,* July 29. https://www.washingtonpost.com/local/public-safety/appeals-court-strikes-down-north-carolinas-voter-id-law/2016/07/29/810b5844-4f72-11e6-aa14-e0c1087f7583_story.html.

Barone, Michael. 2016. "Racial Discrimination on Campus Is Likely to Go on Forever." *National Review,* July 6. http://www.nationalreview.com/article/437500/supreme-courts-fisher-v-university-texas-affirmative-action-case-preserves-race.

Barr, Donald A. 2014. *Health Disparities in the United States: Social Class, Race, Ethnicity, and Health.* Baltimore: Johns Hopkins University Press.

Barreto, Matt A., Benjamin F. Gonzalez, and Gabriel R. Sánchez. 2013. "Rainbow Coalition in the Golden State? Exposing Myths, Uncovering New Realities in Latino Attitudes Toward Blacks." In *Black and Brown in Los Angeles: Beyond Conflict and Coalition,* edited by Josh Kun and Laura Pulido. Berkeley: University of California Press.

Baumgartner, Frank R., and Bryan D. Jones. 1993. *Agendas and Instability in American Politics.* Chicago: University of Chicago Press.

Bayles, Tom. 2000. "NAACP Questions Irregularities." *Sarasota Herald-Tribune,* November 10, 2000.

BBC News. 2016. "What *is* Standing Rock and Why Are 1.4m 'Checking In' There?" November 2, 2016. http://www.bbc.com/news/world-us-canada-37834334.

Bedolla, Lisa Garcia. 2005. "Indelible Effects: The Impact of Women of Color in the U.S. Congress." In *Women and Elective Office: Past, Present, and Future,* edited by Clyde Wilcox and Sue Thomas.

Belz, Herman. 1991. *Equality Transformed: A Quarter-Century of Affirmative Action.* New Brunswick, NJ: Transaction.

Bertrand, Marianne, and Sendhil Mullainathan. 2004. "Are Emily and Greg More Employable than Lakisha and Jamal? A Field Experiment on Labor Market Discrimination." *American Economic Review* 94, no. 4:991–1013.

Black Lives Matter. 2016. http://blacklivesmatter.com.

Blackmon, Douglas A. 2008. *Slavery by Another Name: The Re-Enslavement of Black Americans from the Civil War to World War II.* New York: Anchor Books, Doubleday.

Blake, Aaron. 2012. "Everything You Need to Know About the Pennsylvania Voter ID Fight." *Washington Post,* October 2, 2012. http://www.washingtonpost.com/blogs/the-fix/wp/2012/10/02/the-pennsylvania-voter-id-fight-explained/.

Blalock, Herbert M. 1967. *Toward a Theory of Minority-Group Relations.* New York: John Wiley & Sons.

Blauner, Robert. 1972. *Racial Oppression in America.* New York: Harper & Row.

Blumer, Herbert. 1955. "Reflections on Theory of Race Relations." In *Race Relations in World Perspective,* edited by A. W. Lind. Honolulu: University of Hawaii Press.

———. 1958. "Race Prejudice as a Sense of Group Position." *Pacific Sociological Review* 1, 1 (Spring 1958), pp. 3–7.

Bobo, Lawrence D. and Vincent L. Hutchings.1996. "Perceptions of Racial Group Competition: Extending Blumer's Theory of Group Position to a Multiracial Social Context." *American Sociological Review*: 951–972

Bondl, Chris. 2015. "5 Times the Voting Rights Act of 1965 Has Been Challenged by State Legislation." *Newsmax,* November 8. http://www.newsmax.com/FastFeatures/Voting-Rights-Act-challenges/2015/11/08/id/701175/.

Bositis, David A. 2000. "The Black Vote in 2000: A Preliminary Analysis." Washington, DC: Joint Center for Political and Economic Studies.

———. 2008. "Blacks and the 2008 Elections: A Preliminary Analysis." Washington, DC: Joint Center for Political and Economic Studies.

———. 2012. "Blacks and the 2012 Elections: A Preliminary Analysis." Washington, DC: Joint Center for Political and Economic Studies.

Bosman, Julie, and Monica Davey. 2016. "Republicans Expand Control in a Deeply Divided Nation." *New York Times,* November 11. http://www.nytimes.com/2016/11/12/us/republicans-expand-control-in-a-deeply-divided-nation.html?hp&action=click&pgtype=Homepage&clickSource=story-heading&module=b-lede-package-region&region=top-news&WT.nav=top-news&_r=1.

Boswell, Thomas D., and James R. Curtis. 1983. *The Cuban-American Experience: Culture, Images, and Perspectives.* Totowa, NJ: Rowman and Allanheld.

Bradley v. Milliken. 1975. 402 F. Supp. 1096.

Bradner, Eric, Pamela Brown, and Evan Perez. 2016. "FBI Clears Clinton—Again." *CNN Politics,* November 7. http://www.cnn.com/2016/11/06/politics/comey-tells-congress-fbi-has-not-changed-conclusions/index.html.

Brandt, Katie S. 2015. "Native American Spirit Camp Awaits New Keystone XL Pipeline Decision." *Huffington Post,* September 3, 2015. http://www.huffingtonpost.com/katie-scarlett-brandt/native-american-spirit-ca_b_8085648.html.

Bratton, Kathleen A., and Kerry L. Haynie. 1999. "Agenda Setting and Legislative Success in State Legislatures: The Effects of Gender and Race." *Journal of Politics* 61, no. 3:658–79.

Bratton, Kathleen A., Kerry L. Haynie, and Beth Reingold. 2006. "Agenda Setting and African American Women in State Legislatures." *Journal of Women, Politics & Policy* 28, nos. 3–4:71–96.

Brischetto, Robert. 1996. "Women Lead the Modest Jump in Hispanic Political Representation." Web article. Copyright Hispanic Business, Inc.

Brown, Anna. 2014. "U.S. Hispanic and Asian Populations Growing, but for Different Reasons." Pew Research Center, Fact Tank, June 26. http://www.pewresearch.org/fact-tank/2014/06/26/u-s-hispanic-and-asian-populations-growing-but-for-different-reasons/.

Brown, Anna, and Sara Atske. 2016. "Blacks Have Made Gains in U.S. Political Leadership, but Gaps Remain." Pew Research Center, Fact Tank, June 28. http://www.pewresearch.org/fact-tank/2016/06/28/blacks-have-made-gains-in-u-s-political-leadership-but-gaps-remain/.

Brown, Anna, and Mark Hugo Lopez. 2013. "Mapping the Latino Population, by State, County, and City." Pew Research Center, August 29. http://www.pewhispanic.org/2013/08/29/mapping-the-latino-population-by-state-county-and-city/.

Brown, Emma. 2016. "On the Anniversary of *Brown v. Board,* New Evidence That U.S. Schools Are Resegregating." *Washington Post,* May 17. https://www.washingtonpost.com/news/education/wp/2016/05/17/on-the-anniversary-of-brown-v-board-new-evidence-that-u-s-schools-are-resegregating/.

Brown, Nadia E. 2014. "Political Participation of Women of Color: An Intersectional Analysis." *Journal of Women, Politics & Policy* 35, no. 4 (October 2):315–48.

Brown, Nadia E. and Kira Hudson Banks. 2014. "Black Women's Agenda Setting in the Maryland State Legislature." *Journal of African American Studies* 18, no. 2:164–180.

Brown, Nadia E., and Sarah Allen Gershon. 2016. *Distinct Identities: Minority Women in U.S. Politics.* New York: Routledge.

Brown v. Board of Education of Topeka. 1954. 347 US 483.

———. 1955. 349 US 294.

Brown-Dean, Khalilah. 2007. "Permanent Outsiders: Felon Disenfranchisement and the Breakdown of Black Politics." In *The Expanding Boundaries of Black Politics: The National Political Science Review* 11:103–19.

Brown-Dean, Khalilah, Zoltan Hajnal, Christina Rivers, and Ismail White. 2015. "50 Years of the Voting Rights Act: The State of Race in Politics." http://jointcenter.org/sites/default/files/VRA%20report,%203.5.15%20(1130%20am)(updated).pdf.

Browning, Rufus P., Dale Rogers Marshall, and David H. Tabb. 1984. *Protest Is Not Enough.* Berkeley: University of California Press.

———, eds. 1990. *Racial Politics in American Cities.* New York: Longman.

Burns, Alexander. 2016. "Choice Words from Donald Trump, Presidential Candidate." *New York Times,* June 16. http://www.nytimes.com/politics/first-draft/2015/06/16/choice-words-from-donald-trump-presidential-candidate/?mtrref=www.nytimes.com.

Burrell, Luchy S., Steve Redding, Sonya Schenk, and Marcela Mendoza. 2001. *New 2000 Estimates of the Hispanic Population for Shelby County, Tennessee.* Memphis, TN: Regional Economic Development Center, University of Memphis.

Bush v. Vera. 1996. 517 US 952.

Bystrom, Diane. 2006. "Advertising, Web Sites, and Media Coverage: Gender and Communication Along the Campaign Trail." In *Gender and Elections: Shaping the Future of American Politics*, edited by Susan Carroll and Richard Fox, 169–88. New York: Cambridge University Press.

Cain, Bruce E., and D. Roderick Kiewiet. 1984. "Ethnicity and Electoral Choice: Mexican-American Voting Behavior in the California 30th Congressional District." *Social Science Quarterly* 65:315–17.

———. 1986. "California's Coming Minority Majority." *Public Opinion* 9:50–52.

Cain, Bruce E., D. Roderick Kiewiet, and Carole J. Uhlaner. 1991. "The Acquisition of Partisanship by Latinos and Asian Americans." *American Journal of Political Science* 35:390–442.

Calvo, Maria A., and Steven Rosenstone. 1989. *Hispanic Political Participation.* San Antonio, TX: Southwest Voter Education Project.

Campbell, Colin. 2016. "7 Rural N.C. Counties Flip 'Bloodshot Red,'" *News and Observer,* November 13, A1, 8A.

Capers, K. Jurée, and Candis Watts Smith. 2016. "Linked Fate at the Intersection of Race, Gender, and Ethnicity." In *Distinct Identities: Minority Women in U.S. Politics*, edited by Nadia E. Brown and Sarah Allen Gershon. New York: Routledge.

Capps, Randy, Everett Henderson, John D. Kasarda, James H. Johnson Jr., Stephen J. Appold, Derrek L. Croney, Donald J. Hernandez, and Michael Fix. 2007. *A Profile of Immigrants in Arkansas: Executive Summary.* Washington, DC: Urban Institute.

Capriccioso, Rob. 2012. "Tester, Heitkamp Score Victories with Native Vote." *Indian Country Today,* November 7. http://indiancountrytodaymedia network.com/article/tester-heitkamp-score-victories-with-native-vote-144497.

Carew, Jessica D. Johnson. 2012. "'Lifting as We Climb?': The Role of Stereotypes in the Evaluation of Political Candidates at the Intersection of Race and Gender." http://dukespace.lib.duke.edu/dspace/handle/10161/5527.

———. 2016. "How Do You See Me?: Stereotyping of Black Women and How It Affects Them in an Electoral Context." In *Distinct Identities: Minority Women in U.S. Politics,* edited by Nadia E. Brown and Sarah Allen Gershon. New York: Routledge.

Cargile, Ivy A. M. 2016. "Latina Issues: An Analysis of the Policy Issue Competencies of Latina Candidates." In *Distinct Identities: Minority Women in U.S. Politics,* edited by Nadia E. Brown and Sarah Allen Gershon. New York: Routledge.

Carmichael, Stokely, and Charles V. Hamilton. 1967. *Black Power: The Politics of Liberation in America.* New York: Random House.

Carroll, Susan J., and Ronnee Schreiber. 1997. "Media Coverage of Women in the 103rd Congress." In *Women, Media, and Politics,* edited by Pippa Norris, 131–48. New York: Oxford University Press.

Carson, E. Ann. 2015. "Prisoners in 2014." US Department of Justice: Office of Justice Programs. Washington, DC: Bureau of Justice Statistics.

Castelano et al. v. Rice et al. [undecided].

Catawba Indian Tribe of South Carolina v. United States. 1993. 982 F.2d 1564.

CBC Radio (CBC). 2016. "LaDonna Brave Bull Allard's Land Is Home to Water Protectors at Standing Rock." *CBC,* November 20, 2016. http://www.cbc.ca/radio/unreserved/something -extraordinary-is-happening-at-standing-rock-1.3850506/ladonna-brave-bull-allard-s-land -is-home-to-water-protectors-at-standing-rock-1.3853339.

Center for American Women and Politics. 2008. "Fast Facts: African American Women in Elective Office." http://www.cawp.rutgers.edu/fast_facts/women_of_color/FastFacts_African American Women.

———. 2016. "Women of Color in Elective Office 2016: Congress, Statewide, State Legislature, Mayors." New Brunswick, NJ: Eagleton Institute of Politics, Rutgers University.

Chafe, William H. 1993. *Never Stop Running: Allard Lowenstein and the Struggle to Save American Liberalism.* New York: Basic Books.

Chappell, Bill. 2016. "Police Stop Ends in Black Man's Death; Aftermath Is Live-Streamed on Facebook." *National Public Radio,* July 7, 2016.

Cherokee Nation v. State of Georgia. 1831. 5 Peters 1.

Cheyenne-Arapaho Tribes of Oklahoma v. United States. 1992. 966 F.2d 583.

Children's Defense Fund. 1974. *Children out of School in America.* Washington, DC: Children's Defense Fund of the Washington Research Project.

Cisneros v. Corpus Christi Independent School District. 1970. 324 F. Supp. 599, appeal docketed No. 71–2397 (5th Cir. July 16, 1971).

Civil Rights Cases. 1883. 109 US 3.

Clifford, Harlan C. 1992. "Big Ben." *Boston Globe Magazine,* August 2, 16, 32–34.

CNN. 2000. "Election 2000." http://www.cnn.com/election.2000.

———. 2015. "Donald Trump vs. Univision's Jorge Ramos." http://www.cnn.com/videos /politics/2015/08/26/donald-trump-jorge-ramos-argue-immigration-origwx-bw.cnn/video /playlists/donald-trump-immigration.

———. 2016. "Muslim Woman Ejected from Trump Rally Speaks Out." *CNN Tonight,* January 9. http://www.cnn.com/videos/tv/2016/01/09/rose-hamid-woman-asked-to-leave -trump-event-lemon-intv-ctn.cnn.

CNN Politics. 2016. "Exit Polls." http://www.cnn.com/election/results/exit-polls

Cobb, Roger W., and Charles D. Elder. 1983. *Participation in American Politics: The Dynamics of Agenda-Building.* 2nd ed. Baltimore: Johns Hopkins University Press.

Cohen, Cathy. 2003. "A Portrait of Continuing Marginality: The Study of Women of Color in American Politics." In *Women and American Politics: New Questions, New Directions,* edited by Susan J. Carroll. New York: Oxford University Press.

Cohen, Gaynor. 1982. "Alliance and Conflict Among Mexican Americans." *Ethnic and Racial Studies* 5:175–95.

Colby, Sandra L. and Jennifer M. Ortman. 2015. "Projections of the Size and Composition of the U.S. Population: 2014 to 2060." US Department of Commerce, Economics, and Statistics Administration, U.S. Census Bureau.

Collins, Patricia Hill. 2008. *Black Feminist Thought: Knowledge, Consciousness, and the Politics of Empowerment.* New York: Routledge Classics.

Commonwealth Court of Pennsylvania, 2012. "Stipulation." *Applewhite v. the Commonwealth of Pennsylvania.* July 12.

Confessore, Nicholas. 2016. "For Whites Sensing Decline, Donald Trump Unleashes Words of Resistance." *New York Times,* July 13. http://www.nytimes.com/2016/07/14/us/politics /donald-trump-white-identity.html?_r=0.

Congressional Quarterly. 1991. *Congressional Quarterly Almanac.* Washington, DC: Congressional Quarterly News Features.

Cook, Jennifer. 2016. "North Dakota's Governor Declared a State of Emergency to Deal with Peaceful Oil Pipeline Protesters. We Call It a State of Emergency for Civil Rights." American Civil Liberties Union. September 13.

Cooke, W. Henry. 1971. "Segregation of Mexican-American School Children." In *A Documentary History of Mexican Americans,* edited by Wayne Moquin, with Charles Van Doren, 325–28. New York: Praeger.

Corn, David. 2012. "Secret Video: Romney Tells Millionaire Donors What He Really Thinks of Obama Voters." *Mother Jones,* September 17. http://www.motherjones.com/politics/2012 /09/secret-video-romney-private-fundraiser.

Crenshaw, Kimberlé. 1989. "Demarginalizing the Intersection of Race and Sex: A Black Feminist Critique of Antidiscrimination Doctrine, Feminist Theory, and Antiracist Politics." *University of Chicago Legal Forum*:139.

———. 1991. "Mapping the Margins: Intersectionality, Identity Politics, and Violence Against Women of Color." *Stanford Law Review* 43, no. 6:1241–99.

Crenshaw, Kimberlé, and Andrea Ritchie. 2015. "Say Her Name: Resisting Police Brutality Against Black Women." African American Policy Forum, Center for Intersectionality and Social Policy Studies. http://www.aafp.org.

Crosby, Faye J. 2004. *Affirmative Action Is Dead; Long Live Affirmative Action.* New Haven, CT: Yale University Press.

Cruse, Harold W. 1987. *Plural but Equal: A Critical Study of Blacks and Minorities and America's Plural Society.* New York: William Morrow.

Cumming v. County Board of Education. 1899. 175 US 545.

D'Angelo, Chris. 2015. "U.S. Government Outlines a Path for Native Hawaiian Recognition." *Huffington Post,* September 30. http://www.huffingtonpost.com/entry/native-hawaiian -government-recognition_us_560b28fce4b0768126ffc511.

Dale, C. V. 1995. *Congressional Research Service Report to Robert Dole: Compilation and Overview of Federal Laws and Regulations Establishing Affirmative Action Goals or Other Preferences Based on Race, Gender, and Ethnicity.* Washington, DC: Congressional Research Service, Library of Congress.

Damron, David, and Scott Powers. 2012. "Researcher: Long Lines at Polls Caused 49,000 Not to Vote." *OrlandoSentinel.com,* December 29. http://articles.orlandosentinel.com/2012-12 -29/news/os-discouraged-voters-20121229_1_long-lines-higher-turnout-election-day.

Dao, James, Ford Fessenden, and Tom Zeller Jr. 2004. "Voting Problems in Ohio Spur Call for Overhaul." *New York Times,* December 24, A1.

Davidson, Chandler. 1992. "The Voting Rights Act: A Brief History." In *Controversies in Minority Voting,* edited by Bernard Grofman and Chandler Davidson, 7–51. Washington, DC: Brookings Institution.

Davidson, Chandler, and Bernard Grofman, eds. 1994. *Quiet Revolution in the South: The Impact of the Voting Rights Act, 1965–1990.* Princeton, NJ: Princeton University Press.

Davidson, Osha Gray. 2007. *The Best of Enemies.* Chapel Hill: University of North Carolina Press.

Dawson, Michael C. 1994. *Behind the Mule: Race and Class in African-American Politics.* Princeton, NJ: Princeton University Press.

Decker, Scott H., Cassia Spohn, and Natalie R. Ortiz. 2014. "Criminal Stigma, Race, Gender, and Employment: An Expanded Assessment of the Consequences of Imprisonment for Employment—Final Report to the National Institution of Justice." January. https://www.ncjrs. gov/pdffiles1/nij/grants/244756.pdf.

de la Garza R. O., L. DeSipio, F. C. García, J. A. García, A. Falcón. 1992. *Latino Voices: Mexican, Puerto Rican, and Cuban Perspectives on American Politics.* Boulder, CO: Westview Press.

Delgado et al. v. Bastrop Independent School District of Bastrop County et al. 1948. Docket No. 388, W.D. Tex. June 15.

Deloria, Vine. 1985. *American Indian Policy in the Twentieth Century.* Norman: University of Oklahoma Press.

Democracy Now! 2016. "Dakota Access Pipeline." https://www.democracynow.org/topics/dakota _access.

Dentice, Dianne, and David Bugg. 2016. "Fighting for the Right to Be White: A Case Study in White Racial Identity." *Journal of Hate Studies* 12, no. 1:101–28.

De Sipio, Louis, and Rodolfo O. de la Garza. 2002. "Forever Seen as New: Latino Participation in American Elections." In *Latinos: Remaking America,* edited by Marcelo Suarez-Orozco and Mariela M. Paez. Berkeley: University of California Press.

De Vise, Daniel. 2012. "Student Claims Harvard, Princeton Discriminate Against Asian-Americans." *Washington Post,* February 2. https://www.washingtonpost.com/blogs/college-inc /post/student-claims-harvard-princeton-discriminate-against-asian-americans/2012/02/02 /gIQAkIZYkQ_blog.html.

De Vogue, Ariane. 2016. "North Carolina Counties Must Restore Voters to Rolls, Judges Rule." *CNN Politics,* November 4. http://www.cnn.com/2016/11/04/politics/north-carolina-naacp -voter-registration/.

Diamond, Jeremy. 2016. "Silently Protesting Muslim Woman Ejected from Trump Rally." *CNN Politics,* January 11, 2016. http://www.cnn.com/2016/01/08/politics/donald-trump-muslim -woman-protesting-ejected/.

Dill, Bonnie T., and Ruth Enid Zambrana. 2009. *Emerging Intersections: Race, Class, and Gender in Theory, Policy, and Practice.* New Brunswick, NJ: Rutgers University Press.

Dion, Eryn. 2016. "Group Calls for Reward for Voter Fraud Tips." *Panama City News Herald,* November 2. http://www.newsherald.com/news/20161102/group-calls-for-reward-for-voter -fraud-tips.

Dixon, Brandon J. 2016. "Race-Based Admissions Lawsuit Moves Through Discovery Phase." *Harvard Crimson,* July 8. http://www.thecrimson.com/article/2016/7/8/admissions-lawsuit -discovery-phase/.

DMZ Hawaii/Aloha 'Aina. 2008. Accessed January 21, 2011. http://www.dmzhawaii.org/.

Doherty, Steven J. 1994. "Native American Voting Behavior." Paper presented at the Midwest Political Science Association Annual Meeting, Chicago.

Dowdy, G. Wayne. 2006. *Mayor Crump Don't Like It: Machine Politics in Memphis.* Jackson: University of Mississippi Press.

Draper, Robert. 2012. *Do Not Ask What Good We Do: Inside the U.S. House of Representatives.* New York: Free Press.

Dred Scott v. Sanford. 1857. 19 Howard 393.

Economist 2007. "Race relations: Where black and brown collide." Aug 2nd 2007

Edwards, Julia. 2016. "FBI Agents, Lawmakers Hammer Comey over Clinton Emails Inquiry." *Reuters,* November 7, 2016. http://www.reuters.com/article/us-usa-justice-comey-idUSKBN 1322K6.

Eisinger, Peter K. 1976. *Patterns of Interracial Politics: Conflict and Cooperation in the City.* New York: Academic Press.

Elk v. Wilkins. 1884. 112 US 94.

Entman, Robert M. 1997. "African Americans According to TV News." In *The Media in Black and White,* edited by Everette E. Dennis and Edward C. Pease, 29–36. New Brunswick, NJ: Transaction.

Espiritu, Yen Le. 1992. *Asian American Panethnicity: Bridging Institutions and Identities.* Philadelphia: Temple University Press.

Estrada, Leobardo, F. Chris Garcia, Reynaldo F. Marcias, and Lionel Maldonado. 1981. "Chicanos in the United States: A History of Exploitation and Resistance." *Daedalus* 110:103–32.

Eyler, Janet, Valerie J. Cook, and Leslie Ward. 1983. "Resegregation: Segregation Within Desegregated Schools." In *The Consequences of School Desegregation,* edited by Christine H. Rossell and Willis D. Hawley, 126–62. Philadelphia: Temple University Press.

Falcón, Angelo. 1988. "Black and Latino Politics in New York City." In *Latinos in the Political System,* edited by F. Chris Garcia, 171–94. Notre Dame, IN: Notre Dame University Press.

Fausset, Richard. 2012. "For Romney, Immigration Issue Offers an Opportunity." *Los Angeles Times,* January 18. http://articles.latimes.com/2012/jan/18/nation/la-na-romney-immigration-20120119.

Feagin, Joe R., and Clairece Booher Feagin. 1978. *Discrimination American Style: Institutional Racism and Sexism.* Englewood Cliffs, NJ: Prentice-Hall.

Federal Register. 2016. "Indian Entities Recognized and Eligible to Receive Services from the United States Bureau of Indian Affairs." *Federal Register* 81(January 29):5019.

Feldman, Linda. 2012. "Election 2012: 12 Reasons Obama Won and Romney Lost." November 7. http://www.csmonitor.com/USA/DC-Decoder/2012/1107/Election-2012-12-reasons-Obama-won-and-Romney-lost/Obama-s-superior-campaign.

Fernández, Ricardo R., and Judith T. Guskin. 1981. "Hispanic Students and School Desegregation." In *Effective School Desegregation,* edited by Willis D. Hawley, 107–40. Beverly Hills, CA: Sage.

File, Thom, and Sarah Crissey. 2012. *Voting and Registration in the Election of November 2008,* US Census Bureau (July 2012). https://www.census.gov/prod/2010pubs/p20-562.pdf.

Finnegan, William. 2015. "The Man Who Wouldn't Sit Down." *The New Yorker,* October 5. http://www.newyorker.com.

Fisher v. University of Tex. at Austin. 2016. 758 F. 3d 63.

Flippen, Chenoa, and Parrado Emilio. 2012. "Forging Hispanic Communities in New Destinations: A Case Study of Durham, North Carolina." *City & Community* 11:1–30.

Foner, Eric. 1992. "From Slavery to Citizenship: Blacks and the Right to Vote." In *Voting and the Spirit of American Democracy,* edited by Donald W. Rogers, 55–65. Urbana: University of Illinois Press.

Fraga, Luis Ricardo, and Sharon A. Navarro. 2007. "Latinas in Latino Politics." In *Latino Politics: Identity, Mobilization, and Representation,* edited by Rodolfo Espino, David L. Leal, and Kenneth J. Meier. Charlottesville: University of Virginia Press.

Franklin, Frank George. 1906. *The Legislative History of Naturalization in the United States.* Chicago: University of Chicago Press.

Franklin, John Hope. 1969. *From Slavery to Freedom.* 3rd ed. New York: Vintage Books.

Frey, William H. 2011. "Melting Pot Cities and Suburbs: Racial and Ethnic Change in Metro America in the 2000s." *State of Metropolitan America: Race and Ethnicity.* https://www.brookings.edu/wp-content/uploads/2016/06/0504_census_ethnicity_frey.pdf.

Fuller, Jaime. 2014. "How Has Voting Changed Since *Shelby County v. Holder?*" *Washington Post,* July 7. https://www.washingtonpost.com/news/the-fix/wp/2014/07/07/how-has-voting-changed-since-shelby-county-v-holder/.

Gallup Organization. 2000. "Black Americans Feel 'Cheated' by Election 2000." Poll, December 20.

Garza, Alicia. 2014. "A Herstory of the #BlackLivesMatter Movement by Alicia Garza." *Feminist Wire,* October 7. http://www.thefeministwire.com/2014/10/blacklivesmatter-2/.

———. 2016. "A Herstory of the #BlackLivesMatter Movement." In *Are All the Women Still White?: Rethinking Race, Expanding Feminisms,* edited by Janell Hobson. Albany: State University of New York Press.

Gay, Claudine. 2006. "Seeing Difference: The Effect of Economic Disparity on Black Attitudes Toward Latinos." *American Journal of Political Science* 50, no. 4:997.

Gay, Claudine, and Katherine Tate. 1998. "Doubly Bound: The Impact of Gender and Race on the Politics of Black Women." *Political Psychology* 19, no. 1:169–84.

Gershon, Sarah. 2012. "When Race, Gender, and the Media Intersect: Campaign News Coverage of Minority Congresswomen." *Journal of Women, Politics & Policy* 33, no. 2 (May 1):105–25.

Gershon, Sarah Allen. 2013. "Media Coverage of Minority Congresswomen and Voter Evaluations: Evidence from an Online Experimental Study." *Political Research Quarterly* 66, no. 3 (September):702–14.

Gerstein, Josh. 2016. "Comey Says FBI Stands by Decision to Not Pursue Case Against Clinton." *Politico,* November 6. http://www.politico.com/story/2016/11/fbi-director-comey-says -agency-stands-by-decision-to-not-pursue-case-against-clinton-230842.

Ghumman, Sonia, and Ann Marie Ryan. 2013. "Not Welcome Here: Discrimination Towards Women Who Wear the Muslim Headscarf." *Human Relations* 66, no. 5:671–98.

Giddings, Paula. 1996. *When and Where I Enter: The Impact of Black Women on Race and Sex in America.* New York: HarperCollins.

Giroux, Greg. 2013. "Final Tally Shows Obama First Since '56 to Win 51% Twice." Bloomberg. com, January 4. http://www.bloomberg.com/news /2013–01–03/final-tally-shows-obama-first-since-56-to-win-51-twice.html.

Goldman, Sheldon, and Elliot Slotnick. 1997. "Clinton's First Term Judiciary: Many Bridges to Cross." *Judicature* 80 (May–June):254–73.

Goldman, Sheldon, and Matthew D. Saranson. 1994. "Clinton's Nontraditional Judges: Creating a More Representative Bench." *Judicature* 78 (September–October):68–73.

Gong Lum v. Rice. 1927. 275 US 78.

Gonzales v. Sheely. 1951. 96 F. Supp. 1004.

Gordon, Ann, and Jerry L. Miller. 2005. *When Stereotypes Collide: Race/Ethnicity, Gender, and Videostyle in Congressional Campaigns.* New York: Peter Lang Publishing.

Gordon, Greg. 2008. "More Minorities Voted This Year, but White Turnout Dropped." *McClatchy Washington Bureau* (online), November 18. http://www.mcclatchydc.com/104/story /56113.html.

Government Accountability Office (GAO). 2016. *Better Use of Information Could Help Agencies Identify Disparities and Address Racial Discrimination.* April. http://www.gao.gov/assets /680/676744.pdf.

Graham, Hugh Davis. 1990. *The Civil Rights Era: Origins and Development of National Policy, 1960–1972.* New York: Oxford University Press.

Gratz v. Bollinger. 2003. 539 US 244.

Graves, John William. "Jim Crow in Arkansas: A Reconsideration of Urban Race Relations in the Post-Reconstruction South." *The Journal of Southern History,* 55, no. 3, (August 1989): 421–48.

Grebler, Leo, Joan Moore, and Ralph Guzman. 1970. *The Mexican American People.* New York: Free Press.

Green v. New Kent County School Board. 1968. 391 US 390.

Griggs v. Duke Power Co. 1971. 401 US 424, 91 S.Ct. 849, 28 LEd 2d 158.

Griswold del Castillo, Richard. 1990. *The Treaty of Guadalupe Hidalgo: A Legacy of Conflict.* Norman: University of Oklahoma Press.

Grofman, Bernard, Lisa Handley, and Richard Niemi. 1992. *Minority Representation and the Quest for Voting Equality.* New York: Cambridge University Press.

Grutter v. Bollinger. 2003. 539 US 306.

Guadalupe Organization, Inc. v. Tempe Elementary School District. 1978. 587 F.2d 1022.

Guinier, Lani. 1994. *The Tyranny of the Majority: Fundamental Fairness in Representative Democracy.* New York: Free Press.

Guinn v. United States. 1915. 238 US 347.

Gulick, Sidney L. 1918. *American Democracy and Asiatic Citizenship.* New York: Charles Scribner's Sons.

Gurin, Patricia, Shirley Hatchett, and James S. Jackson. 1989. *Hope and Independence: Blacks' Response to Electoral and Party Politics.* New York: Russell Sage Foundation.

Gutiérrez, José Angel. 1998. *The Making of a Chicano Militant: Lessons from Cristal.* Madison: University of Wisconsin Press.

Gyimah-Brempong, Kwabena, and Gregory N. Price. 2006. "Crime and Punishment: And Skin Hue Too?" *American Economic Review* 96, no. 2:246–50.

Haberman, Maggie, and Alan Rappeport. 2016. "Trump Drops False 'Birther' Theory, but Floats a New One: Clinton Started It." *New York Times*, September 16, 2016. https://www.nytimes.com/2016/09/17/us/politics/donald-trump-birther-obama.html.

Hajnal, Zoltan, Nazita Lajevardi, and Lindsay Nielson. 2017. "Voter Identification Laws and the Suppression of Minority Votes." *Journal of Politics* 79, no. 2.

Halualani, Rona Tomiko. 2002. *The Name of Hawaiians: Native Identities and Cultural Politics.* Minneapolis: University of Minnesota Press.

Hancock, Ange-Marie. 2007. "When Multiplication Doesn't Equal Quick Addition: Examining Intersectionality as a Research Paradigm." *Perspectives on Politics* 5, no. 1:63–79.

Hardy-Fanta, Carol, Pei-te Lien, Dianne M. Pinderhughes, and Christine Marie Sierra. 2006. *Journal of Women, Politics, and Policy,* 28, nos. 3–4:7–41.

Harlan, Chico. 2016. "Inside the Administration's $1 Billion Deal to Detain Central American Asylum Seekers." *Washington Post,* August 14. https://www.washingtonpost.com/business/economy/inside-the-administrations-1-billion-deal-to-detain-central-american-asylum-seekers/2016/08/14/e47f1960-5819-11e6-9aee-8075993d73a2_story.html?utm_term=.35548eec8196.

Harris, Maya. 2014. "Women of Color: A Growing Force in the American Electorate." Center for American Progress. https://www.americanprogress.org/issues/race/reports/2014/10/30/99962/women-of-color/.

Harris, Paul. 2013. "Undocumented Workers' Grim Reality: Speak Out on Abuse and Risk Deportation." *Guardian,* March 28. https://www.theguardian.com/world/2013/mar/28/undocumented-migrants-worker-abuse-deportation.

Hart v. Community School Board of Brooklyn District #2. 1974. 383 F. Supp. 699, aff'd 512 F.2d 37, 1975.

Hauser, Christine. 2016. "Kirk's Retort About Duckworth's Race at Senate Debate Draws Criticism." *New York Times,* October 28, 2016. https://www.nytimes.com/2016/10/29/us/politics/mark-kirk-tammy-duckworth-debate-illinois.html.

Hawkesworth, Mary. 2006. *Feminist Inquiry: From Political Conviction to Methodological Innovation.* New Brunswick, NJ: Rutgers University Press.

Healy, Jack, and Nicholas Fandos. 2016. "Protesters Gain Victory in Fight over Dakota Access Oil Pipeline." *New York Times,* December 4. https://www.nytimes.com/2016/12/04/us/federal-officials-to-explore-different-route-for-dakota-pipeline.html.

Heim, Joe, and Mark Berman. "*Federal Government Moves to Halt Oil Pipeline Construction Near Standing Rock Sioux Tribal Land.*" *Washington Post,* Septembe 9, 2016. https://www.washingtonpost.com/news/post-nation/wp/2016/09/09/federal-judge-denies-standing-rock-sioux-tribes-request-to-stop-work-on-four-state-oil-pipeline/?utm_term=.b8f37260f5cb.

Helekunihi-Walker, Isaiah 2005. "Terrorism or Native Protest?" *Pacific Historical Review,* 74, no. 4 (November 2005):575–602.

Helms, Ann Doss. 2016. "Teen Trump Fan, Ejected from Charlotte Rally, Says He Was Profiled." *Charlotte Observer,* August 19, 2016. http://www.charlotteobserver.com/news/politics-government/election/article96648367.html.

Henderson, Nia-Malika. 2015. "How Black Lives Matter Activists Are Influencing 2016 Race." *CNN Politics.* http://www.cnn.com/2015/08/18/politics/black-lives-matter-2016-presidential-race.

Hennessy-Fiske, Molly, Jenny Jarvie, and Del Quentin Wilber. 2016. "Orlando Gunman Had Used Gay Dating App and Visited LGBT Nightclub on Other Occasions." *Los Angeles Times,* June 13. http://www.latimes.com/nation/la-na-orlando-nightclub-shooting-20160613-snap-story.html.

Henry, Charles P. 1980. "Black and Chicano Coalitions: Possibilities and Problems." *Western Journal of Black Studies* 4:222–32.

Henry, Charles P., and Carlos Muñoz Jr. 1991. "Ideological and Interest Linkages in California Rainbow Politics." In *Racial and Ethnic Politics in California*, edited by Byran O. Jackson and Michael B. Preston. Berkeley: Institute of Governmental Studies, 323–38.

Hernandez v. Driscoll Consolidated Independent School District. 1957. 2 *Race Relations Law Reporter* 329.

Hero, Rodney E. 1992. *Latinos and the U.S. Political System.* Philadelphia: Temple University Press.

Hero, Rodney E., and Caroline J. Tolbert. 1996. "A Racial/Ethnic Diversity Interpretation of Politics and Policy in the States of the U.S." *American Journal of Political Science* 40 (August):851–71.

Herring, Cedric, Hayward Derrick Horton, and Verna Keith. 2004. *Skin Deep: How Race and Complexion Matter in the "Color-Blind" Era.* Urbana: University of Illinois Press.

Higham, John. 1963 [1955]. *Strangers in the Land: Patterns of American Nativism 1860–1925.* Westport, CT: Greenwood Press.

Hill, Mark E. 2002. "Skin Color and the Perception of Attractiveness Among African Americans: Does Gender Make a Difference?" *Social Psychology Quarterly* 65, no. 1:77–91.

Hirschfelder, Arlene, and Martha Kreipe de Montaño. 1993. *The Native American Almanac: A Portrait of Native America Today.* New York: Prentice-Hall.

Hiskey, Jonathan T., Abby Córdova, Diana Orcés, and Mary Fran Malone. 2016. "Understanding the Central American Refugee Crisis: Why They Are Fleeing and How U.S. Policies Are Failing to Deter Them." American Immigration Council. https://www.americanimmigration council.org/sites/default/files/research/understanding_the_central_american_refugee_crisis .pdf.

Hochschild, Jennifer L. 1984. *The New American Dilemma: Liberal Democracy and School Desegregation.* New Haven, CT: Yale University Press.

Hochschild, Jennifer, and Vesla Weaver. 2007. "The Skin Color Paradox and the American Racial Order." *Social Forces* 86, no. 2:643–70.

Hoffman, Thomas J. 1998. "American Indians: Political Participation and Political Representation." Paper presented at the American Political Science Association Annual Meeting, Boston, Massachusetts.

Holland, Jesse J. 2011. "Obama Judicial Nominations Set Record for Women and Minorities." Associated Press, September 13, 2011. http://www.huffingtonpost.com/2011/09/13/obama -judicial-nominees-women-minorities_n_959745.html.

Holloway, Harry. 1969. *The Politics of the Southern Negro.* New York: Random House.

Holt, Len. 1966. *The Summer That Didn't End.* London: Heinemann.

Hong, Y. C. 1995. "A Brief History of the Chinese American Citizens Alliance." *Centennial Celebration and 43rd Biennial National Convention* (Conference Program). San Francisco: Chinese American Citizens Alliance.

Hopwood v. Texas. 1996. 5th Cir. 78 F. 3d 932.

Horne v. Flores. 2009. 516 F. 3d 1140.

Housing and Assistance Council (HAC). 2012. "Race and Ethnicity in Rural America." *HAC Rural Research Brief* April. http://www.ruralhome.org/storage/research_notes/rrn-race-and -ethnicity-web.pdf.

Howell, Kellan. "Muslim Woman Kicked Out of Trump Rally for Staging Silent Protest." *Washington Post,* January 9, 2016. http://www.washingtontimes.com/news/2016/jan/9/rose -hamid-muslim-woman-kicked-out-trump-rally-sta/.

Huffington Post. 2011. "Nikki Haley: Sarah Palin Appears In New Campaign Ad." May 25. http://www.huffingtonpost.com/news/sarah-palin-nikki-haley/

Huffington Post. 2016. "Black Lives Matter." http://www.huffingtonpost.com/topic/black-lives -matter.

Human Rights Campaign and Trans-People of Color Coalition (HRC and TPOCC). 2016. "A Matter of Life and Death: Fatal Violence Against Transgender People in America 2016." http://hrc-assets.s3-website-us-east-1.amazonaws.com//files/assets/resources/A-Matter-of -Life-and-Death-2016.pdf.

Hunter, Margaret L. 2002. "'If You're Light You're Alright': Light Skin Color as Social Capital for Women of Color." *Gender & Society* 16, no. 2 (April 1):175–93.

———. 2007. "The Persistent Problem of Colorism: Skin Tone, Status, and Inequality." *Sociology Compass* 1, no. 1:237–54.

Hylton, Wil S. 2015. "The Shame of America's Family Detention Camps." *New York Times,* February 4. https://www.nytimes.com/2015/02/08/magazine/the-shame-of-americas-family -detention-camps.html.

Ichioka, Yuji. 1988. *The Issei: The World of the First Generation Japanese Americans, 1885–1924.* New York: Free Press.

Imada, Adria L.2004. "Hawaiians on Tour: Hula Circuits Through the American Empire." *American Quarterly*, Vol. 56, no. 1 (March 2004):111–49.

In re Wallace. 1959. 4 *Race Relations Law Reporter* 97.

Independent School District v. Salvatierra. 1930. 33 S.W.2d 790, cert. denied, 284 US 580, 1931.

Indian Country Today. 2016. "Election Day Turmoil in Utah Portion of Navajo Nation." November 14. http://indiancountrytodaymedianetwork.com/2016/11/14/election-day-turmoil-utah -portion-navajo-nation-166443.

INDN's List: Indigenous Democratic Network. 2008. "Elected Officials." http://indnslist.org /elected officials.

Iyer, Sundeep, and Keesha Gaskins. 2012. "Redistricting and Congressional Control: A First Look." New York: Brennan Center for Justice, New York University School of Law.

James, Marlise. 1973. *The People's Lawyers.* New York: Holt, Rinehart, and Winston.

Jardina, Ashley E. 2014. *Demise of Dominance: Group Threat and the New Relevance of White Identity for American Politics.* Ph.D dissertation. University of Michigan.

Jarvis, Sonia R. 1992. "Historical Overview: African Americans and the Evolution of Voting Rights." In *From Exclusion to Inclusion: The Long Struggle for African American Political Power,* edited by Ralph Gomes and Linda Faye Williams, 17–33. Westport, CT: Greenwood Press.

Jiwani, Yasmin, and Mary Lynn Young. 2006. "Missing and Murdered Women: Reproducing Marginality in News Discourse." *Canadian Journal of Communication* 31, no.4:895–917.

Johnson et al. v. Mortham. 1995. 915 F. Supp. 1529, n.d. Fla.

Johnson, Carolyn Y. 2016. "A Black Doctor Barred from Helping on a Flights Get an Apology– And Triggers a Policy Change." *Washington Post.* December 2016. https://www.washingtonpost .com/news/wonk/wp/2016/12/20/a-black-doctor-barred-from-helping-on-a-flight-gets -an-apology-and-triggers-a-policy-change/?utm_term=.35ad8d348768.

Johnson, James H. Jr., and Melvin L. Oliver. 1989. "Interethnic Minority Conflict in Urban America: The Effects of Economic and Social Dislocations." *Urban Geography* 10:449–63.

Johnson v. Miller. 1997. 117 S.Ct. 1264.

Johnson, Kevin. 2016. "Black Lives Matter Finds Canadian Voice." *USA Today,* May 11. http://www .usatoday.com/story/news/world/2016/05/11/black-lives-matter-canada/83827764/.

Joint Center for Political and Economic Studies (JCPES). 2001. "Black Elected Officials: A Statistical Summary 2000." Washington, DC: Joint Center for Political and Economic Studies.

———. 2007. *Annual Report.* Washington, DC: Joint Center for Political and Economic Studies.

Jones, Athena, Jeremy Diamond, and Gregory Krieg. 2017. "Trump Advances Controversial Oil Pipelines with Executive Action." CNN, January 24. http://www.cnn.com/2017/01/24 /politics/trump-keystone-xl-dakota-access-pipelines-executive-actions/.

Jordan-Zachery, Julia S. 2007. "Am I a Black Woman or a Woman Who Is Black? A Few Thoughts on the Meaning of Intersectionality." *Politics & Gender*, no. 2 (June):254–63.

Judd, Dennis R. 1979. *The Politics of American Cities: Private Power and Public Policy.* Boston: Little, Brown.

Junn, Jane, and Natalie Masuoka. 2008. "Asian American Identity: Shared Racial Status and Political Context." *Perspectives in Politics* 6, no.4:729–40.

Kahn, Kim F. 1996. *The Political Consequences of Being a Woman: How Stereotypes Influence the Conduct and Consequences of Campaigns.* New York: Columbia University.

Kauanu Kehaulani, J. 2008. *Hawaiian Blood: Colonialism and the Politics of Sovereignty and Indigeneity.* Durham: Duke University Press.

Keating, Analouise. 2009. "From Intersections to Interconnections——Lessons for Transformation from *This Bridge Called My Back: Radical Writings by Women of Color.*" In *The Intersectional Approach: Transforming the Academy Through Race, Class, and Gender,* edited by Michele Tracy Berger and Kathleen Guidroz. Durham: University of North Carolina Press.

Keneally, Meghan, Veronica Stracqualursi, Shushannah Walshe, Meridith McGraw, and Julia Jacobo. 2016. "2nd Presidential Debate: 11 Moments That Mattered." ABC News, October 9. http://abcnews.go.com/Politics/presidential-debate-11-moments-mattered/story?id=4268 7340.

Keyes v. School District No. 1, Denver, Colorado. 1973. 380 F. Supp. 673.

Kim, Claire Jean. 1999. "The Racial Triangulation of Asian Americans." *Politics and Society* 27, no. 1:105–38.

Kinder, Donald, and Tali Mendelberg. 2000. "Individualism Reconsidered: Principles and Prejudice in Contemporary American Opinion." In *Racialized Politics: The Debate About Racism in America,* edited by David O. Sears, Jim Sidanius, and Lawrence Bobo. Chicago: University of Chicago Press.

King, Deborah K. 1988. "Multiple Jeopardy, Multiple Consciousness: The Context of a Black Feminist Ideology." *Signs* 14, no. 1:42–72.

Kirk, John A. 2002. *Redefining the Color Line: Black Activism in Little Rock, Arkansas, 1940–1970.* Gainesville: University Press of Florida.

Kitano, Harry H. L. 1981. "Asian-Americans: The Chinese, Japanese, Koreans, Filipinos, and Southeast Asians." *Annals of the Academy of Political and Social Sciences* 454:125–38.

Kleppner, Paul. 1990. "Defining Citizenship: Immigration and the Struggle for Voting Rights in Antebellum America." In *Voting and the Spirit of American Democracy,* edited by Donald W. Rogers, 43–53. Urbana: University of Illinois Press.

Kluegel, James R., and Eliot R. Smith. 1986. *Beliefs About Inequality.* New York: Aldine de Gruyter.

Koplinski, Brad. 2000. *Hats in the Ring: Conversations with Presidential Candidates.* North Bethesda, MD: Presidential.

Kousser, J. Morgan. 1992. "The Voting Rights Act and the Two Reconstructions." In *Controversies in Minority Voting,* edited by Bernard Grofman and Chandler Davidson, 135–76. Washington, DC: Brookings Institution.

Kraushaar, Josh. 2010. "Romney backs Haley in S.C.". *Politico.* http://www.politico.com/story /2010/03/romney-backs-haley-in-sc-034504.

Krieg, Gregory. 2016. "14 of Trump's Most Outrageous 'Birther' Claims—Half from After 2011." *CNN Politics,* September 16. http://www.cnn.com/2016/09/09/politics/donald-trump -birther/.

Krogstag, Jens Manuel. 2016. "2016 Electorate Will Be the Most Diverse in U.S. History." Pew Research Center, February 3.

Krupa, Michelle, and Frank Donze. 2008. "Anh 'Joseph' Cao Beats Rep. William Jefferson in 2nd Congressional District." *New Orleans Times-Picayune,* December 6.

KTHV. 2016. "Republican Party of Ark., Stu Stoffer Respond to Lawsuit Claims of Voter Intimidation." November 3. http://www.thv11.com/news/local/repbublican-party-of-ark-stu-stoffer -respond-to-lawsuit-claims-of-voter-intimidation/347245839.

Lakusiak, Mike, Erin Vogel-Fox, Courtney Columbus, and Marianna Haugle. 2016. "Native Americans Still Fighting for Voting Equality." *Indian Country Today,* August 29. https://indian countrymedianetwork.com/news/politics/native-americans-still-fighting-for-voting-equality/.

Larimer, Sarah. 2016. "Disgraced Ex-Cop Daniel Holtzclaw Sentenced to 263 Years for On-Duty Rapes, Sexual Assaults." *Washington Post,* January 22. https://www.washingtonpost.com/news/post-nation/wp/2016/01/21/disgraced-ex-officer-daniel-holtzclaw-to-be-sentenced-after-sex-crimes-conviction/?utm_term=.66935ed7b90c.

Latino Decisions. 2016. "Latino Decisions 2016 National Election Eve Poll." http://www.latinodecisions.com/2016-election-eve-poll/.

Lau v. Nichols. 1974. 414 US 563.

Leadership Conference Education Fund. 2016. "The Great Poll Closures." November. http://civilrightsdocs.info/pdf/reports/2016/poll-closure-report-web.pdf.

Leadership Education for Asian Pacifics. 1996. *Facts About LEAP.* Los Angeles: Leadership Education for Asian Pacifics.

Leal, David L., Matt A. Barreto, Jongho Lee, and Rodolfo O. de la Garza. 2005. "The Latino Vote in the 2004 Election." *PS: Political Science and Politics* 37, no. 1 (January):41–49.

Lee, Curtis. 2015. "Arizona Crowd Welcomes Donald Trump's Tough Stance on Immigration." *Los Angeles Times,* July 11. http://www.latimes.com/nation/politics/la-na-trump-arizona-rally-20150710-story.html.

Lee, Esther Yu Hsi. 2015. "Trump's Bizarre Strategy to Win Back Latino Supporters Is Definitely Not Working." ThinkProgress.org, July 11. https://thinkprogress.org/trumps-bizarre-strategy-to-win-back-latino-supporters-is-definitely-not-working-b1fc831d7f88#.da2w9ryfs.

Lee, Taeku. 2008. "Race, Immigration, and the Identity-to-Politics Link." *Annual Review of Political Science* 11, no. 1:457–78.

Leiderman, Michel. 2007. "Latinos." In *The Encyclopedia of Arkansas History and Culture.* Little Rock: The Central Arkansas Library System. www.encyclopediaofarkansas.net.

Levitt, Justin. 2007. "The Truth About Voter Fraud." *Brennan Center for Justice.* https://www.brennancenter.org/news/truth-about-voter-fraud-0.

Levy, Neil M. 1975. "Native Hawaiian Land Rights." *California Law Review* 63 (4):848–85.

Lewis, Anthony. 1965. *Portrait of a Decade.* New York: Bantam.

Lieb, David A. 2016. "Divided America: Minorities Missing in Many Legislatures." Associated Press, June 16, 2016. http://bigstory.ap.org/article/4c6c0cf4d1aa4c8eba374876b8a24533/divided-america-minorities-missing-many-legislatures.

Liebler, Carol M. 2010. "Me(di)a Culpa?: The 'Missing White Woman Syndrome' and Media Self-Critique." *Communication, Culture & Critique* 3, no. 4:549–65.

Lindblom, Charles E. 1980. *The Policy-Making Process.* 2nd ed. Englewood Cliffs, NJ: Prentice-Hall.

Lineberry, Robert L., and Ira Sharkansky. 1978. *Urban Politics and Public Policy.* New York: Harper & Row.

Liptak, Adam. 2004. "Justice Lets Ohio Ruling on Monitors Stand." *New York Times,* November 3, 6.

Liptak, Kevin. 2013. "South Carolina Gov. Nikki Haley's Husband Deploying to Afghanistan." CNN, January 10. http://politicalticker.blogs.cnn.com/2013/01/10/south-carolina-gov-nikki-haleys-husband-deploying-to-afghanistan/.

———. 2016. "Supreme Court Upholds Affirmative Action Program at University of Texas." *New York Times,* June 23. http://www.nytimes.com/2016/06/24/us/politics/supreme-court-affirmative-action-university-of-texas.html.

Livengood, Chad, Michael Wayland, and Maureen Feighan. 2016. "Trump Narrowly Wins in Michigan." *Detroit News,* November 9. http://www.detroitnews.com/story/news/politics/elections/2016/11/08/michigan-president-election-results/93499404/.

Logan, Rayford Wittingham. 1954. *The Negro in American Life and Thought: The Nadir, 1877–1901.* New York: Dial Press.

Lopez, Mark Hugo. 2008. "The Hispanic Vote in the 2008 Election." Washington, DC: Pew Hispanic Center.

Lopez, Mark Hugo, Ana Gonzalez-Barrera, Jens Manuel Krogstad,and Gustavo López. 2016. "Democrats Maintain Edge as Party 'More Concerned for Latinos,' but Views Similar to 2012." Pew Research Center, October 11.

Lopez. *Los Angeles Times Survey,* June 1993.

Loving v. Virginia. 1967. 388 US 1.

Low, Victor. 1982. *The Unimpressible Race: A Century of Educational Struggle by the Chinese in San Francisco.* San Francisco: East/West Publishing.

Lutey, Tom, and Chris Cioffi. 2015. "Crews to Clean Up Oil Spilled into Yellowstone River from Montana Pipeline." *Billings Gazette,* January 19. http://billingsgazette.com/news/state -and-regional/montana/crews-to-clean-up-oil-spilled-into-yellowstone-river-from/article _89bcd50d-60ed-5a98-9a3d-4cecffa020e4.html.

MacManus, Susan A. and Carol A. Cassel. 1982. "Mexican Americans in City Politics: Participation, Representation, and Policy Preferences," *Urban Interest* (Spring):57–69.

Mai-Duc, Christine. 2016. "Loretta Sanchez Dabbed. Kamala Harris Threw Shade." *Los Angeles Times,* October 5, 2016, http://www.latimes.com/politics/essential/la-pol-sac-essential-politics -updates-what-s-loretta-sanchez-doing-in-the-1475725380-htmlstory.html.

Males, Mike. 2014. "Who Are Police Killing?" Center on Juvenile and Criminal Justice. August 26. http://www.cjcj.org/news/8113.

Mansbridge, Jane. 1999. "Should Blacks Represent Blacks and Women Represent Women?: A Contingent 'Yes'." *Journal of Politics* 61, no. 3: 628–57.

Marcin, Tim. 2015. "Harvard Admissions Discrimination: Coalition Accuses University of Bias Against Asian-Americans." *International Business Times,* May 16. http://www.ibtimes.com harvard-admissions-discrimination-coalition-accuses-university-bias-against-asian-1925779.

Marosi, Richard. 2004. "Arizona Stirs Up Immigration Stew." *Los Angeles Times,* November 6, A11.

Márquez, Benjamin. 1989. "The Politics of Race and Assimilation: The League of United Latin American Citizens." *Western Political Quarterly* 42:355–77.

Marrow, Helen B. 2005. "New Destinations and Immigrant Incorporation." *Perspectives on Politics* 3, no. 4:781–99.

Mason, Jeff. 2008. "Obama Joins American Indian Tribe, Eyes Policy Change." Reuters, May 19.

Matland, Richard and David King. 2002. "Women as Candidates in Congressional Elections." In *Women Transforming Congress,* edited by Cindy Rosenthal. Norman: University of Oklahoma Press.

Matz, Lee. 2016. "Photo Essay: Protesting the Politics of Hate." *Milwaukee Independent,* May 3. http://www.milwaukeeindependent.com/featured/photo-essay-protesting-the-politics-of -hate/.

Mauer, Marc. 2013. "The Changing Racial Dynamics of Women's Incarceration." Sentencing Project. http://www.sentencingproject.org/publications/ the-changing-racial-dynamics-of-womens-incarceration/.

McClain, Paula D. 1993a. "The Changing Dynamics of Urban Politics: Black and Hispanic Municipal Employment—Is There Competition?" *Journal of Politics* 55:399–414.

———, ed. 1993b. *Minority Group Influence: Agenda Setting, Formulation, and Public Policy.* Westport, CT: Greenwood Press.

McClain, Paula D., and Albert K. Karnig. 1990. "Black and Hispanic Socioeconomic and Political Competition." *American Political Science Review* 84:535–45.

McClain, Paula D., and Steven C. Tauber. 2001. "Black, Latino, and Asian Socioeconomic and Political Resources and Urban Electoral Outcomes: Complementary, Competitive, or Independent?" Unpublished manuscript.

McClain, Paula D., Gerald F. Lackey, Efrén O. Perez, Niambi M. Carter, Jessica Johnson Carew, Eugene Walton Jr., Candis Watts Smith, Monique L. Lyle, and Shayla C. Nunnally. 2011. "Intergroup Relations in Three Southern Cities." In *Just Neighbors? Research on African American and Latino Relations in the United States,* edited by Edward Telles, Mark Q. Sawyer, and Gaspar Rivera-Salgado. New York: Russell Sage Foundation.

McClain, Paula D., Jessica D. Johnson Carew, Eugene Walton, and Candis S. Watts. 2009. "Group Membership, Group Identity, and Group Consciousness: Measures of Racial Identity in American Politics?" *Annual Review of Political Science* 12, no. 1:471–85.

McClain, Paula D., Monique L. Lyle, Niambi M. Carter, Victoria M. DeFrancesco Soto, Gerald F. Lackey, Kendra Davenport Cotton, Shayla C. Nunnally, Thomas J. Scotto, Jeffrey D. Grynaviski, and J. Alan Kendrick. 2007. "Black Americans and Latino Immigrants in a Southern City: Friendly Neighbors or Economic Competitors?" *Du Bois Review: Social Science Research on Race* 4, no. 1 (March):97–117.

McClain, Paula D., Niambi M. Carter, and Michael C. Brady. 2005. "Gender and Black Presidential Politics: From Chisholm to Moseley-Braun." *Journal of Women, Politics & Policy* 27, nos. 1–2:51–68.

McClain, Paula D., Niambi M. Carter, Victoria M. DeFrancesco, Monique L. Lyle, Shayla C. Nunnally, Thomas J. Scotto, J. Alan Kendrick, Jeffrey D. Grynaviski, Gerald F. Lackey, and Kendra Davenport Cotton. 2006. "Racial Distancing in a Southern City: Latino Immigrants' Views of Black Americans." *Journal of Politics* 68, no. 3 (August):571–84.

McCool, Daniel. 1982. "Voting Patterns of American Indians in Arizona." *Social Science Journal* 19:101–13.

———. 1985. "Indian Voting." In *American Indian Policy in the Twentieth Century*, edited by Vine Deloria Jr., 105–33 Norman: University of Oklahoma Press.

McCoy, Kevin. 2016. "Bank to Pay $10.6M Over Loan Discrimination Charges." *USA Today*, June 29. http://www.usatoday.com/story/money/2016/06/29/bank-pay-106m-over-loan-discrimination-charges/86526572/.

McDonald, Laughlin, and John A. Powell. 1993. *The Rights of Racial Minorities: The Basic ACLU Guide to Racial Minority Rights.* 2nd ed. Carbondale: Southern Illinois University Press.

McGregor-Alegado, Davianna. 1980. "Hawaiians: Organizing in the 1970s." *Amerasia Journal* 7, no. 2:29–55.

Meier, Kenneth J., and Joseph Stewart Jr. 1991. *The Politics of Hispanic Education.* Albany: State University of New York Press.

Meier, Kenneth J., Joseph Stewart Jr., and Robert E. England. 1989. *Race, Class, and Education: The Politics of Second-Generation Discrimination.* Madison: University of Wisconsin Press.

Memoli, Michael A. 2010. "Mitch McConnell's Remarks on 2012 Draw White House Ire." *Los Angeles Times,* October 27. http://articles.latimes.com /2010/oct/27/news/la-pn-obama-mcconnell-20101027.

Mendez v. Westminster School District. 1946. 64 F. Supp. 544, aff'd 161 F.2d 774, 1947.

Michaelson, Elex. 2016. "Senate Candidates Kamala Harris, Loretta Sanchez Clash in Only Debate." KABC-TV Los Angeles, October 5. http://abc7.com/politics/senate-candidates-kamala-harris-loretta-sanchez-clash-in-only-debate/1541624/.

Michel, Karen Lincoln. 1998. "Fielding a New Clout: Indian Power and Party Politics." *Native Americas* 15, no. 3 (Fall):11.

Miller v. Johnson. 1995. 515 US 900, 115 S.Ct. 2475, 132 LEd, 2d 762.

Min, Jeonghun, and Daniel Savage. 2014. "Why Do American Indians Vote Democratic?" *The Social Science Journal* 51 (2014):167–80.

Minta, Michael D., and Nadia Brown. 2014. "Intersecting Interests: Gender, Race, and Congressional Attention to Women's Issues." *Du Bois Review*, 11, no. 2:253–72.

Mintz, John, and Dan Keating. 2000. "Fla. Ballot Spoilage Likelier for Blacks." *Washington Post,* December 3.

Missouri ex rel. Gaines v. Canada. 1938. 305 US 337.

Mollenkopf, John H. 1990. "New York: The Great Anomaly." In *Racial Politics in American Cities,* edited by Rufus P. Browning, Dale Rogers Marshall, and David H. Tabb, 75–87. New York: Longman.

Montoya, Lisa J. 1996. "Latino Gender Differences in Public Opinion: Results from the Latino National Political Survey." *Hispanic Journal of Behavioral Sciences* 18:255–76.

Montoya, Lisa J., Carol Hardy-Fanta, and Sonia Garcia. 2000. "Latina Politics: Gender, Participation, and Leadership." *PS: Political Science and Politics* 33:555–61.

Moore, Joan, and Harry Pachon. 1985. *Hispanics in the United States.* Englewood Cliffs, NJ: Prentice-Hall.

Moraga, Cheríe, and Gloria Anzaldúa. 2015. *This Bridge Called My Back, Fourth Edition: Writings by Radical Women of Color*. New York: SUNY Press.

Morgan v. Hennigan. 1974. 379 F. Supp. 410.

Morris, Aldon D. 1984. *The Origins of the Civil Rights Movement: Black Communities Organizing for Change*. New York: Free Press.

Morrison, Peter A., and Ira S. Lowry. 1994. "A Riot of Color: The Demographic Setting." In *The Los Angeles Riots: Lessons for the Urban Future*, edited by Mark Baldassare, 19–46. Boulder, CO: Westview Press.

Mullane, Deirdre, ed. 1993. *Crossing the Danger Water: Three Hundred Years of African-American Writing*. New York: Anchor.

Muñoz, Carlos Jr. 1989. *Youth, Identity, Power: The Chicano Movement*. New York: Verso.

Musabji, Heena, and Christina Abraham. 2007. "The Threat to Civil Liberties and Its Effect on Muslims in America." *DePaul Journal for Social Justice* 1, no.1:83–112.

Myrdal, Gunnar. 1944. *An American Dilemma*. New York: Harper and Brothers.

Nagel, Joanne. 1982. "The Political Mobilization of Native Americans." *Social Science Journal* 19:37–45.

Nakanishi, Donald. 1991. "The Next Swing Vote: Asian Pacific Americans and California Politics." In *Racial and Ethnic Politics in California*, edited by Byran O. Jackson and Michael B. Preston, 25–54. Berkeley: Institute of Governmental Studies.

Nakashima, Ellen, Sari Horwitz and Matt Zapotosky. 2016. "For FBI, Email Investigation Yields Little but Criticism." *Washington Post*, November 6. https://www.washingtonpost.com/politics/fbi-director-comey-says-agency-wont-recommend-charges-over-clinton-email/2016/11/06/f6276b18-a45e-11e6-ba59-a7d93165c6d4_story.html.

Naples, Nancy A., ed. 1998. *Community Activism and Feminist Politics: Organizing Across Race, Class, and Gender*. New York: Routledge.

National Asian Pacific American Legal Consortium. n.d. Membership brochure.

National Association for Asian and Pacific American Education. n.d. Membership brochure.

National Association for Bilingual Education (NABE). 2016. "What Is Bilingual Education?" http://www.nabe.org/BilingualEducation.

National Association of Korean Americans. n.d. Membership brochure.

National Association of Latino Elected Officials (NALEO). 1996. "Newly Naturalized Latinos Inspired by Opportunity to Vote and Are Ready to Participate." Press release, October 28, 1996.

———. 2000a. *2000 National Directory of Latino Elected Officials*. Los Angeles: NALEO.

———. 2000b. "Latinos Grab Seats in State Houses Nationwide." *NALEO News*, November 9.

———. 2007. "A Profile of Latino Elected Officials in the United States and Their Progress Since 1996." Los Angeles: NALEO Educational Fund.

———. 2008a. "2008 General Election Profile: Latinos in Congress and State Legislatures After Election 2008: A State-By-State Summary." Los Angeles: NALEO Educational Fund.

———. 2008b. "Latinos Achieve New Political Milestones in Congress and State Houses." Press release, November 5.

———. 2010. "A Profile of Latino Elected Officials in the United States and Their Progress Since 1996." http://www.naleo.org/downloads/NALEOFactSheet07.pdf.

NALEO Educational Fund. 2016. http://www.naleo.org/.

National Center for Education Statistics. 1978. *The Children's English and Services Study*. Washington, DC: Government Printing Office.

National Coalition of Anti-Violence Programs (NCAVP). 2016. "NCAVP 2015 Hate Violence Report Toolkit: 2016 Release Edition." New York City Gay and Lesbian Anti-Violence Project, Inc. http://www.avp.org/storage/documents/ncavp_hvreport_toolkit_201_final.pdf.

National Conference of State Legislatures. 2013. "Voter Identification Requirements." January 14. http://www.ncsl.org/legislatures-elections/elections /voter-id.aspx.

National Council of La Raza. 1990. "Background Paper for Black-Latino Dialogue." Unpublished paper.

National Institute of Education. 1977. *Conference Report: Desegregation and Education Concerns of the Hispanic Community.* Washington, DC: Government Printing Office.

National Public Radio. 2016. "Fact Check: Clinton and Trump Debate for the 2nd Time." October 9. http://www.npr.org/2016/10/09/497056227/fact-check-clinton-and-trump-debate-for -the-second-time.

National Women's Law Center (NWLC). 2014. "Underpaid and Overworked: Women in Low-Wage Jobs." http://www.nwlc.org/sites/default/files/pdfs/final_nwlc_lowwagereport2014.pdf.

———. 2015. "Closing the Wage Gap Is Crucial for Women of Color and Their Families." http://nwlc.org/resources/closing-wage-gap-crucial-women-color-and-their-families/.

Native American Rights Fund (NARF). 1993. *Annual Report.* Boulder, CO: NARF.

Newkirk II, Vann R. 2016. "What Early Voting in North Carolina Actually Reveals." *Atlantic,* November 8. http://www.theatlantic.com/politics/archive/2016/11/north-carolina-early -voting/506963/.

New York Times. 2004. "Playing with Election Rules." September 30, A28.

———. 2015. "What Presidential Candidates Have Said About the Black Lives Matter Movement." *New York Times,* November 19. http://www.nytimes.com/interactive/2015/11/19 /us/19blacklives-listy.html.

News and Observer (Raleigh). 2008a "Black, Female, GOP." November 26, 3B.

———. 2008b. "N.C. Voter Participation Swelled in 2008." December 30, 3B.

Noguera, P. 2007. School Reform and Second-Generation Discrimination: Toward the Development of Equitable Schools. Understanding Educational Equity and Excellence at Scale Project. January. Providence, RI: Annenberg Institute for School Reform.

Nonprofitvote.org. 2008. "Voter Turnout Brief: New Mexico 2008." http://nonprofitvote.org.

North Carolina Board of Elections. 2008. "2008 General Election Absentee Stats for 11/04 /2008." http://www.sboe.state.nc.us/.

———. 2017. "NC Voter Statistics Results. Reporting Period: 01/21/2017." http://enr.ncsbe .gov/voter_stats/results.aspx?date=01-21-2017.

Northcott, Charlie. 2016. "Life in the Native American Oil Protest Camps." *BBC News.* September 2, 2016. http://www.bbc.com/news/world-us-canada-37249617.

O'Connor, Karen, and Lee Epstein. 1984. "A Legal Voice for the Chicano Community: The Activities of the Mexican American Legal Defense and Educational Fund, 1968–82." *Social Science Quarterly* 65:245–56.

Obama, Barack. 2008. "Obama: A Full Partnership with Indian Country." *Indian Country Today,* October 24.

Obergefell v. Hodges. 2015. 576 U.S. Supreme Court.

Oceti Sakowin Camp. 2016. http://www.ocetisakowincamp.org.

Office of Hawaiian Affairs (OHA). 2016. "Governance." http://www.oha.org/governance/.

Office of the High Commissioner, UN Human Rights (OHCHR). 2016. "Native Americans Facing Excessive Force in North Dakota Pipeline Protests—UN Expert." November 15. http://www.ohchr.org/en/NewsEvents/Pages/DisplayNews.aspx?NewsID=20570&Lang ID=E.

Oliver, J. Eric, and Janelle Wong. 2003. "Inter-group Prejudice in Multiethnic Settings." *American Journal of Political Science* 47, no. 4:567–82.

Oliver, Melvin L., and James H. Johnson Jr. 1984. "Inter-Ethnic Conflict in an Urban Ghetto: The Case of Blacks and Latinos in Los Angeles." *Social Movements, Conflicts, and Change* 6:57–94.

Oliver, Melvin, and Thomas M. Shapiro, eds. 2016. *Black Wealth / White Wealth: A New Perspective on Racial Inequality,* 2nd ed. New York, NY: Routledge.

Olsen, Marvin C. 1970. "Social and Political Participation of Blacks." *American Sociological Review* 35:682–97.

Oregonian. 2001. "Rep. Wu's Dilemma: Strange How, Circa 2001, Questions of Race Are Still Uncomfortably Close to the Surface of the Body Politic." May 30, E08.

Orey, Byron D'Andra, Wendy Smooth, Kimberly Adams, and Kisha Harris-Clark. 2006. "Race and Gender Matter: Refining Models of Legislative Policy Making in State Legislatures." *Journal of Women, Politics & Policy*, 28, nos. 3–4:97–119.

Orfield, Gary W. 1969. *The Reconstruction of Southern Education: The Schools and the 1964 Civil Rights Act.* New York: Wiley.

———. 1978. *Must We Bus?* Washington, DC: Brookings Institution.

Orfield, Gary W., with Sara Schley, Diane Glass, and Sean Reardon. 1993. *The Growth of Segregation in American Schools: Changing Patterns of Separation and Poverty Since 1968.* Washington, DC: National School Board Association, Council of Urban Boards of Education.

Organization of Chinese Americans. 1997. "Image." Summer.

Overby, Peter. 2008. "Obama Finished Campaign with Money to Spare." National Public Radio, December 30.

Panaritis, Maria, Dylan Purcell, Chris Brennan, and Angela Couloumbis. 2016. "How Trump Took Pennsylvania: Wins Everywhere (Almost) but the Southeast." *Philadelphia Inquirer,* November 10. http://www.philly.com/philly/news/politics/presidential/20161110_How_Trump_took_Pennsylvania__Wins__almost__everywhere_but_the_southeast.html.

Panetta, Leon E., and Peter Gall. 1971. *Bring Us Together: The Nixon Team and the Civil Rights Retreat.* Philadelphia: Lippincott.

Park, Haeyoun, and Iaryna Mykhyalyshyn. 2016. "L.G.B.T. People Are More Likely to Be Targets of Hate Crimes Than Any Other Minority Group." *New York Times,* June 16. https://www.nytimes.com/interactive/2016/06/16/us/hate-crimes-against-lgbt.html?_r=0.

Patterson, Brandon E. 2015. "Black Lives Matter Just Officially Became Part of the Democratic Party." *Mother Jones,* October 21. http://www.motherjones.com/mojo/2015/10/democratic-national-committee-asks-black-lives-matter-activists-organize-racial-jusitce.

Peltason, Jack W. 1971. *Fifty-Eight Lonely Men: Southern Federal Judges and School Desegregation.* Urbana: University of Illinois Press.

Peralta, Eyder. 2016. "Dakota Access Pipeline Protests in North Dakota Turn Violent." NPR. NPR, n.d. Web. 26 Sept. 2016

Pérez, Efrén O. 2016. *Unspoken Politics: Implicit Attitudes and Political Thinking.* New York: Cambridge University Press.

Pew Hispanic Survey 2007. "2007 National Survey of Latinos." http://www.pewhispanic.org/2007/12/13/2007-national-survey-of-latinos/.

Pew Research Center, 2013. "The Rise of Asian Americans." (Asian American Survey 2013) April 4 http://www.pewsocialtrends.org/2012/06/19/the-rise-of-asian-americans/

———. 2015. "After 200 Years, Native Hawaiians Make a Comeback." Fact Tank, April 6. http://www.pewresearch.org/fact-tank/2015/04/06/native-hawaiian-population/.

———. 2016. "On View of Race and Inequality, Blacks and Whites Are Worlds Apart." June 27. http://www.pewsocialtrends.org/2016/06/27/on-views-of-race-and-inequality-blacks-and-whites-are-worlds-apart/.

Philpot, Tasha S., and Hanes Walton Jr. 2007. "One of Our Own: Black Female Candidates and the Voters Who Support Them." *American Journal of Political Science* 51, no. 1 (January 1):49–62.

Pinderhughes, Dianne. 1982. "Black Women and National Educational Policy." *Journal of Negro Education* 51, no. 3:301–8.

———. 1987. *Race and Ethnicity in Chicago Politics: A Reexamination of Pluralist Theory.* Urbana: University of Illinois Press.

Pinderhughes, Raquel. 1996. "The Impact of Race on Environmental Quality: An Empirical and Theoretical Discussion." *Sociological Perspectives*, 39, no. 2:231–248.

Pipeline and Hazardous Materials Safety Administration (PHMSA). 2016. "Pipeline Incident 20 Year Trends." US Department of Transportation. http://www.phmsa.dot.gov/pipeline/library/data-stats/pipelineincidenttrends.

Plessy v. Ferguson. 1896. 163 US 537.

Pohlman, Marcus. 1991. *Black Politics in Conservative America.* New York: Longman.

Powell, Michael, and Peter Slevin. 2004. "Several Factors Contributed to 'Lost' Voters in Ohio." *Washington Post,* December 15, A01.

Prestage, Jewel Limar. 1977. "Black Women State Legislators: A Profile." In *A Portrait of Marginality: The Political Behavior of African American Women,* edited by Marianne Githens and Jewel Prestage. New York: David McKay.

Purdie-Vaughns, Valerie, and Richard P. Eibach. 2008. "Intersectional Invisibility: The Distinctive Advantages and Disadvantages of Multiple Subordinate-Group Identities." *Sex Roles* 59, nos. 5–6 (September):377–91.

Rainey, Shirley A., and Glenn S. Johnson. 2009. "Grassroots Activism: An Exploration of Women of Color's Role in the Environmental Justice Movement." *Race, Gender & Class* 16, nos. 3–4:144–73.

Ramakrishnan, Karthick. 2005. *Democracy in Immigrant America: Changing Demographics and Political Participation.* Palo Alto, CA: Stanford University Press.

Ramakrishnan, Karthick, Janelle Wong, Takeu Lee, and Jennifer Lee. 2016. "Asian American Voices in the 2016 Election." National Asian American Survey, University of California, Irvine.

Rangel, Jorge C., and Carlos M. Alcala. 1972. "Project Report: De Jure Segregation of Chicanos in Texas Schools." *Harvard Civil Rights–Civil Liberties Law Review* 7:307–92.

Reeves, Keith. 1997. *Voting Hopes or Fears? White Voters, Black Candidates, and Racial Politics in America.* New York: Oxford University Press.

Richmond v. J. A. Croson Co. 1989. 488 US 469, 109 S.Ct. 706, 102 LEd 2d 854.

Rindels, Michelle. 2016. "Cortez Masto Wins in Nevada, Will Be First Latina in Senate." *Washington Times,* November 8, 2016. http://www.washingtontimes.com/news/2016/nov/8/trump-effect-could-shape-3-tight-nevada-congressio/.

Ritt, Leonard. 1979. "Some Social and Political Views of American Indians." *Ethnicity* 6:45–72.

Robertson, David B., and Dennis R. Judd. 1989. *The Development of American Public Policy: The Structure of Policy Restraint.* Glenview, IL: Scott, Foresman/Little, Brown.

Robinson, Donald L. 1971. *Slavery in the Structure of American Politics, 1765–1820.* New York: Harcourt, Brace, Jovanovich.

Robles, Frances, and Geoff Dougherty. 2000. "Ballot Errors Rate High in Some Black Precincts." *Miami Herald* (online), November 15.

Robnett, Belinda. 1997. *How Long? How Long? African-American Women in the Struggle for Civil Rights.* New York: Oxford University Press.

Rodell, Fred. 1968. "The Complexities of Mr. Justice Fortas." *New York Times Magazine,* July 28, 12.

Rodgers, Harrell R. Jr., and Charles S. Bullock III. 1976. *Coercion to Compliance.* Lexington, MA: D. C. Heath.

Romero v. Weakley. 1955. 131 F.Supp. 818.

Rose, Harold M. 1971. *The Black Ghetto: A Spatial Behavioral Perspective.* New York: McGraw-Hill.

Ross v. Eckels. 1970. 434 F.2d 1140.

Roussi, Antoaneta. 2016. "'Sounds Like Black Privilege to Me': Rampant Racism Forces Fox News to Close Comments Section on Malia Obama Article." *Salon,* May 3. http://www.salon.com/2016/05/03/sounds_like_black_privilege_to_me_rampant_racism_forces_fox_news_to_close_comments_section_on_malia_obama_article/.

Ruffin II, Herbert G. n.d. "Black Lives Matter: The Growth of a New Social Justice Movement." BlackPast.org. http://www.blackpast.org/perspectives/black-lives-matter-growth-new-social-justice-movement.

Ruffin, David C. 2004. "The Verdict's in on Black Judges." Blackenterprise.com, October 26.

Rupar, Aaron, and Bryan Dewan. 2016. "Timeline: How Trump Took the Low Road to the Top of the Republican Party," ThinkProgress.org. March 1. http://thinkprogress.org/politics/2016/03/01/3755255/donald-trump-super-tuesday-timeline/.

Russell-Cole, Kathy, Ronald E. Hall, and Midge Wilson. 2013. *The Color Complex: The Politics of Skin Color in a New Millennium*. Rev. ed. New York: Anchor Books.

Rutenberg, Jim. 2015. "What's Left of the Voting Rights Act?" *New York Times*, August 5. http://www.nytimes.com/2015/08/04/magazine/whats-left-of-the-voting-rights-act.html.

San Miguel, Guadalupe, Jr. 1987. *"Let All of Them Take Heed": Mexican Americans and the Campaign for Educational Equality in Texas, 1910–1981*. Austin: University of Texas Press.

Schaffner, Brian. 2002. "The Role of Race and Gender on Local Congressional TV News." Presented at the Annual Meeting of the American Political Science Association, Boston, Massachusetts.

Schattschneider, E. E. 1960. *The Semi-Sovereign People*. Hinsdale, IL: Dryden.

Schneider, David J. 2005. *The Psychology of Stereotyping*. New York: Guilford Press.

Schultheis, Emily. 2014. "How Ethnicity Weighs on Hawaii's Democratic Primary." *Atlantic*, July 16. http://www.theatlantic.com/politics/archive/2014/07/how-ethnicity-weighs-on -hawaiis-democratic-primary/457914/.

———. 2016. "FBI Director to Congress: Still No Charges Recommended After Latest Clinton Emails Reviewed." *CBS News*. November 6. http://www.cbsnews.com/news/fbi-director-comey -congress-new-letter-hillary-clinton-emails-still-no-charges/.

SCOTUSblog. 2016. *Fisher v. University of Texas at Austin*. http://www.scotusblog.com/case-files /cases/fisher-v-university-of-texas-at-austin-2/.

Serna v. Portales Municipal Schools. 1974. 499 F.2d 1147.

Shaw v. Hunt. 1996. 517 US 899.

Shaw v. Reno. 1993. 509 US 630.

Shelby County, Alabama v. Holder 2013, 570 U.S. Supreme Court

Shyong, Frank, Lance Pugmire, Karen Kaplan, Deborah Netburn, Melissa Healy, Christine Mai-Duc, and Matt Hamilton. 2016. "Why This Cop's Conviction Brought Thousands of Asian Americans into New York's Streets." *Los Angeles Times*, April 13. http://www.latimes .com/nation/la-na-liang-brooklyn-shooting-20160413-story.html.

Sigelman, Lee, and Susan Welch. 1991. *Black Americans' Views of Racial Inequality: The Dream Deferred*. Cambridge: Cambridge University Press.

Sigelman, Lee, Steven A. Tuch, and Jack K. Martin. 2005. "What's in a Name? Preference for 'Black' Versus 'African-American' Among Americans of African Descent." *Public Opinion Quarterly* 69:429–38.

Sigler, Jay A. 1975. *American Rights Policies*. Homewood, IL: Dorsey Press.

Silver, Christopher, and John V. Moeser. 1995. *The Separate City: Black Communities in the Urban South, 1940–1968*. Lexington: University Press of Kentucky.

Simien, Evelyn M. 2007. "Doing Intersectionality Research: From Conceptual Issues to Practical Examples." *Politics & Gender* 3, no. 2:264–71.

Simien, Evelyn M., and Rosalee A. Clawson. 2004. "The Intersection of Race and Gender: An Examination of Black Feminist Consciousness, Race Consciousness, and Policy Attitudes." *Social Science Quarterly* 85, no. 3:793–810.

Simmons, Cassandra A., and Nelvia M. Brady. 1981. "The Impact of Ability Group Placement Decisions on the Equality of Educational Opportunity in Desegregated Elementary Schools." *Urban Review* 13:129–33.

Siner, Jeff. 2016a. "Rose Hamid and Jake Anantha Escorted from Trump Rally." *Charlotte Observer*, August 18. http://www.charlotteobserver.com/news/article96525017.html.

———. 2016. "Teen Trump Fan, Ejected from Charlotte Rally, Says He Was Profiled." *Charlotte Observer*, August 19, 2016. http://www.charlotteobserver.com/news/politics-government /election/article96648367.html.

Skrentny, John David. 1996. *The Ironies of Affirmative Action*. Chicago: University of Chicago Press.

Slaughterhouse Cases. 1873. 16 Wallace 36.

Smith v. Allwright. 1944. 321 US 649.

Smith, Candis Watts. 2014. *Black Mosaic: The Politics of Black Pan-Ethnic Diversity*. New York: New York University Press.

Smith, Mychal D. 2014. "How Trayvon Martin's Death Launched a New Generation of Black Activism." *Nation,* August 27. https://www.thenation.com/article/how-trayvon-martins -death-launched-new-generation-black-activism/.

Smith, Robert C. 1990. "From Insurgency to Ward Inclusion: The Jackson Campaigns of 1984 and 1988." In *The Social and Political Implications of the 1984 Jesse Jackson Campaign,* edited by Lorenzo Morris, 215–30. New York: Praeger.

Smith, Robert C., and Richard Seltzer. 1992. *Race, Class, and Culture.* Albany: State University of New York Press.

Smooth, Wendy. 2006. "Intersectionality in Electoral Politics: A Mess Worth Making." *Politics & Gender* 2, no. 3:400–14.

Sonenshein, Raphael J. 1990. "Biracial Coalition Politics in Los Angeles." In *Racial Politics in American Cities,* edited by Rufus P. Browning, Dale Rogers Marshall, and David H. Tabb. New York: Longman, 33–48.

———. 1993. *Politics in Black and White: Race and Power in Los Angeles.* Princeton, NJ: Princeton University Press.

Spickard, Paul R. 1989. *Mixed Blood: Intermarriage and Ethnic Identity in Twentieth Century America.* Madison: University of Wisconsin Press.

Spring, Joel. 1989. *The Sorting Machine Revisited: National Educational Policy Since 1945.* Updated ed. New York: Longman.

Stancill, Jane. 2015. "UNC Applicants' Information to Be Part of Admission Lawsuit." *News and Observer,* November 17. http://www.newsobserver.com/news/local/education/article45278043.html.

Standing Rock Sioux Tribe et al. v. U.S. Army Corps of Engineers et al., Civil Action No. 16–1534.

Steeh, Charlotte, and Maria Kyrsan. 1996. "The Polls-Trends: Affirmative Action and the Public, 1970–1995." *Public Opinion Quarterly* 60 (Spring):128–58.

Stephan, Walter G., C. Lausanne Renfro, Victoria M. Esses, Cookie White Stephan, and Tim Martin. 2005. "The Effects of Feeling Threatened on Attitudes Toward Immigrants." *International Journal of Intercultural Relations* 29:1–19.

Stepler, Renee, and Anna Brown. 2016. "Statistical Portrait of Hispanics in the United States." April 19. http://www.pewhispanic.org/2016/04/19/statistical-portrait-of-hispanics -in-the-united-states-key-charts/.

Stokes, Bruce. 1988. "Learning the Game." *National Journal* 20:2649–54.

Sugrue, Thomas J. 1996. *The Origins of the Urban Crisis: Race and Inequality in Postwar Detroit.* Princeton, NJ: Princeton University Press.

Sundquist, James L. 1968. *Politics and Policy: The Eisenhower, Kennedy, and Johnson Years.* Washington, DC: Brookings Institution.

Swavola, Elizabeth, Kristine Riley, and Ram Subramanian. 2016. "Overlooked: Women and Jails in an Era of Reform." Vera Institute of Justice. http://www.safetyandjusticechallenge.org/wp-content/uploads/2016/08/overlooked-women-in-jails-report-web.pdf.

Takaki, Ronald. 1993. *A Different Mirror: A History of Multicultural America.* Boston: Little, Brown.

Tamari, Sandra. 2015. "From Ferguson to Palestine, We See Us." *Huffington Post,* October 16. http://www.huffingtonpost.com/sandra-tamari/from-ferguson-to-palestine_b_8307832.html.

Tape v. Hurley. 1885. 66 Cal. 473.

Tate, Katherine. 1993. *From Protest to Politics: The New Black Voters in American Elections.* Cambridge, MA: Harvard University Press/Russell Sage Foundation.

———. 2004. *Black Faces in the Mirror: African Americans and Their Representatives in the U.S. Congress.* Princeton, NJ: Princeton University Press.

Taylor, Paul, Mark Hugo Lopez, Jessica Martinez, and Gabriel Velasco. 2012. "When Labels Don't Fit: Hispanics and Their Views on Identity." Pew Research Center. April 4. http://www.pewhispanic.org/2012/04/04/when-labels-dont-fit-hispanics-and-their-views -of-identity/.

Tehekmedyian, Alene, and Melissa Etehad. 2016. "2 Years of Opposition, 1,172 Miles of Pipe, 1.3 Million Facebook Check-Ins. The Numbers to Know About the Standing Rock Protests." *Los Angeles Times*, November 1, 2016. http://www.latimes.com/nation/la-na-standing-rock -numbers-20161101-story.html.

Teitelbaum, Herbert, and Richard J. Hiller. 1977. "Bilingual Education: The Legal Mandate." *Harvard Educational Review* 47:138–70.

Terkel, Amanda. 2012. "Florida Early Voting Fiasco: Voters Wait for Hours at Polls as Rick Scott Refuses to Budge."

Terkildsen, Nayda. 1993. "When White Voters Evaluate Black Candidates: The Processing Implications of Candidate Skin Color, Prejudice, and Self-Monitoring." *American Journal of Political Science* 37, no. 4:1032–53.

Terkildsen, Nayda, and David F. Damore. 1999. "The Dynamics of Racialized Media Coverage in Congressional Elections." *Journal of Politics* 61, no. 3:680–99.

TheGrio. 2016. "Racist Commenters Attack Malia Obama After News of Her Going to Harvard." *AOL News,* May 2. https://www.aol.com/article/2016/05/02/racist-commenters -attack-malia-obama-after-news-of-her-going-to-harvard/21369137/.

Thernstrom, Abigail M. 1987. *Whose Votes Count? Affirmative Action and Minority Voting Rights.* Cambridge, MA: Harvard University Press.

Therrien, Melissa, and Roberto R. Ramierez. 2001. "The Hispanic Population in the United States: Population Characteristics." *Current Population Reports* (March). Washington, DC: US Bureau of the Census, 20–535.

Thielemann, Gregory S., and Joseph Stewart Jr. 1995. "A Demand-Side Perspective on the Importance of Representative Bureaucracy: AIDS, Ethnicity, Sexual Orientation, and Gender." *Public Administration Review* 56:168–73.

Tocqueville, Alexis de. 1966 [1835]. *Democracy in America.* Edited by J. P. Mayer and Max Lerner. New York: Harper and Row.

Toensing, Gale C. 2008. "23 INDN's List Candidates Won." *Indian Country Today,* November 10. http://indiancountrytoday.com/home/content/34082779.

Totenberg, Nina. 2016. "Who is Judge Gonzalo Curiel, the Man Trump Attacked for His Mexican Ancestry?" National Public Radio, June 7, http://www.npr.org/2016/06/07/481140881 /who-is-judge-gonzalo-curiel-the-man-trump-attacked-for-his-mexican-ancestry.

Trahant, Mark. 2012a. "Elections 2012: An Arizona Mystery—Will Native Voters Show Up?" *Indian Country Today,* October 9. http://indiancountrytodaymedianetwork.com /article/elections-2012%3A-an-arizona-mystery-%E2%80 %93-will-native-voters-show-up %3F-138625.

———. 2012b. "Elections 2012: Look at the Numbers and Indian Country Outperformed." *Indian Country Today,* November 8. http://indiancountry todaymedianetwork.com/article /elections-2012-look-at-the-numbers-and-indian-country-outperformed-144886.

———. 2012c. Elections 2012: Saving the Republican Brand in Indian Country." *Indian Country Today,* November 8. http://indiancountrytodaymedia network.com/article/elections-2012 %3A-saving-the-republican-brand-in-indian-country-144708.

———. 2015. "Indian Country Wins with More Representation in the States." *Indigenous Policy Journal,* November 22, http://www.indigenouspolicy.org/index.php/ipj/article/view/353 /346.

Trump, Donald J. [realDonaldTrump]. 2014. Attention all hackers: You are hacking everything else so please hack Obama's college records (destroyed?) and check "place of birth." [Tweet], September 6. https://twitter.com/realdonaldtrump/status/508194635270062080?lang=en.

Tuck, R. 1946. *Not with the Fist.* New York: Harcourt Brace and World.

Turner, C. C. 2002. "Rhetorical Bipartisanship: National Party Platforms and American Indian Politics," *American Indian Culture and Research Journal* 26, no.1:107–22.

Tushnet, Mark V. 1987. *The NAACP's Legal Strategy Against Segregated Education, 1925–1950.* Chapel Hill: University of North Carolina Press.

UCLA Asian American Studies Center. 1993. "CrossCurrents" (Fall/Winter):1, 5.

———. 1996. "CrossCurrents" (Fall/Winter): 1.

———. 2007. *National Asian Pacific American Political Almanac, 2007–08.* 13th ed. Los Angeles: UCLA Asian American Studies Center.

Ueda, Reed. 1997. "Historical Patterns of Immigrant Status and Incorporation in the United States." Paper presented at the Workshop on Immigrants, Civil Culture, and Modes of Political Incorporation: A Contemporary and Historical Comparison. May 2–4, Santa Fe, New Mexico.

Uhlaner, Carole J. 1991. "Perceived Prejudice and the Coalition Prospects of Blacks, Latinos and Asian Americans." In *Ethnic and Racial Politics in California,* edited by Byran O. Jackson and Michael B. Preston, 339–71. Berkeley: Institute of Governmental Studies.

Uhlaner, Carole J., Bruce Cain, and D. Roderick Kiewiet. 1989. "Political Participation of Ethnic Minorities in the 1980s." *Political Behavior* 11 (September): 195–231.

———. 1968. *Political Participation.* Washington, DC: Government Printing Office.

United States v. Cruikshank. 1876. 92 US 542.

United States v. Georgia. 1969. Civil No. 12972, N.D. Ga.

United States v. Harris. 1883. 106 US 629.

United States v. Reese. 1876. 92 US 214.

United States v. Texas Education Agency. 1972. 467 F.2d 848.

United States v. Wong Kim Ark. 1898. 169 US 649.

US Census Bureau. 2016. "2014 National Population Projections: Summary Tables." April 19. https://www.census.gov/population/projections/data/national/2014/summarytables.html.

———. 2010.

———.2011.

US Commission on Civil Rights 1968

US Department of Education Office of English Language Acquisition (OELA). 2015. *Dual Language Education Programs: Current State Policies and Practices.* https://ncela.ed.gov/files/rcd/TO20_DualLanguageRpt_508.pdf.

US Department of Interior. 2015. "Interior Proposes Path for Re-Establishing Government-to-Government Relationship with Native Hawaiian Community." https://www.doi.gov/pressreleases/interior-department-proposes-pathway-re-establishing-government-government.

US Department of Justice. 2015. "About Section 5 of the Voting Rights Act." https://www.justice.gov/crt/about-section-5-voting-rights.

———. 2015. "Justice Department Announces Findings of Two Civil Rights Investigations in Ferguson, Missouri." March 4. https://www.justice.gov/opa/pr/justice-department-announces-findings-two-civil-rights-investigations-ferguson-missouri.

———. 2016. "Justice Department and Consumer Financial Protection Bureau Reach Settlement with BancorpSouth Bank to Resolve Allegations of Mortgage Lending Discrimination." June 29. https://www.justice.gov/opa/pr/justice-department-and-consumer-financial-protection-bureau-reach-settlement-bancorpsouth.

US Government Publishing Office. 2010. *To Express the Policy of the United States Regarding the United States Relationship with Native Hawaiians and to Provide a Process for the Recognition by the United States of the Native Hawaiian Governing Entity.* March 11. https://www.gpo.gov/fdsys/pkg/CRPT-111srpt162/html/CRPT-111srpt162.htm.

———. 1971. *One Year Later.* Washington, DC: Government Printing Office.

US Department of Justice, Civil Rights Division. 2015. "Investigation of the Ferguson Police Department, March 4, 2015." Reported in "Department of Justice Report on the Ferguson, Mo. Police Department." *Washington Post.* https://apps.washingtonpost.com/g/documents/national/department-of-justice-report-on-the-ferguson-mo-police-department/1435/.

US Office of Personnel Management. 1996. *Annual Report to Congress on the Federal Equal Opportunity Recruitment Program (Fiscal Year 1996)* (January). Washington, DC: Employment Service Office of Diversity.

US Senate. 1969. *Indian Education: A National Tragedy—A National Challenge.* Report of Special Subcommittee on Indian Education, Committee on Labor and Public Welfare, 91st Congress, 1st sess., S. Rep. No. 501.

University of Michigan. 2005. "Legislation Related to Bilingual Education." http://www.umich.edu/~ac213/student_projects05/be/legislation.html.

Urbina, Ian. 2009. "Hurdles to Voting Persisted in 2008." *New York Times,* March 11, A14.

Verba, Sidney, and Norman Nie. 1972. *Participation in America.* New York: Harper and Row.

Vigil, Maurilio E. 1987. *Hispanics in American Politics: The Search for Political Power.* Lanham, MD: University Press of America.

———. 1996. "The Political Development of New Mexico's Hispanas." *Latino Studies Journal* 7 (Spring):3–28.

Vose, Clement E. 1958. "Litigation as a Form of Pressure Group Activity." *Annals* 319:20–31.

———. 1959. *Caucasians Only: The Supreme Court, the NAACP, and the Restrictive Covenant Cases.* Berkeley: University of California Press.

Wade, T. Joel, Melanie Judkins Romano, and Leslie Blue. 2004. "The Effect of African American Skin Color on Hiring Preferences." *Journal of Applied Social Psychology* 34, no. 12:2550–58.

Wang, Amy B. 2016. "Trump Booted a Black Man from His Rally and Called Him a 'Thug.' Turns Out He Is a Supporter." *Washington Post,* October 29. https://www.washingtonpost.com/news/the-fix/wp/2016/10/29/trump-booted-a-black-man-from-his-rally-and-called-him-a-thug-turns-out-he-is-a-supporter/?utm_term=.e5ab1d363890.

Wang, Hansi Lo. 2016. "'Awoken' By N.Y. Cop Shooting, Asian-American Activists Chart Way Forward." National Public Radio, April 23. http://www.npr.org/sections/codeswitch/2016/04/23/475369524/awoken-by-n-y-cop-shooting-asian-american-activists-chart-way-forward.

Wards Cove Packing Inc. v. Atonio. 1989. 490 US 642, 109 S.Ct. 2115, 104 L.Ed. 2d 733.

Warren, Christopher L., John G. Corbett, and John F. Stack Jr. 1990. "Hispanic Ascendancy and Tripartite Politics in Miami." In *Racial Politics in American Cities,* edited by Rufus P. Browning, Dale Rogers Marshall, and David H. Tabb. New York: Longman, 155–78.

Washington Post. 1994. May 22, A10.

Watanabe, Teresa. 2008. "Latino vs. Black Violence Drives Hate Crimes in LA County to 5-Year High." *Los Angeles Times,* July 25, 2008.

Weaver, Vesla M. 2012. "The Electoral Consequences of Skin Color: The 'Hidden' Side of Race in Politics." *Political Behavior* 34, no. 1:159–92.

Wei, William. 1993. *The Asian American Movement.* Philadelphia: Temple University Press.

Weinberg, Meyer. 1977. *Minority Students: A Research Appraisal.* National Institute of Education. Washington, DC: Government Printing Office.

Weiser, Wendy, and Margaret Chen. 2008. *Recent Voter Suppression Incidents.* New York: Brennan Center for Justice, New York University School of Law, October 30.

Weiser, Wendy, and Diana Kasdan. 2012. *Voting Law Changes: Election Update.* New York: Brennan Center for Justice, New York University School of Law.

Welch, Susan, Albert K. Karnig, and Richard A. Eribes. 1983. "Changes in Hispanic Local Employment in the Southwest." *Western Political Quarterly* 36:660–73.

Welch, Susan, and Lee Sigelman. 1992. "A Gender Gap Among Hispanics? A Comparison with Blacks and Anglos." *Western Political Quarterly* 45:181–99.

Weyler, Rex. 1982. *Blood on the Land: The Government and Corporate War Against the American Indian Movement.* New York: Everest House.

White House. 2013. "President Obama's Judicial Nominees: Historic Successes and Historic Delays." http://www.whitehouse.gov/infographics/judicial-nominees.

White House. 1995. *Report on the Review of Federal Affirmative Action Programs.* http://www.whitehouse.gov/white_house/EOP/OP/html/aa/aa/aa01.html.

Widner, Daniel, and Stephen Chicoine. 2011. "It's All in the Name: Employment Discrimination Against Arab Americans." *Sociological Forum* 26, no. 4:806–823.

Wilkins, David E. 2002. *American Indian Politics and the American Political System.* Lanham, MD: Rowman & Littlefield.

Wilkins, David E., and Heidi Kiiwetinepinesiik Stark. 2011. *American Indian Politics and the American Political System,* 3rd ed. Lanham: Rowman and Littlefield.

Williams, Linda F. 1987. "Black Political Progress in the 1980s: The Electoral Arena." In *The New Black Politics: The Search for Political Power,* 2nd ed., edited by Michael B. Preston, Lenneal Henderson, and Paul Puryear, 97–135. New York: Longman.

Willis, Kiersten. 2016. "Racist Trolls Come Out the Woodwork to Comment on Malia Obama's College Acceptance." *Atlanta Black Star,* May 2. http://atlantablackstar.com/2016/05/02 /racist-trolls-come-out-the-woodwork-to-comment-on-malia-obamas-college-acceptance/.

Willon, Phil, and Jazmine Ulloa. 2016. "Rep. Loretta Sanchez Implies Obama Endorsed Senate Rival Because They Are Both Black." *Los Angeles Times,* July 22. http://www.latimes.com /politics/la-pol-ca-senate-loretta-sanchez-kamala-harris-president-obama-endorsement-20160722-snap-story.html.

Wilson, Thomas C. 2001. "Americans' Views on Immigration Policy: Testing the Role of Threatened Group Interests." *Sociological Perspectives* 44, no. 4 (Winter 2001):485–501.

Wiltz, Teresa. 2016. "American Indian Girls Often Fall Through the Cracks." *Stateline: Pew Charitable Trusts,* March 4. http://pew.org/1QW9j15.

Wines, Michael, and Alan Blinder. 2016. "Federal Court Strikes Down North Carolina Voter ID Requirement." *New York Times,* July 29. http://www.nytimes.com/2016/07/30/us/federal -appeals-court-strikes-down-north-carolina-voter-id-provision.html.

Wollenberg, Charles M. 1978. *All Deliberate Speed: Segregation and Exclusion in California Schools, 1855–1975.* Berkeley: University of California Press.

Wong, Janelle, S. Karthick Ramakrishnan, Taeku Lee, and Jane Junn. 2011. *Asian American Political Participation: Emerging Constituents and Their Political Identities.* New York: Russell Sage Foundation.

Woodard, Stephanie. 2012. "Blackfeet Voters Hampered by Intimidation, Lack of Ballots." *Indian Country Today,* November 7. http://indiancountrytodaymedianetwork.com/article /blackfeet-voters-hampered-by-intimidation,-lack-of-ballots-144590.

———. 2016. "Election Day Turmoil in Utah Portion of Navajo Nation." Indian Country Media Network, November 14. https://indiancountrymedianetwork.com/news/politics /election-day-turmoil-in-utah-portion-of-navajo-nation/.

Worcester v. Georgia. 1832. 6 Peters 515.

Yamada, Mitsuye. 2015. "Invisibility Is an Unnatural Disaster: Reflections of an Asian American Woman." In *This Bridge Called My Back: Writings by Radical Women of Color.* 4th ed. Edited by Cherríe Moraga and Gloria Anzaldúa. New York: SUNY Press.

Yan, Holly. 2016. "Dakota Access Pipeline: What's at Stake." October 28. http://www.cnn.com /2016/09/07/us/dakota-access-pipeline-visual-guide/.

Yee, Vivian. 2013. "Hispanics in East Haven Are Wary of Kinder Tone." *New York Times,* January 23, 2013. http://www.nytimes.com/2013/01/24/nyregion/in-east-haven-hispanics-are-wary-of-towns-kinder-tone.html?ref=hispanicamericans.

Yee, Vivian, and Nate Schweber. 2015. "Residents of Brooklyn Housing Project Stay Wary After Officer Is Indicted." *New York Times,* February 11. http://www.nytimes.com/2015/02/12/ nyregion/officers-indictment-in-akai-gurleys-death-brings-little-solace-to-brooklyn-resi-dents.html.

Younge, Gary 2003. "It's Time to Take the Men-Only Sign off the White House Door." *Guardian,* March 3, 3.

Zarya, Valentina. 2015. "Founders of #BlackLivesMatter: Getting Credit for Your Work Matters." *Fortune Magazine,* July 19. http://fortune.com/2015/07/19/blacklivesmatter-work-credit/.

Zilber, Jeremy, and David Niven. 2000. *Racialized Coverage of Congress: The News in Black and White.* Westport: Praeger.

Zinn, Maxine Baca, and Bonnie Thornton Dill. 1993. *Women of Color in U.S. Society.* Philadelphia: Temple University Press.

Index

AAPF. *See* African American Policy Form
Abedin, Huma, 139
absentee ballots, 121
Adams, John, 11
affirmative action
  in California, 279–280
  Civil Rights Act (1964) and, 204
  definition of, 287
  in education, 206–208
  in employment, 155, 204–208, 287
  incrementalism and, 206
  landmark cases on, 207–208
  presidency on, 206–207
  public reaction to, 205
African American Policy Form (AAPF), 240
African Americans. *See* blacks
agenda setting, 154, 287
  inside access model of, 155, 289
  mobilization model of, 155, 290
  outside initiative model of, 155, 290
  pluralism and, 155–156
AIM. *See* American Indian Movement
Akaka, Daniel, 62, 63
Alabama, 70–71, 227
Alamilla, Cesar, 257
Alaska Natives, 29 (table)
  See also American Indians
Alternative Right, 274, 284–285, 286n1
An American Dilemma (Myrdal), 2

American Indian Movement (AIM), 55–56
American Indians, 4–5, 68
  BIA, 41, 56
  Catawba Indian Tribe of South Carolina v. United States (1993), 147
  Cherokee Nation v. State of Georgia and, 14
  Cheyenne-Arapaho Tribes of Oklahoma v. United States (1992), 147
  CILS, 147
  citizenship for, 10–15, 22
  civil rights movement, 55–58, 58 (photo)
  Clinton, B., and, 157–158
  in Congress, 173, 175 (table)
  criminal justice system and, 223–224
  elections 2008 and, 125
  elections 2012 and, 134
  in elections 2016, 144–145
  Elk v. Wilkins and, 14, 22
  Five Civilized Tribes, 25
  geographic distribution of, 37 (map)
  interest groups, 147, 149–150
  Jackson, A., and, 157
  NARF, 147
  Obama, B., and, 159 (photo)
  partisan identification, 104–106, 105 (table)
  political history timeline for, 305–313

political ideology of, 90–91, 91 (table)
population and socioeconomic status of, 29 (table), 37 (map), 39, 40 (table), 41–42
Sioux Act, 56
Standing Rock Sioux and Dakota Access Pipeline, 56–58, 242–245, 244 (photo), 271
state elected officials, 186–187, 188 (table), 189 (table), 190 (table)
Trail of Tears, 157
United Nations Declaration on the Rights of Indigenous Peoples, 62–63
voting behavior, 106, 111, 112, 283
voting rights for, 19–22
Wounded Knee Massacre, 55
Anantha, Jake, 153
antimiscegenation laws, 7, 287
Apology Resolution (1993), 62
Arizona, 22
  American Indian population in, 41, 41 (table)
  Proposition 200, 280
  SB 1070 law, 276, 280–281
Arizona v. the United States (2012), 281

Arkansas, 94, 262–263, 263 (photo), 264–265
Ashcroft, John, 118
Asian Americans, 5–6, 239–240
  Asian American label, 82
  citizenship for, 17–19, 274–276
  civil rights movement for, 55
  in Congress, 169, 173, 174 (table)
  discrimination of, 81–82
  education and, 149
  in elections 2000, 119
  elections 2004 and, 120
  elections 2008 and, 125, 128
  elections 2012 and, 132–133, 135
  in elections 2016, 141–142, 142 (table)
  equal educational opportunity for, 198–199
  geographic distribution of, 38 (map)
  group cohesion for, 81–83, 82 (table)
  interest groups, 146–149
  Japanese relocation camps, 157, 158 (photo)
  in Los Angeles, 44 (table)
  partisan identification, 102–104, 102 (table), 103 (table)
  political history timeline for, 327–334
  political ideology of, 86, 88, 89 (table), 90
  population and socioeconomic status of, 29 (table), 31 (table), 32–33, 38 (map), 41–42, 44 (table)
  presidential appointments, 160, 161–162
  state elected officials, 183 (table), 184–186
  voting behavior, 110 (table), 111–114, 114 (table), 115 (table), 283
Asian Pacific American Legal Consortium, 146–147

Baldwin, Tammy, 233 (photo)
BancorpSouth (BXS), 73
banks, 73
Baton Rouge bus boycott, 47–49
Bethune, Mary McLeod, 151n1
Beyoncé, 53
BIA. See Bureau of Indian Affairs
bilingual education, 198, 200–202, 287
birther conspiracy movement, 1, 130, 282
Black and Tan Republicans, 92–93, 287
Black Lives Matter (BLM), 51–53, 237–241, 237 (photo)
Black Twitter, 52
black utility heuristic, 76
blacks
  AAPF, 240
  in Baton Rouge, 47–49
  black-Latino relations and racial threat, 266–268
  black-white relations and racial threat, 266
  citizenship for, 10–15
  civil rights movement for, 46–53, 46 (photo)
  in Congress, 168–169, 170 (table), 171 (table), 247n8
  Congressional Black Caucus, 165–166, 168, 288
  criminal justice system and, 222–223
  in elections 2000, 115–119
  in elections 2004, 120
  elections 2008 and, 124–125, 127–128
  elections 2012 and, 132–137
  in elections 2016, 142–144
  equal educational opportunity for, 191–194
  geographic distribution of, 35 (map)
  group cohesion for, 79 (table)
  in House of Representatives, 168–169
  interest groups, 146, 148
  labeling and terminology for African Americans and, 4
  Los Angeles, 44 (table)
  lynching of, 21 (photo)
  in Memphis, Tennessee, 261–262, 264–268
  in Mississippi, 49–51
  NAACP and, 49–51, 71, 115–116, 239, 290
  partisan identification, 92–94, 95 (table), 96–97
  police brutality and, 1–2, 51–53, 237–241
  political history timeline for, 295–305
  political ideology of, 84, 85 (table), 86
  population and socioeconomic status of, 28, 29 (table), 34, 35 (map), 42
  presidential appointments, 158–163
  presidential candidacies, 163–168
  #SayHerName campaign, 240–241

slavery and, 6–7, 9–10, 292–293
state elected officials, 181–182, 183 (table)
voting behavior, 106–107, 108 (table), 109 (table), 110–115, 110 (table), 114 (table), 115 (table)
voting rights for, 19–22, 49–51, 64
See also affirmative action; discrimination; racism; segregation
Blackwell, Kenneth, 121
Blagojevich, Rod, 168
Blalock, Hubert, 75
Bland, Sandra, 52, 240–241
Blauner, Robert, 76
BLM. *See* Black Lives Matter
Boxer, Barbara, 232, 233
Boyd, Rekia, 240–241
Braun, Carol Moseley, 167–168
Brown, Michael, 51–52
Brown v. Board of Education of Topeka (1954, 1955), 94, 192–193, 203, 290, 293
Bunche, Ralph J., 151n1
Bureau of Indian Affairs (BIA), 41, 56
bureaucracy, 177–179, 228–236, 292
bus boycott, 47–49
Bush, George H. W., 118, 119
Bush, George W., 176, 282
elections 2000 and, 115–119
elections 2004 and, 119–122
No Child Left Behind Act and, 208
presidential appointments of, 160–161
Bush v. Vera (1996), 67
BXS. *See* BancorpSouth

California, 232
affirmative action in, 279–280
education in, 194–196, 198–199
elections 2000 and, 119
elections 2008 and, 126–127
LULAC in, 195–196
political ideology in, 86, 88
Proposition 187, 279–280
See also Los Angeles
California gold rush, 17
California Indian Legal Services (CILS), 147
California Land Act, 18
California Rural Legal Assistance (CRLA), 147
Cambodian Americans, 103 (table)
See also Asian Americans
Canada, 52, 191–192
Cao, Anh "Joseph," 127–128
Carnahan, Mel, 118
Carter, Jimmy, 105
Cary, C. J., 153
Castile, Philando, 238–239
Catawba Indian Tribe of South Carolina v. United States (1993), 147
Chaney, James, 50–51
Chávez, César, 242
Cherokee Nation v. State of Georgia, 14
Cheyenne-Arapaho Tribes of Oklahoma v. United States (1992), 147
Chicago, 41, 41 (table)
Chicano movement, 53–54
Chinese American Citizens' Alliance, 148–149
Chinese Americans, 239–240
citizenship for, 17–18
interest groups, 148–149
Organization of Chinese Americans, 149

partisan identification, 102–103, 102 (table)
political history timeline for, 327–334
political ideology of, 88, 89 (table)
population and socioeconomic status of, 31 (table), 32–33
See also Asian Americans
Chinese Exclusion Act (1882), 18
Chisholm, Shirley, 163–165, 164 (photo)
CILS. *See* California Indian Legal Services
Cisneros v. Corpus Christi Independent School District (1970), 197
Citizens United v. Federal Election Committee, 131
citizenship
for American Indians, 10–15, 22
for Asian Americans, 17–19, 274–276
for blacks, 10–15
Constitution on, 10–19, 287
Declaration of Independence and, 11
defining, 287
Fourteenth Amendment and, 13–14
for Latinos, 15–19, 274–276
naturalization and, 12, 16–17, 18–19, 114, 114 (table), 287, 290
of Obama, B., 1, 130, 282
Proposition 200 and, 280
Civil Rights Act (1866), 20
Civil Rights Act (1964), 181, 193
affirmative action and, 204
Johnson, L., and, 158
Civil Rights Cases (1883), 181

civil rights movement
American Indian, 55–58,
58 (photo)
Asian American, 55
Baton Rouge bus boycott,
47–49
black, 46–53, 46 (photo)
BLM, 51–53, 237–241,
237 (photo)
Latino and Chicano,
53–54
in Memphis, Tennessee,
261–262
in Mississippi, 49–51
Native Hawaiian
movement, 58–63, 63
(photo)
OCR, 193
social movements and,
42–43
classical liberalism, 9, 288
classism, 216, 221–222,
247n4
Clayton, Elias, 21 (photo)
Clinton, Bill, 105, 116–117,
124
on affirmative action, 206
American Indians and,
157–158
presidential appointments
for, 158–160
sexual assault and, 139
Clinton, Hillary, 94, 96,
227–228
elections 2008 and,
122–124
in elections 2016, 104
(photo), 139–146
private e-mail server of,
139–140, 145
coalition politics, 249–251,
288
coalition or competition,
251–256
competition theories and
racial threat, 256–268
interminority group
relations, 251,
266–268, 277–278

COFO. See Council of
Federated
Organizations
Colorado, 198
Colored Women's Club,
218
Comey, James, 139–140
Committee on Fair
Employment Practices,
157
competition theories
coalition or competition,
251–256
racial threat and, 256–268
compromise of 1877, 92
Congress
American Indians in, 173,
175 (table)
Asian Americans in, 169,
173, 174 (table)
blacks in, 168–169, 170
(table), 171 (table),
247n8
Latinos in, 169, 172
(table), 173 (table)
minority representation
in, 168–174, 231–236
Obama, B., in, 168
women in, 168–169,
231–236, 247n8
Congressional Black Caucus,
165–166, 168, 288
Congressional Hispanic
Caucus, 288
conservatives, 83–84, 86
Constitution, US
on black and American
Indian voting rights,
19–22
on citizenship, 10–19,
287
Declaration of
Independence and,
8–11
Equal Protection Clause,
292
Federalist Papers and, 9
Fifteenth Amendment,
20, 64, 181, 247n7

Fourteenth Amendment,
13–14
Nineteenth amendment,
147n7
slavery in, 9–10
three-fifths compromise
in, 10, 292–293
voting rights and, 19–22,
64
Cortez Masto, Catherine, 233
(photo), 234, 236,
247n9
Council of Federated
Organizations
(COFO), 50
Crenshaw, Kimberlé,
240
criminal justice system,
222–224
CRLA. See California Rural
Legal Assistance
Crystal City Revolt, 53
Cuban Americans, 282–283
citizenship for, 16–17
partisan identification,
99 (table), 100
political history timeline
for, 323–327
political ideology of,
87 (table)
population and
socioeconomic status
of, 30 (table), 33
See also Latinos
Cullors, Patrisse, 51, 237,
237 (photo)
cumulative voting, 68–69,
288

Dakota Access Pipeline
(DAPL), 56–58,
242–245, 244 (photo),
271
Davenport, Marilyn, 282
Dawson, Michael, 76
Declaration of Independence,
8–11
Delta Air Lines, 213
democracy, 2–3

Democracy in America
(Tocqueville), 2
Democrats, 281–283
Dixiecrats, 93–94
white primary and, 64,
293
See also partisan
identification
demographic changes,
256–258
Department of Health,
Education and Welfare
(HEW), 193
Department of Justice (DOJ),
US, 223
Dewey, Thomas, 93
discrimination
of Asian Americans,
81–82
by banks, 73
employment and,
225–226
group cohesion and,
77–83
intersectional identity
and, 216–217
against Latinos, 80 (table)
racism and, 291
Roosevelt, F., on,
157
second-generation,
203–204, 292
voting and, 20–22, 64,
69–71
Dixiecrats, 93–94
DOJ. *See* Department of
Justice
Dole, Bob, 117
dominated groups, 42–43,
288
Dominicans. *See* Latinos
Dred Scott v. Sanford (1857),
12–13
DuBois, W. E. B., 93
Duckworth, Tammy, 232,
234–236
Duke, David, 284
Durham, North Carolina,
258–261, 264–268

early voting, 136–137
Eckford, Elizabeth, 263
(photo)
economy, 264–265
education
affirmative action in,
206–208
Asian Americans and, 149
bilingual, 198, 200–202,
287
*Brown v. Board of
Education of Topeka*,
94, 192–193, 203,
290, 293
in California, 194–196,
198–199
equal educational
opportunity, 155, 187,
191–204
Latinos and, 177,
194–198, 200–203
LDF and, 146, 191–192,
290
Native Hawaiian
Education Act, 62
No Child Left Behind
Act, 208
school board
representatives, 68–69
segregation and, 191–195,
202–203
student walkouts, 54
in Texas, 196–198
Edwards, John, 122
Eisenhower, Dwight, 94, 128,
151n2, 193, 263
El Salvadorans. *See* Latinos
elections
intersectional identity
and, 226–237
valence issues in, 167, 293
VRA and, 156–157
white primary and, 64,
293
elections 2000, 115–119, 118
(table)
elections 2004, 118 (table),
119–122
elections 2008

American Indians and,
125
Asian Americans and,
125, 128
blacks and, 124–125,
127–128
California and, 126–127
Clinton, H., and,
122–124
Latinos and, 124–125
McCain in, 125–126
Obama Campaign in,
122–128
racism during, 126–127
results, 118 (table)
voter suppression in, 127
elections 2010, 69
elections 2012, 94
American Indians and,
134
Asian Americans and,
132–133, 135
blacks and, 132–137
Florida and, 136–137
Latinos in, 132–133,
135–137
minorities and, 132–137
Obama, B., in, 128–137
Ohio and, 133, 136–137
Republicans during,
129–132, 135
results, 118 (table)
Romney in, 131–132
Virginia and, 286n2
voter suppression in,
135–137
voting behavior in, 106,
110–114, 110 (table),
114 (table), 115
(table)
whites in, 133
elections 2014, 107, 108
(table), 109 (table),
110 (table)
elections 2016, 94, 96
American Indians in,
144–145
Asian Americans in,
141–142, 142 (table)

elections (*Continued*)
  blacks in, 142–144
  Clinton, H., in, 104
    (photo), 139–146
  controversy surrounding,
    137–146
  immigration and,
    137–138
  Latinos in, 137–138,
    141–142, 142 (table)
  Mexico and, 137–138
  minorities and, 137–146,
    231–236
  overall turnout in, 141
  racism during, 137–138,
    142–146
  Russia and, 145
  Senate races, 231–236
  Trump and, 137–146
  voter suppression in,
    142–144
  whites in, 141
  women in, 141,
    231–236
electoral representation,
  67–69
Elk v. Wilkins, 14, 22
e-mail, 139–140, 145
employment
  affirmative action in, 155,
    204–208, 287
  Committee on Fair
    Employment Practices,
    157
  discrimination and,
    225–226
  federal civilian workforce,
    178, 179 (table)
  immigration and, 226,
    242
  intersectional identity
    and, 225–226
  socioeconomic status and,
    221–222
  unemployment, 128–129
  workers' rights, 241–242
Enforcement Acts, 20
equal educational
  opportunity, 155

for American Indians,
  199–200
for Asian Americans,
  198–199
bilingual education and,
  200–202
for blacks, 191–194
for Latinos, 194–198
for minorities, 187,
  191–204
resegregation and,
  202–203
second-generation
  discrimination and,
  203–204
Equal Protection Clause, 292
equality
  democracy and, 2–3
  separate but equal
    doctrine on, 191, 292
ethnicity
  defining, 7–8, 288
  race and, 3, 6–8, 213–216
Evers, Medgar, 49

Facebook, 52
federal bureaucracy, 178, 179
  (table)
federal civilian workforce,
  178, 179 (table)
federalism, 154–155, 289
  minorities and, 179–181
Federalist Papers, 9
Feinstein, Dianne, 233
Ferguson, Missouri, 51–52
Fifteenth Amendment, 20,
  64, 181, 247n7
Figures, Vivian D., 128
Filipino Americans
  political history timeline
    for, 327–334
  political ideology of, 89
    (table), 90
  population and
    socioeconomic status
    of, 31 (table)
  See also Asian Americans
Fisher v. University of Texas
  (2013), 207–208

Five Civilized Tribes, 25
Fleming, Erik, 128
Florida
  elections 2000 and,
    115–116
  elections 2004 and, 120,
    121
  elections 2012 and,
    136–137
Floyd, Pearl Burris, 128
Fourteenth Amendment,
  13–14
Franklin, Benjamin, 11
free speech, 131
Freedom Riders, 49
Freedom Vote, 49–51

Garner, Eric, 239
Garza, Alicia, 51, 237, 237
  (photo), 241
gender, 6
  intersectional identity
    and, 218–221,
    240–241
  LGBTQ community,
    219–220
  partisan identification
    and, 101, 103–104
  politics and, 77
  sex and, 218–221
  sexuality and gender
    fluidity, 216,
    219–221, 240–241
  voting behavior and, 113,
    114 (table), 227–228
  See also women
George III, King of England,
  9, 11
Georgia, 14, 70, 157
Georgia v. Ashcroft (2003), 70
Gillibrand, Kirsten, 233
  (photo)
Goldwater, Barry, 94
Gong Lum v. Rice (1927), 199
Goodman, Andrew, 50–51
Gore, Al, 105, 115–119
government
  federalism and, 179–181
  minorities and, 8–10

minority representation in, 156–157
grandfather clause, 64, 289
Gratz v. Bollinger (2003), 207
Gray, Freddie, 52
Griggs v. Duke Power Co. (1971), 205
group cohesion, 76, 289
  for Asian Americans, 81–83, 82 (table)
  for blacks, 79 (table)
  discrimination and, 77–83
  for Latinos, 78–80, 80 (table), 81 (table)
group political consciousness, 3, 289
Grutter v. Bollinger (2003), 207, 208
Guinier, Lani, 68
Guinn v. United States (1915), 64
Gurley, Akai, 238, 239–240, 240 (photo)
Gutierrez, Jose Angel, 54

Haley, Nikki Randhawa, 185–186, 186 (photo)
Hamid, Rose, 153
Harris, Kamala, 232–234, 233 (photo), 249
Harris, Luke, 240
Harvard University, 151n1
Hassan, Maggie, 233 (photo)
HAVA. *See* Help America Vote Act
Hawaii
  history and statehood, 59–61
  Kaho'olawe Island, 62
  Native Hawaiian Education Act, 62
  OHA, 60
Hawaiian Homes Commission Act (HHCA) (1921), 59–60
Hawaiian Renaissance, 61–62
Hawaiians, 5
Hui, 61

Native Hawaiian movement, 58–63, 63 (photo)
partisan identification, 104
Hayes, Rutherford B., 20–21, 92
Heitkamp, Heidi, 134
Help America Vote Act (HAVA) (2002), 121, 135
Hernandez v. Driscoll Consolidated Independent School District (1957), 196
Hero, Rodney, 75
HEW. *See* Department of Health, Education and Welfare
HHCA. *See* Hawaiian Homes Commission Act
Hispanics. *See* Latinos
Hmong Americans, 103 (table)
  See also Asian Americans
Holloway, Harry, 76
homosexuality, 216, 219–220
Hoover, Herbert, 93
Horne v. Flores (2009), 201
Huerta, Dolores, 242
Hui, 61

identity. *See* group cohesion; intersectional identity; voter ID laws
Illinois, 41, 41 (table)
immigration
  concern about, 264
  in Durham, North Carolina, 258–261, 264–268
  economic effects of, 264–265
  elections 2016 and, 137–138
  employment and, 226, 242
  for Latinos, 28–29, 224, 258–261, 264–268,

269n2, 269n4, 270n5, 278–279
  politics and, 265–266
  Proposition 187, 279–280
  Proposition 200 and, 280
  refugee status and, 224–225
  SB 1070 law on, 276, 280–281
incarceration rates, 222–223
individualism, 247n1
Ink Fund. *See* Legal Defense and Education Fund
inside access model, 155, 289
interest group activities, 76, 146–150, 289
interminority group relations, 251, 266–268, 277–278
internal colonialism framework, 76
intersectional identity, 23–24, 214–215, 290
  discrimination and, 216–217
  elections, politics, and, 226–237
  employment and, 225–226
  gender and, 218–221, 240–241
  minority representation and, 228–236
  multiple dimensions of, 215–218, 247n3
  salient dimensions of, 218–222, 247n3
  social activism, protest, and, 237–245
  sociopolitical experiences and, 217–218, 222–226
  voting and, 226–228

Jackson, Andrew, 157
Jackson, Elmer, 21 (photo)

Jackson, Jesse, 107
  Congressional Black
    Caucus and, 165–166,
    168, 288
  presidential campaigns,
    165–167
  Rainbow Coalition and,
    166
  on valence issues, 166
Japanese American Citizens
  League (JACL),
  148
Japanese Americans
  citizenship for, 18–19
  partisan identification,
    102, 102 (table)
  political history timeline
    for, 327–334
  political ideology of, 88,
    89 (table)
  population and
    socioeconomic status
    of, 31 (table)
  relocation camps and,
    157, 158 (photo)
  See also Asian Americans
Jefferson, Thomas, 8–10, 11
Jefferson, William, 127–128
Jemison, T. J., 47–48
Jim Crow laws, 222–223
Jindal, Bobby, 184–185
Johnson, Lyndon, 150,
  151n1, 158, 176

Kahoʻolawe Island, 62
Kennedy, John F., 94, 193
Kerry, John F., 119–122
Keyes v. School District No. 1
  (1973), 198
King, Coretta Scott, 94
King, Martin Luther, Jr., 48,
  94, 261
King, Rodney, 1–2, 24,
  249–250, 272
Kirk, Mark, 234–236
Kitchen Cabinet, 93
Korean Americans, 1–2, 149
  partisan identification,
    102 (table)

political history timeline
  for, 327–334
political ideology of, 88,
  89 (table), 90
population and
  socioeconomic status
  of, 31 (table), 32
See also Asian Americans
Ku Klux Klan, 284–285,
  286n1
Ku Klux Klan Act, 181

Latinos, 4–5
  in Arkansas, 262,
    264–265
  black-Latino relations and
    racial threat,
    266–268
  in California schools,
    194–196
  citizenship for, 15–19,
    274–276
  civil rights movement for,
    53–54
  in Congress, 169, 172
    (table), 173 (table)
  Congressional Hispanic
    Caucus, 288
  criminal justice system
    and, 222–223
  discrimination against,
    80 (table)
  in Durham, North
    Carolina, 258–261,
    264–268
  education and, 177,
    194–198, 200–203
  in election 2004, 119–122
  in elections 2000, 119
  elections 2008 and,
    124–125
  in elections 2012,
    132–133, 135–137
  in elections 2016,
    137–138, 141–142,
    142 (table)
  equal educational
    opportunity for,
    194–198

geographic distribution of,
  36 (map)
group cohesion for,
  78–80, 80 (table), 81
  (table)
immigration for, 28–29,
  224, 258–261,
  264–268, 269n2,
  269n4, 270n5,
  278–279
interest groups, 146, 148
labeling and group
  identification for, 8
Latino-white relations
  racial threat, 266
Los Angeles, 45 (table)
LULAC, 148, 195–196,
  290
MALDEF, 146, 197, 287,
  289
in Memphis, Tennessee,
  261–262, 264–268
NCLR, 148
partisan identification, 97,
  98 (table), 99 (table),
  100–101
political history timeline
  for, 313–327
political ideology of, 86,
  87 (table), 88
population size and
  socioeconomic status
  of, 28–29, 30 (table),
  33, 34, 35(map), 39,
  41–42, 45 (table)
presidential appointments,
  159–163
PRLDEF, 146, 201–202,
  290
segregation and,
  211nn2–3
state elected officials,
  181–182, 183 (table),
  184
voting behavior, 106–107,
  108 (table), 109
  (table), 110–115, 110
  (table), 1143 (table),
  115 (table), 282–283

Lau v. Nichols (1974), 199, 202
law enforcement, 177
See also police brutality
LDF. See Legal Defense and Education Fund
League of United Latin American Citizens (LULAC), 148, 195–196, 290
League of Women Voters, 136
Legal Defense and Education Fund (LDF), 146, 191–192, 290
lending, 73
lesbian, gay, bisexual, transgender, and queer (LGBTQ) community, 219–220
Levy-Pound, Nekima, 239
LGBTQ. See lesbian, gay, bisexual, transgender, and queer community
Liang, Peter, 239–240, 240 (photo)
liberalism, 9, 288
liberals, 83–84, 86
Lily White Republicans, 92–93, 290
Little Rock, Arkansas, 94, 262–263, 263 (photo), 264–265
local bureaucrats, 177–178
Locke, Gary, 184
Locke, John, 9, 288
Logan, Rayford W., 151n1
Logan, Willie, 118
Los Angeles
American Indian population in, 41, 41 (table)
Asian American population in, 44 (table)
black population in, 44 (table)
Latino population in, 45 (table)

property crimes in, 1–2
riots in, 1–2, 149
student walkouts in, 54
Louisiana, 47–49
Loving v. Virginia, 7, 287
Lowenstein, Allard, 50
Lujan, Ben R., 127
LULAC. See League of United Latin American Citizens
lynching, 21 (photo)

Madison, James, 74, 150
majority minority districts, 67–68
MALDEF. See Mexican American Legal Defense and Education Fund
marriage, 7, 287
Marshall, Thurgood, 176, 192
Martin, Trayvon, 51, 237
Martinez, Julio, 101 (photo)
McCain, John, 125–126
McCollum, Betty, 127
McCollum, Bill, 118
McConnell, Mitch, 130
McGhie, Isaac, 21 (photo)
McKenna, Natasha, 240–241
McKesson, DeRay, 52
media coverage, 230–231
Memphis, Tennessee, 261–262, 264–268
Mendez v. Westminster School District (1946, 1947), 195–196
Mexican American Legal Defense and Education Fund (MALDEF), 146, 197, 287, 289
Mexican Americans
citizenship for, 15–16
elections 2016 and, 137–138
partisan identification, 97, 98 (table)
political history timeline for, 313–320

political ideology of, 86, 87 (table)
population and socioeconomic status of, 30 (table)
segregation and, 211nn2–3
See also Latinos
Mexico, 137–138
Mikulski, Barbara, 233 (photo)
Mill, John Stuart, 288
Miller v. Johnson (1995), 67
Minnesota, 238–239
minorities, 1–3, 27–28
in election 2000, 115–119
in election 2004, 119–122
in elections 2008, 122–128
elections 2012 and, 132–137
elections 2016 and, 137–146, 231–236
equal educational opportunity for, 187, 191–204
federalism and, 179–181
government and, 8–10
interminority group relations, 251, 266–268, 277–278
political behavior of, 76–77
political ideology of, 83–91
population size, socioeconomic status, and concentration of, 28–42, 44 (table), 45 (table)
presidential appointments of, 158–163
race relations and targeting of, 279–281
voting by, 29, 32, 63–71, 226–228
See also specific minorities; specific topics

minority representation
  in bureaucracy, 177–179,
    228–236, 292
  in Congress, 168–174,
    231–236
  in government, 156–157
  intersectional identity
    and, 228–236
  media coverage and,
    230–231
  presidency and, 157–168
  in state elective office,
    181–190, 247n7
  stereotyping and,
    229–230
  in Supreme Court,
    174–177
minority women. See women
Mississippi, 49–51, 73
Missouri, 51–52, 118–119
Missouri ex rel. Gaines v.
  Canada (1938),
  191–192
mobilization model, 155, 290
Mochida family, 158 (photo)
moderates, 83–84
modernization/developmental
  framework, 76
Monroe Doctrine (1823), 16
Montana, 112, 134
moral dilemma framework,
  75
Moral Monday movement,
  71
Moses, Robert, 49, 50
Muslim Americans, 281
Myrdal, Gunnar, 2, 75

NAACP. See National
  Association for the
  Advancement of
  Colored People
NARF. See Native American
  Rights Fund
National Association for the
  Advancement of
  Colored People
  (NAACP), 239, 290
  in election 2000, 115–116

in Mississippi, 49–51
  Moral Monday movement
    and, 71
National Council of La Raza
  (NCLR), 148
Native American. See
  American Indians
Native American Rights Fund
  (NARF), 147
Native Hawaiian Education
  Act, 62
Native Hawaiian movement,
  58–63, 63 (photo)
nativist movement, 4–5
naturalization, 12, 16–17,
  18–19, 287, 290
  voting behavior and, 114,
    114 (table)
Naturalization Act (1790),
  12
Navajo Nation. See American
  Indians
NCLR. See National Council
  of La Raza
Nelson, Bill, 118
New Deal, 93
New Mexico, 22, 41, 41
  (table), 112, 125
New York, 41, 41 (table)
Nineteenth amendment,
  147n7
Nixon, Richard M., 94, 105,
  193, 205
No Child Left Behind Act
  (2001), 208
North Carolina, 71,
  124–125, 142–144,
  258–261, 264–268,
  285

Obama, Barack, 94, 96, 105,
  129 (photo), 157, 176
  on affirmative action, 207
  American Indians and,
    159 (photo)
  birther conspiracy
    movement and
    citizenship of, 1, 130,
    282

campaign strategy of,
    124–127, 131–133
  in Congress, 168
  elections 2008 and,
    122–128
  elections 2012 and,
    128–137
  Harris, K., and, 233, 249
  opposition to, 129–130
  presidential appointments
    of, 161–163
  on SB 1070, 281
  unemployment and,
    128–129
  on United Nations
    Declaration on the
    Rights of Indigenous
    Peoples, 62
Obama, Malia, 27, 129
  (photo)
Obama, Michelle, 129
  (photo)
Obama, Sasha, 129 (photo)
Obergefell v. Hodges (2015),
  220
OCR. See Office for Civil
  Rights
OFCCP. See Office of Federal
  Contract Compliance
  Programs
Office for Civil Rights
  (OCR), 193
Office of Federal Contract
  Compliance Programs
  (OFCCP), 204–205
Office of Hawaiian Affairs
  (OHA), 60
office-holding. See minority
  representation
OHA. See Office of Hawaiian
  Affairs
Ohio, 121–122, 133,
  136–137
Oklahoma, 41, 41 (table),
  147
Oregon v. Mitchell (1970), 70
Organic Act, 59
Organization of Chinese
  Americans, 149

outside initiative model, 155, 290
Ozawa, Takao, 18–19

PACs. *See* Political Action Committees
#Palestine2Ferguson campaign, 52
Palin, Sarah, 126
partisan identification, 76, 290–291
American Indians, 104–106, 106 (table)
Asian Americans, 102–104, 102 (table), 103 (table)
blacks, 92–94, 95 (table), 96–97
gender and, 101, 103–104
Latinos, 97, 98 (table), 99 (table), 100–101
PASSO. *See* Political Association of Spanish-Speaking Organizations
PATRIOT Act, 281
Pennsylvania, 136, 205
perceptions, 229–230
Philadelphia Plan, 205
Plessy v. Ferguson (1896), 22, 191–192, 292
pluralism, 74–76, 155–156, 291
police brutality, 1–2, 51–53, 237–241
policymaking, 23
adoption in, 154, 287
agenda setting in, 154–156, 287, 289–290
evaluation, 154, 288
formulation in, 154, 289
implementation in, 154, 289
public policies and, 154, 291
Political Action Committees (PACs), 131

Political Association of Spanish-Speaking Organizations (PASSO), 53
political behavior
data and surveys on, 77
group cohesion and discrimination, 77–83
of minorities, 76–77
political frameworks, 74–77
political history timelines
for American Indians, 305–313
for Asian Americans, 327–334
for blacks, 295–305
for Cuban Americans, 323–327
for Latinos, 313–327
for Mexican Americans, 313–320
for Puerto Ricans, 320–323
political ideology, 76, 291
of American Indians, 90–91, 91 (table)
of Asian Americans, 86, 88, 89 (table), 90
of blacks, 84, 85 (table), 86
in California, 86, 88
conservatives, 83–84, 86
of Latinos, 86, 87 (table), 88
liberals, 83–84, 86
of minorities, 83–91
moderates, 83–84
political incorporation, 291
politics
free speech in, 131
gender and, 77
immigration and, 265–266
intersectional identity and, 226–237
See also coalition politics
population, of minorities, 28–42, 44 (table), 45 (table)

Pottinger, Stanley, 197
power relations framework, 75
presidency
on affirmative action, 206–207
black presidential candidacies, 163–168
minority presidential appointments, 158–163
minority representation and, 157–168
women presidential candidacies, 163–164, 167–168
See also specific presidents
private e-mail server, 139–140, 145
PRLDEF. *See* Puerto Rican Legal Defense and Education Fund
property crimes, 1–2
property ownership, 19
Proposition 187, 279–280
Proposition 200, 280
protesters
Dakota Access Pipeline and, 56–58, 242–245, 244 (photo), 271
intersectional identity and, 237–245
riots and, 1–2, 149, 249–250
of Trump, 153
public policies, 154, 291
See also policymaking
Puerto Rican Legal Defense and Education Fund (PRLDEF), 146, 201–202, 290
Puerto Ricans
citizenship for, 16
partisan identification, 97, 98 (table)
political history timeline for, 320–323
political ideology of, 87 (table)

Puerto Ricans
  citizenship for
    (*Continued*)
  population and
    socioeconomic status
    of, 30 (table)
  See also Latinos

race, 3, 6–8, 213–216
race relations, 2, 272–274
  dilemmas revisited,
    274–279
  future of, 281–285
  interminority group
    relations, 251,
    266–268, 277–278
  targeting of minorities
    and, 279–281
  VRA and, 281–284
racial gerrymandering, 67
racial group identification,
    7–8, 215–216, 291
racial threat
  black-Latino relations
    and, 266–268
  black-white relations and,
    266
  competition theories and,
    256–268
  demographic changes and,
    256–258
  Latino-white relations
    and, 266
racism, 6, 213
  defining, 291
  discrimination and, 291
  during elections 2008,
    126–127
  during elections 2016,
    137–138, 142–146
Rainbow Coalition, 166, 291
Ramos, Jorge, 138
Reagan, Ronald, 104,
    281–282
redistricting process, 69
refugee status, 224–225
Rehberg, Denny, 134
relocation camps, 157, 158
    (photo)

representative bureaucracy,
    177–178, 292
Republicans, 281–282
  Black and Tan, 92–93,
    287
  during elections 2012,
    129–132, 135
  Lily White, 92–93, 290
  Tea Party, 130–131
  See also partisan
    identification
resegregation, 202–203
Reynolds, Diamond,
    238–239
Rice v. Cayetano, 63
riots, 1–2, 149, 249–250
Rock the Vote, 136
Romney, Mitt, 131–132
Roosevelt, Eleanor, 93
Roosevelt, Franklin D., 93,
    128, 157
Russia, 145

Sánchez, Linda, 232–234,
    247n8
Sánchez, Loretta, 232, 249
#SayHerName campaign,
    240–241
SB 1070 law, 276, 280–281
scapegoating, 239–240
school board representatives,
    68–69
schools. *See* education
Schwerner, Michael, 50–51
second-generation
  discrimination,
    203–204, 292
segregation
  with all deliberate speed
    concept and, 293
  in Arkansas, 262–263,
    263 (photo)
  *Brown v. Board of
    Education of Topeka*
    on, 94, 192–193, 203,
    290, 293
  education and, 191–195,
    202–203
  Latinos and, 211nn2–3

  in Mississippi, 49–51
  resegregation, 202–203
  Southern Manifesto and,
    193, 292
Senate races, 2016, 231–236
separate but equal doctrine,
    191, 292
SES. *See* socioeconomic status
Sessions, Jeff, 128
sex, 218–221
sexual assault, 138–139
sexuality, 216, 219–221,
    240–241
Sharpton, Al, 167–168
Shaw v. Hunt (1996),
    67
Shaw v. Reno (1993), 61
Shelby County v. Holder,
    70–71, 227, 276–277
shootings, 51–53, 186,
    220–221, 237–241
Sioux Act, 56
slavery, 6–7, 9–10, 292–293
Smith v. Allwright (1944), 64,
    293
SNCC. *See* Student
    Nonviolent
    Coordinating
    Committee
social activism, 237–245
  See also interest group
    activities; protesters
social hierarchy, 214, 241,
    247n4
social media, 52, 237–238,
    240–241
social movements, 42–43,
    292
socioeconomic status (SES),
    6, 292
  American Indian
    population and, 29
    (table), 37 (map), 39,
    40 (table), 41–42
  Asian American
    population and, 29
    (table), 31 (table),
    32–33, 38 (map),
    41–42, 44 (table)

black population and, 28, 29 (table), 34, 35 (map), 42

classism and, 216, 221–222, 247n4

defining, 28

employment and, 221–222

Latino population and, 28–29, 30 (table), 33, 34, 35(map), 39, 41–42, 45 (table)

pluralism and, 74

population size and, of minorities, 28–42, 44 (table), 45 (table)

white population and, 39 (table)

sociopolitical experiences, 217–218, 222–226

Solis, Hilda, 127

Sotomayor, Sonia, 176–177

South Carolina v. Katzenbach (1966), 70

Southern Manifesto, 193, 292

Standing Rock Reservation, 56–58, 242–245, 244 (photo), 271

state elective office

American Indians in, 186–187, 188 (table), 189 (table), 190 (table)

Asian Americans in, 183 (table), 184–186

blacks in, 181–182, 183 (table)

Latinos in, 181–182, 183 (table), 184

minority representation in, 181–190, 247n7

stereotyping, 229–230

Sterling, Alton, 238

Student Nonviolent Coordinating Committee (SNCC), 49

student walkouts, 54

suffrage, 10–11, 19–22, 63–71, 292

See also voting rights

Summer Project, 50–51

Supreme Court, 174–177

See also individual cases

Taney, Roger, 12–13

Tape v. Hurley (1885), 198–199

Tea Party, 130–131

Tennessee, 261–262, 264–268

Tester, Jon, 134

Texas

American Indian population in, 41, 41 (table)

Crystal City Revolt, 53

education in, 196–198

elections 2000 and, 116–118

Fisher v. University of Texas (2013), 207–208

Thomas, Clarence, 176

three-fifths compromise, 10, 292–293

Tocqueville, Alexis de, 2, 274

Tometi, Opal, 51, 52, 237, 237 (photo)

Trail of Tears, 157

transgender identity. *See* gender

Treaty of Guadalupe Hidalgo (1848), 17

Truman, Harry, 93

Trump, Donald, 94, 96, 228, 234, 236, 281, 284–285

Alternative Right and, 274, 286n1

birther conspiracy movement and, 1

elections 2016 and, 137–146

presidential appointments of, 163

protesters of, 153

on Standing Rock Reservation and Dakota Access Pipeline, 58

supporters of, 101 (photo), 153, 282

Twitter, 52

two-tiered pluralist framework, 75

UDL. *See* United Defense League

unemployment, 128–129

See also employment

United Defense League (UDL), 47

United Nations Declaration on the Rights of Indigenous Peoples, 62–63

United States v. Cruikshank, 20

United States v. Harris (1883), 181

United States v. Reese (1876), 20–21, 151

United States v. Wong Kim Ark, 18

Utah, 22

valence issues, 167, 293

video evidence, 238–239

Vietnamese Americans

partisan identification, 103 (table)

political ideology of, 89 (table), 90

population and socioeconomic status of, 31 (table), 32

See also Asian Americans

Virginia, 7, 286n2, 287

vote dilution, 66–67, 293

voter ID laws, 71, 135–136

voter suppression, 227

in elections 2008, 127

in elections 2012, 135–137

voter suppression (*Continued*)
  in elections 2016,
    142–144
voting
  absentee ballots,
    121
  cumulative, 68–69,
    288
  discrimination and,
    20–22, 64, 69–71
  early, 136–137
  Freedom Vote, 49–51
  HAVA, 121, 135
  intersectional identity
    and, 226–228
  League of Women Voters,
    136
  by minorities, 29, 32,
    63–71, 226–228
  racial gerrymandering
    and, 67
  Rock the Vote, 136
  See also elections
voting behavior, 76, 293
  American Indians, 106,
    111, 112, 283
  Asian Americans, 110
    (table), 111–114,
    114 (table),
    115 (table), 283
  blacks, 106–107, 108
    (table), 109 (table),
    110–115, 110 (table),
    114 (table),
    115 (table)
  in elections 2012, 106,
    110–114, 110 (table),
    114 (table),
    115 (table)
  in elections 2014, 107,
    108 (table), 109
    (table), 110 (table)
  gender and, 113, 114
    (table), 227–228
  Latinos, 106–107, 108
    (table), 109 (table),
    110–115, 110 (table),
    113 (table), 114
    (table), 282–283

  naturalization and, 114,
    114 (table)
  whites, 107, 110 (table)
voting rights
  for American Indians,
    19–22
  for blacks, 19–22, 49–51,
    64
  Civil Rights Act (1866)
    and, 20
  Constitution and, 19–22,
    64
  in election 2000, 115–116
  electoral representation
    and, 67–69
  Fifteenth Amendment
    and, 20, 64, 181,
    247n7
  grandfather clause and,
    64, 289
  majority minority districts
    and, 67–68
  property ownership and,
    19
  suffrage, 10–11, 19–22,
    63–71, 292
  for women, 227–228,
    247n7
Voting Rights Act (VRA)
  (1965), 23, 276–277,
  293
  in Alabama, 70–71,
    227
  description of, 64–65
  elections and, 156–157
  race relations and future
    of, 281–284
  Section 5, 69–71

Warren, Earl, 94, 151n2
water protectors, 56–58,
  242–245, 244 (photo),
  247n12
Weaver, Robert C., 151n1
white primary, 64, 293
white superiority,
  213–214
white supremacy, 274,
  284–285, 286n1

whites
  black-white relations and
    racial threat, 266
  bus boycott and, 47–48
  in elections 2012, 133
  in elections 2016, 141
  Latino-white relations
    racial threat, 266
  Lily White Republicans,
    92–93, 290
  population and
    socioeconomic status
    of, 39 (table)
  scapegoating and,
    239–240
  voting behavior, 107, 110
    (table)
  women, 218–219
  See also police brutality
Wilson, Darren, 51–52
Wilson, Woodrow, 93
with all deliberate speed
  concept, 192, 293
women
  Colored Women's Club,
    218
  in Congress, 168–169,
    231–236, 247n8
  in elections 2016, 141,
    231–236
  League of Women Voters,
    136
  presidential appointments,
    162
  presidential candidacies,
    163–164, 167–168
  #SayHerName campaign,
    240–241
  voting rights for,
    227–228, 247n7
  white, 218–219
Worcester v. Georgia, 157
workers' rights, 241–242
Wounded Knee Massacre, 55

Yanez, Jeronimo, 238–239

Zimmerman, George, 51,
  237